Enabling Peace
in Guatemala

■ ■ ■

HISTORIES OF UN PEACE OPERATIONS

A project of the International Peace Institute

Enabling Peace in Guatemala

THE STORY OF MINUGUA

■ ■ ■

William Stanley

LYNNE
RIENNER
PUBLISHERS

BOULDER
LONDON

Published in the United States of America in 2013 by
Lynne Rienner Publishers, Inc.
1800 30th Street, Boulder, Colorado 80301
www.rienner.com

and in the United Kingdom by
Lynne Rienner Publishers, Inc.
3 Henrietta Street, Covent Garden, London WC2E 8LU

Library of Congress Cataloging-in-Publication Data
Stanley, William.
 Enabling peace in Guatemala : the story of MINUGUA / by William Stanley.
  p. cm.
 Includes bibliographical references and index.
 ISBN 978-1-58826-656-9 (hc : alk. paper)
 ISBN 978-1-58826-681-1 (pb : alk. paper)
 1. Misión de Verificación de las Naciones Unidas de Guatemala. 2. Human rights—
Guatemala. 3. Peace-building—Guatemala. 4. Guatemala—Politics and government.
5. Guatemala—Social conditions. I. Title.
 JC599.G8S83 2012
 972.8105'31—dc23

                                                          2012044241

British Cataloguing in Publication Data
A Cataloguing in Publication record for this book
is available from the British Library.

Printed and bound in the United States of America

The paper used in this publication meets the requirements
of the American National Standard for Permanence of
Paper for Printed Library Materials Z39.48-1992.

5 4 3 2 1

Contents

Foreword

Terje Rød-Larsen
President, International Peace Institute

THE INTERNATIONAL PEACE INSTITUTE (IPI) is proud to present *Enabling Peace in Guatemala: The Story of MINUGUA,* by William Stanley of the University of New Mexico. This book chronicles the critical role played by the United Nations in the immediate aftermath of the Guatemalan civil war, which ended in 1996 after more than thirty years of fighting and more than 200,000 lives lost. After playing an active part in mediating the peace, the UN mission, under a General Assembly mandate, took on the challenge of verifying the full accords. As Stanley tells it, this is a story of principled diplomacy under difficult circumstances. The agreement that ended the war included comprehensive goals to build a lasting peace, but it lacked a clear mechanism to implement the policies necessary for success. As Stanley shows, neither party to the conflict had both the political leverage and the determined will to effect the comprehensive change called for by the peace accords. This made the job of MINUGUA (UN Mission for the Verification of Human Rights and of Compliance with the Comprehensive Agreement on Human Rights in Guatemala) all the more difficult. Stanley details the key challenges faced by the mission and the tough decisions made by UN staff over the course of ten years, as they walked the fine line between enabling the government to institute change and sanctioning it to discourage obstructionism and backsliding.

Enabling Peace in Guatemala is the second volume in IPI's Histories of UN Peace Operations, a project initiated by the UN's Department of Political Affairs (DPA) and Department of Peacekeeping Operations (DPKO) with the strong support of then Secretary-General Kofi Annan. It arose out of a recognition that, for all the academic literature about UN peace operations, the inside story of individual UN missions often went untold. IPI was asked to fill that gap by producing an ongoing series of histories that would capture UN perspectives and pay particular attention to the environment of opportunities and constraints within which major strategic decisions were made, with the goal of providing an independent assessment of each mission. Each book in the series benefits from the author's access to internal UN documents and personnel. In the course of researching each volume, the authors have been made privy to previously undisclosed internal correspondence, memoranda, and reports. IPI is deeply grateful for this level of cooperation from the UN Secretariat.

The book reflects IPI's continuing engagement with issues related to peacekeeping and peacebuilding, the core competencies of the United Nations. In the coming years we hope to further this engagement. IPI's Histories of UN Peace Operations will continue with forthcoming volumes on the United Nations Protection Force (UNPROFOR) for Croatia and Bosnia-Herzegovina and the United Nations Operation in Somalia (UNOSOM I and II). We hope that these volumes provide a learning tool for UN staff as they navigate the complex challenges of future peace operations, and provide insight for all those interested in the work of the United Nations.

IPI owes a debt of thanks to all of its generous donors who make publications like this one possible. In particular, IPI would like to thank the original donors to this project—the governments of France, Ireland, the Netherlands, and the United Kingdom.

Acknowledgments

THIS PROJECT WAS made possible by an extraordinary act of transparency: the United Nations Departments of Political Affairs (DPA) and Peacekeeping Operations (DPKO) agreed to open their files to outside researchers for the International Peace Institute's series, Histories of UN Peace Operations. While working on research for this book, I was allowed to read memoranda about high-level meetings, reports of boards of inquiry, and all cable traffic between the UN mission in Guatemala and UN headquarters. When MINUGUA closed in 2004, all the records of regional offices had been boxed up, sent to New York, and stored in a facility outside the city. While the sheer volume of material from a ten-year mission with thirteen regional offices made it impracticable to review everything, the UN archive recalled sample boxes from storage and gave me space to rummage. This was an extraordinary opportunity to see how decisionmakers responsible for the mission described the choices available to them and how they explained the choices made. I am grateful to the UN Secretariat for making this kind of research possible, and I hope that the final product validates the decision to let an outside researcher read the organization's mail.

Of course, not everything is written down, and hindsight sometimes brings new perspective on past events. I was fortunate to have the opportunity to interview two former special representatives of the Secretary-General for Guatemala, Jean Arnault and Tom Koenigs. Mr. Arnault was especially generous with his time in corresponding with me and sharing his own academic writings and talks. The director of the Americas Division at DPA, Martha Doggett, provided invaluable insights into the dynamics of MINUGUA's final years. Assistant Secretary-General for Political Affairs Alvaro de Soto spoke with me when MINUGUA was still in the field, as did numerous members of the MINUGUA staff, generally off the record. I am very grateful for their generosity with their time and their candor in discussing the external and internal challenges that faced the mission. I was fortunate to speak with a number of Guatemalans who were close observers of the peace process. Retired general

Julio Balconi, former secretary of the presidency Gustavo Porras, and former government negotiator Hector Rosada stand out. I would have been lost in the complexities of Guatemalan politics without guidance from my friends David Holiday and Edmundo Urrutia. Guatemalan scholars Tania and Mayra Palencia helped me understand finer points of the peace accords and the fiscal impasse. In New York, Jared Kotler, Denise Cook, Marcie Mersky, and others shared recollections of the mission. Teresa Whitfield at the Social Science Research Council filled in key historical details and provided analytical perspective. I could not have done this project without the help of Annie Mazaud at DPA, who showed me how to navigate the files. Most important, without the careful record-keeping efforts of Ms. Mazaud and other administrative staff members in DPA, DPKO, and MINUGUA, there would not have been a clear documentary record on which to base this account.

The International Peace Institute has been steadfast in its support for this project. IPI provided financial backing that enabled me to take a year-long sabbatical to do the initial document research, encouraged me at every stage of the project, and dealt seamlessly with the editorial process. I particularly want to thank IPI senior director of research Francesco Mancini, who stuck with me despite delays; former program officers Vanessa Wyeth, Jenna Slotin, and Amy Scott, who guided the early stages of the project; senior editor Adam Lupel, who saw the manuscript through to production; and Paul Romita, Till Papenfuss, and Ellie Hearne, who provided editorial guidance along the way. At Lynne Rienner Publishers, Lesli Brooks Athanasoulis and Jennifer Top caught many of my mistakes and inconsistencies, and patiently corrected my willful ignorance of the style guide.

Colleagues at the University of New Mexico (UNM), including Mark Peceny, Mala Htun, Richard Wood, and Kendra Koivu, read and commented on portions of the manuscript, as did Elisabeth Wood, Michele Leiby, Amelia Hoover, Nancy Robinson, and Meghan Lynch. UNM graduate students Michael Wolff, Steve Samford, and Jessica Jones combed through and summarized human rights reports, public UN documents, and a variety of sources covering the period since MINUGUA closed. An anonymous reviewer provided invaluable comments and corrections, which I have attempted to fully incorporate. The remaining errors are entirely mine.

The Gene Gallegos Lectureship at UNM funded my earlier work on the Guatemalan peace process, especially police reform, and a one-year sabbatical provided by UNM released me from teaching duties and allowed me to spend time in New York.

My wife, Judy Bieber, and daughters, Ruth and Rosa, supported and inspired me throughout the project, put up with physical and sometimes mental absences, and kept me focused on the sovereign importance of getting it done. I am grateful for their patience and indulgence as I endeavored to get this story right.

—*William Stanley*

1 How to Play a Weak Hand

IN 1994 THE UNITED NATIONS stepped in to salvage stalled peace talks between the government of Guatemala and a group of Marxist revolutionaries who had been waging a sputtering insurgency since 1960. The revived peace talks eventually led to a settlement in late 1996. Almost two years before that final deal was reached, the United Nations took a chance and deployed a mission to monitor human rights in Guatemala—the United Nations Mission for the Verification of Human Rights and of Compliance with the Comprehensive Agreement on Human Rights in Guatemala (MINUGUA). The United Nations hoped that the mission would help improve human rights conditions enough for the rebels to feel safe putting down their arms. Once the final accords took effect, MINUGUA took over primary responsibility for verifying compliance with the full package of peace accords.[1] The mission would stay in Guatemala for a decade. When MINUGUA closed in 2004, it left behind a more consolidated democracy, better human rights conditions, and modest reforms to key institutions such as the judiciary, prosecutors, and police. Compared to the catastrophic outcomes of some other peacekeeping efforts in civil wars such as in Angola and Rwanda, Guatemala looks like a peacekeeping success story. Yet the results fell short of the United Nations' goals for "peacebuilding" in post–civil war societies (remediating the root causes of the conflict), and far short of the high-sounding goals laid out in the Guatemalan peace accords themselves (which in the view of one UN official amounted to turning "Guatemala into Switzerland").[2]

Guatemala was among the most unequal societies in a very unequal region. Its indigenous majority suffered from terrible economic, health, and educational disparities. Its economic elite exercised remarkable privileges and political powers, while resisting the formation of a working state. Its military had dominated political life for decades, killing over 100,000 non-combatants, and committing atrocities while its officer corps became

1

Map created by Chris Perry

increasingly corrupt and effectively immune from prosecution. Guatemala needed a makeover, and the peace accords superficially promised at least a significant down payment on the needed changes.

Unfortunately, three consecutive Guatemalan governments either failed or chose not to implement the majority of promised reforms. In the face of these failures, the United Nations used its verification mandate in an effort to uphold the norm that the government should comply with its commitments. MINUGUA pressured the government to do more by drafting critical reports that were published under the names of Secretary-General Boutros Boutros-Ghali and his successor Kofi Annan. It probably saved many lives by deterring human rights violations. Where possible the mission worked with government agencies to improve their performance, and it worked with grassroots groups to help them advocate more effectively for their own interests. At key moments, MINUGUA very likely prevented backsliding and even a possible democratic breakdown. But to a distressing extent, it verified and reported on a decade of governmental failure, including a perilous period during which organized crime appears to have controlled the state at the highest levels.

The United Nations' mission in Guatemala was the softest of soft peace-keeping. In contrast to the "black helicopter" imaginings of folks in Idaho, the United Nations is far from all-powerful, especially in peacekeeping operations. While under Chapter VII of the UN Charter, the Security Council can authorize one country to invade another if it is a threat to "international peace and security," in practice—even after the end of the Cold War—it has been difficult to gain the support of all five veto-wielding permanent members for peacekeeping actions that challenge sovereignty. Most UN peace-keeping operations involving countries with civil wars operate under carefully circumscribed mandates to monitor, report, advise, and attempt to protect civilians within strict rules of engagement. Where UN soldiers have been deployed, they have generally gone with the consent of the host government. For reasons explained in the next chapter, in Guatemala the United Nations had to settle for a General Assembly mandate for MINUGUA rather than a stronger Security Council mandate, with the very limited exception of the military observer component that monitored the rebels' rapid demobilization. There was no international coercion, nor even a hint of coercion: the United Nations got involved because the Guatemalan government and rebels invited it to, and maintained the observer mission for a decade because it was repeatedly invited to do so. The Security Council studiously avoided framing the United Nations' involvement as a matter of international peace and security. The United Nations was just there to help.

As anyone knows who has ever tried to help a recalcitrant person solve a deep problem, being a helper is not a strong bargaining position. What do you do when the intended beneficiary of your help rejects advice, reneges on promises, reverts to bad old patterns of behavior, complains about what you do, tells you to get lost, and then pleads for more help? More specifically, faced with such a person, about whom for some reason you continue to care, how do you maximize your leverage? Obviously the dynamics of interpersonal relations do not provide a valid model for understanding relations between an international organization and a sovereign state. Yet descriptively, the analogy seems to fit the interplay between the United Nations and Guatemala around the peace accords. The United Nations and its supportive member states continued to help Guatemala because, no matter how galling the conduct of the Guatemalan government, military, economic elite, or former rebels, the whole point was to create better conditions for the majority of Guatemalans and, to the extent possible, reduce the likelihood of future violent conflict. That concern for the Guatemalan majority created an asymmetry of motivation, in which the United Nations was generally more committed to implementing accords than the relatively narrow slice of Guatemalan society that had the constitutional political power to do so. The government and its constituents could assert sovereignty and ignore the United Nations' complaints, but such assertions lacked much normative legitimacy since the government was often defending practices that had helped fuel civil war in the first place. Because much of the Guatemalan public was poorly educated, uninformed about the accords, and politically terrorized after three decades of mayhem, the United Nations often found itself advocating for agreements that it understood to be in the best interests of a Guatemalan majority that was itself politically passive. It could not count on a groundswell of popular support to push the elites along, unless it found a way to trigger such a groundswell itself. In fact, in a shocking reversal early in the peace process, key provisions of the accords were *voted down* in a public referendum.

The Guatemalan accords were especially difficult for the United Nations to verify because they were both sweeping in scope and comparatively lacking in measurable commitments by either of the parties. The design of the accords was not the United Nations' idea. The earliest stages of the Guatemalan peace talks—before the United Nations began mediating and before the government even began talking directly with the rebels—involved a broad consultation with civil society groups including peasants, labor unions, cooperatives, businesses of various sizes, and so forth. The groups collectively generated a broad negotiating agenda that the government and the rebels agreed to adopt when direct talks got under way in 1991. The agenda included constitutional reforms; reform of the military; strengthening of civilian courts and prosecutors; indigenous cultural and linguistic rights; government tax policy; government services in education, housing, and health; agricultural extension; land availability, surveying, registration, and markets; labor rights; resettlement and development for refugees and displaced people; administration of elections; legal accountability for past acts of political violence; and reincorporation of the former rebels.[3]

This agenda accurately captured the range of things that needed to change for Guatemala to become a more functional, stable, and just society. If the opposing sides in the civil war had been powerful and coherent actors, they might have been able to cut a substantive deal and implement it. But the four consecutive governments that participated in the negotiations, as well as their rebel counterparts, were all weak. The first government faced two military coup attempts; the second carried out an "auto-coup" to seize dictatorial powers and was thrown out by civil society protests and international sanctions; the third was a provisional caretaker; and the fourth depended politically on support from the business community, which was not very interested in reforms that would create a functioning state that could collect taxes. None of these governments had the capacity to plan or carry out major changes. The rebels of the Guatemalan National Revolutionary Unity

(URNG) were weaker still: substantially defeated in the early 1980s, by the late 1990s they were a small movement that was more of a military nuisance than a serious threat to the state, and they faced a near lethal combination of eroded popular support, internal divisions, financial shortfalls, and erratic leadership. The combination of a sweeping agenda (generated by civil society) and weak national political actors resulted in final accords that were a mile wide and an inch deep, symbolically important as an expression of desires for a better country but short on concrete, measurable commitments to which anyone could be held accountable.

Though the United Nations drew a weak hand in Guatemala, it did have a few high cards. With offices around the country, it had better information about what was going on than any other institution, with the possible exception of Guatemalan military intelligence. It had a mandate to report on its human rights and other findings, and these reports had the potential to either improve or damage the government's international reputation. It had a mandate from the outset to help strengthen institutions of justice and human rights accountability, and this gave it some capacity to bargain with government agencies. It also had a mandate to communicate directly with the public about the peace accords and human rights. MINUGUA staff had expertise on how to take testimony, conduct investigations, manage legal cases, assess the impact of tax and other economic measures, manage and evaluate government programs, and write legislation. Government agencies needed this expertise, and this gave MINUGUA points of leverage within the state, even when the government as a whole was uncooperative. And while MINUGUA lacked the power to impose conditions on most international aid programs, its public reporting and behind-the-scenes lobbying could either help or hurt the government's prospects for major grants and loans.

The focus of this book is how the United Nations played the cards it was dealt, with secondary consideration of whether there are some hands the United Nations just should not play in the future. That is, given the powers the United Nations had in Guatemala, which strategies worked and which ones fell short? Were there ways that the mission's leverage could have been either strengthened or better used? In the historical chapters that follow, I look at the interactions between the United Nations and the Guatemalan parties as a bargaining process. Faced with recalcitrance on the part of the implementing governments, MINUGUA needed to concentrate its limited leverage on those issues where progress was either most likely or most important, and it needed to enhance its leverage whenever possible through savvy use of its mandate. As readers will see in the chapters that follow, the mission did not always do this. Rather than formulating a strategy that matched its goals to its capabilities, it generally spread its limited leverage across the full range of issues in the peace accords. The one issue it did focus on, increasing tax collections, was probably the single issue on which it was least possible to make progress because doing so went against the core interests of the most entrenched and powerful constituencies in the country. The mission was also prone to depending on the same kind of broad civil society consultation that produced the broad accords in the first place. MINUGUA's default "strategy" in the face of government noncompliance was to convene diverse civic groups and grope toward consensus, in the absence of any strategy to generate sufficient political power to get anything done.

In the wake of the various scandals that have affected other UN peace missions, it seems like a cheap shot to note that MINUGUA was not always well managed. But the mission's internal difficulties were significant and did interfere materially with its ability to make decisions and implement them. The core problems were unprofessional selection processes for high-level personnel, and an administration that was organizationally and culturally divorced from the substantive work of the mission. These problems were deeply rooted in the ways the United Nations does business and were not easily remedied.

To some extent, MINUGUA may have faced Mission Impossible. One conclusion this book draws is that the United Nations needs to find a way to give peacebuilding missions more capacity to impose political conditions on international aid. There are, of course, many institutional barriers to doing so, but the history of MINUGUA shows the potential futility of un-conditionally shoveling money toward governments that are (predictably) more interested in their own short-term political success than in solving their country's long-term structural problems.

▌ Outline of the Book

The conditions and choices facing the mission changed during its ten years in Guatemala. Moreover, each head of mission (HOM) brought a distinct analysis of the situation, a distinct leadership style, and distinct preferences. As a result, I have organized the chapters around the different HOMs, with one exception. Chapter 2 traces the negotiation process from its first stages of indirect talks to direct talks mediated by Archbishop Quezada, to the final stage of mediation by Jean Arnault (France) on behalf of the United Nations. Chapters 3 and 4 (jointly covering the period May 1994 through March 1997) overlap chronologically with the negotiations process described in Chapter 2. Since these were separate but related processes, they are treated as separate narratives here, with references in all three chapters to interactions between the negotiations and the mission. Chapter 3 addresses the initial deployment of MINUGUA as a human rights verification mission, under the leadership of Leonardo Franco (Argentina). During Franco's period, the mission established a reputation in Guatemala for evenhanded and authoritative assessments of human rights conditions. Chapter 4 traces nine months during which MINUGUA was headed by David Stephen (UK), who oversaw ongoing human rights verification while dealing with demands for on-the-ground mediation within Guatemala and preparing for the mission's future role as verifier of the full accords. Chapter 5 examines the challenging verification of the full accords, with MINUGUA under the leadership of Arnault, who became HOM and special representative of the Secretary-General (SRSG) in charge of MINUGUA after completing the negotiations.[4] Chapter 6 covers the work of MINUGUA under SRSG Gerd Merrem (Germany), who came out of retirement to lead the mission as it sought to maintain momentum in the face of numerous setbacks during the presidency of Alfonso Portillo. Chapter 7 covers the final stage of the mission, as SRSG Tom Koenigs (Germany) prepared the mission for departure, focusing on capacity building while helping to add stability during a sometimes violent election campaign and the transition to a new Guatemalan president, Oscar Berger. The concluding chapter reviews the choices that faced the mission, highlights the main lessons of Guatemala for civilian peacemaking and peacebuilding, and suggests how this challenging and partially successful experience can guide the United Nations and member states in the future.

Readers should bear in mind that the story of MINUGUA is not an action thriller. There were some suspenseful and physically dangerous moments during the mission, including kidnappings and hostage situations, close brushes with gunfire, and a tragic helicopter crash. However, this is mainly a story about principled diplomacy on behalf of peaceful resolution in the face of deep political differences. Much of the important work of the mission took the form of conversations with political figures in Guatemala; painstaking investigations into singular events as well as broad patterns of social, economic, and cultural equity; and carefully crafted statements and reports. The parsed language of these conversations and documents figures prominently in this account.

Readers will probably detect a tone of frustration and cynicism at times with regard to the conduct of Guatemalan political actors and state officials at all levels. Whereas this book is necessarily critical of some decisions and actions by the UN, it does find that MINUGUA and its staff, as well as key officials in New York, consistently worked with goodwill to promote peace and real democratization in Guatemala. The unavoidable truth is that, with some shining exceptions, many Guatemalans in positions of power did the opposite. Among those with a share of power in a highly unequal and violent society, altruism seems to be in short supply, while opportunism abounds. To paraphrase former US defense secretary Donald Rumsfeld, the United Nations must make peace with the national elites that exist, not the national elites it might want or wish to exist at a later time. Obviously much of this behavior was conditioned by institutions that made altruism difficult: consider, for example, the incentives facing a well-intentioned prosecutor of human rights cases whose life or family members are threatened by other state officials. The central challenge of peacebuilding is how to build national institutions that will secure future peace, while working through the preexisting institutions and the people accustomed to working within them. The institutions of the United Nations are themselves not above reproach, and I hope that my criticisms of Guatemalan institutions and actors herein are counterbalanced by frank assessments of internal changes needed in how the United Nations operates.

This book cannot tell the whole story of MINUGUA. Most of the research for this project took place after the mission had closed and depended on the United Nations' own files, interviews with key actors, and secondary sources. Because of the sources used, it tends to privilege a headquarters perspective (both the UN Secretariat and MINUGUA), and cannot fully capture the diverse experiences of MINUGUA field offices. My hope, however, is that the book, by highlighting key challenges, interactions, and decision points, captures the flavor of this extraordinary mission, the dedication of its staff and the tough choices that they faced, and some of the main lessons to be learned from their collective experience.

▮ Notes

1. With the assumption of its comprehensive verification mandate, the mission's name changed to the United Nations Verification Mission in Guatemala, with the same acronym.

2. Remark by Assistant Secretary-General Danilo Türk to incoming head of mission Tom Koenigs, "Note to the File: Meeting on Guatemala with Mr. Tom Köenigs and Mr. Gerd Merrem," Martha Doggett, June 7, 2002.

3. For an online collection of documents including all the Secretary-General's verification reports, human rights reports, various thematic reports, and related UN resolutions, see http://en.wikisource.org/wiki/Portal:United_Nations_Verification_Mission_in_Guatemala.

4. The United Nations did not appoint a special representative of the Secretary-General (a higher-status title than head of mission) until the final peace accords were signed. This reflected misgivings in the Department of Political Affairs and the Secretary-General's office regarding whether the process would actually go forward, especially in 1995.

2 | Negotiating the End of an Asymmetrical War

THE UNITED NATIONS became actively involved in the Guatemalan peace process late in the game. Negotiations had been going on for six years, and the dynamics of the talks, and important precedents, were already set before the United Nations began mediating. Two key features distinguished the Guatemalan negotiations process from others. First, the rebels were politically and militarily weak. Their main source of leverage was their willingness and ability to continue the fighting indefinitely. Seldom has a civil war between two such unequal forces been settled by negotiation. Second, civil society groups were extensively involved, especially during early stages when the government would not meet directly with the rebels. Special forums were set up for the purpose of generating consensus views on what political and economic reforms were needed. These forums prompted healthy debate and participation. Their emphasis on consensus, however, meant that, in the language of political science game theory, there were many "veto players" whose views needed to be accommodated.[1] The result was an exhaustively comprehensive negotiating agenda whose scope greatly exceeded the political leverage available to actually implement change. Because the civil society–influenced agenda was so broad, the URNG was never in a position to strategically focus its very limited political resources on one issue—say, the rule of law or demilitarization—and instead had to spread it over all possible issues of concern to civil society. Not only was the agenda very broad, but also the demands of civil society groups (as well as of factions within the URNG) were quite radical and out of step with political reality. This radicalism was driven by frustration, by the isolation of civil society groups from practical politics, and by a sense that decades of death and sacrifice needed to be morally counterbalanced by significant accomplishments at the bargaining table. Thus the URNG as a negotiating party was caught between its very limited politico-military leverage and a need to satisfy potential constituencies that wanted major

9

changes. The only way to satisfy these contradictory forces was to gravitate toward comprehensiveness in the negotiations, regardless of political realism.

The United Nations inherited this dynamic when it assumed the role of mediator in 1994. Just as the URNG could not focus its energies on key issues during the talks, the breadth of the accords later entrapped the United Nations as verifier into a process in which it had to address a wide range of issues and was seldom able to concentrate its own limited political resources on priority concerns.

This chapter traces the peace process. It begins with a brief history of the civil war itself, and then turns to the early efforts at indirect negotiations, direct talks, UN-mediated talks, and the final settlement. It provides a fairly detailed description of the content of each of the accords, which is essential for understanding the later challenges of verification. Events in this chapter (from mid-1994 through early 1997) coincide with the human rights verification phase of MINUGUA described in Chapters 3 and 4.

■ Effects of Asymmetrical Warfare

By the time peace talks began, the URNG—which had once posed a serious threat to the state—could no longer muster the force to carry out major, sustained actions against the Guatemalan military. The rebels could at most hope to disrupt some regions. The rebels' political support base had atrophied in much of the country, although they retained pockets of intensely loyal supporters, and had strong influence within some civil society organizations. Despite these setbacks, the URNG was not defeated. Because its forces were so small, and because it was no longer attempting to maintain a presence nationwide, the URNG's logistical needs were modest. It could continue to fight almost indefinitely. Its core members, having sacrificed so much already, were reluctant to compromise their goals and willing to keep fighting.

The government was reluctant to make concrete concessions to a weak enemy and had little sense of urgency. Social elites and the army viewed the URNG as defeated, thus increasing the domestic political costs to Guatemalan governments for even holding talks with the URNG. Foreign countries paid comparatively little attention to the Guatemalan conflict because it was unlikely to spill over into neighboring countries. By the latter years of the conflict, relatively few members of the Guatemalan public were directly affected by fighting that was largely confined to specific areas of the country and quite intermittent. In a sample survey conducted in 1996, for example, 85 percent of respondents said that neither they nor a family member had suffered as a result of the war.[2]

Under these circumstances, the war, however small in scale, could continue for many more years. Besides interfering with Guatemala's ability to attract investment and tourists, ongoing fighting would provide the military with an excuse to dominate society and political life. Military repression distorted and suppressed civil society. The military often viewed civil society groups as subversives and treated them accordingly. For years, the military had pursued a policy of suppressing indigenous cultures, promoting a homogeneous Hispanic or "Ladino" culture.[3] The army appointed "military commissioners" who collected intelligence and threatened, beat, and in some cases murdered suspected subversives. Holders of military commissioner ID cards could get away with almost anything, and could eliminate commercial or personal rivals simply by making unfounded accusations of involvement in subversion. The army organized almost a million men in rural communities into "voluntary" Community Self-Defense Patrols (Patrullas de Autodefensa Civil [PACs]) that forced all able-bodied men from communities to report to the army, receive antiquated weapons, and patrol the surrounding areas.[4]

As a military force, the PACs were ineffectual and the URNG rebels usually just avoided contact with them, but they were a powerful mechanism of social control and surveillance. Through the PACs, the army in several instances also forced indigenous peasants to murder their neighbors, thereby dividing communities against one another and making the patrollers complicit in the army's mass murder. Effectively protected from arrest and prosecution, some PAC members—and many of the military commissioners—indulged in crime with impunity, including kidnapping, rape, and murder.

Members of civilian political parties were subject to threats and violence. Economic elites used the war as a pretext to call for state violence against labor organizers, whom they treated as subversives. The military was able to call for a disproportionate share of the national budget, while the civilian state—never well developed—atrophied and fell far short of the capacity needed to provide education, health services, justice, support for agricultural and industrial development, or basic infrastructure. Without an end to the war, Guatemala would have little chance of deepening its incipient democracy, developing economically, or achieving greater social justice.[5]

The Guatemalan peace process was limited from the outset by the weakness of Guatemalan political actors, as well as the inherited social and institutional context. Yet the involvement of the United Nations, first as an observer to the talks, and later as mediator and verifier of the accords, also shaped what domestic actors chose—and were able—to do. UN involvement prevented backsliding at crucial moments, and helped to bridge deep political and ideological gaps. By the final stages of the negotiations in 1996, the parties were able to move rapidly toward settlement and established confidence-building measures of their own—such as direct military contacts inside of Guatemala—that sometimes went beyond what the United Nations was attempting or willing to arrange. UN mediation and technical assistance helped shape peace agreements that, if fully implemented, would have corrected many of the key flaws in Guatemala's politics, state institutions, economy, and social structure.

Stepping into the Guatemalan crisis brought political risks for the United Nations. By the mid-1990s, the United Nations had moved toward a doctrine of peacebuilding that involved addressing root causes of conflict once the fighting stopped.[6] In Guatemala, the causes of conflict were plain enough, but powerful figures within the military as well as the civilian aristocracy were unwilling to carry out any significant institutional or economic change. There needed to be *some* organized domestic counterweight to these forces of stasis. Despite its military and political weakness, the URNG was the only actor capable of playing this role in the near term. During the negotiations, the United Nations defended the URNG's central role against efforts to marginalize it, and against charges by conservative elites (and even at one point the government's chief negotiator) that the rebels were illegitimate and irrelevant. This, in turn, brought frequent accusations from the far right in Guatemala that the United Nations (along with the Catholic Church, many academics, portions of the national press corps, human rights organizations, and so forth) was a stalking horse for the URNG. This perception of the United Nations as an ally of the left—simply because of its support for substantive negotiations with the URNG and implementation of substantive reforms—shadowed it throughout its involvement in Guatemala.

▊ A Legacy of Social Inequality

Guatemala carried a heavy burden of social inequalities, racial and ethnic divisions, and authoritarian institutions that, with no exaggeration, were traceable back to Spanish colonialism and the early years of Guatemalan independence. Spanish colonial administration established elaborate mechanisms for extracting labor services and material tribute from indigenous communities, while the Catholic Church sought to regulate their private and spiritual lives. Along with control came norms of state and Church responsibility for the welfare of indigenous people. After Central America broke away from Spain, however, even these dubious protections eroded, creating perilous conditions for indigenous peoples. Under liberal reforms begun in the 1870s, new laws expropriated and privatized indigenous lands in the western piedmont for the purposes of coffee cultivation. Draconian labor laws, enforced by newly expanded military and police forces and supplemented by mechanisms of debt peonage, forced indigenous people to work on the new coffee farms, and later on coastal sugar, banana, and cotton plantations.

The result was a society that by the early twentieth century suffered the triple curses of segregation and discrimination against indigenous peoples (who made up at least half of the population); an overgrown military and internal security apparatus; and highly concentrated land ownership that left most of the population landless or land poor, while oligarchic families underutilized their vast holdings. After decades of alternating oligarchic rule and military dictatorship, a transition to democracy took place in 1944, part of a region-wide political opening in the wake of World War II. A second civilian government was elected in 1950 under President Jacobo Arbenz. Advised by members of the communist Guatemalan Workers Party (PGT), Arbenz attempted a massive land reform that, had it remained in place, would have constituted a significant step toward a more equitable society. However, Arbenz was overthrown in 1954 by the US Central Intelligence Agency (CIA), operating in collaboration with disloyal sectors of the army.[7] The United States installed a military regime that remained in de facto power for more than thirty years. US security assistance in the 1960s deepened the repressive capacity of the Guatemalan police state, while the reformism of the Alliance for Progress years made barely a dent in the country's economic elitism.

Three Decades of Civil War

With this background, it was not surprising that civil war broke out in Guatemala in the 1960s. In an ironic legacy of the US-led 1954 coup, the catalyst for the civil war was nationalist resentment against gringo domination. The first shots of the war were fired on November 13, 1960, as some 120 junior officers and 3,000 enlisted men seized army bases in the eastern part of Guatemala and demanded the resignation of military president Miguel Ydígoras Fuentes. The rebels were offended that Ydígoras had allowed the United States to train Cuban agents for the planned Bay of Pigs operation on Guatemalan soil. Yet US power prevailed in 1960 once again: B-26 bombers owned and operated by the CIA flew from Honduran and Guatemalan bases and bombed the rebels into submission.

Survivors of the 1960s mutiny fled the country, regrouped in Honduras, and returned in 1962 to begin an insurgency under the rubric Revolutionary Movement of November 13, or MR-13. While never very successful militarily, the MR-13 for a time galvanized popular opposition to the military regime, and helped prompt formation of other, more ideologically motivated rebel groups. The PGT formed an insurgent group called the Revolutionary Armed Forces (FAR). FAR and MR-13 merged and waged a small insurgency centered in the eastern province Zacapa.

Once again, US power trumped revolutionary ambitions: alarmed by the FAR rebellion in the wake of the Cuban revolution, the United States deployed special forces advisers to train and reinforce the government's counterinsurgency apparatus. This included the formation of a paramilitary network of intelligence gatherers and enforcers who multiplied the strength of the government's regular army. Major landowners in the east enthusiastically supported this system, and were deputized by the state to suppress subversion, which often equated to killing anyone with an inclination to organize farm workers. Government forces and paramilitaries killed some eight thousand civilians in and around Zacapa in the mid-1960s in pursuit of a few hundred FAR combatants. By the late 1960s, the FAR was defeated, splintered, and driven out of the country.[8]

Survivors of this failed attempt shifted their focus from the Spanish-speaking eastern departments to the more expansive, remote, and mostly indigenous western highlands and north. Rebel operatives learned indigenous languages and began organizing from the ground up so as to have a more thoroughly integrated civilian support base. They shifted away from the Ché Guevara–style *foco* (focal point) strategy of the early days, which had emphasized showy military operations designed to inspire popular revolt, toward a more careful, political approach based on organizing and ideological training. Two new groups emerged to supplement the FAR: the Organization of the People in Arms (ORPA) operated in the western highlands, in the capital city, and along the Pacific coast; and the Guerrilla Army of the Poor (EGP) operated in the central highlands, in the "northern transversal strip" near the border with Mexico, and in the remote province of Petén in the northeast. Some urban cells began armed operations again in the early 1970s, but the rural insurgency did not resume in earnest until the late 1970s after several years of preparation.

By this point, the United States had pulled back from its very active involvement in building up Guatemalan counterinsurgency forces, but the apparatus it left behind was more than capable of suppressing internal challenges. In 1977, the Guatemalan government unilaterally severed its military aid ties to the United States in response to President Jimmy Carter's human rights policies. This freed the Guatemalan state to use as much violence as it wished, without regard to the sensibilities in Washington. Small amounts of US military assistance trickled back in during the 1980s under "counterterrorism" waivers that allowed US agencies to overlook human rights problems. The CIA maintained ties in the Guatemalan military. The state of Israel stepped in as provider of small arms and technical advice.[9]

It is difficult to overstate the extent of military domination of Guatemalan government and society by the late 1970s. Officers controlled vast land holdings in the north, as well as key positions in the state bureaucracy and state-controlled companies. Military bases around the country maintained paramilitary forces including "military commissioners," PACs, and other intelligence networks. Army special forces troops known as Kaibiles were trained in counterinsurgency methods and steeped in an ideology that categorized much of the civilian population as the enemy. The military intelligence service was devoted almost entirely to identifying and killing regime opponents. Even local and regional governments were dominated by the military. The military had its own munitions factory and its own financial institutions. This entire apparatus was, at the same time, spectacularly corrupt. The same impunity from prosecution deemed necessary for state forces to carry out violent counterinsurgency opened the door to criminality on a massive scale and at all levels of government.

As the new, highlands-based insurgency got under way, the army ramped up a campaign of terror. Security forces identified and swept up rebel safe houses in the cities, with the help of US, Israeli, and Argentine intelligence advice.[10] Army forces swept through rural communities where rebels were operating and killed tens of thousands. Troops forced indigenous villagers to murder their neighbors and to witness horrendous acts. The military destroyed and depopulated some 440 villages, and the death toll has been estimated (using multiple-source estimation techniques) at 132,000, with most of the deaths occurring between 1978 and 1983.[11] Hundreds of villages were at least temporarily abandoned (between 70 and 80 percent in the Ixil highland area). Survivors were herded into multiethnic resettlement camps under intense military scrutiny, in an effort to break down indigenous cultures and loyalties. The UN-sponsored Commission for Historical Clarification (the Guatemalan truth commission) would later characterize the army's campaign as genocide.[12]

The rebels were once again caught unprepared by the strength of the state's reaction. The three main rebel groups (FAR, ORPA, and EGP) did not form a unified command until 1982. In part because they had not previously unified, and in part because of logistical challenges, the three groups received only tepid Socialist Bloc support through Cuba and Nicaragua. This was in contrast to the Farabundo Martí National Liberation Front (FMLN) in neighboring El Salvador, which received massive flows of weapons, help with secure communications equipment and techniques, and highly specialized training for attacks against military bases and economic targets.[13] Lacking much outside assistance, the Guatemalan insurgents were forced onto the defensive by the government's onslaught. Unable to protect their civilian supporters, they rapidly lost the organized social base they had spent years constructing. By the time the URNG unified, it was already in serious trouble. Although the group was able to continue the fight (in contrast to the FAR's defeat in the 1960s), it was never able to muster decisive force against the state. After the pogroms of the early 1980s, revolutionary victory of the kind achieved by the Sandinistas in Nicaragua was out of reach, and the URNG lacked the military leverage available to the Salvadoran FMLN as it began peace talks in 1990.

The onslaught of government violence also decimated organized civil society. Remnants of the PGT and of various peasant organizations that had supported the 1952 land reform never abandoned the idea of working through the state to achieve greater social equity. Through the 1950s and early 1960s, they sought to build on what political space was (sporadically) available. However, the repressive apparatus systematically eradicated most of the surviving Arbenz supporters and forced prodemocratic people on the left toward armed struggle.[14] In the center of the political spectrum, the Christian Democratic Party (DCG) gained representation in the national Congress and in municipal offices in the 1960s. Yet the DCG paid a terrible price, as security forces murdered hundreds of its members. State repression systematically eliminated community members with the skills and initiative to lead. By the mid-1980s, Guatemala's civil society was terrorized and atomized. Very few people participated in public organizations of any kind, focusing instead on family life and economic survival.

■ The Path to Settlement

Conditions for a negotiated settlement began to fall into place in the mid-1980s. With the URNG no longer an imminent threat to the state, the Guatemalan armed forces took a step back from direct control over government. A group of officers around General Héctor Alejandro Gramajo favored a tightly controlled transition to civilian rule. This faction argued that there needed to be political safety valves—channels for popular participation in governance—in the absence of which Guatemala would likely face more violence and instability. This was no democratic vision: on the contrary, the army simply wanted, for its own reasons, to have civilian leaders and parties run interference with the general public, so that the army as an institution would not be subject to the wear and tear of daily governance.[15]

A controlled transition began with an election in 1984 for a Constituent Assembly that would write a new constitution. Then an election was held in 1985 that brought to office in January 1986 a civilian president, Vinicio Cerezo from the DCG, as well as a new Congress in which the DCG held a narrow majority. With civilians ostensibly in power, the army kept its tentacles wrapped closely around civilian authorities. A military staff group called the Presidential General Staff (Estado Mayor Presidencial [EMP]) oversaw daily operations of the presidential house, including agenda setting, briefings of the president, and presidential security. While managing—and closely controlling—the civilian presidency, the EMP also ran a domestic spying organization called The Archive (El Archivo). The Archive staff tortured suspects and informants, operated one of the most active death squads in the country, and coordinated the activities of other death squads.[16]

Before his inauguration, Cerezo made overtures to the URNG through contacts in Costa Rica. He signaled that he would like to meet formally, but that the military and US president Ronald Reagan would be opposed. Indirect contacts continued in Madrid between URNG representatives and Guatemala's ambassador to Spain, and later Cerezo offered (through his foreign minister) to meet with rebel commanders in Mexico.[17] That meeting didn't happen, but the offer prompted the URNG to propose conditions for future talks. The rebel *comandancia* declared that if the government were serious, it would restructure the armed forces; purge the high command of the army and police; eliminate paramilitary groups; punish state personnel responsible for killings, torture, and disappearances; dissolve the PACs; and eliminate oppressive resettlement camps.[18] This was a somewhat ridiculous set of conditions to impose prior to even opening discussions. Because all of these measures would directly affect the military, they were also among the things that were impossible for the Cerezo government to do. In what would become a refrain for Guatemalan governments in the next few years, Cerezo responded that he would be happy to talk to the URNG as soon as they put down their arms.

After this inauspicious start, however, more concrete steps toward peace took place during 1987. First, the URNG leaders backed away from their a priori demands for military reform and proposed a more modest set of conditions that would humanize the war and reduce civilian casualties. They called for a conversation aimed at forming "the greatest and broadest alliance in our history . . . with the objective of shaping an advanced democracy that is popular and independent . . . a new historical commitment."[19] This was the first expression of a view that subsequent Guatemalan governments came to at least partially accept: that the country needed a new social pact that would address the needs of much of the population and form the basis for social peace. It was a view that did not necessarily insist upon revolutionary change in Marxist/Leninist terms, and thus seemed to open the way to a compromise. Reaching agreement on the specific terms of that new social compact would take several more years, and even that would be an elite pact with little societal backing.

The main accomplishment in 1987 was the signing by five Central American presidents of a document entitled Procedure for Establishing a Firm and Lasting Peace in Central America, also known as the Esquipulas II agreement. This pact, in which Costa Rican president Oscar Arias played a leading role, was an effort by the Central American states to reassert control over their own territories. Central America faced ongoing US military intervention in support of Nicaraguan counterrevolutionaries (contras) operating from Honduras, as well as ongoing east bloc assistance to insurgents in El Salvador. Regional powers Mexico, Venezuela, Panama, and Colombia had earlier led the so-called Contadora effort to demilitarize Central America.[20] However, the Contadora effort focused on halting outside arms flows and military aid to the region, and thus ultimately depended—futilely—on cooperation from the United States, Cuba, and the Soviet Union.

President Arias took a different tack that exploited US prodemocracy rhetoric. Instead of making demands of the superpowers, the Central American states would settle their own internal differences through democratic means. Each country was to form a National Reconciliation Commission that would convene a national dialogue and oversee a transition to full democracy. Alienated sectors would be brought back into the fold. Each country would provide amnesty for former insurgents, facilitate the return of refugees, and hold free elections as a means of settling internal conflicts. The plan also called on Central American states to prevent the use of their national territories by neighboring insurgencies, and to stop assisting irregular forces. Finally, the agreement called for international verification.[21]

Esquipulas II brought the United Nations into Central America in a peacemaking role. The United Nations deployed an observer mission, ONUCA (United Nations Observer Group in Central America), to monitor international arms shipments; it participated in a joint UN/Organization of American States (OAS) operation to oversee the demobilization of Nicaraguan contra forces under the name International Verification and Assistance Commission (CIAV); and it deployed, for the first time in UN history, a mission to monitor conditions for, and the conduct of, an election in a sovereign state—the United Nations Observer for the Verification of Elections in Nicaragua (ONUVEN), which monitored the 1990 elections.

▌ Oslo, March 1990

Despite the framework provided by Esquipulas II, the Cerezo government could not hold direct peace talks with the URNG and expect to survive. In 1989, Cerezo weathered two coup attempts led by army officers who were opposed—among other complaints—to any compromise with the URNG. These factions felt that the army had already won the war, and were unwilling to see the government give anything away at the negotiating table. Although the plotters were suppressed, their rebellions sent a clear warning to Cerezo not to go too far. Cerezo conspicuously wore a sidearm to work each day, and declared he would shoot the army officer who came to inform him of a coup.[22]

Because of these constraints, the National Reconciliation Commission (CNR) emerged to play a vital role.[23] The Guatemalan CNR was composed of a Guatemalan bishop, Rodolfo Quezada y Toruño; Vice President Roberto Carpio Nicolle; Jorge Serrano Elías, head of the Solidarity Action Movement (MAS); and journalist Teresa Bolaños de Zarco. Quezada was elected president of the CNR. The CNR convened a "Grand National Dialogue," which involved fifteen different commissions within which various sectors of Guatemalan society began discussions about what a reformed society ought to look like. From the point of view of the army, these indirect discussions were tolerable and "constitutional": conversely, direct talks would amount to recognition of an illegal terrorist group, and the army arrogated to itself the authority to judge such negotiations unconstitutional and perhaps treasonous.[24]

Unfortunately, the main business and growers' associations boycotted these talks, claiming that most of the civil society groups were in the service of the URNG and dismissing these groups' legitimacy. To some extent, the business groups had a point, as the URNG did have significant influence among some of the grassroots associations, but the boycott prevented frank dialogue between those groups and business interests—a dialogue that could have been salutary for both.

The first important accomplishment of the CNR-led process was the Oslo Agreement, the subtitle of which was Basic Agreement for the Search for Peace Through Political Means, signed in March 1990 by the CNR (not the government) and the URNG. The Oslo Agreement called upon Quezada to serve as "conciliator," empowered to convene the parties and mediate between them.[25] In a first step toward UN involvement in the nascent peace process, it also called upon the Secretary-General of the United Nations to observe the talks. The Secretary-General accepted and sent Francesc Vendrell (Spain) as his representative. Conciliator Quezada hosted a meeting of the URNG with the political parties then represented in the Guatemalan Congress, as well as a series of meetings between the URNG and various sectors of Guatemalan society, including representatives of the leading business associations, small businesses, churches, labor unions, cooperatives, academics, and professionals. Mayan groups, who make up a majority of the Guatemalan population, were conspicuously underrepresented in the Oslo process. Some Mayans participated through the "popular organizations" group, but the major indigenous groups such as the Coordination of Mayan Peoples' Organizations (COPMAGUA) were not directly included, a major oversight.

The conversations held under the Oslo process varied in their results, from a complete failure (the Ottawa meetings between the URNG and business groups) to a substantive endorsement of the URNG's pursuit of democracy, justice, human rights, and socioeconomic equity (the Metepec, Mexico meetings with popular sector groups). The overall effect of the Oslo process was to establish the principle that civil society must have input into any subsequent negotiating process, while also highlighting the tendency of such consensus-building efforts to generate very expansive proposals.

■ Direct Talks

Following his brief service on the CNR, Jorge Serrano Elías took office in January 1991 as the first elected civilian president to succeed another since the inauguration of Jacobo Arbenz in 1951. Serrano used his inaugural address to propose a renewed process of negotiations toward "total peace." He called for peace that was not "just a truce," but rather a comprehensive peace that would remove the original causes of war. The URNG greeted this overture with increased military activity.[26] In response, the government fell back on the refrain that the URNG must disarm prior to any direct talks.

Back-channel communications took place, however, and in April Serrano agreed to discuss any topic without preconditions, issuing the Initiative for Total Peace, which, though brief and vague, laid out a broad agenda including increased social and economic equity, reinforced rule of law, and deepened democracy. The army, which had blocked direct talks during Cerezo's government, initially gave the more conservative Serrano greater latitude.[27] Serrano formed the Presidential Peace Commission (COPAZ) consisting initially of five civilian officials and five army officers (three of whom were thought to favor a negotiated settlement), and sent them to meet with the URNG in Mexico at the end of April 1991.[28] A key appointment to the government's peace commission was Serrano's personal adviser and friend Amilcar Burgós, who had been a student leader and a member of the DCG in the 1960s. Burgós had some sympathy with the social justice concerns of the left. He played a key role in drafting the Agreement on the Procedure for the Search for Peace by Political Means (referred to as the Mexico Agreement), signed on April 26, 1991, in which the parties committed to negotiate without interruption until a final accord was reached, to maintain the secrecy of the negotiations, and to send delegations with authority to make decisions.[29] Under the agreement, the conciliator would convene direct and indirect negotiations, serve as depository of documents produced during the negotiations, designate his own advisers, and call recesses as needed.

The most significant aspect of the Mexico Agreement was its incorporation of an agenda much broader than that laid out in the Esquipulas II framework: in addition to questions around the demobilization and reincorporation of the URNG, the parties agreed to take up an ambitious, substantive agenda that was heavily influenced by the civil society–driven Oslo process. The eleven-point agenda was as follows: democratization and human rights; strengthening of civilian power and the role of the armed forces in a democratic society; the identity and rights of indigenous peoples; constitutional reforms and the electoral regime; socioeconomic issues; access to land and rural development; resettlement of refugees and displaced people; reincorporation of the URNG into the political life of the country; arrangement for a definitive ceasefire; timetable for implementation, compliance, and verification of the agreements; and final signing of a "firm and lasting peace." With minor word changes, these agenda points defined the content of the accords that would be negotiated over the following five years and eight months.

The Mexico Agreement was followed quickly by an agreement on democratic principles signed at Queretaro, Mexico, on July 25, 1991, which called for "the pre-eminence of civil society, the development of democratic institutions; . . . the permanent elimination of political repression, electoral fraud and coercion, military abuses and pressures, and anti-democratic, destabilizing actions; . . . [and] subordination of the role of the armed forces to civilian authority."[30]

This precedent-setting launch gave way to disappointment over the next two years. Through thirteen rounds of direct talks, the government and the URNG sparred about a handful of central issues. Human rights were the first item on the agenda, and the URNG had a series of demands that the government was unwilling to consider. The rebels wanted a truth commission to investigate past crimes; they wanted the army to be purged and dramatically reduced in size; and they wanted the PACs demobilized. The government initially rejected all of these positions, and fell back on the refrain that since Guatemala was now a democracy, the URNG could simply put down their arms and work for their goals through the existing constitutional order. Serrano's posture became a combination of intransigence and impatience, as if he expected the URNG to go along with whatever he proposed and viewed them as illegitimate if they did not. Since the legitimacy of the Guatemalan state (and thus the legitimacy of taking arms against it) was the crux of the matter, this self-serving framing did not motivate the URNG to make concessions. For their part, the rebels still viewed the talks largely as a tactic to buy time and delegitimate the government, rather than as a serious way of achieving some of their goals.[31]

During 1991, 1992, and early 1993, the international community applied increased pressures on Serrano to improve human rights conditions. The United Nations Human Rights Commission and its independent expert, Christian Tomuschat, reported severe human rights abuses and asked the government to abolish the PACs. The US group Human Rights Watch issued a report on the role of the EMP in coordinating and carrying out systematic human rights violations, including murder, disappearance, unlawful imprisonment, and torture. The Inter-American Commission on Human Rights (CIDH) of the OAS sent an investigative delegation to Guatemala to look into the imprisonment of an EGP militant.[32] Guatemala's own human rights counsel, Ramiro de León Carpio, condemned state forces as the primary violators of human rights and criticized them for failing to respond to complaints.[33]

The United States and the European Union (EU) both issued travel advisories that would hurt tourism. An EU parliamentary delegation proposed new human rights conditions on trade and aid programs. In March 1992, the consultative group of main international aid donors to Guatemala called on Serrano to demonstrate progress on human rights and the negotiations.[34]

There were counterpressures from within the armed forces, as well as from conservative civilian circles. Someone began to set off bombs targeting civilians in Guatemala City. The government accused the URNG of responsibility, but the pattern, frequency, and easy access to targets in the capital city were more consistent with the resources and priorities of the extreme right within the military. Many observers at the time assumed that right-wingers were using the bombings to frighten the public, and to suggest that the URNG was more capable in the capital city than it really was. A group calling itself the Officers of the Army issued death threats and bombed offices of the DCG and the Democratic National Union (UDN) after party officials met independently with the URNG in Mexico to discuss constitutional reforms.[35]

Rumors about possible coups d'état circulated, and senior army officials made statements that signaled their intent to veto any compromise with the URNG. In May 1992, defense minister José Domingo García Samayoa said the army was not prepared to dissolve the PACs and stated, "what we need is reinforcement of the army, not reduction. . . . The Guatemalan Army is the only [institution] for getting serious projects done in the country."[36] In January 1993, an army spokesman called the URNG's demands "risible."[37]

The government and the URNG jockeyed over the mediation process itself in ways that generated confusion. Both sides called for a greater role for the UN.[38] In late May 1992, when the government suddenly agreed to a proposed human rights agreement, the URNG backed away from it. The proposal provided for a truth commission and immediate UN verification. Although immediate UN human rights verification would have been highly favorable to the URNG, the rebels nonetheless rejected this out of hand, in the process subjecting themselves to considerable criticism in the media.[39]

Despite all the talk from both sides about expanding the United Nations' role, when UN observer Vendrell helped draft elements of a proposed human rights agreement and assisted Quezada with shuttle diplomacy, the government charged that Vendrell had overstepped his observer role and asked the United Nations to remove him.[40] Vendrell was recalled.[41] Serrano then optimistically asked UN Secretary-General Boutros Boutros-Ghali to replace Vendrell with a very senior official, "to give greater seriousness and responsibility to the process."[42] Boutros-Ghali instead appointed a then comparatively junior desk officer from the Department of Political Affairs, Jean Arnault.[43]

Arnault stepped in as the UN observer at a dark moment in the negotiating process. Besides the signals of resistance from the army, the main private sector organizations in the country, including the leading private sector association, the Coordinating Committee of Associations for Agriculture, Commerce, Industry, and Finance (CACIF), rejected negotiations with the

URNG on the grounds that it was an illegal group. After the thirteenth round of direct talks, Serrano's secretary of the presidency (and head negotiator) Manuel Conde Orellana declared that "the government will seek to crush the URNG militarily: President Serrano cannot give any more."[44]

■ Serrano's Coup d'État

Ironically, after wrapping his government in constitutionality and adherence to law, and demanding self-righteously that the URNG lay down arms and join the legal order, Serrano proceeded three weeks later to completely discard the constitution. On May 25, 1993, facing possible indictment for "illicit enrichment," Serrano issued an executive decree (Temporary Norms of Government) closing Congress, the Constitutional Court, and the Supreme Judicial Court, and suspending essentially all aspects of the constitution relating to civil liberties or constraints on executive authority.[45] The army, internally split and aware of the political risks of Serrano's move, issued a tepid statement of obedience to the commander in chief. Apparently, the constitutional scruples that earlier justified army rejection of talks with the URNG did not extend to blocking a flagrantly unconstitutional seizure of power by the executive. Army forbearance was not enough, however, and Serrano's position quickly eroded.

Serrano's self-coup (*autogolpe*) triggered massive political resistance. Remarkably, CACIF joined with labor, popular organizations, and the political parties in calling for Serrano's removal. Elite sectors—that had historically supported or at least tolerated coups—bought full-page ads in newspapers, as well as airtime on television and radio, to condemn the coup. The daily newspaper *Siglo XXI* (*21st Century*) published a special issue *Siglo XIV* (*14th Century*) to protest censorship. Grassroots organizations demonstrated against Serrano, and circulated an open letter calling for his resignation. The Catholic Episcopal Conference condemned Serrano, as did the government human rights ombudsman. An unprecedented cross-class alliance formed under the name National Consensus Body (Instancia Nacional de Consenso [INC]), with business organizations providing active leadership. International pressures came into play as well. The United States suspended economic assistance, and the OAS convened under the terms of the Santiago Accord to condemn the suspension of democratic governance.

The "dissolved" Constitutional Court met in defiance of Serrano's order, and issued a ruling that Serrano had acted outside the constitution. The Constitutional Court called on the ministers of defense and governance to enforce its order. This got the army off the hook for having initially tolerated the coup since they could now help remove him in response to a court order. The Supreme Judicial Court then issued a statement that Serrano's actions were potentially criminal.[46] Out of options, Serrano resigned on June 1, one week after his coup. Vice President Gustavo Espina Salguero briefly tried to succeed Serrano, but he faced overwhelming opposition. On June 2, 1993, the attorney general indicted both Serrano and Espina on multiple charges. Serrano fled to Panama, where he was able to evade repeated attempts to extradite him.[47]

Under constitutional provisions, Congress was required to elect an interim president to serve out the remainder of Serrano's term. The INC produced a list of three candidates, and after five days of intense negotiations, Congress selected former human rights counsel Ramiro de León Carpio. De León had strong support from grassroots organizations that viewed him as having acted courageously in condemning the army's human rights record. Modernizing elements of both the private sector and the army supported him because he had a favorable international reputation and might be able to restore some measure of Guatemala's international image. Despite this broad support, de León did not belong to a political party and would face great difficulty in getting legislation passed by Congress, where the parties would inevitably begin positioning themselves for the next round of elections.

■ The United Nations "Moderates": A New Phase of Direct Talks

The failure of the Serrano coup and the installation of de León signaled a change in Guatemalan politics. Although the INC lasted only a few months, the fact that business and popular sectors had gotten together to defend democracy opened up new possibilities. While authoritarian impulses and practices persisted, somehow democratic norms had gained a toehold in Guatemala. As the peace process resumed, for the first time both sides began to take it seriously, rather than using it as a tactic en route to an imagined military victory.

Within a month of de León's inauguration he made an overture to the URNG to reopen talks. This plan, however, drafted by the new head of the government negotiating team, Héctor Rosada, proposed to segment the talks so that the government would not have to discuss substantive issues with the URNG. A commission of the OAS or the United Nations would broker an end to the armed conflict, focusing narrowly on demobilizing and reintegrating the URNG (the Esquipulas II agenda). Negotiating all the substantive issues previously laid out in the Mexico Agreement would be shifted to a Permanent Forum for Peace, functionally replacing the CNR and still under the leadership of Quezada. The Permanent Forum would convene a broad national dialogue, in which representatives of the URNG could participate only as one "sector" among many.[48]

Rosada's proposal sought to diminish the standing of the URNG. He did not think that the organization was entitled to special status simply by virtue of having taken up arms, and felt that Serrano had given the URNG too prominent a role in the peace talks given its military weakness.[49] Of course Rosada was right that the URNG lacked the military capacity and social base to negotiate with much authority. Yet the URNG did have the capacity to keep fighting, and it had a small but dedicated social base. Attempting to ignore these facts was unlikely to lead to peace. Moreover, Rosada's proposal, however justified in raw power terms, reneged on the Mexico Accord, in which the previous government had agreed to negotiate substantive issues with the URNG. If prior commitments of state could be tossed out, what was the point of negotiating further, especially with an interim government?

In practice, the Rosada Plan was stillborn. The URNG strenuously opposed being marginalized from substantive discussions. The government presented the plan before the UN General Assembly, where it was received coolly. Various members of the diplomatic community told Rosada and the president that the reaffirmation of democracy after Serrano's coup created a key moment of opportunity that must be seized, and this implied taking the URNG's perspective seriously. Diplomats recommended a process with an active, impartial, non-Guatemalan mediator with authority to propose solutions, and early agreement on human rights protections and verification.[50]

While these discussions were under way, Quezada sought to jump-start the talks by proposing that the parties accept all previous agreements (an obvious dismissal of the Rosada Plan), immediately take up the question of human rights, and agree to a new, more robust civil society consensus-building forum that would feed proposals to the formal negotiations. Quezada's initiative did not get far, however. Both sides had begun conversations about the possibility of internationally sponsored talks with a stronger role for the United Nations. Undersecretary-General for Political Affairs Marrack Goulding met with URNG representatives in New York to discuss what more the United Nations could do to facilitate and later verify an agreement. Despite military and private sector resistance to an expanded UN role, de León agreed to send a government delegation to Mexico City in January 1994 to discuss a new approach. The UN Secretary-General invited Quezada to attend, but he declined.[51]

In Mexico, the parties converged on a plan that incorporated Quezada's idea for a reinvigorated civil society forum that would play an advisory role. It established what came to be called the Civil Society Assembly (ASC) that would attempt to reach consensus positions on as many substantive issues as possible and communicate those to the government, the URNG, and the United Nations. The ASC's consensus views would be nonbinding, and the core negotiations on the Mexico Agreement's substantive agenda would continue to be between the government and the URNG.[52]

Most importantly, the parties invited the United Nations to provide a "moderator" for the talks, and specifically asked for Jean Arnault to play that role.[53] They agreed that they would continue to negotiate secretly (to allow compromises without interference from constituents), and that they would complete the entire negotiating process as quickly as possible in 1994. It was never resolved how the parties could negotiate secretly while also keeping civil society informed enough to make substantive recommendations that would dovetail with the official negotiations. This would prove to be a source of constant problems in the remaining years of negotiations.[54] The parties asked the governments of Colombia, Mexico, Norway, Spain, the United States, and Venezuela to form a group of friends to support the process. Most importantly for the future, they agreed to invite the United Nations to verify any agreements reached. These points were formalized in the Framework Agreement for the Resumption of the Negotiating Process Between the Government of Guatemala and the Unidad Revolucionaria Nacional Guatemalteca (URNG) signed on January 10, 1994.

Overall, the reformulation of the process was deft. The United Nations' engagement added visibility and political pressures not to fail. The ASC allowed for a broad civil society dialogue, while keeping the URNG central to the substantive negotiations.[55] The friends states engaged actively with the process, especially Norway, which hosted some of the talks and leaned heavily on the parties to settle.

The parties' preference for Jean Arnault as moderator caused mild unease back at UN headquarters because he was still relatively junior, having at that point about ten years of UN experience in a range of posts. On January 10, 1994, Marrack Goulding wrote to Arnault congratulating him on his "triumph" in brokering the Framework Agreement, but expressing some concerns "on hierarchical grounds."[56] For perspective, note that as a P-5—that is, a senior political officer—Arnault was only one to two ranks above the political officers who would head up small regional and subregional offices of the UN mission once it deployed, and around three ranks below the seniority usually associated with a major peace negotiations effort (typically an assistant secretary-general or equivalent). In a follow-up memo to the Secretary-General, Goulding expressed concerns about Arnault's seniority and his lack of management experience "to handle what will, if all goes well, become quite a substantial negotiation, with a United Nations team of as many as ten people." Goulding recommended that the United Nations support the parties' choice, but appoint a veteran UN official, Gilberto Schlittler (Brazil), to serve as a special envoy at the assistant secretary-general level. Arnault would handle the negotiations, formally under Schlittler's supervision.[57]

The intensity of the Guatemalan parties' shared support for Arnault is striking. The government and the URNG were, after all, very far apart ideologically and in terms of their political interests, yet they converged in wanting Arnault as their broker. Documents from the negotiations, as well as interviews with the parties and with Arnault himself, point to possible reasons. First, Arnault was intrinsically respectful of the Guatemalans. While other political observers, including some senior UN officials, expressed impatience and irritation with the often-recalcitrant Guatemalan parties, Arnault was deeply sympathetic with the challenges they faced. He also held views that were favorable from the point of view of each side, for different reasons. For instance, he supported the URNG's general view that Guatemala's political economy needed profound changes and that if the war was to end, the URNG needed to be taken seriously despite their political and military weakness. He knew that an asymmetrical war would not necessarily be easy to end. He also understood the nationalist sensitivities of the government's constituencies, and agreed that the United Nations as mediator and verifier needed to make concessions to those sensitivities.

The entire moderation effort operated on a shoestring through the UN Department of Political Affairs (DPA). Goulding need not have worried about Arnault's lack of experience in managing a large team, as none was ever formed. The Department of Peacekeeping Operations (DPKO), which has generally had the lead in peacemaking efforts, declined to provide regular staffing to the negotiating effort. It offered only to assign temporary staff on short notice as needed. A single political officer at DPA maintained liaison among Arnault, Schlittler, Goulding, Assistant Secretary-General Alvaro de Soto, and the head of the Americas and Europe division (a position that underwent turnover during the period of the negotiations and played little role). At any given meeting, Arnault had one or two support staff persons to take notes and help manage the sessions. Technical specialists were drawn in from other agencies to consult on human rights, legal, and economic development questions. UN budget shortfalls sometimes restricted staff travel, and accommodations and meeting spaces were not always adequate. The Mexican government provided hotel accommodations for the URNG delegation and supported the logistics of the talks in innumerable ways (and at one point, quietly threatened to withhold this support if the URNG did not pick up the pace of negotiations). A trust fund was set up to collect voluntary contributions from member states, but its administration proved cumbersome and disbursements were often delayed by red tape. On the positive side, Goulding maintained an active interest in the process, and occasionally traveled to the region to signal the Secretariat's support for the process and to lean on the parties to make more rapid progress.

▌ The Human Rights Agreement

Once the Framework Agreement was in place the parties made relatively rapid progress on the first item on their agenda, human rights. It came first because it was a comparatively easy agreement to reach: preliminary drafts mainly required the government to uphold rights that it had ratified under existing international human rights declarations and conventions. It was also a critical starting point from the URNG's point of view. Without that agreement in place, the rebels could not consider addressing other issues.

The main sticking point for the government was the commission on the past, or truth commission. The army wanted no such commission, and if it were unavoidable, wanted its findings sealed for twenty years. One of the URNG leaders, Rodrigo Asturias, suggested moving the commission on the past to a separate agenda so that the agreement on human rights could move ahead. The government agreed. The government, in turn, indicated that it could give up its prior demands that the talks address the ceasefire before other issues.[58] The other thing the government wanted in exchange for agreeing to immediate human rights verification was that the UN verification mission would not merely criticize: it would *help* the government to improve human rights performance by strengthening institutions such as police, prosecutors, courts, and the human rights ombudsman.[59]

These talks, while promising, also foreshadowed difficulties to come. Arnault wrote,

> While not unsatisfactory, the 3–8 March meeting *raised a serious question as to URNG's capacity to make the kind of concessions that would allow a compressed negotiation as envisaged in the Framework Agreement.* One has the distinct impression that, as was the case in March–May 1993, Rodrigo Asturias is willing and able to engage in a dynamic process of mutual concessions while Rolando Moran and Pablo Monsanto (militarily stronger) are suspicious of the negotiating process, and perhaps the peace process in general, in which they see a potential trap.[60] (emphasis in original)

With the broad outlines of the human rights accord nearing completion, one question facing the United Nations was what the conditions should be for a UN verification mission. The government asked for language that would require government approval for future extensions of the mission's mandate. Arnault wrote to New York suggesting that the United Nations agree to such language. Although the procedure would be cumbersome, it would reassure the government that the commitment to international human rights verification was not open-ended, and Arnault thought that in practice, government support for renewals would not be a problem. He wrote,

> The fact is that for the Government of Guatemala, the pre-ceasefire deployment of the UN is a major step (for some even a risky leap of faith). . . . I think they should be helped to "take the plunge"—if only because the Government's cooperation is a critical pre-condition for the Mission's effectiveness—as long as doing so does not jeopardize the viability and credibility of UN verification.

The near-final draft also limited the mission's authority to inspect government facilities: "should there be any reasonable indication pointing to a violation of human rights, the mission will conduct its visits without prior notice." Human rights specialists from the UN mission in El Salvador had reviewed this provision and thought it was acceptable. However, a higher-up in DPA, Michael Möller (Denmark), strongly objected to any restrictions on the mission's authority to go anywhere, anytime, without prior notice. That provision, along with the provision for a government veto over mandate renewal, was stricken from the final version.[61] In retrospect, this was a close brush with disaster: one can only imagine the use that Guatemalan rightists would have made of a requirement that MINUGUA demonstrate probable cause prior to investigating secret government detention centers.

After a final two-day negotiating session, the parties finally signed the Comprehensive Agreement on Human Rights on March 29, 1994, in Mexico City, along with a joint statement agreeing to take up the question of a truth commission at a later date, and a timetable committing the parties to reach final accords by December 1994.

In broad terms, the human rights agreement required the government to comply with international human rights instruments to which it was already a party. More specifically, it called on the government to police its own human rights conduct more effectively by strengthening the Human Rights Ombudsman's Office (Procuraduría para la Defensa de Derechos Humanos [PDH]) as well as the Public Ministry (which carried out attorney general functions) and the courts. The PDH was to verify that the PACs were really voluntary—something of a joke since they patently were not—but the question of demobilizing the PACs was deferred for later. Other requirements included a halt to forced military conscription, greater protection of individuals working in human rights advocacy, and compensation for human rights victims. The agreement called on both the government and the URNG to reduce the suffering of the civilian population.

In accordance with the earlier Framework Agreement, it called for UN verification of the parties' compliance with their commitments. The agreement gave the anticipated UN verification mission sweeping powers to establish itself throughout the country, to go anywhere—including government facilities—without prior notice, to receive denunciations and to collect any information it needed to determine whether rights violations were taking place, and to determine whether government authorities were living up to their responsibilities.[62] It also called on the UN mission to strengthen state agencies responsible for human rights, making the mission both a critic and partner of the government. The parties called on the United Nations to deploy a mission before hostilities stopped, acknowledging that this might require extra security precautions. They asked the United Nations to send a preliminary mission as soon as possible.

The brief passage about reducing the suffering of the civilian population proved politically significant. Other than a general commitment by both parties to protect individuals' rights, it was the only part of the agreement that placed demands on the URNG. As discussed in the next chapter, MINUGUA actively investigated whether the URNG was complying with this commitment, and criticized the rebels when they detained people for propaganda, collected war taxes, or sabotaged infrastructure. This helped balance the mission's inevitable criticism of the government and made the mission's presence more tolerable to conservative sectors and the military.

While the government appeared to make the greatest concessions in signing the Comprehensive Agreement, the greatest political impact was felt by the URNG. By agreeing to suspend attacks affecting civilian populations, the URNG limited itself to attacking only military targets (unless it were to openly violate the Comprehensive Agreement). Since the rebels had very little capacity to attack military targets, in the two years and nine months of negotiations remaining, they found themselves with few means to ratchet up military pressure on the government. Most of the actions that were within their military grasp exposed them to criticism from MINUGUA.

▌ Back to Oslo

After the breakthrough on human rights, negotiations entered a troubled period. The next two items on the agenda were resettlement for refugees and displaced persons, and the truth commission. Impasses developed quickly on both. The URNG wanted an autonomous agency to handle resettlement and development programs for uprooted populations. The government opposed this, wanting to control these resources and activities. Issues also lingered regarding the mandate for the truth commission, including whether it would be headed by international commissioners or by Guatemalans, whether it would begin work immediately or only when a final accord was signed, and whether it would single out individuals responsible for human rights crimes.

After unproductive talks in Puebla, Mexico, in late May, the parties reconvened in June in Holmenkollen, an idyllic former Winter Olympics site outside of Oslo, Norway, complete with ski jump. The agenda included final details of the Agreement on Resettlement of the Population Groups Uprooted by the Armed Conflict, and the Agreement on the Establishment of the Commission to Clarify Past Human Rights Violations That Have Caused the Guatemalan Population to Suffer.

Arnault had shuttled between the parties after the Puebla round, and had worked out most of the details on the resettlement agreement. The government agreed to the formation of a Technical Committee, with two representatives of government, two designated by uprooted populations, and two from international donors and cooperating agencies. The last two would have only advisory status. The Technical Committee would be the policymaking entity for resettlement, charged with implementing the participatory, context-sensitive, integrated development philosophy laid out in the resettlement agreement.

With that agreement in hand, the talks turned to the question of the "commission on the past" or Historical Clarification Commission (CEH). As hosts, the Norwegian government, as well as other national diplomats present, put intense pressure on the parties to stay on schedule and complete an agreement. The URNG was in the hot seat: it had received pressure from civil society groups to insist on a strong, immediate, and internationally led CEH that would name individual culprits and feed into eventual prosecutions. This was a strongly emotional issue, because so many horrific abuses had taken place during the war. Nonetheless, the URNG decided in favor of pragmatism. The agreement signed at Holmenkollen stated that the commission would not attribute individual responsibility for past violence, and would not lead to any judicial process. It is doubtful that the URNG could have obtained government consent without these limitations. The army would never have tolerated a CEH that would name individual perpetrators or that led directly to prosecutions. The wobbly Guatemalan judiciary would in any case have been unlikely to convict and sentence many human rights perpetrators in the near term.

Ironically, when the CEH issued its report in February 1999, it turned out to be far more forceful and effective than expected. It found the armed forces responsible for the vast majority of violence against civilians, including a systematic policy of genocide against indigenous peoples. Because there is no statute of limitations under international law for prosecution for genocide, the report laid the groundwork for potential prosecutions if the Guatemalan courts were ever to have enough independence and strength. It also limited the international mobility of former military officers by potentially encouraging arrests and prosecution by other countries under universal jurisdiction for crimes against humanity.

However, this future was unknown to Guatemalan popular organizations at the time of the agreement, and their immediate reaction was that the URNG had given away far too much. In the wake of so much suffering, they wanted members of the army held accountable, just as they expected concrete economic benefits to help justify the sacrifices associated with the war. The URNG's pragmatic decision was completely unacceptable.

A somewhat discomforting aspect of the CEH agreement from the United Nations' point of view was that it named Arnault to head the CEH. There were concerns within the Secretariat that this role could create a conflict of interest for Arnault as moderator, and his superiors decided that he should not become involved in any preparatory work for the CEH. The talks dragged on for over two more years, and by the time final accords were signed the parties wanted Arnault to be appointed SRSG to head the full verification mission instead of the CEH. Human rights expert Christian Tomuschat (Germany) was tapped to head the CEH.

▌ Stalemate Pending Deployment of MINUGUA

After the Comprehensive Agreement was signed, the United Nations sent a delegation to Guatemala to assess what would be required to verify that agreement. Once this was done, however, the Secretariat held back from establishing the mission. Goulding was concerned that further progress at the table was unreliable. Arnault's reporting on the internal difficulties of the URNG was a factor, as was the acerbic style of the government's COPAZ. After the June CEH agreement, there were further signs of trouble, as the URNG backed away from the talks, worked on repairing relationships with popular groups, and blamed the United Nations for the delays.

By midsummer, a new source of delay emerged: a political debate between the UN Secretariat and member states about whether the mission should be mandated by the Security Council or the General Assembly. The Secretariat favored the Security Council route, since this would greatly facilitate the budgeting process and give the mission greater political clout. It was also thought to be more appropriate from a "constitutional" point of view. The UN Charter gave the Council responsibility for international peace and security. Strictly speaking, human rights verification did not involve international peace and security, but the language of the Comprehensive Agreement made it clear that the human rights mission would be only the first stage of a multidisciplinary peace mission (though the government later claimed not to see it this way), so it was appropriate to go through the Security Council from the outset, as had been done in the case of the United Nations Observer Mission in El Salvador (ONUSAL).

The Secretariat's argument for a Security Council mandate was offset, however, by the Guatemalan government's strong preference for a General Assembly mandate. Some government constituencies were worried about losing control of the peace process if a stronger, Council-mandated mission were deployed.[63] The Guatemalan political elite had by this point gotten a close look at the UN presence in neighboring El Salvador, and wanted to do whatever they could to reduce the authority of any UN mission. Moreover, Mexico, Colombia, Venezuela, and the United States, as friends states, strongly favored the General Assembly route, for different reasons. Mexico, Colombia, and Venezuela claimed that they wanted an Assembly mandate because it was the appropriate venue for a human rights mission. The real reason was more likely that they would have more influence over a General Assembly–mandated mission.[64] The United States wanted the Assembly mandate for purely budgetary reasons, since the peacekeeping scale of assessments would not apply and thus the United States' share of costs would be lower.

Faced with a firm position on this issue from the host government, three regional powers, and the United States, Goulding had no choice but to ask the Secretary-General, with regret, to present a report to the General Assembly proposing the mission. Goulding noted that the Assembly route would be slower and "will entail further complicated procedures once a final peace agreement has been signed and international verification by the United Nations is expanded to include all the commitments contained in it."[65]

During the three months of debate on the mandate, Arnault had become increasingly alarmed that the peace process was losing momentum and that the United Nations needed to commit more seriously to the process. He wrote to Schlittler in July in an almost desperate tone, arguing that the United Nations must promptly appoint an SRSG to provide greater weight to the negotiating process and to integrate the negotiation and verification roles. He wrote that the moderator *"cannot function without the necessary authority and full political support from Headquarters"* (emphasis in original). He offered to step aside as moderator, suggesting that the Secretary-General may need to appoint a high-level representative, "as is done usually in similar cases, to take over the functions of moderator."[66]

Arnault added,

> *It is a paramount consideration for the Secretariat, based on previous experiences, that negotiation and verification should be closely integrated. This requires the appointment of an official who would accumulate responsibilities in both areas. . . . It is only natural that the official who would have responsibility for facilitating negotiation and overseeing verification of those agreements should be of a high-level.* (emphasis in original)

Arnault also called for a prompt decision regarding the choice of Security Council or General Assembly mandate, insisting that the Guatemalan government be consulted closely on this question. He was aware that the Secretariat favored the Security Council route while the government wanted a General Assembly mandate, and he warned Schlittler that failure to consult adequately could trigger powerful political pushback in Guatemala.[67]

The Secretary-General did not appoint a senior SRSG. However, Arnault's plea did garner some attention, as Under-Secretary-General Marrack Goulding soon became more directly involved in preparations for MINUGUA. Meanwhile the parties continued to stall. The URNG pointed to ongoing human rights violations, while the government helpfully suggested that the rebels put down their arms and join Guatemalan democracy. At the end of August, the URNG suddenly added deployment of MINUGUA as a formal precondition for resuming talks. Arnault flatly told them this was unacceptable and they withdrew the demand.[68]

On September 12, 1994, the United Nations sent the parties an aide-mémoire proposing an interlocking timetable of steps by the parties and by the United Nations. A preparatory meeting would take place in the next week. The General Assembly would approve the mission before September 20, and the moderator would announce the reconvening of talks on September 26. The memo closed with the diplomatic observation that, "While there is no formal linkage between these measures, the Secretary-General considers that a delicate equilibrium exists between them and that their synchronized unfolding in the manner described would help to ensure that they all have the desired effect."[69]

The URNG strongly rejected the (so delicately) implied ultimatum, and civil society groups piled on. A UN adviser attending a meeting of Guatemalan civil society groups in Oslo on September 14 described the discussion as "devoted to frantic UN-bashing by representatives of civil sectors, with the support of Monseñor Quezada. The UN is accused of inefficiency and bad faith for mishandling the verification mission. A first draft of the Oslo final declaration criticizes the UN for its 'lack of interest' and 'having failed the Guatemalan people.' The statement may be changed."[70] Government negotiator Rosada wrote to Schlittler taking strong exception to the aide-mémoire, saying that "if anything has negatively impacted the peace process, it has been the delay by the United Nations" in presenting the proposal for MINUGUA to the General Assembly.[71]

The Secretary-General and his advisers decided to take the risk of further involvement in the Guatemalan process, and issued a report to the General Assembly recommending that MINUGUA be established. At the end of its forty-eighth session, on September 28, 1994, the General Assembly approved the creation of the United Nations Mission for the Verification of Human Rights and of Compliance with the Commitments of the Comprehensive Agreement on Human Rights in Guatemala (MINUGUA).[72] A preparatory mission followed immediately, and the UN presence began to be felt through press conferences held by head of mission–designate Leonardo Franco calling on the parties to reduce the level of violence.[73] During the first week of October, a month before MINUGUA would formally open and several months before it was fully deployed, the head of the Presidential Human Rights Commission (COPREDEH) pronounced MINUGUA's staffing levels "elevated and excessive." The government's negotiator, Rosada, announced (erroneously) that MINUGUA was not authorized to carry out investigations (see Chapter 3).[74] Thus, after the government had pushed for months and criticized the United Nations for delays in deploying the mission, its representatives promptly and shamelessly maneuvered to minimize the MINUGUA's authority. This proved to be a harbinger of things to come.

▌ The Indigenous Accord

Despite the United Nations' renewed investment in Guatemalan peace, little if any progress followed. The group of friends grew tired of the game and issued a communiqué in October calling on the parties to start talking soon. On December 22, 1994, Secretary-General Boutros Boutros-Ghali wrote to both parties asking them to indicate what they would do to get the process moving again. The government, suddenly filled with enthusiasm, proposed to wrap up the negotiations in sixty days, leaving most substantive issues to be worked out within Guatemalan institutions. The URNG responded with equal surrealism, calling for final peace "in a day," arguing that all the government needed to do was agree to the proposals of the Civil Society Assembly on all substantive issues and the war would end.[75] Neither side's response advanced the process.

At this juncture, the Civil Society Assembly imploded. The ASC had made significant contributions, having fulfilled its mandate under the Framework Agreement to prepare consensus recommendations on the remaining substantive areas of negotiation. But the URNG's declaration that the government should just accept the ASC's positions linked the ASC to the URNG in a way that was unacceptable to the Catholic Church. On January 27, 1995, the Guatemalan Conference of Bishops wrote to Jean Arnault, announcing that Quezada would withdraw from his role as President of the ASC, citing concerns about the political games being played. The URNG's endorsement of the ASC's recommendations called into question the Church's impartiality as long as Quezada continued to lead the ASC. Quezada's withdrawal left an ad hoc steering committee in charge at a moment of great tensions and centrifugal pressures within the Assembly.[76]

With the situation deteriorating rapidly, the UN Secretariat lost patience and issued an overt ultimatum. Goulding wrote to the two parties on February 18, 1995, presenting a new timetable for talks that would lead to signing a final peace accord in August 1995. The letter pointed out that the United Nations had deployed a human rights mission to Guatemala with the expectation that it would accelerate the peace talks. Since that had manifestly not taken place, and if the parties did not accept and act upon the new timetable, the Secretary-General would have to report to the General Assembly "that the modalities for the participation of the United Nations in the peace process would have to be reconsidered."[77]

Although the parties complained about the UN ultimatum, they nonetheless began to meet and signed the Agreement on Identity and Rights of Indigenous Peoples on March 31, 1995. It acknowledged a history of abuse and oppression against indigenous peoples, recognized shared elements of the "cosmovisión" of indigenous peoples, and explicitly recognized their distinctive collective and subgroup identities.[78] It called for a constitutional reform to recognize Guatemala as multicultural, multiethnic, and multilingual. It called on the government to take steps to criminalize discrimination against indigenous people (especially indigenous women), and to create state legal offices charged specifically with defending their rights. The government agreed to uphold indigenous cultural rights to use native languages in education, official business, and court proceedings; to be consulted in the management of indigenous archaeological sites; to use indigenous dress and enjoy freedom to conduct religious practices and celebrations; to have nondiscriminatory access to the media and particularly to radio frequencies needed for community radio broadcasts; to administer their own communities in accordance with customary practices; and to apply norms of customary law to conflicts and crimes within indigenous communities "provided that the latter are not incompatible with the fundamental rights defined by the national legal system or with internationally recognized human rights."[79]

It also recognized the question of indigenous peoples' access to and control over land, but deferred specifics on these issues to a future socioeconomic accord. It called upon the government to regularize the legal status of indigenous land rights and, in a potentially expansive and explosive provision, to both suspend the statute of limitations on "the plundering of indigenous communities," and, where the statute of limitations had already run out (as would be the case for the extensive plundering of indigenous lands in the late-nineteenth and early- twentieth centuries!) to compensate plundered communities with "lands purchased for that purpose."[80] The agreement called on the government to decentralize administration of education, health, and cultural services in accordance with indigenous linguistic boundaries. It called for improved mechanisms to ensure indigenous participation in governmental decisions affecting indigenous communities, as well as access to public service positions.

While some of these measures were self-explanatory and within the grasp of the executive to carry out, the majority of the provisions begged the question of how, exactly, the provisions would be implemented, what agencies of the state would be responsible, and what priorities would be set given limited resources. On such issues as the use of indigenous languages in education, participation and representation in government, and land rights, the agreement called for the creation of a series of joint commissions, composed of equal numbers of government and indigenous representatives, which would be charged with working out details and means of implementation. The accord said nothing about which state agencies would be responsible for implementing whatever the "parity commissions" recommended. This omission would later result in a series of dead ends.

While most of the agreement would take effect upon the signing of final accords, the United Nations was to immediately begin verifying those aspects of the accords that related to human rights. This would apply mainly to racial discrimination, which was already unlawful under the International Convention on the Elimination of All Forms of Racial Discrimination.

The government agreed to advocate in Congress for ratification of the International Labour Organization Convention 169 Concerning Indigenous and Tribal Peoples in Independent Countries (ILO 169), which contained a series of norms that substantially overlapped with the Agreement on Identity and Rights of Indigenous Peoples.

Legal specialists for the United Nations began analyzing the difficulties in verifying the accord, especially the human rights components. Two key challenges emerged: first, unlike most human rights verification, which involved investigation of individual claims, the indigenous rights accord would require MINUGUA to examine broad patterns of interactions between indigenous societies and the state to assess whether discrimination was occurring and whether cultural rights were being protected. Secondly, the call to recognize indigenous customary law and to integrate it with the country's existing liberal legal framework was extraordinarily challenging from a practical point of view and raised significant human rights questions.[81]

Public response to the accord was muted. Indigenous groups greeted the agreement with caution since it was not *their* agreement. Ultimately what remained of the ASC as well as the main indigenous associations endorsed it. In a signal of elite reserve about the agreement, however, the national newspapers, which had published the full text of all the previous accords, neglected to publish the indigenous accord.[82]

Electoral Dynamics Delay Peace

The signing of the indigenous rights accord proved to be the high point for peace talks under President de León. He had spent most of his political capital, and the coming elections began to overshadow the peace process. The next item on the agenda was the accord on socioeconomic and agrarian questions. Given the extreme social inequalities in Guatemala, and the state's exceptionally low capacity to deliver basic social services and public goods, this agreement would be central to the country's future prospects. It was also, of course, politically controversial. After decades of suffering economic hardships and violence, social sectors supportive of the URNG had high expectations and were disinclined to settle for half measures. Major landowners and many business interests wanted to preserve the status quo.

Anticipating difficulties, the United Nations had put in place in mid-1994 an exemplary process for supporting the parties in negotiating this critical agreement. The World Bank, the Inter-American Development Bank, the UN Development Programme (UNDP), and the Development Program for Displaced Persons, Refugees, and Returnees in Central America (PRODERE) were all engaged from the earliest stages in discussions around the architecture of the accord, analyzing such issues as land tenure, taxation, and legal bases for redistributive reforms. Assistant Secretary-General for Political Affairs Alvaro de Soto had been eager that the UN system not repeat the mistakes made in El Salvador, where the UN Secretariat found that the international financial institutions were often working at cross-purposes with the peace process, calling for austerity measures at moments when conflict resolution called for increases in social services.[83] Arnault worked closely with the parties and advisers from the international financial and development organizations, and by July 1995 he was drafting components of an agreement.

Guatemalan electoral politics soon overtook this process, however, and the URNG in particular began to show signs of deliberate stalling. Arnault kept pushing, but his reports and those of Schlittler increasingly sounded a note of caution. The Supreme Electoral Tribunal (TSE) ruled that former dictator Efraín Ríos Montt could not run for the presidency because he had previously taken power in a coup d'état. His party, the Guatemalan Republican Front (FRG), put forward a new candidate, Alfonso Portillo, from the more populist branch of the party. With Ríos out of the running, the URNG gambled that Alvaro Arzú from the National Advance Party (PAN) would win the coming elections. Since Arzú represented the more modern and internationally oriented sector of the business community, the URNG slowed the negotiations in hopes of getting a better deal from Arzú than they could expect from the lame-duck de León.[84]

One of the few positive steps during this period was a decision by all of the Guatemalan political parties (even the FRG) to sign a statement, the Contadora Declaration, committing them to support all agreements previously reached between the government COPAZ and the URNG. Key language in the agreement recognized the power of the executive to make commitments and committed the parties to accept these as "agreements of state." Thus, at least in principle, regardless of which party won, the new government would implement previous agreements and, by implication, keep negotiating until a definitive settlement (as provided in the Mexico accord). In the same agreement, the URNG agreed to suspend offensive military operations for two weeks in November to safeguard the electoral process.[85]

During negotiations in September and October, the URNG was often poorly prepared, drafting incomplete and unresponsive proposals. Although Rodrigo Asturias continued to push for making a deal on socioeconomic matters with the current government, his URNG colleagues grew increasingly reluctant. The October 5, 1995, massacre of eleven returned refugees by army forces at a resettlement community in the province of Alta Verapaz gave the URNG further reason to hesitate. Resistance on the right began to increase as well. A group of agricultural producers and ranchers, rubber growers, and disaffected conservatives formed a new group known as the National Coordinating Committee for the Agricultural Sector (Coordinadora Nacional Agropecuaria [CONAGRO]), which brought a personal lawsuit against the government's lead negotiator, Rosada, as well as a constitutional challenge against COPAZ.[86]

President Alvaro Arzú and the Final Phase of Negotiations

Despite the frustration caused within the United Nations by the URNG's strategic delay, the Secretariat's patience—and Arnault's persistence—paid off over the following year. After winning a plurality (but not a majority) in the first-round elections in November 1995, Alvaro Arzú won the January 1996 runoff in what a UN report described as a "heart-stoppingly close race."[87] The margin of victory was 31,900 votes, in the context of low (37 percent) voter turnout. Despite winning a slim majority of the vote (51.22 percent), Arzú actually lost in eighteen out of twenty-two districts in the country, and was elected on the basis of strong margins in his favor in Guatemala City, where he had been a popular mayor. This led Alfonso Portillo to facetiously declare himself president of Guatemala while announcing that Arzú had been elected president of Guatemala City.[88] Despite the wobbly mandate, Arzú's political position was at least somewhat stronger than de León's had been. Arzú's party, the PAN, had won forty-three out of eighty seats in Congress, giving Arzú a working legislative majority, at least at the outset. PAN was a new party, however, and not well institutionalized. It was thus vulnerable to defections and legislative vote buying. Arzú would have to proceed somewhat carefully to avoid losing congressional support, and the main threat came from powerful landowner interests.

These political constraints would later hamper peace implementation, but for the negotiations, Arzú's government brought a fresh, constructive approach and an early willingness to take bold steps. Even before the runoff elections on January 7 and Arzú's inauguration, he and a delegation of senior advisers met secretly at least four times with the URNG. To the first meeting, Arzú brought Gustavo Porras, whom he tapped to be his chief negotiator. Porras's participation was groundbreaking, because he was a former militant from one of the factions of the URNG (the EGP).

The tone of meetings between Arzú's team and the URNG was completely different from that under the previous government. Whereas de León's negotiator Rosada had sought to marginalize the URNG, Arzú's approach was the opposite: he and his team treated the URNG with perhaps more regard than their deteriorating political and military leverage required. Although there continued to be deep philosophical differences between the government and the rebels, there was an element of partnership in the negotiations as the two negotiating teams jointly sought to craft socioeconomic and state institutional reforms that would address long-standing problems.

In other words, the URNG's demands became a vehicle for Arzú's team to pursue reforms that they considered good for the country but would have had political difficulty pursuing were it not for the internationally sponsored peace talks. It would prove easier for this team to incorporate elements into the agreements than to implement them (see Chapter 5).

For Arnault and the Secretariat, there was a significant sense of relief as the unmovable obstacles began to fall away. Goulding and Arnault visited Guatemala on January 24 to signal high-level UN support for resumption of peace talks, and to meet with members of the new government and the political parties. They then met with the URNG in Mexico on January 28 for the same purpose.[89]

Arzú's COPAZ operated under the minister of foreign relations, Eduardo Stein, signaling that it was an integral part of the government rather than a sideshow. The composition was different from de León's COPAZ as well: besides Porras, the team consisted of two former ministers of finance, Richard Aitkenhead and Raquel Zelaya, and only one representative of the army, Otto Pérez Molina. Arzú's newly appointed minister of defense, Julio Balconi, had previously served on COPAZ and was an outspoken and unwavering supporter of a negotiated settlement. Pérez, as former head of the EMP, was more right-wing than Balconi, but strongly supported military hierarchy and obedience to civilian authority.[90] He is viewed as having played a constructive role in the negotiations.

■ The Socioeconomic and Agrarian Accord

On February 21, the Constitutional Court dismissed CONAGRO's lawsuit against COPAZ and formal talks resumed on February 22. The parties would reach an agreement on socioeconomic and agrarian issues in just over two months. Before finalizing the socioeconomic accord, however, the parties stunned many observers by effectively ending the war on March 21, 1996. In an orchestrated rollout of reciprocity, both sides announced a halt to military operations against the other. The URNG went first, announcing a unilateral, temporary halt to offensive military operations. Their forces would engage only in political and propaganda activities, and would not attack military or economic targets. On the same day, Arzú, speaking at an event in Ixcán, Quiché province (one of the hardest-hit regions during the war), announced the suspension of counterinsurgency operations. Defense Minister Balconi signaled the military's support for this measure, though he noted that there would need to be some clarification about what the URNG meant by their stated intent to continue political and propaganda activities. Depending on how the URNG actually implemented their ceasefire, he predicted that the army would be prepared to demobilize the PACs in some areas.[91] Although many important issues remained to be discussed, aside from isolated acts of violence, the fighting was over.

The ceasefire reduced tensions between the two sides at the negotiating table, and talks progressed relatively rapidly. The socioeconomic accord was, as noted, among the most politically fraught agreements. Business groups were hostile to anything smacking of socialism or expropriation, while the URNG was under pressure from constituents to obtain substantial measures addressing inequalities. The parties bridged this divide by identifying a set of commitments by the state that would substantially increase the efforts and capacity of the government to address inequality and poverty, without challenging the essentially market-based nature of the economy.

Progress was facilitated by the fact that the parties had inherited significant previous work on the socioeconomic accord (negotiations on these issues had begun about a year earlier), as well as a detailed and well-argued proposal from the ASC.[92] Arnault and the parties were advised by a team of economists and development specialists on loan from the development banks and UN agencies. The Agreement on Social and Economic Aspects and Agrarian Situation was signed on May 6, 1996, in Mexico City, in the presence of the Mexican foreign minister, representatives of the friends states, and members of the ASC. Goulding signed the agreement along with Arnault.

The agreement was a significant departure from the original revolutionary, socialist aims of the URNG. Most of its content was drawn from the development banks' repertoire of "best practices" in economic development, as well as from the agenda laid out by the ASC. It called for participatory mechanisms that would allow local stakeholders to shape what projects were implemented and how. In addition, the agreement called for significant increases in the delivery of health and education services, decentralization of their administration, and a reorientation of each to primary-level services. Primary health care was to be available at the local level, and the government would seek to ensure universal availability of primary education by 2000. Literacy programs were to be offered in as many languages as feasible, with the goal of a 70 percent literacy rate by 2000. The government committed to improving availability of housing, and particularly to addressing uncertainty of land ownership, even in urban areas, which had prevented families from building permanent houses.

As with the indigenous accord, the socioeconomic agreement highlighted the need to eliminate discrimination against women through reforms of existing laws and regulations.[93] There was a brief section on labor rights calling for the government to revise regulations and promote legislation to increase penalties against firms that withhold lawful payments to workers, violate minimum wage laws, or violate workplace health and safety rules. It also called in vague terms for strengthening inspection and enforcement mechanisms. This fell well short of the provisions recommended by the ASC, which included such things as penalties for *maquiladora* plants that closed in efforts to prevent collective bargaining; maternity leave rules; child care provisions; and creation of an insurance or compensation program to protect workers who are injured on the job.

A major section of the agreement addressed rural development, and began with acknowledgment of grave historical wrongs: "From the conquest to the present, historic events, often tragic, have left deep traces in ethnic, social and economic relations concerning property and land use. These have led to a situation of concentration of resources, which contrasts with the poverty of the majority and hinders the development of Guatemala as a whole."[94]

The measures to correct these historic wrongs were modest and mostly financial in nature. The government was to establish a land trust fund, whose role would be to make financing available to micro, small, and medium producers with minimal down payments. The financial mechanisms would promote a transparent land market as well as more efficient and sustainable use of lands. The government was to give priority to "rural men and women who are organized for that purpose," thus responding to demands from peasants that cooperatives—as opposed to individual farmers—be given recognition and support. The land market would be facilitated by "an efficient decentralized multi-user land registry system that is financially sustainable, subject to compulsory updating and easy to update."[95]

The land trust fund was to confine its activities to only certain kinds of properties, including unused state lands, state-owned farms, illegally settled public lands, land acquired with foreign donations, and undeveloped land expropriated under Article 40 of the constitution (eminent domain), along with a few other very specific categories. This list was supposed to reassure major landowners that the land trust fund would not finance, or be involved in, any mandatory expropriation of lands. From the outset, observers wondered how poor rural Guatemalans would be able to service loans to purchase land: given the inherited extreme inequalities, the proposed financial and administrative mechanisms were hardly transformative, at least within the time scale of a decade or more.

Perhaps the most potentially transformative aspect of the agreement was the state's formal acknowledgment of a responsibility to provide for the basic needs of *all* of the public. A few specific provisions of the accord made this commitment concrete: the state would increase spending on health and education by 50 percent versus 1995 levels by the year 2000, measured as a share of GDP. These increases would be paid for by a 50 percent increase in the tax burden by 2000. These increases were expected to be even larger in absolute terms, because the government agreed to take measures to ensure a 6 percent per annum growth rate in GDP. This was an absurdly high target that the state had no capacity to deliver or even influence. Its inclusion in the accord cast some doubt on the seriousness of other quantitative targets, and as implementation began, the government's inability to achieve favorable growth numbers quickly became an excuse for backing away from the tax goals.

A commitment to raise taxes may seem to be a strange requirement to put in a peace agreement, and indeed the Secretariat was advised not to highlight this feature in publicizing the peace agreement in the United States, since tax increases were politically anathema to some sectors in Washington.[96] But for a state that had been crippled in its ability to provide public goods by a lack of revenue, and where tax increases had been repeatedly defeated by elite interest groups, the commitment to expand the state and its revenue base was a bold and, as it turned out, politically risky move for Arzú.[97]

Surprisingly, the increased taxation and spending enjoyed the support of the international financial institutions (IFIs) such as the International Monetary Fund and the World Bank that often pressure developing countries to reduce public spending. This was important, because in El Salvador, the IFIs had called for austerity measures just at the moment when the government needed to spend more to ameliorate social conflicts in the immediate aftermath of the war.[98] For Guatemala, the IFIs could support tax-and-spend policies because Guatemala's state was far below regional norms in its public spending and capacity to address poverty. The UN Secretariat had astutely brought the IFIs into an advisory role early in the negotiating process. They had been able to shape the content of the accord and therefore took a degree of ownership in it.[99]

As the socioeconomic accord took shape, skepticism about the peace process within political parties and elite interest groups began to fall away. For the most part, the business community heaved a collective sigh of relief at the content of the accord. The head of the business association CACIF, Humberto Preti, expressed his satisfaction with the agreement. This was a significant shift, as Preti had been pessimistic in his statements about the peace process until that point. One exception was the grower's association CONAGRO, which raised yet another legal objection to the peace process, this time on the risible grounds that URNG commanders had signed agreements with their *noms de guerre* rather than their legal names.

In contrast to the complacent elite response, some popular sectors were angry about the accord. Regional office coordinators of MINUGUA (now in its second year in the field) noted the grassroots anger and predicted an increase in potentially violent confrontations, land occupations, and other protests.[100] Even ex-COPAZ head Rosada chided the URNG for renouncing all their demands and signing on to the PAN's political platform, though this commentary was rather cynical given his prior efforts to cut the URNG out of the negotiations altogether.[101] Popular disappointment with the agreement also generated internal divisions within the URNG. On June 9, Rolando

Morán of the URNG *comandancia* announced that the rebels' "political diplomatic commission" was being dissolved. Future negotiations would be carried out by a small group of top commanders without a second tier of support.[102] It appeared that the political support base on the left for the talks was narrowing, even as the way had opened to more rapid negotiations.

▌ Agreement on the Military and Police

The next and final substantive topic of negotiation included the future role of the military, its subordination to civilian political authorities, separation of military and police functions through creation of a civilian police force, and various measures to strengthen the civilian side of the state, including the legislature, executive, and judiciary. In a society long afflicted by military domination and official criminality, this was possibly the most crucial accord.

The Agreement on the Strengthening of Civilian Power and on the Role of the Armed Forces in a Democratic Society (AFPC) was signed September 19, 1996, in Mexico City. The accord was innovative in its combination of measures to defang the military and to strengthen civilian official institutions, especially those responsible for justice.

The text began with general proposals intended to strengthen the legislature, although for some reason it included a congressional term limit, a measure that would inevitably make Congress less competent. The accord provided only general guidelines, however, and details were to be worked out by a multiparty negotiating forum over the course of a year.

Turning to the justice system, the agreement laid out in general terms (that is, without providing draft language) a set of constitutional reforms that would clarify the responsibilities of the judiciary and establish standards for appointment, duties, compensation, and discipline of judges and magistrates. It called for creation of a public defender's office that was required by the 1994 Criminal Procedure Code but had never been implemented.[103] It called for strengthened witness and prosecutor protection programs (desperately needed) as a step toward reducing impunity. Echoing the socioeconomic accord, it stated that the government "intends" to increase net public expenditure on courts and prosecutors by 50 percent versus 1995 levels. Finally, it left the elaboration of additional specific reforms to the Commission on the Strengthening of the Justice System, which would have six months to make recommendations to improve accessibility, speed of reaching decisions, quality of judicial personnel and decisionmaking, and caseload administration.

The section on the executive branch laid out institutional reforms to be implemented, including creation of a new National Civil Police (PNC), which would incorporate the functions of all three existing security forces, under the Ministry of Interior (Ministerio de Gobernación). It provided specific constitutional reform language that would establish that the PNC was

> the only armed police force competent at the national level whose function is to protect and guarantee the exercise of the rights and freedoms of the individual; prevent, investigate and combat crime; and maintain public order and internal security. It shall be under the direction of the civil authorities and shall maintain absolute respect for human rights in carrying out its functions.

That was as specific as the agreement got on the police, however. Where the comparable agreement in El Salvador had incorporated the full text of the needed secondary legislation, complete with details regarding police doctrine, training, qualifications of applicants, and internal disciplinary mechanisms, the Guatemalan accord said only, in the passive voice, that there should be "submission of a bill on security and police," and that "a new Act on Public Order shall be promoted."[104] Regrettably, this left the Arzú government and its successors with a great deal of wiggle room to leave elements of the existing, militarized police system intact. Later paragraphs called on the government to deploy 20,000 PNC cops by late 1999, a very ambitious goal apparently motivated by a desire to avoid a security vacuum after the transition to the new force.[105]

The section on the military began starkly with the statement that "The role of the Guatemalan armed forces is defined as that of defending Guatemala's sovereignty and territorial integrity; they shall have no other functions assigned to them." It then laid out, article by article, specific constitutional reforms that would effect this basic change in the military's role, stripping away the many domestic political powers the military had accumulated.[106] The balance of the section called for revisions to the military's doctrine and educational system, transfer of gun control administration to civilian authorities, and a change to universal voluntary service that would include alternatives to military service. A later section shrewdly entitled Operational Considerations Resulting from the End of the Armed Conflict called for abolition of the PACs, demobilization of the Mobile Military Police, and cuts of 33 percent in both the personnel and budget of the military. Putting these cuts under this section heading allowed them to be framed rhetorically as a result of the military's victory in the war. Success leads to downsizing.

A fourth section proposed measures to strengthen the civilian presidency. The president was empowered to abolish the notorious EMP and replace it with an entity of his choice. The military's general staff and intelligence division were forbidden to engage in domestic intelligence activities, and that task was to be assigned instead to a Civilian Intelligence and Information Analysis Department that would focus mainly on organized crime.

A new Strategic Analysis Secretariat would provide general analysis and strategic advisement to the president. All state agencies involved in intelligence were to observe a strict firewall between intelligence gathering and operations, but no constitutional reform or secondary legal language was included to this effect. Existing intelligence archives would be shifted to the civilian agencies. A proper civil service career system would strengthen the executive overall.[107]

With the benefit of hindsight, it is clear that while the AFPC laid out a powerful agenda for change, it was too vague on key issues regarding the police as well as domestic intelligence institutions. Several factors conspired to produce an agreement that was considerably less concrete than the one in El Salvador, and one that was thus more easily circumvented during implementation. First, during the months leading up to the agreement, the Arzú government pressured the URNG to sign all the remaining accords by September 15 (independence day), no doubt because of the potential political rewards to the government of such an achievement. The URNG (and Arnault) considered this unrealistic, but the government's insistence created a sense of urgency. Second, the URNG had relatively few ideas to offer on the details of reforming state institutions such as the police and judiciary. In fact, negotiators for the URNG later acknowledged that they knew so little of police matters that they consented to having the Spanish Civil Guard be the lead international agency for helping to develop the new police, thinking, on the basis of the name, that it was a genuinely civilian force when in fact it is a paramilitary force.[108] A similar problem had afflicted the FMLN guerrillas in El Salvador, whose initial ideas for police reform amounted to their becoming local sheriffs in their own areas of influence. The UN negotiating team in that case, however, brought in international consultants who drafted the secondary legislation on police organizational design, doctrine, training, and personnel selection.[109]

International guidance for the police component of the Guatemalan AFPC was more limited. Some international consultants had been brought in earlier to assess the characteristics of the existing police and make recommendations, but the assessment of the woeful status quo was more thorough than the recommendations for how to fix it.[110] The outside consultants and MINUGUA's own police advisers reached similar conclusions: the police were weakened by subordination to the military, acute lack of resources, poorly educated and largely untrained personnel, lack of accountability, and a grossly deficient investigative capacity. Multiple police agencies including the PNC, the Military Mobile Police, and the Treasury Guard, needed to be replaced by a single, distinctly civilian force.[111]

A political officer on loan from MINUGUA to the negotiating team, Jan Perlin, had opportunities to advise the parties, but she and other consultants were not in a position to incorporate many details into the agreements. This contrasted with the rather extensive influence of outside advisers on the socioeconomic accord. In a written report for discussion purposes, Perlin advocated clear separation of military and policing functions and a reconceptualization of policing as guaranteeing the safety of citizens rather than as a mechanism of control and repression (elements that were incorporated into the AFPC). The brief report contained only four pages of text in the section on "practical considerations with respect to the institutional picture on citizen security in Guatemala." This contrasted with the draft police law prepared largely by international consultants and incorporated into the Salvadoran accords, which specified organizational design, doctrine, entry requirements, training, and internal disciplinary mechanisms.[112]

One of the reasons for the truncated UN input into the police reform content of the AFPC was that the government had already jumped ahead and negotiated a bilateral deal with Spain to reform and develop the police. It had, in effect, preempted the negotiation on future police reforms by choosing an international partner and moving ahead with a major reform project, even before the AFPC had been negotiated and signed.[113] Having observed the way international advice and assistance programs had shaped the development of a new civilian police force in El Salvador, the Arzú government had its own ideas. The Salvadoran process had, according to Interior Minister Rodolfo Mendoza, resulted in a cacophony of contradictory advice from different nations' police advisers. Mendoza also observed that the transition from the old police to the new PNC in El Salvador had created a security vacuum that had contributed to a postwar crime wave.[114] As a result, within a week of taking office in January 1996, Mendoza told MINUGUA that he was in conversations with the Spanish government and that plans were already under way to bring in a Spanish Civil Guard (GCE) advising team to redevelop the police.[115]

Guatemalan human rights nongovernmental organizations (NGOs) objected strongly. They, unlike the naïve URNG, recognized the GCE as a militarized force that had been closely linked to the Franco dictatorship in Spain, and viewed it as definitely *not* a suitable model for a future Guatemalan police force. The ASC objected to Mendoza's announced plans, calling it a set of "dispositions and initiatives outside of the peace negotiations and accords, which contradict and undercut their spirit and objectives."[116]

A few days later, Mendoza met with David Stephen (UK), who had just arrived to replace Leonardo Franco as head of MINUGUA. Mendoza asserted that the decision to adopt the Civil Guard model "was the firm and sovereign decision of the Government of Guatemala, and no one would change it." In the wake of the ASC press release, he had been told that MINUGUA staff members were critical of the GCE deal, and he was concerned that any negative comments from MINUGUA could be harmful since the international community "looked to MINUGUA for guidance." He wanted any concerns within MINUGUA expressed to him privately. Stephen, and his deputy Leila Lima, both reassured Mendoza that MINUGUA had expressed no opinion, and that it was not its role to do so.[117]

While at that moment, that was probably the correct response for MINUGUA as a human rights mission, it was certainly the role of DPA, or the moderation team, to raise some questions. While going through the motions of negotiating with the URNG about future military, police, and justice institutions, the government had unacceptably narrowed the possibilities for reform by proceeding with the GCE package. With a project already in motion, the government resisted incorporating detailed police reform plans into the relevant peace accord. DPA political officer Denise Cook (Spain) apparently became uncomfortable with the direction things were going. She wrote to Arnault that "agreeing to a watered-down version of the military and public security and judiciary issues for the sake of a quick peace would ultimately weaken the process." Referring to the Salvadoran peace accords signed at Chapultepec castle in Mexico, she wrote,

> An agreement which does not set down detailed guidelines for the doctrine, selection procedures, training, deployment and funding of the National Police is bound to run up against major problems; Chapultepec had a clear cut programme for the demobilization of old police forces and the creation of a new force. Even so, the most corrupt elements and those guilty of human rights abuses tried constantly and sometimes succeeded in bending or ignoring the rules in order to retain their power within the New Policía Nacional Civil; Two years after Chapultepec PNC agents were still being accused of torturing detainees. Now lets [sic] apply the picture to the current Guatemalan Police . . .[118]

Asked about this memo later, neither Cook nor Arnault could remember the specific circumstances that gave rise to it. But it turned out to be prescient, as the lack of details in the accord, combined with the determination of the government to do things its own way, led to an expedient and sloppy police reform that missed a critical window of opportunity to fix long-standing problems.[119]

The final stages of talks coincided with an intense campaign of threats and intimidation directed against MINUGUA (discussed in detail in Chapter 4). The government exploited this nationalist outburst by sending a high-level delegation to New York to warn against future intrusions into Guatemalan affairs. Goulding deflected this strategy. However, the government had shown that it was determined to preserve as much policy flexibility for itself as possible on the police issue, it had already committed to an approach to police reform, and it had strong support from Spain, which reacted sharply to any criticism of the GCE project.

There are indications that international NGOs interested in demilitarization reforms—who might have contributed to a stronger accord—were caught off guard by the speed and direction of the negotiations. The Washington Office on Latin America (WOLA), which had helped rally US congressional support for the peace process at earlier stages, belatedly engaged with the issue on September 12, 1996, just a week before the accord was signed. WOLA forwarded a draft document containing a series of recommendations by a working group of NGO staff and international specialists on police reform. The document, which had been drafted in November 1995 but never finalized, laid out such useful details as screening procedures and criteria for new recruits, educational standards for entry into various ranks of the police, exclusion of former military intelligence personnel from the new police, projections of realistic time periods for training of personnel, priority to recruitment of indigenous and female police officers, and an increase in MINUGUA's police division to monitor and advise the transition.[120] These recommendations were exactly the kind of details needed in the accord, but they had no chance of being included in a deal that was almost finalized.

The ASC, despite its official role as generator of consensus advisory positions on substantive issues, found it particularly difficult to be heard on this set of issues. It had issued an updated consensus position on June 21 (having issued a previous version back in September 1994). The ASC called, among other things, for creation of a new Technical Investigations Police following the model of a new detective corps that had been created in neighboring Honduras. This group would be made up entirely of university graduates, would receive intensive training in investigative and forensic techniques, and would report directly to the Public Ministry (which, under a new Criminal Procedure Code adopted in 1994, was responsible for directing investigations and prosecutions). This would have gone a long way toward addressing the most serious weaknesses of the postwar police reform effort and might have helped prevent the descent into mass criminality and near state failure that occurred over the next decade. Instead, the parties ignored the ASC and went ahead with their expedient deal, and the United Nations went along with them.

■ The Novella Kidnapping

With the signing of the AFPC, the parties had finished negotiating the entire substantive agenda laid out as a result of the Oslo process back in March 1990 and codified in the Mexico Agreement of April 1991. All that remained were the "operational" questions of how the URNG would be demobilized, the conditions under which they would be incorporated into the legal political life of the country, and the timetable for implementation. This could have been the smoothest part of the peace process, since the war was effectively over and there was by this point little controversy about the "recycling" of the Guatemalan insurgents as citizens and legal political actors. A tragic and, in retrospect, potentially avoidable event intervened, however.

On August 25, 1996, a small group of urban insurgents associated with the ORPA, dressed in National Police uniforms and using a fake police car, kidnapped Olga Alfaro de Novella, who was at the time eighty-seven years of age.[121] Mrs. Novella happened to be a close family friend of President Arzú. He immediately called upon a special antikidnapping unit that was part of the EMP to assume responsibility in the case. It bears mentioning that the EMP antikidnapping unit had no legal standing: it could not collect evidence for use in a court of law, and it could not legally make arrests except in flagrante delicto. Yet it was considered by many wealthy Guatemalans to be the only unit operationally competent to investigate and use force in sensitive kidnapping cases.

The EMP's investigation finally bore fruit nearly two months later, when it apprehended two members of ORPA, Rafael Augusto Valdizón Núñez (known as Comandante Isaías) and Juan José Cabrera Rodas (known as Mincho) shortly after they had placed telephone calls to Novella's family regarding the ransom. The capture was not exactly a smooth operation: EMP personnel chased the two kidnappers' car around Guatemala City in two SUVs and a panel van. Once Isaías and Mincho were cornered, EMP operatives bludgeoned them with batons and took them into custody. Mincho was struck in the head and the Historical Clarification Commission later suggested that he might have incurred injuries at the time of capture sufficient to cause his death. Regardless, Mincho became the first and only state-sponsored disappearance to occur during the Arzú government.

Isaías survived capture, and the negotiations quickly shifted from money to the question of a prisoner exchange. Arzú was alarmed that Novella would be killed upon Isaías's capture, and indeed the combatants in charge of holding her were under orders to kill her if anyone involved in the operation were captured. Isaías got his comrades on the phone, however, forestalling her murder, and the two were exchanged a few days later on October 20, 1996. The incident was made public on October 28, at which point MINUGUA learned about it for the first time.[122]

The kidnapping brought a halt to the peace talks. Once the exchange had been arranged, and news regarding the case reached the public, Arzú contacted Arnault in New York and asked him to demand from the URNG an explanation of its involvement in the kidnapping. The case was damaging to Arzú on a number of levels. He had staked a great deal of his political capital on negotiating with the URNG and ending the war. For the URNG to kidnap an elderly member of a prominent family was a gross breach of the incipient trust that had developed between the two parties. It made Arzú look naive for having bargained with the URNG. Moreover, the far-right FRG party, as well as Arzú's own attorney general, immediately pounced on the prisoner exchange, accusing Arzú of acting in an unconstitutional manner. The FRG also accused the government of concealing the truth about the second ORPA combatant, whose presence the government had not acknowledged.[123]

The URNG *comandancia* denied having any knowledge of the kidnapping, and claimed it was a rogue operation. The CEH later questioned this claim. Given the duration of Novella's captivity, and the resources brought to bear for the operation, top commanders had to have known about it. The *comandancia* did accept "political responsibility" for the kidnapping, whatever that meant, and, after some delay, Asturias (who as head of ORPA was the individual most responsible) withdrew from the negotiating table. The URNG also immediately suspended "armed propaganda" actions that had irritated the military (see Chapter 4), and offered to negotiate the ceasefire agreement next as a signal of good faith.

Thus, in the final stage of the talks, the URNG lost its most able negotiator and the person who had most consistently pushed for compromise, concessions, and progress in the talks. The rebels were also weakened politically, since public opinion was generally appalled by their crime. The kidnapping reinforced right-wing discourse that equated the URNG with criminal gangs.

The disappearance of Mincho also implicated the EMP in a serious crime. The EMP claimed that he had escaped, or been allowed to escape due to insufficient EMP personnel at the scene. This claim strained credulity, especially in view of witness statements describing a second guerrilla having been struck in the head and taken into custody. As the attorney general, and later MINUGUA and the CEH, began to investigate the case, EMP officials referred all inquiries to their superiors in the Ministry of Defense, who stonewalled any further inquiry.[124] The Mincho case would later create problems for Arnault (as SRSG) and for MINUGUA (see Chapter 5).

In its review of the Novella kidnapping, the CEH noted that a contributing factor was probably the URNG's lack of alternative financing mechanisms. The rebels had, under pressure from MINUGUA on the basis of the Comprehensive Agreement, halted war tax collection. This left the URNG with no regular source of revenue, at a moment when the organization was preparing for the transition from insurgency to political party—a costly undertaking. The precedent of the Mozambican National Resistance (RENAMO) might have called attention to the financial needs of former insurgencies during their transition to legal party status. The UN SRSG in Mozambique, Aldo Ajello, used a discretionary fund to finance RENAMO's conversion, and this had been widely credited in the peacekeeping community with preventing RENAMO from withdrawing from the peace process and resuming violence. Looking back on this episode in an interview in

2008, Jean Arnault remarked that the urgency of the URNG's financial needs had not been clear to him at the time. Nor had the rebels brought up that issue as a bargaining point—an unfortunate omission on their part. Had they asked, something could have been done.[125] As discussed in the next chapter, MINUGUA's decision to pressure the URNG to halt war tax collection seemed to be a principled, as well as politically astute, position. Yet halting this activity, without replacing it with some other more transparent financing source, helped create conditions for the Novella kidnapping and a near collapse of the peace process.

■ The Race to Final Accords

Asturias's withdrawal from the URNG negotiating team proved sufficient to bring the government back to the table. From this point onward, talks proceeded rapidly. Having missed the government's cherished September 15 deadline, the parties now felt urgency to complete the talks by the end of the year. Secretary-General Boutros Boutros-Ghali would be stepping down then, so it seemed important for both domestic and international political reasons to close the deal. Three accords were signed in quick succession in European capitals to acknowledge the support of the host countries during the talks, as well as to potentially attract the support of donors. These included the Agreement on the Definitive Ceasefire, signed in Oslo, Norway, on December 4, 1996; the Agreement on Constitutional Reforms and the Electoral Regime, signed in Stockholm, Sweden, on December 7, 1996; and the Agreement on the Basis for Legal Integration of the Unidad Revolucionaria Nacional Guatemalteca, signed in Madrid, Spain, on December 12, 1996. Two final agreements were signed in Guatemala City on December 29, 1996: the Agreement on the Implementation, Compliance, and Verification Timetable for the Peace Agreements, and the Agreement on a Firm and Lasting Peace, which put all the other agreements into effect (except the human rights accord and the human rights component of the indigenous accord, which had taken immediate effect).

The main source of controversy during the negotiation of these final agreements was the question of amnesty. Human rights advocacy organizations were concerned that the conditions for legalizing the status of the URNG would also provide an amnesty for members of the armed forces, making it impossible to achieve accountability for past abuses. Observers were alarmed that the agreement on reincorporation of the URNG proposed "extinction of legal responsibility" for some common crimes as well as political crimes. The challenge facing Congress was to craft a law that was sufficiently broad that it would enable former URNG combatants and militants to rejoin society without fear of prosecution, while still leaving open the possibility of prosecutions of either side for extreme abuses. In the end, the National Reconciliation Law passed on December 27, 1996, was only a partial amnesty. For both agents of the state and the URNG, the law excluded acts of genocide, torture, or forced disappearance; excessive force against prisoners; crimes unrelated to the armed confrontation; and crimes committed for personal goals. This meant that the military, police, and intelligence services could potentially still be held accountable for many murders of activists who were clearly noncombatants (both targeted death squad killings and indiscriminate rural massacres), not to mention many for-profit crimes such as robberies, kidnapping, theft, drug and arms trafficking, and murders for hire. The law called for compensation for victims, which potentially left the government on the hook for substantial payment.[126]

The definitive ceasefire agreement was comparatively uncontroversial, but would have serious political implications. It laid out the plan for separating forces, concentrating the URNG in eight areas, and demobilizing their forces in three phases over sixty days. The accord called upon the United Nations to deploy unarmed military observers to coordinate this process, monitor the movements of military forces, maintain communication, and approve and coordinate any special movements by either side that might be misinterpreted. It called on the United Nations to receive URNG weapons, and to later turn them over to the government. The sixty-day timetable for demobilization was quite rapid, and it meant that whatever military leverage the URNG still had would disappear very early in the implementation phase of the peace process. Thereafter, the rebels would depend heavily on the United Nations to ensure that the government actually delivered on its promises. Rebel leader Rodrigo Asturias later remarked that it would have been wiser to withhold demobilization until the constitutional reforms had been passed.[127]

The constitutional accord itself merely cataloged all of the constitutional measures called for in the other accords. In a few cases, it proposed more specific language to replace or supplement existing constitutional articles. It also distinguished between those reforms that were already specified and those that would need to be developed by the various joint commissions created by the accords to address such questions as judicial system reform, Mayan languages as official languages, education reform, and so forth.

The section on the electoral regime deferred entirely to the constitutional authority of the TSE, called on that body to set up a commission on electoral reforms, and proposed a series of measures for that commission to consider. These measures included such things as creation of a single national photo identification card, which would simplify maintenance of voter rolls. These were merely suggestions, however, and the government made no promises or commitments.

The Agreement on the Implementation, Compliance, and Verification Timetable for the Peace Agreements contained serious flaws with respect to political process, and reflected the haste and sudden weakness of the URNG that had also undercut the AFPC. The accord announced that the government had decided to place coordination of peace implementation under a technical Peace Secretariat (SEPAZ), which would report directly to the presidency. This would prove to be a weak mechanism in that SEPAZ had no direct executive, regulatory, or legislative authority. Its powers were limited to coordination.[128] The primary domestic verification mechanism would be a Follow-Up Commission (Comisión de Acompañamiento). The Follow-Up Commission would consist of an equal number (not specified but in practice two) of representatives from each of the parties to the accords; four citizens from different sectors of the population, invited by mutual agreement of the parties; one representative chosen by Congress; and the head of the UN verification mission (with voice, but without vote). This composition proved to be a serious mistake: since the other political parties in the Congress were not represented in the commission (except by the single representative of Congress), they had little sense of ownership over the peace process. The four "citizens" on the Follow-Up Commission did not represent any sector or party. The other political parties did not assume a shared responsibility for implementing the accords, developed no vested interest in preparing the ground for passage of necessary legislation, and did not have to confront the inherent challenges in implementation. They could stand apart, and tended to do so since the government's decision to exclude them from the Follow-Up Commission suggested its intent to appropriate whatever political benefits might accrue from the peace accords. Why should they help the PAN do that? In practice, the leading figures in the Follow-Up Commission were drawn from the same small group that negotiated the peace accords, including Arnault (representing MINUGUA), Zelaya and Porras for the government, and Pablo Monsanto and Arnoldo Noriega for the URNG. Once implementation began, it would become clear that while Zelaya and Porras were committed to implementing the peace process, the government they represented was not. The Follow-Up Commission devolved into a conversation among friends that was increasingly isolated from the political realities of the country.[129]

Another key aspect of the Timetable Agreement was that it expanded MINUGUA's role beyond verification to include making recommendations to remedy noncompliance; "good offices" assistance to resolve problems; advisory services and technical support to facilitate compliance, including support for "other bodies involved in the implementation of the Peace Agreements"; and public information about the accords and their implementation. The agreement made MINUGUA, in a word, a "partner" in peace implementation, which would subsequently make it more difficult for MINUGUA to assess the government's role in peace implementation at arm's length.[130]

The entire Timetable Agreement was strangely worded, with a large majority of commitments stated in the passive voice with no indication of who was responsible to implement them. This is, of course, a common construction in Spanish, but nonetheless reflected an underlying vagueness about agency and responsibilities. Only in a few cases did the phrasing obligate the president or the executive to take specific actions, and in most instances that amounted to introducing legislation to Congress or forming commissions. This reflected deeper flaws in the Timetable Agreement: it did not realistically take account of the political processes that would be involved in implementing the accords (such as, for example, increasing taxes or implementing multilingualism in schools and government services). Moreover, some elements of the accords implied social changes that would have to unfold over a decade or more. Failure to comply was built into the timetable from the moment it was signed.[131]

Most troubling, the Timetable Agreement made no distinction between elements that were critical to the value of the accords as a whole and elements that were "nice to have" but not essential. It set up a "flat" verification scheme in which verification would take place commitment by commitment, without regard to relative importance or difficulty. It also front-loaded many of the easiest tasks, and back-loaded the more difficult ones. Given that the Arzú government's political leverage would inevitably decline in its final years in office, this sequencing made complete implementation less likely.[132]

■ Conclusion: A Diffuse Peace Process

As we turn to the question of implementation of the peace accords, several important features of the Guatemalan accords emerge: the accords were broad in their coverage of issues; many of the commitments required actions by institutions and groups other than the executive, and insufficient time and mechanisms were available to ensure that most of these would be implemented; some of the government's concrete commitments were politically implausible; many details of reform were delegated to joint commissions; among the most important measures were constitutional reforms that would have to be approved both in Congress and through popular referendum, with unpredictable results; and the parties to the final accords were both politically weakened by the time they were signed.

The United Nations had inherited in Guatemala a negotiating process that was slow, diffuse, asymmetrical in terms of the power of the two parties, and extraordinarily broad in scope. It was also a process that was very distant from the priority concerns of much of the public, as revealed in public opinion surveys. The accords had become a project of the Arzú government and the URNG, with other parties, social groups, and the general public increasingly disengaged.[133] UN moderator Arnault had probably brokered the best agreements that were possible under the circumstances, with two exceptions. First, stronger international guidance and less haste might have produced a better Agreement on the Strengthening of Civilian Authority. Second, the Timetable Agreement incorporated serious architectural flaws that undercut prospects for implementation and effective verification by the United Nations.

The United Nations' involvement had clearly saved the peace process on a number of occasions. UN diplomacy helped head off Rosada's dead-end strategy; UN mediation reinvigorated the stagnated talks; MINUGUA's deployment helped mute the URNG's main excuse for stalling and helped create a human rights climate in which the rebels and their supporters could safely disarm without risk of being slaughtered; and the February 1995 ultimatum probably prevented a complete breakdown. However, the final agreements created deficient mechanisms for follow-up and verification by both the Follow-Up Commission and MINUGUA, and the domestic political context in which they would be implemented was inauspicious and deteriorating. The United Nations was in for a rough ride.

▌ Notes

1. George Tsebelis, *How Political Institutions Work* (Princeton, NJ: Princeton University Press, 2002).

2. Luis Pásara, *Paz, ilusión, y cambio en Guatemala: El proceso de paz, sus actors, logros, y límites* (Ciudad de Guatemala: Universidad Rafael Landívar, 2003), 67.

3. Tanya Palencia Prado, *Peace in the Making: Civil Groups in Guatemala* (London: Catholic Institute for International Relations, 1996), 3–4.

4. Typically the PACs were armed with rusty 1940s vintage bolt-action Mauser rifles, whose small capacity and very slow rate of fire made them no match for modern assault rifles used by the URNG.

5. A transition to formally elected civilian rule took place in 1986, but the military retained extensive de jure and de facto authority. The constraints on civilian authority are discussed in detail below.

6. Boutros Boutros-Ghali, *An Agenda for Peace: Preventive Diplomacy, Peacemaking, and Peace-Keeping,* United Nations, 1992, at www.un.org/Docs/SG/agpeace.html; and *Supplement to an Agenda for Peace,* United Nations, 1995, at www.un.org/Docs/SG/agsupp.html.

7. See Piero Gleijeses, *Shattered Hope: The Guatemalan Revolution and the United States, 1944–1954* (Princeton, NJ: Princeton University Press, 1991).

8. Michael McClintock, *The American Connection: State Terror and Popular Resistance in Guatemala* (London: Zed Books, 1985), 49–109.

9. Milton Jamail and Margo Gutierrez, *It's No Secret: Israel's Military Involvement in Central America* (Belmont, MA: Association of Arab-American University Graduates, Inc., 1986), 48–61; McClintock, *American Connection,*192–196.

10. McClintock, *American Connection,* 219.

11. For a presentation of how multiple human rights reporting sources can be used to generate an overall estimate of the numbers of civilians killed during a

conflict, see Patrick Ball, "The Guatemalan Commission for Historical Clarification: Generating Analytical Reports, Inter-Sample Analysis," in *Making the Case: Investigating Large Scale Human Rights Violations Using Information Systems and Data Analysis,* edited by Patrick Ball, Herbert F. Spirer, and Louise Spirer, 259–286 (Washington, DC: American Association for the Advancement of Science, 2000), at http://shr.aaas.org/mtc/index.html.

12. Comisión de Esclarecimiento Histórico, *Guatemala: Memoria del Silencio* (Guatemala: United Nations Office of Project Services [UNOPS], 1999).

13. For example, Cuba constructed a mock-up of a Salvadoran military base on which FMLN commandos could practice an assault before infiltrating back into El Salvador. I am not aware of any comparable assistance to the URNG.

14. Greg Grandin, *The Last Colonial Massacre: Latin America in the Cold War* (Chicago: University of Chicago Press, 2004).

15. Jennifer Schirmer, *The Guatemalan Military Project: A Violence Called Democracy* (Philadelphia: University of Pennsylvania Press, 1998), 185–257. Gramajo was moderate by the standards of the Guatemalan military, but nonetheless was found responsible by a US court in 1995 for human rights violations and ordered to pay US$47.5 million in damages. He died on his farm in Guatemala in 2004, attacked by Africanized bees. See http://harvardwarcriminals.blogspot.com/2007/05/hector-gramajo.html.

16. Rachel Garst, *Military Intelligence and Human Rights in Guatemala: The Archivo and the Case for Intelligence Reform* (Washington, DC: Washington Office on Latin America, 1995).

17. Pásara, *Paz, ilusión, y cambio,* 13.

18. Inforpress Centroamericana, *Guatemala 1986–1994, Compendio del Proceso de Paz I: Cronologías, análisis, documentos, acuerdos* (Guatemala: Inforpress Centroamericana, 1995), 9–11.

19. Ibid., 13.

20. Named after the Panamanian island of Contadora where the first such regional agreement was signed in 1983.

21. William Goodfellow and James Morrell, "Esquipulas: Politicians in Command," in *Political Parties and Democracy in Central America,* edited by Louis W. Goodman, William M. LeoGrande, and Johanna Mendelson Forman, 267–287 (Boulder, CO: Westview Press, 1992).

22. See Jean-Marie Simon, *Guatemala: Eternal Spring, Eternal Tyranny* (New York: W. W. Norton, 1987), 230.

23. Héctor Rosada-Granados, *El lado oculto de las Negociaciones de Paz: Transición de la Guerra a la Paz en Guatemala* (Guatemala: Friedrich Ebert Stiftung, 1998), 19.

24. "El Ejercito ante la Pacificación," *Inforpress Centroamericana,* no. 894 (July 12, 1990).

25. Quezada was bishop of Zacapa at the time he served as president of the CNR and conciliator. He was appointed archbishop of Guatemala in 2001 and elevated to cardinal in 2003. In the narrative I will follow Guatemalan practice in referring to him as monseñor.

26. "Propuesta de paz genera expectativas," *Inforpress Centroamericana,* no. 929 (April 11, 1991); also Inforpress, *Compendio I,* 81.

27. Serrano's presidential candidacy had taken off after former general Efraín Ríos Montt was excluded as a candidate on constitutional grounds (he had previously come to power by coup d'état), and Serrano had inherited much of the conservative political support originally directed at Ríos. He thus had some political capital with

the military that Cerezo lacked. Historically, the Christian Democratic Party had opposed military rule, and although Cerezo himself had given the military few grounds for complaint, the institution—particularly its far-right wing—was hostile. Thus Serrano could take steps that Cerezo could not.

28. Interview, UN official, New York, January 2008.

29. Pásara, *Paz, ilusión, y cambio,* 20.

30. Acuerdo de Querétaro, Querétaro, México, July 25, 1991.

31. Palencia Prado, *Peace in the Making,* 14.

32. The activist, Maritza Urrutia, was fortunate to have international ties through her brother, Edmundo Urrutia (later Guatemala's ambassador to the UK), who mobilized various networks on her behalf and helped obtain her release. For a detailed, personal account of this remarkable episode, see Dan Saxon, *To Save Her Life: Disappearance, Deliverance, and the United States in Guatemala* (Berkeley: University of California Press, 2007).

33. Inforpress, *Compendio I,* 110.

34. Ibid., 94.

35. Ibid., 110.

36. Ibid., 101.

37. Ibid., 109.

38. Ibid., 91.

39. Jean Arnault, "Note for the File: Guatemala Peace Process, Preparation for a New Round of Negotiations Between the Guatemalan Government and the Unidad Revolucionaria Nacional Guatemalteca (URNG)," July 1992.

40. Inforpress, *Compendio I,* 88–92.

41. Francesc Vendrell, "Participation of the UN Observer in Indirect Meetings Between the Government of Guatemala and the Unidad Revolucionaria Nacional Guatemalteca," to Vladimir Petrovsky, September 18, 1992.

42. Inforpress, *Compendio I,* 99.

43. Alvaro de Soto, "Note to the File," June 15, 1992. At the time of his appointment, Arnault had ten years of experience in the United Nations, initially in language services, but thereafter as a political officer in various posts in Namibia, Afghanistan, Pakistan, and Western Sahara.

44. Inforpress, *Compendio I,* 113.

45. Rosada-Granados, *El lado oculto,* 30–34.

46. Ibid., 33–35. Note that the Constitutional Court and Supreme Judicial Court are separate entities with distinct jurisdictions, with the latter ruling on criminal and civil matters.

47. Espina voluntarily returned in 1997 to face trial for violating the constitution.

48. The proposal was widely referred to as the "Rosada Plan."

49. Rosada-Granados, *El lado oculto,* 54.

50. Ibid., 59–61.

51. Interview, UN official, New York, January 2008.

52. Ibid.

53. The term "moderator" was chosen to soften opposition among conservative Guatemalans to the sort of strong mediation role the United Nations had played in El Salvador.

54. Personal communication, UN official, New York, January 2008.

55. Ibid., 68–80.

56. Marrack Goulding, "Note to Mr. Arnault: Peace Making in Guatemala," January 10, 1994.

57. Marrack Goulding, "Note to the Secretary-General: Guatemala: Appointment of a 'Moderator,'" February 3, 1994.

58. Jean Arnault, "Note to the File: First Round of Guatemalan Talks (3–8 March 1994)," March 10, 1994.

59. Ibid.

60. Ibid.

61. Michael Möller, Officer in Charge, Americas Division, DPA, "Note to Mr. Goulding," March 24, 1994.

62. In this regard, MINUGUA's mandate was close to that of the International Commission Against Impunity in Guatemala (CICIG) in that the authority to collect information verged on subpoena power.

63. Marrack Goulding, "Note to the Secretary-General, Guatemalan Peace Process: Establishment of Verification Mission," August 3, 1994.

64. "Letter from Representatives of Colombia, Mexico, and Venezuela to Secretary-General Boutros Boutros-Ghali," July 27, 1994.

65. Marrack Goulding, "Note to the Secretary General, Guatemalan Peace Process, Establishment of a Verification Mission," August 10, 1994.

66. Jean Arnault, "Note for M. Schlittler: Guatemalan Peace Process," July 14, 1994.

67. Ibid., and Jean Arnault, "Note to Mr. Schlittler, Human Rights Verification Mission in Guatemala," July 15, 1994.

68. Jean Arnault, "Summary on the Consultations on the Resumption of the Guatemalan Peace Talks," September 10, 1994.

69. "Ayuda Memoria," Nueva York a 12 de septiembre de 1994. Author's translation.

70. Jean Arnault, "Note to Mr. Schlittler," September 14, 1994.

71. "Letter from Héctor Rosada Granados to Gilberto Schlittler," September 13, 1994, original in Spanish, translation by author.

72. "Establishment of a Human Rights Verification Mission in Guatemala, Report of the Secretary-General," A/48/985, August 18, 1994. Resolution Adopted by the General Assembly: Mission for the Verification of Human Rights and of Compliance with the Comprehensive Agreement on Human Rights in Guatemala. United Nations Document A/Res/48/267, September 28, 1994. All public UN documents of this kind can be searched and recovered by symbol (such as in this case A/48/267) through the UN Official Document System at http://documents.un.org/simple.asp.

73. Inforpress, *Compendio I, 221.*

74. Ibid., 225.

75. Inforpress, *Centroamericana, Guatemala 1995–1996, Compendio del Proceso de Paz II: análisis, cronologías, documentos, acuerdos* (Guatemala: Inforpress Centroamericana, 1996), 13–15.

76. Personal communication, UN official, New York, January 2008.

77. See "The Situation in Central America: Procedures for the Establishment of a Firm and Lasting Peace and Progress in Fashioning a Region of Peace, Freedom, Democracy and Development: Report of the Secretary-General," A-49/857-S/1995/168, March 1, 1995, for a summary of measures taken and transcripts of correspondence.

78. Reflecting an intense debate among indigenous groups about pan-Mayan identity, the agreement recognized the shared elements of identity of peoples descended from Mayan culture, but also the distinctiveness of the contemporary sociocultural groups, as well as the distinctive identity of Xinca and Garífuna peoples.

79. "The Situation in Central America: Procedures for the Establishment of a Firm and Lasting Peace and Progress in Fashioning a Region of Peace, Freedom, Democracy and Development: Letter dated 5 April 1995 from the Secretary-General to the President of the General Assembly and to the President of the Security Council," A/49/882-S/1995/256, April 10, 1995, 13–14.

80. Ibid., 14–16.

81. Roger Plant, Adviser, Indigenous Affairs, "Discussion Paper, Verification of the Indigenous Agreement," April 17, 1995.

82. Management Systems International (Kenneth Coleman et al.), "An Assessment of the State of Democratic Consolidation and Governance in Guatemala: Late 1996," prepared for Office of Democratic Initiatives, USAID/Guatemala, (Washington, DC: MSI, November 15, 1996), 11, no. 32, cited in Pásara, *Paz, ilusión, y cambio,* 65.

83. Alvaro de Soto, "Note to Mr. Goulding: Guatemala," April 13, 1994.

84. Inforpress, *Compendio II,* 9–10, 70–71.

85. "Declaración de Contadora," 22 de agosto de 1995. Signed by members of COPAZ, the URNG, six political parties, and three members of the Central American Parliament. Accessed from MINUGUA website mirror disk "Diez Años" through section on Proceso de Paz.

86. The peak business association, CACIF, explicitly disagreed with the CONAGRO suit and many members of the business community, and opinion leaders in the press, criticized the lawsuits.

87. MINUGUA, "Weekly Situation Report," January 2–15, 1996.

88. Ibid., and Leonardo Franco, "Briefing Paper for Your Visit," to Marrack Goulding, January 23, 1996, cable GUANY 182.

89. Inforpress, *Compendio II,* 86–87.

90. Ivan Briscoe, *A Criminal Bargain: The State and Security in Guatemala* (Madrid: FRIDE, 2009), 9.

91. Ibid., 95–97.

92. "Posición de la Asamblea de la Sociedad Civil ante el tema socioeconomico y situación agraria," Guatemala, marzo de 1996. Facsimile transmitted from ASC to DPA/NY March 26, 1996.

93. Agreement on Social and Economic Aspects and Agrarian Situation, Part I, Section B, paragraph 13. Accessed from MINUGUA website mirror disk "Diez Años" through section on Proceso de Paz.

94. Ibid., Part III, paragraph 28.

95. Ibid., Part III, Section G, paragraph 38.

96. Leila Lima, Officer in Charge, MINUGUA, "Op-Ed Piece on Guatemala," to Marrack Goulding, May 24, 1996.

97. For a detailed a sobering account of the difficulty of changing Guatemala's regressive and inadequate tax system, see J. Fernando Valdez and Mayra Palencia Prado, *Los dominios del poder: La encrucijada tributaria* (Guatemala: FLACSO, 1998).

98. Alvaro de Soto and Graciana del Castillo, "Obstacles to Peacebuilding," *Foreign Policy* 94 (Spring 1994): 69–83.

99. Susan Woodward, *Balkan Tragedy: Chaos and Dissolution After the Cold War* (Washington, DC: Brookings, 1995); and Stephen Samford, "IMF Lending Arrangements, Social Development Spending, and Civil War," manuscript, Albuquerque, NM, 2009, on file with author.

100. MINUGUA, "Weekly Situation Report," April 30–May 16, 1996.

101. Edelberto Torres-Rivas, *Negociando el futuro: La paz en una sociedad vi-*

olenta, la negociación de paz en 1996 (Guatemala: Facultad Latinoamericana de ciencias sociales [FLACSO], 1997), 77.

102. Ibid., 83–84.

103. The 1994 code implemented adversarial, oral trial–based criminal procedure, but the judicial system had been very slow to adopt it in practice.

104. "Agreement on the Strengthening of Civilian Power and on the Role of the Armed Forces in a Democratic Society," Section IV. Accessed from MINUGUA website mirror disk "Diez Años" through section on Proceso de Paz. Paragraphs 24 and 25 were particularly bereft of detail.

105. Ibid., paragraph 30.

106. Ibid., paragraphs 35 and 36.

107. Ibid., paragraphs 46–55.

108. United Nations Development Programme, "UNDP Security Sector Reform Assistance in Post-Conflict Situations: Lessons Learned in El Salvador, Guatemala, Haiti, Mozambique, Somalia and Rwanda" (New York: UNDP Emergency Response Division, June 20, 2001), 40.

109. Author conversation with Blanca Antonini, San Salvador, El Salvador, July 8, 1993.

110. "Estudio realizado por la Comisión Multinacional sobre las Instituciones que Brindan Seguridad Pública en la República de Guatemala," del 24 de octubre al 4 de noviembre de 1994, DPA files, hand-labeled "Borrador" or "draft."

111. MINUGUA, Asesoría Policial, "Análisis presituacional sobre organización y problematica de la Policía Nacional," July 1995.

112. "Consideraciones de la Misión respecto a la institucionalidad de la seguridad ciudadana," undated, author not indicated, handwritten notes indicate "from Jan Perlin" and "Aug 96." Previous personal communications with Jan Perlin confirm that she provided advisement to the "moderation" and the party on police matters during this time period.

113. "UNDP Security Sector Reform Assistance," 40.

114. Rodolfo Mendoza, minister of interior, public presentation hosted by Washington Office on Latin America, Washington, DC, November 10, 1997.

115. MINUGUA, "Weekly Situation Report for the period 16–22 January, 1996."

116. ASC, "Pronunciamiento público de la Asamblea de Sociedad Civil," Comunicado de prensa 12-96, June 28, 1996.

117. David Stephen, "Meeting with Interior Minister," to Marrack Goulding, July 3, 1996, GUANY 1425.

118. Denise Cook, "Note to J. A.," July 30, 1996.

119. William D. Stanley, "Business as Usual? Justice and Policing Reform in Postwar Guatemala," in *Constructing Justice and Security After War,* edited by Charles T. Call, 113–155 (Washington, DC: United States Institute of Peace Press, 2007); and William D. Stanley, "Building New Police Forces in Guatemala and El Salvador: Learning and Counter-Learning," *International Peacekeeping* 6, no. 4 (Winter 1999): 113–134.

120. "Propuesta de reforma policiaca para Guatemala," WOLA, November 20, 1995, conveyed by Rachel Garst to Jean Arnault by fax, September 11, 1996.

121. This was the second such experience for the Novella family: Mrs. Novella's daughter had been kidnapped by EGP rebels in 1976.

122. Comisión de Escalacimiento Histórico (CEH), *Guatemala, Memoria del Silencio,* Tomo IV, Casos Ilustrativos (Anexo I), (Guatemala: UNOPS, June 1999), 269–284.

123. Torres-Rivas, *Negociando el futuro,* 118.

124. CEH, *Guatemala, Memoria del Silencio,* Tomo IV, 269–284.

125. Author interview with Jean Arnault, New York, January 2008.

126. Decreto number 145-1996, Ley de reconciliación nacional, December 27, 1996; also David Stephen, "Análysis de la Ley de Reconciliación Nacional," to Denise Cook through Marrack Goulding, December 19, 1996.

127. Pásara, *Paz, ilusión, y cambio,* 183–184.

128. Hilde Salvesen, "Guatemala: Five Years After the Peace Accords," A report for the Norwegian Ministry of Foreign Affairs (Oslo: International Peace Research Institute [PRIO], March 2002), 26.

129. Pásara, *Paz, ilusión, y cambio,* 178–182; see also Salvesen, "Guatemala," 29.

130. Confidential interview, MINUGUA official, Guatemala City, June 1998.

131. Pásara, *Paz, ilusión, y cambio,* 178–192; author conversation with Tania Palencia, Guatemala City, May 1998.

132. Ibid.

133. Pásara, *Paz, ilusión, y cambio,* 67–72.

3 Defending Human Rights and Fighting Impunity, 1994–1996

DEPLOYING A HUMAN RIGHTS mission in the midst of the peace talks was a risky undertaking. It was probably necessary to the success of the peace process, but it also had the potential to scuttle the talks or drag the United Nations into a morass. Jean Arnault would later write that the United Nations should only undertake human rights verification if the United Nations is also conducting the peace talks.[1] Mediating the talks at least gave the United Nations some measure of influence over the content of the agreements, what the United Nations would be asked to verify, as well as an inside view of progress (or lack thereof). Combining the two functions, for all the risks, gave the United Nations more leverage in each area than it would have had otherwise.

That said, the particular tasks outlined for the United Nations by the Comprehensive Agreement on Human Rights were challenging and contradictory. The Comprehensive Agreement gave the United Nations responsibility for two tasks. One was to verify the parties' compliance with their commitments under the accord to protect individual rights and to halt actions that caused civilians to suffer. The other was to strengthen those state institutions responsible for protecting human rights, including the police, the Public Ministry, the Human Rights Ombudsman's Office (PDH), and the Presidential Human Rights Commission (COPREDEH). Each of these tasks would be challenging, and the combination placed the United Nations in the position of both criticizing and attempting to build up the government.

International human rights verification was unfamiliar in Guatemala and potentially perceived by the military and right-wing civilian groups as a violation of sovereignty, even though the government had invited the United Nations in. This meant that the way the mission handled its work could have a significant impact on the course of the ongoing negotiations. On one hand, it could reassure the rebels. On the other, it could alarm some elements of the government, as well as important nationalist constituencies, so as to make a final settlement and later comprehensive peace verification impossible.

Human rights work also faced a public relations problem. Despite the fact that the Guatemalan constitution enshrined such principles as equal protection under the law, actual practice had seldom if ever upheld these norms and much of the public did not particularly value them. In the face of serious crime problems, the public often favored iron-fist measures against criminals. Human rights verification—which inevitably stressed equal protection and due process, even for accused criminals—often put the UN mission at odds with public demands for summary justice. Human rights verification in Guatemala presented logistical challenges: much of the country was very remote, mission personnel would need to travel to be accessible to the public in areas that lacked transportation services, and many of the potential victims of government abuse spoke indigenous languages rather than Spanish, meaning that the mission would need to depend heavily on translators to assist in its work.

The "institutional strengthening" component of the mission's mandate was also challenging. Guatemalan repressive and justice institutions were designed to preserve impunity for state agents engaged in a dirty counterinsurgency war. As the war had cooled down to a simmer, these institutions remained unchanged. Impunity had given rise to extensive criminal activities involving the police, military personnel, and other state agents, creating powerful financial interests in favor of preserving impunity. Despite the stated intentions of provisional president Ramiro de León Carpio and his successor, President Alvaro Arzú, to achieve reforms and end impunity, actual presidential authority over these institutions was tenuous. Finally, there was, at the time of the United Nations' initial deployment of a human rights mission, no agreement in place regarding major structural reforms to police, prosecutors, intelligence organizations, or the courts. That agreement wasn't signed until late September 1996, and did not take effect until early 1997. Thus for over two years, the United Nations would be responsible for strengthening deeply flawed institutions, but without a formal roadmap for how to do this, and without an explicit, binding commitment on the part of the government to accept major changes. Of course, at the time the United Nations deployed the mission, it could not know how long the delay would be. However, it was understood within the Secretariat that at least several months would elapse before agreements on major state reforms would be in effect. While the willingness of the United Nations to help build and not just criticize state institutions was helpful in convincing the government to sign the Comprehensive Agreement, in practice this combination was hard to pull off, particularly prior to completion of the accord on strengthening civilian power.

■ Preparing the Mission

Within a month of the signing of the Comprehensive Agreement, the Secretariat sent a preliminary mission to Guatemala and Mexico to assess the scope of the verification challenge, clarify the expectations and priorities of the parties, and design the structure and geographic deployment of the mission. The preliminary mission consisted of six experienced UN officials led by Leonardo Franco, who was then head of the International Protection Division of the United Nations High Commissioner for Refugees (UNHCR).

Having moved swiftly to send the preliminary assessment team, headquarters moved slowly in seeking a mandate for the actual mission. There was internal debate as to whether the United Nations should take this on, because there seemed to be a contradiction between the impartiality required of any peacekeeping operation and the likelihood that human rights verification activities would often involve monitoring the government. The then head of the Department of Peacekeeping Operations, Kofi Annan, in a memo on June 29, 1994, described "an alternative approach" to such situations, whereby organizations such as the Organization of American States (OAS) or Organization of African Unity (OAU) could be assigned human rights verification responsibilities.[2] This would have the additional advantage of involving regional organizations in field activities, an evolving priority that had recently been voiced by the Secretary-General.

However, Annan's suggestion was not applied to Guatemala. Both the Framework Agreement and the Comprehensive Agreement were explicit in calling for UN verification (though the government later tried to dodge this). The OAS, dominated by the United States, did not have the reputation for impartiality enjoyed by the United Nations and was therefore not an option. The United Nations would need to somehow balance the competing demands of human rights reporting and peacemaking, a tension that would prove to be a key challenge for MINUGUA.

As described in Chapter 2, there were a number of issues that had to be resolved before the mission could deploy. The Secretariat had to reach the decision to go ahead, despite the lack of progress at the negotiating table. After deciding to proceed, the Secretariat then needed to come to terms with member-state resistance to a Security Council mandate.

Once the General Assembly approved the mission's mandate on September 28, personnel questions built in further delay. There was a strong consensus within the Department of Political Affairs (DPA) that UNHCR's Leonardo Franco would be the ideal head of mission. Franco was an Argentine lawyer with a long and distinguished record in human rights and refugee protection. He had extensive UN and executive experience through the UNHCR. The only problem was that the UNHCR was reluctant to let him go, and since the UNHCR was autonomous of the UN Secretary-General, his loan to DPA for the Guatemala mission had to be negotiated. The main question was timing, since a major international conference was coming up in October for which Franco had significant responsibilities. It was eventually agreed between Secretary-General Boutros Boutros-Ghali and High Commissioner Sadako Ogata that Franco could move to DPA and Guatemala in late October.

There were also discussions regarding at what rank Franco should be appointed. One option would be to appoint him as special representative of the Secretary-General (SRSG), as had been done when the United Nations Observer Mission in El Salvador (ONUSAL) deployed initially as a human rights mission prior to the end of that conflict. This would have the advantage of giving him somewhat greater political weight. Another option would be to appoint someone else as SRSG while Franco headed the human rights mission. A third option was to appoint Franco as head of the mission and delay appointment of an SRSG until the final peace was decided. The Guatemalan government had not expected the head of mission to also be an SRSG at this stage, so the Secretariat ultimately followed option three and waited until later to appoint an SRSG.[3]

While all these deliberations continued, Franco was permitted some time away from UNHCR to lead a second advance team to Guatemala in September. Arriving in Guatemala amid intensive press coverage, Franco encountered the tremendous pent-up demand for international human rights monitoring. He wrote, "Much of our time in the past two days has been spent explaining that the Technical Advance Team (Equipo Técnico Preparatorio, ETP) does not for the time being have a mandate to verify human rights violations." Many people seemed to be investing a great deal of hope in the forthcoming mission. Franco described a downbeat national mood shaped by a "deep economic slump," government budget cuts, rising social unrest, considerable increases in both human rights violations and common crime, and pessimism about the stalled peace process. "In the midst of this, the arrival of the Mission is seen as the only real hopeful sign of change." Franco also reported that "most sectors are frustrated and impatient with what is perceived as sluggishness by the United Nations."[4]

Pending the formal opening of the mission planned for November, Franco suggested the ETP remain in Guatemala to "bridge the gap." He also expressed concern that even the November time frame for starting the mission might be unrealistic unless New York strengthened its administrative capacity to support the mission, and unless personnel recruitment processes were greatly accelerated. Franco and DPA political officer Denise Cook (Spain) had drawn up a list of core staff members who needed to arrive in Guatemala within a month to remain on schedule, but there were signs that the administrative wheels were turning too slowly. Franco was particularly concerned that a chief administrative officer (CAO) needed to arrive in Guatemala as soon as possible to arrange quarters for Guatemala City and regional offices, communications, transportation, and further hiring.

A key factor, which would ultimately work out in MINUGUA's favor, was that ONUSAL in El Salvador was by this point expected to close in April 1995, to be replaced by a much smaller follow-on political mission

(MINUSAL). ONUSAL's drawdown (as well as that of the International Civilian Mission in Haiti [MICIVIH]) potentially freed up experienced human rights verifiers and political officers. Franco hoped that the head of ONUSAL, Enrique Ter Horst, would be willing to let some of his best staff members leave early to help set up MINUGUA, to which Ter Horst ultimately agreed. Thus as the core staff formed in Guatemala, it included a good number of professionals who had extensive experience in Central America, good knowledge of the UN system, and a number of lessons they had learned in El Salvador that could be immediately applied in Guatemala. The downside of this arrangement was that Guatemalan elites were opposed to a "repeat performance of ONUSAL" and the transfer of personnel from El Salvador heightened that sensitivity.[5]

▌ Deploying MINUGUA

The United Nations Mission for the Verification of Human Rights and of Compliance with the Comprehensive Agreement on Human Rights in Guatemala (MINUGUA) opened its doors on November 21, 1994, in a ceremony attended by representatives of the diplomatic community in Guatemala and of other UN agencies. In keeping with past UN practice, and to avoid politicizing the event, neither the government nor the URNG were invited to attend. This invited some unfavorable comments from Guatemalans and somewhat lowered the profile of the event. The mission's opening was also eclipsed in national media coverage by the frenzied attention to the hunger strike by US activist Jennifer Harbury, who camped out in front of the National Palace to demand that the government clarify the whereabouts of her husband Efraín Bámaca, a URNG combatant who had been captured by the army in 1992 and "disappeared."

The quiet opening fit a general effort by the mission to maintain a low profile to avoid a nationalist backlash. It was unavoidable that in verifying human rights complaints and therefore criticizing government conduct, MINUGUA would elicit hostility from some sectors of Guatemalan society. However, the mission tried to avoid gratuitously antagonizing Guatemalans as the UN mission in El Salvador had too often done. For example, MINUGUA staff members were asked to avoid congregating conspicuously at restaurants and bars, and to be particularly alert to the number of white UN vehicles parked at any one location. In El Salvador, fleets of white SUVs with ONUSAL license plates routinely parked outside fashionable restaurants, or at popular beach resorts. This led to jokes about "Vacaciones Unidas" (United Vacations) and a good deal of resentment about the economic privileges of UN staff. To the extent possible, MINUGUA registered its cars with "MI" (international mission) license plates, deliberately creating ambiguity about whether a given car on the road was part of the verification mission (and thus potentially viewed as intrusive) or part of an international aid mission (just there to help).[6]

One of the greatest initial challenges for the new mission was the physical remoteness of much of Guatemala, especially many of the areas that had seen the most armed conflict and that therefore required the most careful monitoring of human rights conditions. The road network was in very poor condition aside from the main arteries, the telephone network was sparse, and mountainous terrain interfered with line-of-sight radio communications until repeater stations could be installed. Thus, when the mission opened, its ability to collect and investigate complaints in much of the country was quite limited. Plans laid out by the advance team called for establishment of eight regional offices, in Guatemala City (separate from the mission headquarters), Quetzaltenango (Guatemala's second largest city), Sololá, Huehuetenango, Santa Cruz del Quiché, Cobán, Zacapa, and Flores/Santa Elena. Because of the rugged terrain and poor roads, there would also be subregional offices in Jutiapa (later changed to Escuintla, reporting to Guatemala City region), San Marcos (Quetzaltenango), Barillas (Huehuetenango), Nebaj (Santa Cruz del Quiché), and Cantabal (Cobán).[7] Even with thirteen offices around the country, each office would cover a tremendous area. In the meantime, representatives of the mission traveled throughout the country to verify complaints received at the Guatemala regional office. This wasn't fully satisfactory, since people had to somehow travel to the capital to make their initial complaints, but even this was an improvement over the previous lack of international scrutiny.

MINUGUA scaled up over the remaining weeks of 1994, adding one or two regional or subregional offices each week. Some of the regional and subregional offices offered austere accommodations, difficulty in accessing potable water, and limited and monotonous food. Road travel was punishing, and often the only way into rural communities was by foot. These physical difficulties were compounded by periodic threats, and in some cases violence, directed against the mission.

Overall, the field presence of MINUGUA was very junior. Each regional office was headed by a regional coordinator (at the P-3 or P-4 level) assisted by a political affairs officer (PAO) (at the P-3 or P-2 level). There were a handful of police or military observers, and the rest of the human rights verification staff were United Nations Volunteers (UNVs), who began arriving in December 1994. A higher proportion of substantive staff members were UNVs than in any previous UN mission, and they held very large responsibilities in a difficult working environment. The UNVs typically were either well educated but lacking in field experience, or field-experienced with nongovernmental organizations but lacking advanced degrees.

■ Budget Problems

As the mission was deploying, there was an intense behind-the-scenes struggle about the mission's budget between, on one side, the Advisory Committee on Administrative and Budgetary Questions (ACABQ) as well as the so-called Fifth Committee (the General Assembly committee-of-the-whole responsible for budgetary decisions), and the Field Operations Division of the Department of Peacekeeping Operations (FOD/DPKO) on the other side. FOD was responsible for developing the mission budget. While the mission reported politically to DPA, DPKO was more accustomed to setting up and managing missions and therefore handled many operational matters. The Fifth Committee, which was under tremendous pressure at this time to achieve savings (mainly because of US arrears and demands for reforms), had rejected the initial MINUGUA budget as padded. On November 21, the day that MINUGUA opened its doors, the Director of the Programme, Planning, and Budget Division (a division of the UN Treasury, part of the UN Secretariat) Jean-Pierre Halbwachs wrote that somehow more cuts had to be made. The reaction of the Fifth Committee to the initial MINUGUA proposal was the "most negative" he had ever encountered. DPKO was asking far too much, especially in terms of staffing. He cited the examples of missions in Haiti and South Africa (MICIVIH and the United Nations Observer Mission in South Africa [UNMOSA]) whose actual expenditures were far below the original estimates. The Secretariat's credibility was at stake. Specifically, the Fifth Committee wanted MINUGUA to cut ten junior professional positions deemed superfluous, and wanted to see about a 30 percent cut in the number of vehicles assigned to the mission.[8]

In retrospect, the negative reaction of the Fifth Committee reflected a deficient understanding of what was involved in verifying human rights throughout a country such as Guatemala, and perhaps a failure by the committee members to consult a map of the country. MINUGUA seems to have been caught up in a complicated game between the Secretariat and member states. While planners for some other missions might have overestimated costs, the planning for MINUGUA had been very scrupulous, reflecting the United Nations' financial constraints at the time and awareness that a General Assembly mission would be particularly closely scrutinized. The mission was designed to be as lean as possible. Yet the member states on the Fifth Committee assumed that the Secretariat was padding its figures. This created a catch-22: having kept MINUGUA lean in the first place, there were few concessions the Secretariat could make when the Fifth Committee raised objections.

Director of Mission (DOM) Franco wrote back to Halbwachs that cutting the ten junior professional positions was unacceptable. The junior political affairs officers were to be deputies to the regional coordinators, and would be responsible for regional offices whenever coordinators were out of the area. Franco was not prepared to leave such responsibilities to UNVs, especially during the politically vital first stages of the mission.

Not mentioned in Franco's argument, but equally important in retrospect, was the fact that civilian authority over police and military components had been tenuous in some other peace missions (ONUSAL comes immediately to mind, where separate military and police divisions had their own de facto chains of command). MINUGUA placed military and police officers in the mission under the authority of the civilian coordinator in the region to which they were assigned. This was a very good idea that in practice helped to avoid the formation of parallel military and police command and information channels that had plagued many other UN missions. But it would have been completely unrealistic to place police and military officers, who generally had at least several years of professional experience, under the command of green UNVs.

Franco also challenged the Fifth Committee's view that MINUGUA was asking for too many vehicles. MINUGUA staff would have to travel constantly on "roads which are little more than mountain tracks and which further deteriorate during the 6-month rainy season." Staff would be working in an area of armed conflict. They needed mobility for their own safety. MINUGUA needed at least 132 vehicles (not the proposed 109). Comparison to other missions would reveal that the requested number was modest.[9]

While this may seem a mundane issue, the mission (or rather, the Guatemalan "road" system) was in fact very hard on vehicles, and subsequent reporting showed that even with its full complement of vehicles, the mission was sometimes hampered by breakdowns in remote areas and delays in obtaining spare parts. The original request appears not to have been padded, and had the Fifth Committee succeeded in imposing a smaller fleet, the mission would have had trouble functioning.

On other issues, Franco simply asserted that the budget was already "at a minimum level. Any lower level of funding will not allow us to implement the mandate given to us." DPKO supported this position. Franco traveled to New York on December 7 to make the case to ACABQ in person. In the end, MINUGUA won the initial budgetary arguments, but its dependence on General Assembly budget processes would make it subject to strong questioning and great uncertainty every six months.

■ First Reactions

On December 5, MINUGUA opened its regional office in Santa Cruz del Quiché, in the heart of one of the most militarily contested regions the country. Between 1,500 and 2,000 people showed up for the event, signaling the strong local interest in having international human rights monitoring. As the mission continued opening additional regional offices, public attention gradually increased, and opening ceremonies began to be attended by increasing numbers of representatives of government, including the armed forces. The general tone of these events was hopeful and positive.

In the first week of December, MINUGUA successfully resolved its first human rights case in a way that suggested just how helpful the mission could be in individual situations. Military forces had arrested a young man for carrying a carbine. When his family inquired after him, the local military post said they didn't have him. When MINUGUA inquired, the military admitted that he was in custody (since of course MINUGUA could inspect their base if they lied), and soon released him. MINUGUA also responded to Jennifer Harbury's high-visibility protest by beginning its own search for disappeared URNG combatant Bámaca, making first use of its authority to make unannounced inspections of government facilities.

Some local NGOs responded to MINUGUA's initiative in the Bámaca case in a way that sadly would characterize their posture toward the mission—by remarking that having set the precedent of looking for this one disappeared individual, MINUGUA should actively pursue the other 45,000 cases of disappeared individuals. A national NGO called the Mutual Support Group (GAM) claimed to have presented three hundred similar cases to the courts, though it provided MINUGUA with documentation on only about half that number. MINUGUA avoided comment on this request, and proceeded with its deployment and investigation of individual cases brought to it by the public.

MINUGUA experienced its first minor act of intimidation on December 21, when members of a local PAC unit, operating under orders from military commissioners, forcibly confiscated a MINUGUA representative's notebook, hurled insults, and broke up a meeting. The mission responded with a *note verbale* to the Foreign Relations Ministry, reminding the government that the mission considered military commissioners and their agents to be "acting public authorities." The government had promised in the Comprehensive Agreement to ensure the safety of MINUGUA personnel, so the mission was holding the government responsible for delivering on that promise. The mission finished out the year without further incident.

■ Methods and Politics of Human Rights Verification

Verifying the Comprehensive Agreement

The Comprehensive Agreement gave the UN verification mission the following tasks:

- Receive and investigate complaints regarding possible human rights violations;

- Ensure that national institutions were carrying out investigations effectively in accordance with the Guatemalan constitution and applicable international human rights norms;
- Determine when human rights violations had taken place, with particular emphasis on "the rights to life, to integrity and security of person, to individual liberty, to due process, to freedom of expression, to freedom of movement, to freedom of association and to political rights";
- Determine whether the agreement was being fully implemented by the parties;
- Make recommendations to the parties;
- Meet regularly with each of the parties to discuss the mission's findings and recommendations;
- Report regularly to the Secretary-General.[10]

Almost all of the obligations in the agreement fell on the government. The URNG was required only to halt actions that caused the civilian population to suffer. The asymmetry in responsibilities combined with the historically atrocious human rights conduct of government forces meant that there was no way that the mission could avoid making devastating public criticisms of the government, and this brought political risks for the mission. Compounding this fact was the imbalance between the two sides with respect to the number of combatants. With around ten times the personnel of the URNG, the government was simply more likely to commit actions that violated the agreement.

The one thing that balanced the tables somewhat was that MINUGUA interpreted Article IX, paragraph 1 of the agreement (on preventing civilian suffering) to mean that the URNG should halt the collection of "war taxes," as well as all acts of coercion, threats, retaliation, destruction of property, and temporary detentions of civilians during war tax collection. MINUGUA repeatedly called upon the rebels to stop these actions and documented cases in which such activities had continued and resulted in violence or property damage.

While this was no doubt a principled position on the part of the mission, it also proved politically fortuitous. It established the mission's impartiality, even to skeptical audiences within the government and private sector. This in turn gave the mission the political space to continue operating in a country where it might easily, under only slightly different circumstances, have faced such a hostile environment that its operations would have to cease. The mission's personnel lacked any real protection from attacks, and their work required being easily accessible to the public. Thus the decision to criticize the URNG and pressure it to halt war tax collections may have made the difference between continuation of the mission and its collapse within a year or so. The downside of this decision, in retrospect, was that in the absence of alternative (perhaps voluntary international) funding sources for the URNG as a political party, the suspension of war tax collection left the rebels insolvent and contributed to the decision in 1996 to kidnap Mrs. Olga de Novella—an incident that almost derailed the entire peace process.[11]

The Case of the Missing Information System

A key weakness of MINUGUA in the first year and a half of its human rights work was that there had been no planning for an electronic database. Human rights cases were recorded on paper forms. A first sheet established a case with a unique number, when and where the violation occurred, name of the deponent or deponents, and a description of the event. A second sheet recorded personal identity and profile information. A third sheet provided for coding the violations (only up to three violations per case) in accordance with the categories set out in the verification manual. The office coordinator would then decide which of the three violations was most serious, and the case was then reported to headquarters and tabulated there, based on this "most serious" violation.

There were numerous problems with this approach. First, it meant that all the other violations that took place in a given case were not tabulated for the purposes of counts. If, for example, a person were illegally detained, beaten, and then killed, only the extrajudicial execution would be recorded. Since multiple violations of this kind were very common, MINUGUA underreported the incidence of detention and excessive force in its early reports. Moreover, details regarding multiple victims, witnesses, and alleged perpetrators were found only in the descriptive narrative for the case. This made it impossible to track with any ease the human rights records of individual perpetrators, whether army officers, police agents, prosecutors, or members of PACs. All of this contextual information resided mainly in the memories of individual employees of the mission. Many of those employees were either UNVs, who generally rotated among regional and subregional offices every six months, or civilian police officers, who typically remained with the mission for only six months. Unless new personnel arriving at a regional office had the time to read the hundreds of pages of narratives describing previous cases, there was no way for them to know which local officials already had a track record of abuses, which individuals had been previously victimized, and so forth.[12] These problems were compounded by the fact that while members of PACs generally remained in their local areas, army officers were often transferred from one part of the country to another, in some cases precisely because they had generated controversy for previous abuses. Unless regional coordinators happened to share this information verbally, MINUGUA staff might not know when a serial human rights violator moved into their area.

The overall effect of this paper system was that MINUGUA's reporting could not systematically identify patterns in abuses by either side. Until a database was implemented in late 1995, the mission's reports were primarily anecdotal, with interpretive observations added based on the mission staff. It is astonishing that the technical team sent to Guatemala in 1994 to prepare for the mission did not foresee the need for a computerized database. Such tools had already been used in El Salvador for ONUSAL, the UN Truth Commission for El Salvador, and the Ad Hoc Commission that identified officers who needed to be purged from the military after the end of the Salvadoran war. No budget was allocated for database programming, and no plans were made.

Within the first year, the head of the Human Rights Division recognized the need for a database, a view that Franco supported. Yet the CAO of MINUGUA would not authorize any spending for this purpose, even though human rights monitoring was the entire purpose of the mission. The administration claimed that the existing information technology staff could handle this job, even though they were understaffed, had no specialized expertise in human rights database design, and had minimal programming skills.

By coincidence, one of the UNVs in the mission, Ken Ward, had previous experience with programming and had built a human rights database for an NGO in El Salvador. At the insistence of the Human Rights Division, the UNV office agreed to his transfer to MINUGUA headquarters in October 1995, almost a year after the mission opened. Ward proceeded to work 16–18 hours a day, seven days a week, and completed the database in about one month. The result was a "relational" database system that could record and track the relationships among cases, individual persons (who could be victims, witnesses, or perpetrators in relation to any incident or violation), and violations. Ward designed a tolerably user-friendly interface that regional office staff could use reliably after training. The system made it possible to accurately tabulate multiple violations against a single individual, multiple victims in a given incident, multiple perpetrators, and the involvement of perpetrators in multiple violations. Data were sent in every month (and later every two weeks) by regional offices, and incorporated into a central database. Encrypted data storage and transmission techniques were used to ensure the safety of deponents.[13]

Ward trained regional office staff on the database in November and December of 1995, and by January the system was in use. A month later, all previous case information had been brought into the new system, so that comparisons could be made later across different reporting periods to identify trends. The first analysis using this system appeared in the fourth human rights report in February 1996, attributing over 44 percent of abuses to the National Police. Full comparisons of violation trends across categories and perpetrating agencies appeared for the first time in the fifth report in July 1996.

As Ward has pointed out, the clear lesson to be learned is that human rights mission planning needs to include budget and personnel for database creation. It was dumb luck that MINUGUA happened to have a UNV on hand who had the requisite skills. Without Ward, the mission might have gone many more months without any ability to detect trends. This was a serious oversight, and the CAO's resistance to correcting it shows a fundamental failure to prioritize the operational success of the mission.

MINUGUA's First Human Rights Report

MINUGUA issued its first human rights report on March 1, 1995. The report began with a description of the situation in which the mission was operating. This included a rather bleak but accurate summary of the human rights climate, the pervasiveness of paramilitary counterinsurgency networks, the inefficiency and weakness of the National Police, the recent history of political instability, the low voter turnout in recent elections, and the fragile economic conditions. The report went through each of the priority rights named in the Comprehensive Agreement and provided a general assessment of how well the government protected those rights (poorly in most cases). It then described individual cases. Almost 35 percent of the substantiated complaints related to violations of the right to life, including twenty-two extrajudicial executions (murders), ten attempted executions, and sixty-eight death threats. Many of the murder cases also involved obvious misconduct by the police, either committing the killings themselves, failing to investigate, or taking active measures to prevent an effective investigation. Most of the killings appeared to be politically motivated, as the victims were members of unions, civil society organizations, human rights groups, or one of the more socially active churches.

A sample case from the section on torture illustrates the content of the report:

> On 26 November 1994, a person who asked that his name be withheld was stopped and detained by a military patrol who accused him of being a guerrilla member. The next day, the military authority of the zone denied that he was being held, but two days later he was released after MINUGUA contacted the General Staff and the military base. The then chief of the military zone admitted in writing to the Mission that the victim had been detained for arms possession. The victim informed MINUGUA that he had been tied up and interrogated under torture, in which a plastic bag had been placed over his head so that he could not breathe, a spike had been inserted in his palate and he had been beaten on the soles of his feet. In the course of his interrogation about the alleged origin of a rifle and while he was still blindfold [sic] and chained to a metal bed, a gold crown had been removed from one of his teeth with a sharp knife. MINUGUA confirmed

the signs of physical abuse. The Mission has asked COPREDEH and the military authorities repeatedly for information on the follow-up to this case, to ensure that it does not go unpunished. So far, the only reply it has received is that "the case has been handed over to the public prosecutor" by the Ministry of Defence. The commander of the military zone at the time of the incident was assigned to another military zone.

The report addressed various other problems, including illegal security forces and clandestine armed groups, illegal forced conscription, intimidation against local human rights groups, failure to provide compensation to victims, and (under Commitment IX) actions that perpetuated civilian suffering. While the overwhelming failure to comply with commitments fell on the government, MINUGUA did note URNG violations of Commitment IX through its destruction of electric power posts as well as retaliatory destruction of installations at farms that had refused to pay war taxes.

President de León and most agency heads characterized the report as objective and fair, and as identifying areas where improvements were needed. The minister of defense was alone among relevant cabinet members in not commenting on the report. Sadly the Presidential Human Rights Commission, COPREDEH, which could have viewed MINUGUA as an ally, instead responded defensively and failed to take the report's contents seriously.

The first report established MINUGUA as a serious, professional, objective presence in the country. For the first time it provided the Guatemalan public with an undisputed account of just how bad the human rights situation was, despite the fact that the civil war was nearly over. Subsequent reports, three more during Leonardo Franco's period as director of MINUGUA, reinforced this contribution. This was, as described by a UN official who worked in the mission, a period of "building political capital" through authoritative and unflinching documentation of human rights conditions.[14]

"Defending Criminals"

Even as it strove to demonstrate its objectivity, however, MINUGUA faced a public relations problem of a different nature. Many Guatemalans barely perceived that the country was at war, but they did perceive that crime was on the rise; indeed as one social movement leader remarked to a MINUGUA consultant, "people don't see the arrival of MINUGUA in the context of peace, they see it in the context of rising crime."[15] In a society so brutalized by years of repression and lawlessness, the idea of the rule of law was so remote as to seem absurd and many members of the public, feeling vulnerable, wanted quick, violent retribution against perceived criminals. However, the mission was there to promote and protect the rule of law and some people took offense when it sometimes intervened to protect accused criminals from lynching, or criticized the police or courts for failing to afford due process. Critics of the mission pounced on such cases in newspaper and

TV editorials, as well as in graffiti, charging that MINUGUA defended "criminal rights."

In the highland department of Quetzaltenango, anger over MINUGUA's perceived role in protecting criminals led to threats against the mission. Threats started with graffiti calling the mission "parasites," "agitators," and "URNG," and telling the mission to leave. Someone shouted from a car at the regional coordinator, saying "MINUGUA is shit." None of this alarmed the mission leadership much, until a note signed by the "Urban Command for Immediate Action" was handed to a British citizen at a local bar, to be passed on to the mission. The note threatened to kill members of the mission, citing as precedent the name of a Mexican national, Lucina Cárdenas, who had worked for UNDP and been murdered in the area in December 1995. MINUGUA took this seriously, all the more because Cárdenas had been threatened by a note before she was killed. The Quetzaltenango regional office (ORQUE) restricted the movements of its staff, improved physical security at the office and staff residences, chose a local hotel as a rallying point in case of emergency (chosen because it had a soccer field next to it where a helicopter could land), and put in an emergency requisition for razor wire, none of which would have helped much against a determined assailant.

Then the regional office began addressing the underlying problem. A local committee of middle- and upper-class people was very angry about the lack of security in the region. Some had lost close relatives, killed along the highway connecting Quetzaltenango to Sololá (and the capital). Many robberies and killings were clustered in an area along the highway known as "Alaska." Members of the committee were frustrated with the police, whom they called cowards, and had been extremely aggressive toward the mission in meetings, accusing it of racism against Ladinos in favor of indigenous people, of "only getting thieves out of jail," and of getting in the way of what needed to happen, which was torture, beatings, and killings directed against criminals. Among their remarks had been that "If the mission doesn't change its ways, there's no telling what could happen," and "MINUGUA doesn't care about crime because nothing has happened to them yet." ORQUE staff suspected that behind the scenes, state officials were fanning the flames of hostility toward the mission. One ORQUE analyst wrote that "the cumulative result of state incompetence is so disastrous that the only excuse that state institutions can put forward is to blame the mission—confidentially and anonymously—for the current situation." The mission offered various kinds of help to this local group, including publicizing the violent crimes and pressuring the government to act. None of this impressed the citizens' committee very much.[16]

What did impress them, and ultimately quieted their hostility toward the mission, was that MINUGUA used its investigative capacity to identify who was carrying out the killings and robberies in the Alaska area.

MINUGUA handed this information to the National Police, who carried out two operations, scooping up suspects in the Alaska violence, as well as a former army soldier suspected in the Lucina Cárdenas murder.[17] Notwithstanding this important local success, accusations of favoritism toward criminals would haunt the mission continuously, especially when MINUGUA weighed in publicly on the question of the death penalty (addressed in Chapter 4).

Public alarm over rising crime gave rise to a new problem: lynching. This posed an awkward problem for the mission. The perpetrators were almost always civilians rather than official state agents, putting this phenomenon potentially outside the mission's formal mandate. On March 22, 1996, for example, a group of church women (!) beat and set fire to a man whom they accused of robbing their church.[18] This was fairly typical: many of those killed (often by being burned to death) were accused by the mob only of property crimes. Clearly lynching reflected the complete failure of the state to provide any protection to people living in remote areas, but it also constituted a failure by the state to protect the targets of lynching, who were denied due process and often received punishments grossly disproportionate to their alleged crimes. Moreover, the mission found evidence in several cases that paramilitary forces, including military commissioners and civilian patrollers, had provoked the mobs. The mission reported regularly on lynching, condemned the practice, and tried to prevent further incidents. MINUGUA alerted the police to transfer prisoners away from unprotected facilities, and pushed the government to deploy police to underserved communities. Despite these efforts, periodic waves of lynching continued throughout MINUGUA's deployment.

Property Rights as "Human Rights"

The other third-rail issue for the mission—in this case affecting its relationship with the business community—was its role in dealing with land invasions and other agrarian conflict. If the general public was mainly worried about crime, the top echelons of the agrarian elite were worried about their property. They had been historically unwilling to contemplate anything resembling land reform. The wealthiest families had their own aircraft and landing strips, fleets of armored vehicles, their own security forces, proficient attorneys, enough funds to educate their children at elite schools at home or abroad, and access to all the private services they could need. For them, the main utility of the state was to protect private property. This led them generally to resist the peace process, from which they expected no benefits and in which they saw considerable risks.

In early meetings with MINUGUA, leaders of CACIF chastised the mission for failing to guarantee property rights. The right to property was, from their point of view, a priority human right (think John Locke) and the mission should do something about illegal land invasions by peasants. In February 1995, the head of a CACIF delegation asked MINUGUA to intervene to prevent the expected occupation of a farm in Quetzaltenango by a newly formed peasant group, calling this "a test of the mission's usefulness."[19] Franco of course declined. The mission repeatedly found itself explaining the limits of its mandate: the Comprehensive Agreement listed the priority rights it was to verify, and property rights were not among these. What it could offer was to receive and investigate complaints of war tax collection, as well as threats or violence related to war taxes. Some members of the private sector appreciated and followed up on this offer.

The mission made other gestures in an effort to build a relationship with the private sector. When gunmen tried to kill the Guatemalan Industries Association chairman (who was saved by the armor installed in his car), private sector associations accepted and publicized MINUGUA's offer to investigate. When a member of the National Coffee Association was killed in a plane crash on a remote mountainside, MINUGUA offered to use its helicopter to recover the body. These gestures, and the mission's general efforts to keep lines of communication open, led to some degree of acceptance and cooperation from elements of the private sector.

Yet in this ideologically charged environment, the wave of land occupations and rural labor conflicts presented a complicated challenge. Since MINUGUA was protecting people—especially poor and indigenous people—and not protecting landowners' interests, it was all too easy for critics to accuse the mission of having leftist sympathies. Moreover, conservative Guatemalans may have had a point about the political leanings of at least some mission staff. Naturally enough, some of the idealistic young people recruited to serve as UNVs were more sympathetic to the disadvantaged social classes than to the elite. Some UNVs chafed at, or ignored, the restrictions implicit in working for the United Nations in a verification role.[20] When land conflicts occurred, landowners saw the mission as biased in favor of peasants and even as instigators, because they perceived MINUGUA staff as having friendly relations with organized peasants and agricultural workers.[21]

Mission policy on how to respond to land occupations and evictions was ambivalent and inconsistent over time. Initially, when the de León government asked MINUGUA in March 1995 to observe what the government claimed were lawful evictions, the mission demurred, saying this was outside its mandate. But by later in 1995, the mission yielded to pressure from all the parties to begin monitoring evictions, on the grounds that the presence of mission personnel might reduce the risk of excessive violence by the police and that the mission's good offices might in some cases defuse conflicts. In practice, this proved to be tricky because both the landowners and the occupiers tended to view the mission's presence as a threat. In a few cases, violence broke out and damage was done to mission vehicles, though fortunately no mission staff members were ever injured. Often, the police did nothing to protect mission staff; at an April 2006 eviction in San Sebastian, for example, the police retreated in the face of two hundred enraged peasants, leaving MINUGUA personnel dangerously exposed. MINUGUA increasingly found that its presence seemed not to contribute to moderation on either side, and became more selective about observing evictions, while also urging the government to seek a more comprehensive set of solutions to land conflicts.[22]

There were also many labor and land conflicts that arose at the local level without much prior warning, and to which it was difficult to apply any sort of formal policy. On February 14, 1996, for example, UNV Kenneth Ward (coincidentally the same UNV who had programmed the mission's human rights database) from the San Marcos subregional office in Quetzaltenango stepped in to protect a landowner's representative, who was being beaten with sticks by angry *campesinos*. The representative and his two bodyguards, knowing a good thing when they saw it, took Ward hostage, calculating that the workers would not attack as long as they held the UNV. MINUGUA's regional coordinator, chief security officer, and a police adviser came to the scene, offered themselves as alternative hostages and arranged for a commitment from the police not to intervene and from the peasants not to attack further. With the situation (temporarily) defused, MINUGUA staff withdrew, but the incident demonstrated that neither side in local disputes respected the mission's neutrality.[23]

Despite the willingness of mission staff to in some instances take personal risks on behalf of landowner interests, some portions of the private sector never accepted MINUGUA. Twice in 1995, national newspapers printed full-page advertisements, which sharply criticized the mission and accused it of trampling Guatemalan sovereignty. The second of these appeared in the aftermath of the mission's high visibility condemnation of an army massacre of repatriated refugees at Xamán (see below) and was entitled "Hasta aquí, ya no Más" (This Far, No Farther). It was placed by CONAGRO, the same a group mentioned in Chapter 2 for having sued the government's peace negotiator. The timing reflected the fact that the government's negotiations with the URNG had finally taken up the question of socioeconomic reforms, including taxation, documentation of land ownership, agricultural credit, and social spending—incendiary issues in the eyes of some agrarian capitalists. MINUGUA was an easy scapegoat for groups disaffected with the broader political process.

Coincident with the first publicity campaign against the mission in May, the owner of the hotel that housed the MINUGUA headquarters first demanded increased rent and then began to block the elevators and the parking garage, threatening to embargo the mission's equipment.[24] The mission eventually vacated, crowding the "substantive" (nonadministrative) head-quarters staff into the Guatemala City regional office until new office space could be arranged.

Somewhat reassuring was the response of several newspaper colum-nists, as well as CACIF, who criticized CONAGRO's stance. After discus-sions with various elite opinion leaders, Franco concluded that the anti-MINUGUA campaign reflected "a genuine fear among the private (agricultural) sector of the peace process, which they view as a real threat to their economic and social wellbeing."[25] Perhaps Franco was a bit gener-ous in this assessment: indigenous peasants whose families had been mas-sacred had well-founded fears; the agrarian elites had privileges that they wished to retain, a somewhat different emotion.

Military Outreach

The private sector right was not the only constituency the mission had to mollify in order to carry out its mandate effectively. Given the Guatemalan army's history and reputation, there was a substantial risk that the military could impede MINUGUA's ability to monitor human rights conditions. Civilian authority was, after all, quite tenuous, and the military itself had long accepted international opprobrium as the cost of pursuing its agenda. Fortunately, there had been a degree of change within the upper ranks of the military, toward being more mindful of the costs of international isolation.[26] However, the moderation in the institution's policies was very much con-tested. The military had initially supported President Jorge Serrano's seizure of power in 1993, later reversing itself as a more internationally ori-ented faction asserted itself in the face of prompt OAS and US sanctions. Shortly after de León had taken office as president, a faction within the mil-itary had overtly interfered in his selection of a minister of defense, forcing him to temporarily sideline his choice, General Mario René Enríquez. En-ríquez did eventually take the post and signaled support for MINUGUA's mission. He invited the mission's military adviser Juan Yagüe to give in-formative talks to officers at military bases around the country regarding MINUGUA's mandate. These talks did not always go smoothly, however. At a presentation in June 1995, an officer in the audience launched into a tirade against MINUGUA and particularly against Franco, characterizing him as an Argentine who, because of his nationality, must be antimilitary. This brought thunderous and sustained applause from the 200 or so mid-ranking officers in the audience. Yet Defense Minister Enríquez apologized for the incident and assured MINUGUA that it did not represent "an institu-tional attack against the Mission" (just a personal attack against its head).[27]

Other gestures from the military high command included arranging permission for MINUGUA's helicopters to land and refuel at military bases, which added to the mission's operational flexibility. This may have been self-serving as it gave the military intelligence about MINUGUA's movements. The talks in regional barracks also gradually convinced some officers not to view the mission as an enemy. In meetings with the minister of defense and with the army chief of staff, General Marcos Antonio González Taracena, representatives of MINUGUA were necessarily blunt in challenging the army over egregious human rights cases and impunity. One weekly "Sitrep" from September 1995 describes a "grueling" two-hour meeting characterized by "strong discussion" on a specific case.[28] However contentious these meetings were, they at least involved active engagement by the highest level of the army in discussions with military colleagues from other countries. The Guatemalan officers were told, persistently and forcefully, that the army's conduct was not acceptable under both Guatemalan and international law. For a time, González Taracena resisted these meetings by canceling them at the last minute, but he ultimately accepted the obligation to meet regularly with the mission.

The army high command was often at pains to restrain disorderly subordinates. When MINUGUA set about investigating a case of attempted kidnapping and attempted murder in Santa Lucia Conzumalguapa involving the National Police, an army officer threatened to "get" Leonardo Franco if the mission did not back off. Defense Minister Enríquez ordered the officer "to report to DOM [Franco] the following day for the purpose of explaining his alleged [*sic*] statements and objectionable behavior, in general. The colonel, somewhat subdued and perspiring profusely, spread his hands in 'disbelief' that someone should misquote him in such a manner, given that he was MINUGUA's 'best friend.'" Although this incident was temporarily resolved in the mission's favor, it signaled the deep and potentially dangerous divisions within the military. The sweating officer would go on to threaten MINUGUA again, and was eventually subject to an arrest warrant after police agents searching his house found cars with illegal plates and a lab for testing the purity of cocaine.

The Xamán Massacre

The greatest early test of MINUGUA's ability to verify human rights conditions and deal effectively with the army came in October 1995, when an army patrol massacred eleven civilians, including two children, at a community of returning refugees at Xamán in Alta Verapaz. The patrol entered the village in contravention of an agreement from October 1992 prohibiting military incursions into resettlement communities. A crowd of outraged villagers surrounded and heckled the patrol. Someone in the crowd grabbed the barrel of one of the soldiers' weapons and a sergeant ordered the patrol to open fire. Their firing was uncoordinated and they shot three of their own soldiers, later attempting to blame these casualties on (unarmed) civilians. The soldiers continued firing as they departed. One soldier went out of his way to murder an eight-year-old boy.[29] MINUGUA responded very promptly to this incident, demonstrating the importance of the mission's deployment around the country and its mobility. Two observer teams met and questioned the soldiers on their way back to base, learning that the soldiers had already been given instructions about what to say about the incident (which they apparently violated in describing events to MINUGUA staff). MINUGUA personnel reached the massacre site within two hours, and were able to observe physical evidence of the violence as well as take prompt testimony from witnesses, including many of those who were wounded and evacuated. The army gave permission for MINUGUA to carry out additional interviews with members of the patrol.

MINUGUA never found evidence pointing to high command involvement in the massacre, and its reports attesting to these findings gave the mission new standing with the army high command. As embarrassing as the incident was for the military, it appeared to have been a local-level misstep rather than a high-level policy. MINUGUA's willingness to say so made the more politically savvy members of the military aware that the mission could actually help the army with its pariah image.[30] But Defense Minister Enríquez made ill-considered remarks in the immediate aftermath of the incident, and de León called for his resignation. Army chief of staff González Taracena replaced Enríquez as defense minister. This gave rise to some speculation that the military would now shift in a more hard-line direction, a concern shared by some in the mission in light of González Taracena's earlier dismissive conduct toward the mission. In practice, González Taracena maintained a satisfactory working relationship with the mission, stressing in subsequent meetings with MINUGUA that he wanted the army to "learn from Xamán," that he expected justice to be done in the case, and that he accepted MINUGUA's report on Xamán as accurate and "had ordered the Army to view it as a basic document."[31] At the end of October, as MINUGUA military adviser Juan Yagüe prepared to return to Spain, González Taracena informed the mission that the army wanted to award Yagüe the *Monja Blanca* medal for "exceptional service."[32]

MINUGUA's reporting on Xamán was revolutionary in the sense that almost all of the violence against rural civilians during the war had taken place in isolation and secrecy. No other massacre had been immediately reported to the public, with details about who did what to whom, and medical evacuation of wounded civilians by helicopter. As DPA political officer Denise Cook put it, "These were people who had been nameless, and all of a sudden they were individuals. Proof. This is what happened. This is who did it. This was a major change." This incident, more than any other, demonstrated the value of having a mobile international human rights verification presence, and it clearly taught the army that it was operating in a new environment.[33]

It remains difficult to assess the lasting effects of human rights lectures, persistent public exposure of the army's wrongdoing, and public acknowledgment by senior Guatemalan officers of the norms promoted by MINUGUA. The hard-line, antidemocratic, anti-accountability factions within the military would soon reassert themselves, and at the end of MINUGUA in 2004, the army remained largely unreformed. At a minimum, however, these initial openings to international human rights norms, contested as they were within the army, helped to build a foundation for army acceptance of the final stage of the peace talks and a de facto end to hostilities during the next presidential administration.

▌ Institutional Strengthening

Political Context for Institutional Reform

The whole point of human rights verification was to create incentives for the government to improve its performance. Moreover, MINUGUA had a direct mandate to help the government to do so. Provisional President de León had previously served as human rights counsel and in that capacity had developed a reputation for personal courage in confronting the army over its egregious abuses. He was personally motivated to improve human rights conditions, and in general viewed the mission as an ally in achieving these goals. His main problem, however, was a profound lack of power to influence the conduct of the army, or to overcome the numerous shortcomings of key institutions such as the National Police, the Public Ministry, and the courts. His administration faced crippling shortages of money: previous mismanagement had left state coffers empty and the private sector did everything it could, including repeated lawsuits, to prevent de León from increasing and actually collecting taxes.

De León was sometimes surprisingly frank in admitting that Guatemala was still afflicted by impunity despite the efforts of his government.[34] Once the first MINUGUA human rights report was out, de León met with Franco and expressed his appreciation for the mission's work, saying that he "hated to imagine what things would be like now without its presence." Nonetheless, he also remarked that ironically the report had in some ways caused him to lose ground against the far right groups, since his enemies had disingenuously appropriated MINUGUA's criticisms to attack him politically. He was not faulting the report, which he called "tough but objective" and "reflecting the harsh reality," but rather alerting the mission to the fact that given his opponents' willingness and capacity to manipulate information, the report had hurt him. The president told Franco about an encounter with a group of students, who had advised de León to "get out while you can" because "you don't belong there." The president had found this depressing, and it had captured his sense of frustration as institutions he had worked hard to build were crumbling. Franco described the president as "overwhelmed, fed up and dangerously close to resigning."[35]

MINUGUA's highest-level ally faced deep divisions within his own government. The military continually sent mixed messages about its commitment to the peace process and to reforms. Foreign minister Maritza Ruiz de Vielman seemed to represent private sector interests that were skeptical of the peace process, and was at times out of step with the president. In a meeting and subsequent phone call with Assistant Secretary-General for Europe and the Americas Rosario Green, Vielman observed that there was significant opposition to the mission within Guatemala claiming that "the need for a large number of UN staff in Guatemala, as compared to similar missions in other parts of the world, was being questioned publicly. She had, in fact, had to travel around Guatemala herself to 'sell MINUGUA.'"[36] There was reason to question her salesmanship. In a June 1995 meeting with Franco, Vielman complained that the pressures on the government from the international community were far too strong. She asserted that Guatemala would not be "taken over" like El Salvador, and claimed that the "vast majority of Guatemalans were against MINUGUA, which was perceived as defending the rights of only one of the parties." Franco shut down this line of argument, noting that MINUGUA was there at the government's request, and that the mission would not tolerate "wave after wave of slander and insults." Vielman stepped down as foreign minister shortly after this encounter.[37]

Even de León himself, despite his background as a human rights advocate, was sometimes unsteady in his commitment to that cause when political expediency required. For example, when the Guatemalan Congress passed a law extending the death penalty to a wider range of crimes including kidnapping, de León told MINUGUA that he would never sign the bill, pointing out that the extended death penalty presented serious human rights and due process questions, but also that in practice it would lead kidnappers to more often kill their hostages. Instead of vetoing the bill, however, he referred it to the Constitutional Court hoping it would die there, which it did not. Moreover, in September 1995, faced with public outrage when the kidnappers of an eight-year-old boy rejected his parents' ransom offer and demanded more money, de León called for application of the death penalty if the kidnappers were caught.[38] In another instance, he announced that the murder of his own cousin Jorge Carpio Nicolle had been a common crime, despite significant evidence pointing to involvement by agents of the state.[39]

MINUGUA also needed cooperation from Congress, and found a surprising ally in Pablo Duarte, who represented the Guatemalan Republican Front (FRG) on the Peace Committee of Congress. He met with MINUGUA officials regularly, expressed support for the human rights mission, and served as liaison between the United Nations and the FRG. He brought to Jean Arnault FRG proposals for resolving problems in the peace talks. Duarte, like other centrist figures in the very conservative FRG, was not always fully representative of his party, however. The depth of division within the FRG was evident in a meeting held by UN special envoy Gilberto Schlittler with several FRG leaders in November 1995, during which the president of Congress from the FRG (and former military dictator) Efraín Ríos Montt bickered openly with FRG presidential candidate Alfonso Portillo on such topics such as human rights, the military, and communism.[40]

As the electoral campaign got under way in 1995, the mission was somewhat disheartened to note that "three presidential candidates are under investigation for misappropriation of funds, larceny, embezzlement, illegal removal of documents, kidnapping and rape, among other crimes and five candidates to Congress or PARLACEN . . . have pending legal problems related, *inter alia,* to charges of assault, murder, misappropriation of public funds, kidnapping . . . 30 candidates, including some to the presidency, have received death threats." The candidates' slogans did not elicit much confidence in their breadth of vision, ranging from promising "every monkey in his swing," "do away with privileges," "it is time for a change," "together we will build a new Guatemala," "the best way of saying things is to do them," and the promise to "govern with brains, heart, and balls" (cabeza, corazón, y cojones).[41]

The mission had an interest in anticipating future prospects of pro–human rights reforms, and therefore carefully monitored opinion polls published in Guatemala. During the early stages of the campaign, Ríos Montt was the declared candidate of the FRG, and this generated some concern given his history of involvement in a period of particularly horrific human rights violations, including the mass forced resettlement of indigenous peoples. The courts barred him from running, and the less reactionary Alfonso Portillo emerged as the FRG candidate. Despite his populist rhetoric, Portillo nonetheless represented a party that was very close to the traditional agrarian oligarchy and to the social control networks established by the counterinsurgency state. Portillo's opponent was Alvaro Arzú from the National Advance Party (Partido de Avanzada Nacional [PAN]), who represented the more internationally oriented elements of the business community, as well as portions of the middle class. Given his affiliations, he seemed more likely to create a favorable climate for pro–human rights reform, though little was known about his stances on human rights. The mission reported to New York with thinly veiled relief as polls showed Arzú rising in popularity while Portillo sank somewhat.

The "Results Oriented" Arzú Government

In the first-round elections in November 1995, the PAN won forty-three out of eighty seats in the legislature, while Arzú won 36.6 percent of the popular vote in the presidential race—well short of the 50 percent needed to avoid a runoff election. Portillo came in second with 22.1 percent. The second-round election in early January 1996 resulted in a narrow victory for Arzú based largely on the urban vote. Although Arzú was assumed to be preferable to Portillo from a human rights point of view, during the campaign he had said little if anything about human rights or the peace process. The mission remarked in a report to New York, "One wonders whether the omission of these points during the campaign was deliberate, given the low priority accorded to these issues by the population to whom Arzú owes his very slim victory."[42]

Franco and his staff were somewhat reassured regarding Arzú's agenda after they met with Gustavo Porras, Arzú's close adviser who was soon to be appointed lead negotiator on behalf of the government. Pressed by Franco to move quickly to address particularly egregious cases of impunity, Porras signaled that he understood the mission's concerns, but added that he wasn't sure how quickly and decisively the government could move, "because we can't open too many fronts at outset, given the complexity of established corruption, narcotics traffickers, bands of kidnappers and car thieves, all linked to powerful actors."[43] In fact, Arzú moved early and aggressively. He fired 118 officers and agents from the National Police on grounds of corruption. He appointed General Julio Balconi as his minister of defense, one of the most openly pro-peace officers within the upper ranks of the military. In September 1996, Arzú, with Balconi's support, moved to arrest one senior officer and dismiss nine others, including two generals, as well as senior officials from the Defense and Interior Ministries, National Police, and customs. The military part of the purge was directed mainly against a group of officers known as the Cofradía, who had been central players in the counterinsurgency and domestic intelligence war of the early 1980s, and who had allegedly developed an extensive criminal network centering in the customs service. Significantly, Arzú did *not* take on other military clandestine networks thought to exist, including some allegedly linked to current and former military intelligence officers.[44] This was far from the comprehensive anticorruption strategy that was needed to break up the nexus of semiprivatized violence and intimidation that was emerging already as the primary source of human rights violations in Guatemala.[45] It was, however, politically strategic, and reflected a good sense on Arzú's part of the limits on his power.

Arzú's government showed little expertise or interest in improving human rights per se. There were early signs of a single-minded focus on attracting foreign loans, grants, and investments. Newly appointed foreign minister Eduardo Stein warned human rights organizations that they should be careful how they used negative information regarding the human rights situation, since this could hurt Guatemala's international relations, "including in the economic field."[46] In other words, human rights violations were a public relations problem to be managed, not an outrage requiring public denunciation. It wasn't initially clear whether he was referring to MINUGUA or only to nongovernmental groups, but he would soon make clear that he thought the United Nations in Guatemala ought to certify the government's accomplishments, facilitate receipt of international money, and little else.

Leonardo Franco would step down as director of MINUGUA before the Arzú government had shown the full scope of its resistance to international human rights (and other) verification. But even on the basis of early indications, Franco was concerned. His two meetings with Arzú were strangely unsubstantive. The new president seemed to treat these encounters as social events, in contrast to the serious and business-like tone that Franco had become accustomed to with de León. Worse, in his remarks, Arzú seemed oddly naïve, or dismissive, about institutionalized impunity, especially given his courageous initial steps to purge the police. A possible explanation was the president's nationalism, which came more fully into view in the following year (see Chapter 4). In one instance, Arzú mentioned to Franco a case in which an ex-military commissioner, who was wanted for multiple serious crimes, had turned himself in and promptly been released on bail. The president claimed that the case could now no longer be considered "within the framework of impunity." Franco was "somewhat taken aback by this apparently overly-naïve statement, [and] pointed out that impunity was greatly favoured by precisely such actions and that this unfortunate development highlighted even more the need for genuine cooperation among all the state institutions." In the final days of his term as director of mission, Franco suggested that the mission needed to develop a more robust approach "in its dealings with our new entrepreneur and result-oriented counterparts."[47] Franco's use of "result-oriented" as a pejorative was more than just a snide riposte to contemporary attacks on the "process-oriented" United Nations: he correctly recognized that in its haste to achieve some measure of change (and bring in foreign money), the Arzú government was inattentive to fundamentals.

These early interactions with both the executive and legislative branches signaled one of the fundamental challenges facing MINUGUA: all the governments the mission would deal with over ten years were internally divided, and each of the parties in Congress was in turn internally divided. Within this chaotic context of political weakness and ambiguous political programs, moderates seeking some measure of reform often turned to MINUGUA as a political ally. Yet the Guatemalan parties' own weakness meant that their support for the mission was utterly unreliable. Writing in a February 1995 assessment of the upcoming election campaigns, UNDP analyst Ricardo Stein described an "absence of evident political alternatives that could galvanize the country on the basis of a national project shared by a majority."[48] Within each party, nationalist impulses (often unaccompanied by national vision) opposed allowing MINUGUA to have the kind of tutelary role the United Nations played in El Salvador. Thus the mission's ability to effect change depended entirely on the political intentions and efficacy of Guatemalan political actors. Too often their intentions were ambiguous and their efficacy limited.

Governmental Human Rights Agencies

MINUGUA faced perhaps insurmountable obstacles in implementing its mandate to strengthen state human rights agencies, especially during the early years of the mission. Because of misallocation of resources and a feud between two competing agencies, there was essentially no effective domestic counterpart agency to which MINUGUA could transfer its expertise in human rights verification. MINUGUA's official counterpart within the government was the Presidential Human Rights Commission (COPREDEH), which had been established some years earlier in response to a recommendation by the UN independent expert on human rights Christian Tomuschat. COPREDEH included a personal representative of the president, plus the ministers of foreign relations, defense, interior, the attorney general (head of the Public Ministry), and the government's head peace negotiator. The human rights ombudsman, who headed the other government human rights agency (referred to as the PDH), was not a member of COPREDEH. This was obviously a flawed arrangement, since the PDH had a constitutional mandate to investigate human rights cases and call to the attention of the courts and the Public Ministry those cases that required criminal investigation and prosecution.

The ostensible purpose of COPREDEH was to impose some meaningful collective response to human rights matters, much as US presidents periodically create "czar" posts in efforts to solve interagency coordination problems. There is little evidence that COPREDEH ever served this function effectively. In practice, despite President de León's history of commitment to human rights causes, COPREDEH was little more than an institutional apologist for the government's poor performance on human rights issues.

Compounding the problem created by two overlapping agencies, COPREDEH got most of the government resources devoted to human rights, while the PDH, which, unlike COPREDEH, had a mandate to maintain an effective field presence, was starved for funds. This was a direct violation of the government's commitment in the Comprehensive Agreement to adequately fund the PDH. Moreover, as MINUGUA opened offices around the country, COPREDEH opened offices nearby, eventually establishing seven regional offices in addition to its headquarters in the capital. These offices performed no discernible service for the public, and drew attention and potential resources away from the PDH.

With the PDH critically underfunded, it had little hope of scaling up to replace MINUGUA as a national human rights monitor. Thus MINUGUA was unable to provide the scope of on-the-job training and accompaniment that might have helped the mission to work itself out of a job by building up the PDH. The head of the PDH at the time, Jorge Mario García Laguardia, complained continuously about the misallocation of resources to COPREDEH, and charged that the commission's regional offices served only to help the government "control" MINUGUA's activities at the local level, while eclipsing the PDH and confusing the public.[49] MINUGUA substantially agreed with his analysis of the situation. Yet unfortunately García Laguardia also felt eclipsed by MINUGUA and was initially very hostile toward the mission. There seemed little the mission could do to build a working relationship with him. Franco wrote in January 1995 that García Laguardia had

> misread the acceptance enjoyed by the Mission to mean his removal from the limelight. In at least one case, MINUGUA was bluntly informed that the Counsel had issued orders "not to provide any information" to the Mission. Despite efforts to demonstrate the Mission's goal of strengthening his institution . . . García Laguardia feels threatened and completely overshadowed. In a conversation I had with him today, he was overtly defensive. I invited him to request anything that he felt would strengthen his institution—with the exception, of course, of inaction by MINUGUA.

As the mission's institution-building activities began to bring money into the PDH, García Laguardia's attitudes softened somewhat. Yet in his end of mission report, Franco noted with disappointment that García Laguardia "has never succeeded in overcoming his feeling of inadequacy and . . . is openly envious of the Mission and its attributes, while complaining—quite justifiably—about the meagre resources at his disposal."[50]

This impasse was particularly disappointing given the fact that senior MINUGUA staff members were well aware of the importance of working effectively with the PDH. In El Salvador, ONUSAL had largely failed to build up the PDH there, mainly because for most of the mission's time in country the PDH leadership would have nothing to do with the mission. Senior MINUGUA staff with prior experience in El Salvador were very sensitive to the importance of building institutional capacity in Guatemala from the get-go, and yet they were stymied by the lack of a working relationship with the PDH, and the lack of governmental financial support to the one institution that could have most directly carried on a credible human rights monitoring role in the long run. In retrospect, it appears that the United Nations should have insisted that the government make a robust financial commitment to the PDH prior to the United Nations' agreeing to engage in "institutional strengthening." This would not have eliminated the problem of erratic leadership at the PDH, but would have helped ameliorate the gnawing resentment that poisoned MINUGUA/PDH relations for a decade. It might also have been helpful if MINUGUA could have been seen to provide substantial material help to the PDH in addition to technical advice that was so easily seen as patronizing.

Prosecutors, Defenders, Police, and Courts

As with the human rights agencies, MINUGUA encountered significant, homegrown obstacles in its efforts to strengthen the capacity of criminal justice institutions to provide equal protection to all Guatemalans and to hold state agents accountable for abuses. Part of the problem was that there was, in the first two years of the mission's deployment, no explicit political agreement that the government would undertake specific measures. Lessons that senior ONUSAL officials had learned in El Salvador included (1) an outside agency will have difficulty developing an institution that won't cooperate with it; (2) successful development of police as well as other rule of law institutions requires a concrete, agreed-upon framework—that is, making reforms up as you go along gives home-court advantage to those resistant to change; and (3) development of functioning institutions requires radical change, including change in leadership and substantial change in personnel.[51] Yet for the first two years of MINUGUA's work, there was no commitment from the government to bring in new leadership or staffing, no criteria that personnel should meet, no draft of new legislation for what reformed institutions would look like, and no new financial commitment from the nearly bankrupt state. Some agencies, such as the Public Ministry, were simply overwhelmed and were at least potentially responsive to advisement, reorganization, and better training. Other state agencies, such as the National Police, were so flawed in their doctrine, design, organizational culture, internal discipline, and choice of personnel that no amount of strengthening would be likely to produce improvements in human rights performance. Instead, fundamental redesign, and new personnel, were essential. Lacking an explicit political agreement to carry out such changes, "strengthening" efforts were predictably futile.

MINUGUA set up an Institutional Strengthening division (Fortalecimiento Institucional [FORIN]), with subsections for carrying out different parts of the mandate. The FORIN division gradually began placing MINUGUA-hired advisers in the key institutions and also undertook a human rights education program. In a way, the FORIN mandate was consistent with the lessons learned in El Salvador: that it was important to build local capacity from the outset. However, the political circumstances were different in a key way. Whereas in El Salvador the FMLN rebels were the change agents (with behind-the-scenes help from UN technical advisers) demanding specific reforms as a condition for ending the war, in Guatemala the FORIN mandate placed MINUGUA in the position of change agent. Rather than verifying specific reforms negotiated by the rebels and accepted by government, the Comprehensive Agreement asked MINUGUA to undertake institutional reforms on its own initiative. This was, of course, exactly what nationalistic Guatemalans were most resistant to. Notwithstanding the mission's efforts to maintain a low profile, its FORIN role was inherently intrusive and tutelary.

The scope of the challenge is revealed in one of FORIN's own reports.[52] The section on police, for example, diagnosed the many deficiencies of the National Police and argued that the mission should not even attempt to strengthen the National Police unless it purged itself of "elements that generate citizen insecurity" (read: criminals, corrupt cops, and those who have carried out actions "against the rule of law," which presumably meant interfering with investigations; threatening witnesses, prosecutors, or judges; or destroying evidence). In addition to a purge, for the police to be effective would require both basic and advanced training, much greater transparency, new doctrine and training regarding the use of force, more congenial public relations, and a clear separation of police and military functions.

Despite the obstacles, MINUGUA was obligated to do something to strengthen the police in accordance with the Comprehensive Agreement. Thus it deployed five advisers to work with the police, focusing initially on criminal investigations (despite the government's lack of commitment to recruiting appropriate personnel for that function), basic police training, and the design and curriculum for the police academy. The mission undertook all of this before the government and URNG had signed an accord on police reform that would presumably address such issues as doctrine, training, personnel selection, and so forth, and even before the Arzú government struck its bilateral deal with Spain to develop the police. In this sense, anything the mission did with respect to the police in the first two years of the mission was premature. One example was a series of intensive training courses the mission held for members of the Treasury Guard (Guardia de Hacienda)—a police force that would later be abolished under the Agreement on Strengthening Civilian Power. It is difficult to see how these courses had any value, as the personnel who received them were to be cashiered.[53]

Work with the judiciary was similarly out of phase: MINUGUA carried out a diagnostic of the judiciary, but the scope of problems was so great that it was difficult to identify things that the mission could usefully do in the absence of an overarching framework for reform. The judiciary's problems included absolute legal and administrative control over lower courts by the Supreme Judicial Court; clientelistic rather than professional merit-based recruitment and selection of most judges; a gross lack of legal education on the part of judges; unfamiliarity by judges with the heavily revised 1994 criminal procedure code; information systems that were antiquated, mutually incompatible, or simply not used; and insufficient administrative capacity to deal with the case load.[54]

Other elements of the FORIN mandate at least involved activities in which the mission could make a contribution within existing institutional frameworks. For example, MINUGUA and UNDP formed the joint Program of Institutional Assistance and Legal Reform (PROLEY), which worked with the legislature to develop new laws related to human rights, most of them designed to bring national legislation in line with Guatemala's existing, ratified international human rights commitments. The mission also placed advisers in the PDH where they did such things as draft manuals on applicable national and international laws, as well as procedures for investigating human rights violations including due process questions. As already noted, the effectiveness of this work was hampered by the PDH's lack of money for staff, transportation, communications, and office space.

The two institutions where the mission was able to achieve the quickest, most measurable results were the Public Ministry and the public defender's office. When MINUGUA began its work, the Public Ministry was nearly paralyzed. The 1994 criminal procedure code gave the Public Ministry sole responsibility for investigating and prosecuting crimes (previously the job of judges under the inherited Napoleonic Code–based legal system). There was a 350 percent increase in the ministry's budget from 1994 to 1995, but given the quantum leap in the ministry's workload, this was not enough. Perhaps most crippling was the fact that the Public Ministry's attorneys, lacking any experience with adversarial criminal procedures, did not know how to manage cases. The courts were similarly flummoxed, and there had been only ten oral trials during the first eight months that the new criminal procedure code was in effect. During this same period, the Public Ministry in the metropolitan district had brought only thirty-four indictments. The system was near collapse. MINUGUA stepped in with an advisory team that drafted a procedures manual, gave seminars to prosecutors on case management, and accompanied prosecutors in their daily work until some of them got the hang of what they needed to do. In the first six months of the project, the Public Ministry issued more than 120 indictments, a nearly fivefold increase. After the initial year, FORIN focused on training a group of prosecutors to become an internal advisory unit within the Public Ministry.[55]

MINUGUA found the public defender's office to be similarly inchoate. Although the new criminal procedure code required free public legal representation to be available, the office got off to a shaky start. The idea of prosecutors and defenders playing out adversarial roles in an oral trial to arrive at a just outcome was unfamiliar, and the idea that the state should provide lawyers at no cost to people whom the police and prosecutors considered to be criminals was anathema. This resistance within the legal community translated into tepid initial support for the public defender's office. The office was created as a unit of the judiciary, and thus was administratively subordinate to the Supreme Judicial Court (CSJ). The defenders had to request CSJ approval for every personnel action and every expenditure, an arrangement that was completely unworkable. There were only twenty-nine public defenders in the entire country, and none at all in the largely indigenous highland departments of El Quiché and Huehuetanango. MINUGUA provided advisement on basic procedures, suggesting for example that to find clients, public defenders should visit the prisons! Mission personnel felt they were able to have a comparatively big initial impact because the office began in such disarray. But FORIN's role had limited potential until the public defender's office was allowed its own administrative leadership, enabling legislation that would formally create the office, adequate budget, and political backing.

Part of improving human rights performance is ensuring access to the justice system for people from lower socioeconomic strata, and particularly for indigenous peoples. The mission therefore undertook projects that trained court interpreters to translate between Spanish and indigenous languages, developed terminological dictionaries in two of the most common languages (Quiché and Mam), and worked with judges to establish procedures for using interpreters in court. In an effort to improve the integration of police, prosecutors, defenders, and the courts, MINUGUA helped sponsor an "integrated justice center" in the Ixíl area. It also launched a pilot project called the Popular Law Firm (Bufete Popular), which was intended to provide pro bono legal advice to low-income clients who faced disputes about land ownership, tenancy, or rental agreements.

These institutional strengthening activities were all funded by voluntary contributions to a trust fund. Sweden, Norway, the United States, the Netherlands, and Denmark collectively contributed over US$4 million for 1995 and 1996. Other states considered contributions, but held off because of the high overhead rate the United Nations charged for this type of account (13 percent), well in excess of that charged by some other UN agencies. This would become a significant point of tension between the mission and DPA (interested in maximizing trust fund contributions) and the controller (under tremendous financial pressures from member states and loath to lower the rate). Eventually (as discussed in later chapters) management of the trust fund was transferred to the UN Office for Project Services (UNOPS), in part to get a lower overhead rate as requested by some donors such as Japan, and in part to increase efficiency and agility.

Until this change took place, the mission's management of trust fund money was often cumbersome. This was a by-product of the way the Secretariat itself operated. The Secretariat's procedures had been created to serve the needs of an organization whose main activity was holding international conferences. Now, these systems were being asked to oversee field activities that needed flexibility and speed. The Secretariat's response to new challenges had been bureaucratic retrenchment. The inherent rigidity of Secretariat systems had been compounded by member-state micromanagement and withholding of financial assessments, to the point of near paralysis.

The lack of speed and flexibility was particularly problematic for projects such as the Popular Law Firm, which raised public expectations and required prompt follow-through. Leonardo Franco remarked in his final report that the mission needed greater flexibility in spending voluntary funds, and noted that in general the work of the mission's administrative office "does not always reflect a priority commitment to the goals of the mission," for which the refusal to fund database programming was a prime example.[56]

Occasionally, ambassadors of countries friendly to MINUGUA—including major donors to the trust fund—raised questions about the efficacy of the FORIN projects. In general, Franco dismissed these criticisms as unrealistic, and argued that it was unsurprising that institutional reforms were moving slowly. Yet the question of evaluation could not be ignored, and in 1996 the mission called in an outside consultant, David Holiday, to lead an effort to assess the mission's impact.[57] The report, based on dozens of interviews with government officials, staff of nongovernmental organizations, business leaders, and community and social movement leaders, challenged the way the mission had been assessing its projects. The report's main criticism was that the FORIN division sometimes measured its accomplishments on the basis of its activities: that is, if it held twenty-five training sessions, or gave seventy-five public talks on human rights, this was taken to be an accomplishment in its own right. The report urged the mission to look more to qualitative indicators of real change in *how* institutions were functioning, and to more systematically use its verification reporting to assess the results of its FORIN efforts. The mission never fully adopted these recommendations. Although individuals working on FORIN projects could observe changes in the attitudes and practices of their Guatemalan counterparts, it was frankly difficult to discern major changes in the functioning of the justice system overall, even after years of effort by the mission.[58]

The broader question was, what should be the division of labor between the human rights verification mission (with its FORIN mandate), and the various agencies of the highly decentralized UN system, which included the UN Development Programme and dozens of specialized development agencies? Weren't issues such as rule of law essentially long-term development questions? Or were some institutional development activities uniquely appropriate to a human rights or peace verification mission? There were no clear answers to these questions, a fact that contributed to considerable tension between the leadership of MINUGUA and that of UNDP during Franco's term.

One argument for combining verification and FORIN within MINUGUA was that the combination of hard-nosed verification of human rights performance and efforts to fix Guatemalan institutions might have provided a basis for financial and political leverage over the government by making the continuation of the development projects directly contingent on meeting certain qualitative indicators of improved institutional performance. Nothing of this nature emerged in the first eighteen months of MINUGUA's deployment. MINUGUA never attempted to make the continuation of FORIN projects contingent on improvements in human rights performance. MINUGUA's first four human rights reports described the deficient performance of state agencies, as well as the mission's own FORIN activities, without explicitly acknowledging that the continued human rights problems called into question the justification for FORIN projects.

Assessing MINUGUA's First Phase

When the parties asked the United Nations to deploy a human rights mission before most of the peace accords had been signed, they were asking the organization to take a major risk. Unlike in El Salvador, where the initial human rights deployment of ONUSAL came at a moment when negotiations were moving rapidly and most observers were confident that an agreement would soon be reached, in Guatemala the talks were lagging, the (interim) president was nearly a lame duck, there was significant elite and military resistance to making any concessions to the URNG, and the rebels themselves were showing political weaknesses.[59] Thus the United Nations stepped into a very open-ended commitment that was fraught with hazards. In his report to the General Assembly calling for MINUGUA to be established, the Secretary-General argued that deploying a human rights mission would increase the confidence of the parties and help facilitate peace.[60] This argument was premised on an idea borrowed from the Salvadoran experience: that the main obstacle to civil war settlement would be the reluctance of rebels to disarm. While such concerns were certainly salient, in Guatemala there was another set of obstacles to peace: because the military had essentially won the war in the early 1980s, it was unmotivated to make concessions to the URNG, and likewise many private sector opinion leaders saw no reason to change anything to appease a militarily insignificant rebel force. In May 1994, UN moderator Jean Arnault wrote to New York, fretting that the mission would be "*a most delicate political exercise* and a significant factor in the strengthening or weakening of the negotiating process" (emphasis in original).[61] The human rights mission could undermine peace talks if the presence of the UN mission were too irritating to the government and conservative elites.

By these criteria, the initial phase of MINUGUA was clearly a success. The United Nations established its credibility, provided unprecedented nationwide scrutiny of human rights conditions, and shined a spotlight on the weaknesses of key state institutions, while remaining carefully within its mandate. Although some members of the military and the social elite remained hostile to the mission, the United Nations appeared to successfully cultivate support or at least acquiescence from those individuals who were open-minded and willing to see the potential benefits that the mission could bring. Although the institution-building portion of the mission's mandate asked for the impossible, the fact that the United Nations brought collaboration and expertise to the table (in addition to all the unwelcome criticism) helped soften opposition and thereby helped make the human rights verification role possible.

Despite these successes, however, the public perception of the mission in Guatemala was not uniformly positive. Probably the greatest error committed by the mission in its early phase was its failure to adequately explain its role and its mandate to the general public. Its problems were symptomatic of a broader syndrome for the United Nations—that it often succeeds at the work it does, but fails to demonstrate these accomplishments effectively to local people or to global publics. The mission was slow to make use of mass media outlets—especially radio—to explain itself, with the result that many people, particularly in remote areas of the country, did not understand why the mission was there or what to expect from it. This lack of understanding extended to local human rights NGOs, who, for example, expressed great frustration with the fact that MINUGUA did not share the information it collected on human rights cases with local NGOs. There were generally good reasons for the mission's policies, since in some cases the mission had offered assurances of confidentiality, and because information collected had to be judged for credibility and checked against other sources. Yet the mission seems not to have made these arguments effectively to local NGOs.

With the mission's low profile in public communications, the views and practices of the national press corps took on added weight. The Guatemalan press was not particularly fastidious about accuracy, and Franco found himself needing to publish corrections and engage in damage control. During the May 1995 CONAGRO publicity campaign against the mission, for example, Franco was "quoted" in the paper as saying "the invasion of private property is not a human rights violation, but the shortage or lack of access to private property is." In response to this particularly incendiary "total invention," Franco had to make the rounds of CACIF leaders to set the record straight.[62] The mission's political reporting throughout the period focused sometimes excessively on taking the political temperature of editorials, assessing whether the mission was making progress in gaining elite acceptance, and gauging the depth and breadth of opposition. Weekly "situation reports" characterized critical coverage as "aggression" against the mission. To some extent this hypersensitivity to how the mission was treated in the press might have been unnecessary had the mission run a more intensive public communications campaign of its own.

Ultimately, however, the mission could not avoid the basic structure of its role: it was simultaneously asked to carefully and truthfully document human rights conditions in a very violent and oppressive country, contribute to reforming state institutions to hold wrongdoers accountable, and avoid generating a political backlash against the peace process. Managing these contradictions successfully for eighteen months was a singular achievement.

▌ Notes

1. Jean Arnault, "Panel on United Nations Peace Operations," to Iqbal Riza for Lakhdar Brahimi, April 27, 2000, 5.

2. Kofi Annan, "Note to Mr. Goulding: Human Rights Verification," June 29, 1994.

3. Jean Arnault, "Note to Mr. Schlittler, Human Rights Verification Mission in Guatemala," July 15, 1994.

4. Leonardo Franco, untitled FAX to Marrack Goulding, September 21, 1994.

5. Leonardo Franco, "End of Mission Report," memo to Marrack Goulding, May 9, 1996.

6. Author interview, UN official, Guatemala City, June 1998.

7. The Guatemala City subregional office was relocated from the planned location in Jutiapa to Escuintla because so many serious human rights problems, as well as labor and social tensions, were focused in the Escuintla area.

8. Jean-Pierre Halbwachs, "MINUGUA—Revised Cost Estimates," memo to Denis Beissel, November 21, 1994.

9. Leonardo Franco, "MINUGUA—Revised Cost Estimates for Proposed Budget Covering the Period 1 October 1994–31 March 1995," memo to Iqbal Riza, November 23, 1994.

10. Comprehensive Agreement on Human Rights, Section X, paragraphs 5–15; see also "Report of the Director of the United Nations Mission for the Verification of Human Rights and Compliance with the Commitments of the Comprehensive Agreement on Human Rights in Guatemala," A/49/856 March 1, 1995, paragraph 24.

11. As noted in Chapter 2, one precedent to follow was the use of voluntary donations by the Italian government in support of the Mozambican peace process to help the Mozambican National Resistance (RENAMO) complete its conversion to a civilian political party. Apparently, the URNG never asked for such assistance.

12. Ken Ward, "The United Nations Mission for the Verification of Human Rights in Guatemala: Database Representation," in *Making the Case: Investigating Large Scale Human Rights Violations Using Information Systems and Data Analysis,* edited by Patrick Ball, Herbert F. Spirer, and Louise Spirer, 137–150 (Washington, DC: American Association for the Advancement of Science, 2000).

13. Ibid.

14. Author interview, UN official, Guatemala City, June 1998.

15. "Evaluación del impacto de MINUGUA," Unidad de Análisis y Documentación (ANDOC), MINUGUA, March 15, 1996. David Holiday was the lead author on this report.

16. Leonardo Franco, "Security-Related Developments," to Marrack Goulding, February 8, 1996.

17. "MINUGUA Weekly Situation Report 5–12 March 1996."

18. "MINUGUA Weekly Situation Report 19–25 March 1996."

19. "MINUGUA Weekly Situation Report 7–13 February 1995."

20. Luis Pásara, *Paz, ilusión, y cambio en Guatemala: El proceso de paz, sus actors, logros, y limites* (Ciudad de Guatemala: Universidad Rafaél Landívar, 2003), 298.

21. "Evaluación del impacto de MINUGUA," p. 26.

22. "MINUGUA Weekly Situation Report 30 April–13 May 1996."

23. Leonardo Franco, "MINUGUA Staff Detained at Finca," to Marrack Goulding et al., February 14, 1996.

24. "MINUGUA Weekly Situation Report 9–15 May 1995"; "MINUGUA Weekly Situation Report 4–10 July 1995"; and "MINUGUA Weekly Situation Report 11–17 July 1995."

25. Leonardo Franco, "Campaign Against MINUGUA and the Peace Process," to Marrack Goulding, October 19, 1995.

26. See Jennifer Schirmer, *The Guatemalan Military Project: A Violence Called Democracy* (Philadelphia: University of Pennsylvania Press, 1998).

27. "MINUGUA Weekly Situation Report 6–12 June 1995."

28. "MINUGUA Weekly Situation Report 20–25 September 1995."

29. "Fourth Report of the Director of the United Nations Mission for the Verification of Human Rights and of Compliance with the Commitments of the Comprehensive Agreement on Human Rights in Guatemala (MINUGUA)," A/50/878, February 24, 1996, paragraphs 25–32.

30. This insight from "Evaluación del impacto de MINUGUA."

31. "MINUGUA Weekly Situation Report 24–30 October 1995."

32. Leonardo Franco, "Request to Accept Decoration," to Kofi Annan, October 26, 1995.

33. Author interview, DPA political officer Denise Cook, New York, February 1, 2007.

34. "MINUGUA Weekly Situation Report 21–28 February 1995."

35. Leonardo Franco, "Meeting with President," memo to Marrack Goulding and Kofi Annan, March 29, 1995.

36. Rosario Green, "Note to Mr. Goulding, Guatemala," memo to Marrack Goulding, February 2, 1995.

37. "MINUGUA Weekly Situation Report 6–12 June 1995."

38. "MINUGUA Weekly Situation Report 5–11 December 1995."

39. Carpio's widow, for one, rejected the president's view. "MINUGUA Weekly Situation Report 30 May–5 June 1995."

40. Gilberto Schlittler, untitled FAX memo to Marrack Goulding, November 22, 1995. Schlittler oversaw the DPA Guatemala Unit, as described in Chapter 2.

41. "MINUGUA Weekly Situation Report 17–23 October 1995."

42. "MINUGUA Weekly Situation Report 17–23 January 1996."

43. Leonardo Franco, "Meeting with Gustavo Porras," memo to Marrack Goulding, January 15, 1996.

44. Susan C. Peacock and Adriana Beltrán, *Hidden Powers in Post-Conflict Guatemala: Illegal Armed Groups and the Forces Behind Them* (Washington, DC: Washington Office on Latin America, 2003), 14–26.

45. Adriana Beltrán, *The Captive State: Organized Crime and Human Rights in Latin America* (Washington, DC: Washington Office on Latin America, 2007), 23.

46. "MINUGUA Weekly Situation Report 17–23 January1996."

47. Leonardo Franco, "Meeting with the President of the Republic," memo to Secretary-General Boutros Boutros-Ghali, May 4, 1996.

48. Leonardo Franco, "Electoral Analysis," memo to Marrack Goulding, February 21, 1995, with untitled attachment prepared by Ricardo Stein, UNDP.

49. "MINUGUA Weekly Situation Report 15–22 August 1995."

50. Leonardo Franco, "End of Mission Report" memo to Marrack Goulding, May 9, 1996.

51. See, for example, Gino Costa, *La Policía Nacional Civil de El Salvador (1990–1997)* (San Salvador: UCA Editores, 1999). Costa was a senior political officer in ONUSAL.

52. Sección de Fortalecimiento Institucional (FORIN), "Informe Especial," MINUGUA, 1996.

53. "MINUGUA Weekly Situation Report 23–29 January, 1996."

54. FORIN, "Informe Especial."

55. Ibid.

56. Leonardo Franco, "End of Mission Report," memo to Marrack Goulding, May 9, 1996, paragraph 24(d).

57. "Evaluación del impacto de MINUGUA."

58. William D. Stanley, "Business as Usual? Justice and Policing Reform in Postwar Guatemala," in *Constructing Justice and Security After Wars,* edited by Charles T. Call, 113–155 (Washington, DC: USIP, 2007).

59. "Evaluación del Impacto de MINUGUA," 29–32.

60. "Establishment of a Human Rights Verification Mission in Guatemala, Report of the Secretary-General," A/48/985, August 18, 1994.

61. Jean Arnault, "Note for the File: Situation of the Guatemalan Peace process, 15 May 1994," May 16, 1994.

62. Leonardo Franco, "Campaign Against MINUGUA," memo to Marrack Goulding and Kofi Annan, May 11, 1995.

4 | Preparing for Comprehensive Verification, 1996–1997

LEONARDO FRANCO'S DECISION to step down as head of MINUGUA was a disappointment at UN headquarters. He had distinguished himself as a principled advocate for human rights protection in Guatemala, and had navigated the shoals of Guatemalan politics and reactive nationalism. He had been firm and outspoken on issues as necessary, but had also been tactful not to alienate the host government (or right-wing social groups) unnecessarily. He had found ways to reach out to some of the social elites who were initially unwelcoming to the mission. There had been an expectation that he would be named the SRSG once the peace process was complete. However, family priorities called him back to Geneva, and the Secretariat needed to find a new head of mission on short notice. This was not easy. Highly qualified specialists on human rights with enough experience in the UN system and the seniority to head a mission were scarce. Finding such a person who spoke Spanish well enough for a mission that operated almost entirely in Spanish was more difficult still.

The Secretary-General's staff looked inside the Secretariat for someone who could be called in on short notice. Mr. David Stephen (UK) had been working in the executive office of the Secretary-General in New York for about four years. His background was largely in development work rather than human rights, and he was comparatively new to the United Nations. His most recent position before coming to the United Nations had been as director of corporate relations for the Commonwealth Development Corporation, which makes concessional loans for development projects, mainly in British Commonwealth countries. He had some years of experience in Latin America running a university exchange program (two decades earlier), and he had done a stint as a journalist and editor. In sum, Stephen's UN, diplomatic, human rights, and field mission résumé was notably thinner than his predecessor's, but he seemed to have the needed skills. Having worked in the Secretary-General's office, he was a known quantity, and he was eager to take on MINUGUA.

Under-Secretary-General (USG) Marrack Goulding wrote to Stephen at the beginning of his assignment, providing eight pages of instructions regarding how Stephen should implement the mission's mandate. Details included reporting lines and how to keep New York informed as well as how to relate to the parties, other parts of the UN system, other international actors and NGOs, the media, and the UN "moderation." The detailed guidance, apparently unmatched for any of the other heads of MINUGUA, reflected the complex moment that Stephen was stepping into, as well as perhaps an intuition that he in particular might need clear guidelines.[1] Because the peace negotiations were suddenly on a faster track under the Arzú government, Guatemalan political actors and the press were beginning to ask questions about when a comprehensive peace accord would be signed and what the UN mission's role would be after that. How large would it be? How assertive? The Guatemalan press was also fixated on the question of the death penalty: popular opinion favored the death penalty, as did elite right-wing opinion. The public was outraged by an intense crime wave. Reporters knew that MINUGUA would oppose the death penalty, and baited the mission with questions about its position, knowing that any comment would set the mission up for accusations of interference in domestic affairs.

Right-wing Guatemalans began to speak out against the prospect of a UN "occupation," calling it a "parallel government."[2] This mimicked elites in El Salvador who had found ONUSAL's presence too heavy-handed. The Arzú government wanted the Guatemalan peace verification mission to have a lighter footprint. Yet the accords were so broad that any mission that did a conscientious verification of so many aspects would unavoidably be intrusive. Given the squishiness of the accords and the eroding political power of the URNG, as well as the strong political challenge to the incumbent PAN from the right, the UN verification mission would need to have some form of power, either through leverage over foreign assistance or strong diplomatic and public information tools, to be in a position to insist that the government actually implement its commitments. Thus the situation inevitably generated tensions between the government and the United Nations about the nature of the future mission, and Stephen needed to be careful about what he said.

The reciprocal ceasefire that began in March 1996 had begun to change the relationship between MINUGUA and the parties. Whereas previously MINUGUA had maintained its liaison with the URNG *comandancia* in Mexico, by July 1996 MINUGUA had made 24 local-level contacts with the URNG across seven different regional offices.[3] The army also asked MINUGUA to help orchestrate meetings between local military and URNG field commanders. Since the Secretariat's intent had been to maintain a firewall between MINUGUA (human rights verification *only*) and the moderation (negotiations *only*), this increasingly unavoidable local-level mediation began to blur the boundaries between negotiations and verification.

Given this messy context, Goulding's letter cautioned Stephen:

> You should bear in mind that the United Nations' involvement in internal political issues is a matter of considerable sensitivity in certain circles in Guatemala. This inevitably affects the Government's attitude to the Mission. The Director of MINUGUA therefore has to tread the narrow path of conscientiously carrying out the mandate entrusted to him by the parties, the Secretary-General and the General Assembly, while at the same time taking care not to cause the Government surprises or otherwise complicate its difficult task of building a consensus in Guatemala in favour of the peace process and the United Nations' role in it.[4]

Thus, implicitly, the Arzú government was the United Nations' ally, and the United Nations needed the goodwill and cooperation of Arzú to continue to have a role in the peace process. The United Nations would lose that cooperation if it did things that inflamed the Guatemalan right. Effectively, the nationalism of the Guatemalan right made the United Nations politically dependent upon the host government.

Regarding the relationship between MINUGUA and the moderation, Goulding wrote that DPA would keep Stephen informed about developments in the talks, and asked Stephen to share any information that he or his senior colleagues "may happen to pick up about the attitudes of the Guatemalan parties," while asking him not to actively solicit such information. He asked Stephen to provide analytical reports on aspects of the Guatemalan scene that could be relevant to the negotiations. Finally, he cautioned Stephen as follows: "unless specifically asked to do so, you should not take any initiatives in relation to the negotiations, i.e. you should not float ideas on a personal basis."[5]

With these guidelines freshly in hand, Stephen met a week later on June 6 with President Arzú and a group of government ministers and advisers including the foreign minister, finance minister, central bank president, and the newly appointed presidential commissioner for international cooperation for peace, Richard Aitkenhead. The topic was foreign assistance, and the government made an appeal for donors to act more swiftly to commit peace-related funds or else the government would have difficulty implementing the socio-economic accord. Stephen cabled New York describing the meeting and reporting that after Arzú's brief remarks, "I floated the idea that the international community might wish to make its financial support for the peace process in part conditional on progress in the process itself and that the United Nations might have a role to play in some form of certification process. This was, I think, a new idea to them, but they are clearly going to think seriously about it."[6] No doubt the Guatemalan leaders thought about this very seriously. It was exactly the sort of arrangement they hoped to avoid. Arzú's government wanted international assistance and cooperation, not tight conditionality with a UN supermission controlling the flow of money.

Stephen's cable must have caused at least a ripple in New York. His remarks were hard to reconcile with his instructions not to "float ideas on a
personal basis." Five days after Stephen floated his ideas, Guatemalan foreign minister Eduardo Stein was in New York to meet with Goulding to discuss the format for the future verification mission. Stein made it clear that
the government did not want an overbearing UN "institutional presence" in
Guatemala. Goulding's response had been conciliatory: the United Nations
"envisaged a division of labour, with the bulk of the work being done by
specialized agencies, programmes, funds and offices, many of whom were
already represented in Guatemala. We would not assign to a United Nations
peace-keeping operation activities which could be as well, or better, done
by more specialized institutions within the United Nations system." Goulding
insisted, however, that the UN mission did have a unique role to play: "All
that we would ask would be that we should have the lead in defining the tasks
to be performed, in suggesting who should do what and, given our responsibilities under the framework agreement, in verifying what was done."[7]

This was obviously a softer approach than the financial conditionality
that Stephen had proposed, and it would limit the United Nations' future
leverage over quality of implementation. It was probably as strong a model
as was politically realistic at that time, however, even within the United Nations. The development and financial agencies, which did not report to the
Secretariat, would certainly have resisted giving the mission formal powers
to turn off the financial spigot.

After the meeting with Stein, Goulding wrote back to Stephen, "better
not to pursue with your interlocutors the idea in your GUANY 1222 that
the UN could certify progress in the peace process as a condition for the
release of donors' financial support for that process. Attractive though the
idea is in many ways, it is highly controversial and could compromise our
current efforts to get everyone to work together in a coordinated way with
a common purpose."[8] Notwithstanding the questionable tact and timing of
Stephen's remarks, he had identified, within days of his arrival in
Guatemala, the one leverage point that—had it been feasible—might have
enabled the mission to make the Guatemalan government carry through on
its commitments under the peace accords. The government was fully
aware of the mission's potential power, and was doing everything it could
to prevent it.

◼ Military Matters

Shortly after Stephen's arrival in Guatemala, MINUGUA received a request
from a senior Guatemalan army officer from the Presidential General Staff
(EMP) to arrange a meeting between the army's "military zone" commanders and their URNG counterparts. This was obviously outside the boundaries

of human rights verification. Nonetheless, Stephen wrote to New York asking permission to have the mission's military adviser preside over the meeting. He saw this as an opportunity to further the United Nations' goal of making peace in Guatemala, and as part of the mission's de facto good offices role. Meetings between zone-level commanders could help prevent misunderstandings, address points of tension, and help preserve the ceasefire. Stephen proposed, somewhat optimistically, that it could be interpreted formally as "a continuation and an extension of the ongoing work carried out by the Military Adviser in verifying complaints of infringements of existing agreements."[9]

Goulding wrote back immediately, denying approval for the meetings in strong terms. He had several concerns. First, it was inappropriate that the request had come directly out of the EMP. Consultations with the government's chief negotiator, Gustavo Porras, confirmed that he and the president were in the dark. Furthermore, such "informal talks" could put at risk the broader agreement on the army that was currently under negotiations. Even as a confidence measure, "such a meeting could backfire badly." Goulding then took Stephen to task for suggesting that the military adviser had verification functions. The mission's only verification mandate at that stage involved human rights, and the military adviser was not supposed to have any role in that. The March ceasefire between the government and the URNG was the parties' own initiative and MINUGUA had no role in verifying it.[10]

Stephen hastened to clarify: this initiative did come out of the EMP and it had Defense Minister Balconi's full support. It had not, however, been shared with the president or the rest of his government because of a perceived need within the military for secrecy. He acknowledged that his language about the military adviser could have been tighter, but the fact was that despite the formal organization of the mission into two operational areas (verification and institutional strengthening) and five advisory groups (human rights, legal, military, police, and indigenous affairs), "In practice this distinction is hard to observe."[11] In a small mission with a limited number of highly qualified professional staff supplemented by UNVs, having a solid firewall between verification work and advisory work was unrealistic. Regardless, Stephen was unable to convince New York to allow him to go ahead.

In the end, the army and the URNG arranged the meetings on their own, without incident. Balconi had surprised Leonardo Franco and his staff back in April 1996 by telling them that he was in regular telephone contact with URNG commanders.[12] Thus although UN coordination might have made direct contacts safer, it was not essential. At their own initiative, field commanders met, with maps in hand, to discuss the disposition of their forces and thereby avoid inadvertent contacts. They shared cell phone and pager numbers, and arranged procedures for communicating with one another. A degree of trust began to take hold between the two military forces. Initial meetings took place outside the country, but subsequent meetings took place within Guatemala.[13] These meetings were part of an initiative by Defense Minister Balconi to make the peace process irreversible as soon as possible. It would later become clear that he had climbed a bit too far out on a political limb within the military, and a more hard-line officer replaced him. But during the critical peacemaking phase in 1996 and early 1997, he was able to assert his peace agenda and appeared to have the support of many of his field commanders.

One of Balconi's other initiatives in support of Arzú's peace agenda was to begin demobilization of the infamous civilian self-defense patrols or PACs (referred to in UN documents as Voluntary Civil Defense Committees [CVDCs]).[14] Elimination of the PACs had been an early demand of the URNG because of the PACs' atrocious human rights record and because of their ability to potentially suppress grassroots political work by the rebels. The issue had been put aside back in 1994 because the army refused to discuss it. The human rights accord had only called on the army not to create more PACs, and gave the Human Rights Ombudsman's Office (PDH) the responsibility of verifying that the PACs were "voluntary." In mid-1996, the URNG was pushing to have formal arrangements for PAC demobilization built into the agreement on strengthening civilian powers and the role of the military. The army preempted this and set about demobilizing the PACs on their own terms.

This presented MINUGUA with a conundrum. Since the army was carrying out the demobilizations outside of the terms of any of the peace agreements, MINUGUA did not have a formal mandate to verify that the PACs were actually being disarmed and demobilized. Yet this process, whatever its flaws, was moving ahead and it was important to public trust in the peace process overall for MINUGUA to monitor and report on the demobilizations. The URNG was suspicious that the PACs would not really be demobilized, and there were immediately rumors (mostly true as it turned out) that the army was reorganizing the PACs into "peace and development committees" designed to be yet another mechanism for military social control. PACs had been one of the most frequent sources of human rights violations, so their full and genuine demobilization was a priority concern for much of rural society.

On July 16, 1996, army spokesman Otto Noack met with Stephen to inform him that the army would begin formally demobilizing the PACs at the end of the month. The army would be asking MINUGUA to verify the PACs' dissolution and disarmament, and to receive their arms. By this point, MINUGUA regional offices had already detected that PACs were being demobilized and disarmed, and had received similar requests from local army commanders to help verify their demobilization. In at least one instance, a unit from the URNG had disarmed the local PAC and sought help from MINUGUA in disposing of the weapons. MINUGUA could not help—outside the mandate again—and so the insurgents had to get in touch with the army (!) to hand over the weapons confiscated from the PAC. The actual pacification process on the ground was getting ahead of the legal framework for its implementation.[15]

Stephen wrote Goulding that

> we have come to the conclusion that, while "verification" of the disarming of CVDCs may not fall within the Mission's mandate, verification of compliance with commitment IV of the Comprehensive Agreement (that there should be no illegal security forces and clandestine machinery, and that there shall be regulation of the possession, bearing and use of firearms), clearly does. The disarming/dissolution of the CVDCs could also have an important effect on the Mission's verification of commitment V (regarding voluntary membership of CVDCs, their involvement in human rights violations and establishment of new CVDCs).

Having established an argument for actually verifying the demobilization of the PACs, however, Stephen went on to propose that the mission should merely "observe" the process. He explained,

> The difference between "verifying" and "observing" is that the verifier must certify officially that the disarming has, in each case, been genuine and reliable, for example, that the arms recovered are the same, in number and type, as those originally distributed by the Army to the CVDCs. He/she must then form an opinion which [sic] is the basis of a report on each case. The observer, on the other hand, limits him/herself to being present at the disarming ceremonies and forms a general opinion on the process, to be taken into account, as a contextual element, in situations that are verified in line with the mandate.[16]

There was no immediate written comment on this proposal from New York, and Stephen went ahead with observation of the demobilizations. In early August, the government announced that it would demobilize the PACs in three phases, completing the process by November 15, 1996.[17] This would be a major undertaking, involving hundreds of thousands of men and thousands of weapons.[18] One of the first formal demobilization ceremonies, at Colotenango in Huehuetenango in the northwestern highlands, set the tone. MINUGUA observers noted obvious tensions between the patrollers and the community. The head of the presidential human rights commission COPREDEH, Marta Altolaguirre, made a speech assuring the community that those who had committed abuses would be held accountable. Then the army's chief of staff Sergio Camargo set that straight, speaking warmly of the patrollers and their future.[19] Later in August, MINUGUA observers at

the demobilization in Comalapa in the highland department of Chimalte-
nango, just west of the capital, were taken aback by the military master of
ceremony's remarks that "this isn't a good-bye, it's a see-you-soon" ("no es
un adiós, sino un hasta pronto"). At the end of the ceremony, the army released a covey of doves that, apparently overcome by their confinement,
plummeted to earth rather than flying away.[20]

MINUGUA lacked the mandate to collect PAC guns, thus the government had set up a commission headed by the interior minister to oversee the
process. The commission was then to hand the guns over to the army, which
still had legal responsibility for the control of arms and munitions. Since
the army had set up the PACs in the first place, this gun recycling hardly
confirmed the end of the PACs.[21]

In October, the various ambiguities in the demobilization process
sparked a war of words. The human rights ombudsman Jorge Mario García
Laguardia commented that the demobilizations amounted to little more than
"a chain of 'tributes' paid to ex-patrollers rather than their effective demobilization." García's comments were aimed mainly at COPREDEH, which
was overseeing the process on behalf of the civilian government. As noted
in the previous chapter, García saw COPREDEH as an "unwelcome com-
petitor." But his remarks also prompted a communiqué from MINUGUA
clarifying that "the Mission's presence at CVDC demobilization ceremonies did not constitute verification either of these elements' effective demobilization or disarming." This, in turn, brought a strongly worded letter
from the foreign minister alleging that MINUGUA's communiqué had "cast
doubts on the Government's genuine efforts to demilitarize Guatemala."[22]

In retrospect, MINUGUA's "observing" the PAC demobilizations without
actually verifying them served little purpose other than to allow MINUGUA
to collect some intelligence about what various officials said at these
events. As of November 1996, some 200,000 PAC members had been demobilized, yielding a total of 9,000 weapons. MINUGUA had expected at
least 13,500 weapons, so there were concerns about the authenticity of demobilization.[23] Behind the scenes, however, MINUGUA's human rights
verification efforts did uncover anecdotal information about the activities of
former PACs, their involvement in criminal activity, and particularly the efforts of some elements of the military, acting against high command instructions, to pressure PAC members not to demobilize or to immediately
rejoin other (illegal) armed groups. The mission also confirmed that many
PAC members were retaining weapons, despite the lack of licenses for these
arms. This information was incorporated into MINUGUA's sixth human
rights report published in early 1997. However, the mission had not carried
out a comprehensive verification that would have allowed them to estimate
the scope of this problem or publicly identify illegal armed groups.[24]

MINUGUA eventually backed away from another similarly ambiguous
form of "observation." In October, Stephen decided to stop sending

MINUGUA staff to observe evictions of peasants from occupied lands. This practice had started during Franco's term as head of mission, and questions about its utility had arisen early on. There had been a number of incidents of peasant hostility toward MINUGUA during evictions, and the mission wasn't really in any position to take preventive action if the police acted improperly. Stephen concluded that the mission was coming to be associated in the popular eye with unpopular evictions, while landowners saw it as interfering with lawful efforts by the government to protect property rights. Given this lose-lose political context, and the dubious benefits in terms of rights protection, it was time to reconsider the policy.[25]

▌ URNG Armed Propaganda

Another novel feature of the situation MINUGUA faced in 1996 was that the URNG, having called a halt to its "offensive military operations" and war tax collection, was still carrying out armed propaganda. Typically, URNG combatants would enter a community, disarm the police, gather people in the square, and make political speeches. Here again, MINUGUA had an ambiguous mandate. The Comprehensive Agreement called on the parties to halt activities that adversely affected the civilian population. Based on this, MINUGUA had successfully pressured the URNG to halt most war tax collections. Armed propaganda was less clear-cut: it was clearly an inconvenience, but the incidents since the ceasefire had not led to bloodshed or any serious suffering.

Defense Minister Balconi remarked to Stephen in a meeting in early June that he thought the URNG's armed propaganda violated their commitment to cease military operations. Overall, Balconi was "almost disturbingly positive," and proposed to have army specialists collaborate with URNG combatants in removing minefields, as a confidence-building measure. But his message was clear: the armed political *charlas* (chats) were a problem for him politically within the army.[26] There were reports during that same week that in some instances of armed propaganda, URNG combatants had been saying positive things about President Arzú, Balconi, and his chief of staff Camargo. But in other instances, they had been more confrontational.[27]

Later in June, officials of the Escuintla subregional office (which covered a gritty industrial city south of Guatemala City as well as the surrounding commercial agricultural area) met with local URNG leaders and urged them to keep their public propaganda actions brief and to avoid an aggressive tone. This was important to avoid their being perceived as provocative. The URNG received this advice favorably. Reports from the regional offices indicated some efforts by the rebels to tone down their actions.[28]

Following conversations with Balconi, David Stephen became convinced that local army commanders felt their honor was at stake in having to sit idle while the URNG occupied villages and towns. Stephen decided to do what he could to reduce tensions. He gave an interview to the newspaper *Prensa Libre* in which he remarked that the army had responded with restraint to "provocations" in which the URNG had occupied villages for up to four hours, essentially daring the army to intervene. President Arzú later quoted him approvingly in a speech. Explaining his actions to New York, Stephen wrote that, "As you know, we are taking the view that, while it is clear that the URNG may see such activities as political campaigning, local army commanders may see them in military terms and may react accordingly. These are very delicate moments of transition and such ambiguities are potentially dangerous."[29] Stephen's statement on this issue was arguably outside of the mission's human rights mandate. Yet it was almost certainly helpful to the pro-peace faction within the military in restraining demands for actions against the URNG.

Other aspects of the *Prensa Libre* interview did not work out so well. The article published on July 1, 1996, was titled "MINUGUA Intensifies Contacts with URNG for a Virtual Demobilization." The article quoted Stephen as saying that the increasing contacts between the mission and the URNG involved discussions of the next military demobilization phase, during which international cooperation would be key to achieving reconciliation. Writing to New York about the story, Stephen characterized it as pure fabrication. He had told the reporters about the contacts with the URNG, but the supposed quotes about "virtual demobilization" were false. He had accepted this interview and a few others in response to three weeks of requests from the press, and the advice of the mission spokesman. He was now feeling stung. "[I]t seems to be asking too much of local journalists to differentiate between MINUGUA, on one hand, and the negotiations and the work of the Moderator on the other. The Mission Spokesman is writing to the Editor today to clarify the position." Stephen closed his message with the observation that "We will learn from this experience. With the publication of the Fifth Report, which we hope will take place in early August, we will try to focus again on the actual work of MINUGUA."[30]

■ Verifying Human Rights

Indeed, MINUGUA's job was to verify human rights conditions in Guatemala, and it was doing that work more effectively. As noted in the previous chapter, MINUGUA had finally developed a computer database system by the beginning of 1996 that allowed for some analysis of patterns and trends. That database had been used in very limited fashion in the fourth report issued in February 1996. The Arzú government's response to MINUGUA's fourth report had been mild: that report had covered the latter portion of the de León government, and so its criticisms did not really affect the Arzú administration. The fifth report, issued in July 1996 a little over a month after Stephen arrived, produced an entirely different response.

The "Fifth Report of the Director of the United Nations Mission for the Verification of Human Rights and of Compliance with the Commitments of the Comprehensive Agreement on Human Rights in Guatemala" [A/50/1006] opened in a positive tone, complimenting the government on a series of measures it had taken during its early months in office, including passing legislation that subjected military personnel to civilian laws for ordinary infractions; achieving passage and ratification of ILO 169 as called for in the indigenous rights accord; taking steps to reform the penal code to criminalize racial discrimination; and carrying out replacements of senior personnel within the military, police, public prosecutor's office, and COPREDEH. It also remarked favorably on efforts to pursue criminal gangs, including some involved in kidnappings. However, subsequent paragraphs were pretty tough on the government.

Based on cases admitted and verified during the period covered (January 1 through June 30, 1996), the report also noted very serious problems with the government's compliance with the Comprehensive Agreement. MINUGUA noted numerous cases in which state agents had used violence against civilians inappropriately, and in which state agencies responsible for investigating these abuses had failed to follow up in any meaningful way. There were numerous cases of excessive violence in making arrests; postarrest beatings and torture, and signs of class and racial bias in making arrests and in the use of force. Effective access to the justice system was still denied to indigenous people. On some plantations, landowners and their agents were denying workers the basic rights afforded by the constitution, while the state did nothing to protect them.

In a section on impunity, the report acknowledged the government's efforts to strengthen accountability of state agents, but noted many remaining weaknesses, exemplified by an emerging pattern of involvement of state agents in "social cleansing" operations in which homeless children and suspected youth gang members were summarily executed. There were too many instances of judges' releasing state officials and members of PACs—pretrial—despite strong evidence of their involvement in major crimes. It criticized the government's focus on increasing penalties rather than dealing with systemic problems. Particularly unhelpful, according to the report, was the decision to apply the death penalty to kidnappers, which of course would create incentives for kidnappers to kill their captives if threatened with discovery and arrest. The National Police had reported an increase in kidnappings since this reform was implemented, so obviously it was not having the desired deterrent effect.

The mission noted disturbing systemic trends. In order to combat impunity effectively, "it is essential to professionalize the National Police and

. . . this, in turn, requires the separation of police and military functions." In March, the government had issued a decision decree establishing that the Interior Ministry would oversee all police strategy and operations, with *support* from the armed forces. Yet the mission had "observed not only that members of the army and of its intelligence branches have taken part in a number of operations which were clearly police tasks, but also that in some cases the army took the lead or acted first and independently, excluding the National Police" (paragraph 77). Other trends included proliferation of weapons in civilian hands and indications that despite the army's formal commitment to demobilize the PACs, new groups were forming, armed, and encouraged by the military.

The report included a critique of "human rights culture" in Guatemala. It noted a contradiction among the constitution, primary school curriculum, and the Comprehensive Agreement, all of which highlighted individual rights and due process of law, and a de facto "streak of intolerance and discrimination" combined with a "culture of violence." "In this context, defending human rights is said to amount to defending criminals, the death sentence is proclaimed to be the solution to the crime wave and there are instances, which are not strongly condemned in the press, of criminals being lynched as an alternative means of dispensing justice" (paragraph 156).

The report concluded with a balanced assessment that while the government had taken significant measures, and while tackling impunity was a difficult job, there was a long way to go. It noted in particular

> (a) the lack of an integral policy against impunity; (b) the defective functioning of the judicial branch, the Public Prosecutor's Office and the security forces; (c) insufficient cooperation from the army with these bodies when its members appear to have been involved in illegal acts, and indeed the protection it affords such persons; (d) the alarming proliferation of and failure to control firearms in the possession of private individuals; and (e) the tenuous social awareness that every person accused of a crime has inalienable human rights, including the presumption of innocence. (paragraph 166)

Overall, the fifth report differed in minor ways from its predecessors. There was more critical commentary about the failures to effectively address impunity. The database allowed a more detailed and valid tabulation of abuses. The main new element was the critique of human rights culture, as well as the negative commentary on the death penalty. The substantive observations about misconduct by state institutions were little changed from the fourth report. In view of Guatemala's later postwar domination by organized crime and the nearly complete collapse of the rule of law, this report was prescient and on-target. Unfortunately, it did not trigger corrective action by the Arzú government while there was still time to fix these problems. Instead, the government attacked the messenger.

Shortly after the report was issued, Foreign Minister Stein met with Stephen and

> launched a long and unexpected tirade against the report, including a thinly-veiled threat to convey these feelings to the Secretary-General. In an intervention marked by inaccuracies and misreadings of the text, Stein accused the Mission of reaching unsubstantiated conclusions, undervaluing the positive steps taken by the Arzú Government, and making unconstructive recommendations. This is particularly regrettable, said Stein, given how influential the MINUGUA reports are in forming international perceptions about the situation in Guatemala. He said we had failed to take account of the fact that Guatemala is a poor country, with limited resources. The Mission should make more realistic recommendations, and do more to convey a sense of priorities and expected timetables, thus giving the Government a better sense of what is expected.[31]

Stein's complaints were not completely unfounded: the report might have been more effective without the vague, passive-voice generalizations about Guatemala's culture of violence, which after all was in and of itself neither an act nor an omission by the state. Stein's outrage at MINUGUA's fifth human rights report coincided with the beginning of a government campaign—centered around Guatemala's use of the death penalty—to limit the scope of MINUGUA's verification powers following signing of the final accords.

▌ The Death Penalty Dilemma

Before the fifth report was released, there had been growing pressure on the mission to take a public position on the death penalty. The public mood was angry about a series of widely publicized homicides and kidnappings, and both the government and the press were beating the drum of harsher penalties. Stephen wrote that the mission was refraining from commenting on the issue because the "public mood is such that an ill-judged intervention by MINUGUA could be seen as provocative and might back-fire."[32]

The issue would soon become impossible to sidestep, however. In fulfillment of the mission's human rights mandate, the Guatemala City regional office of MINUGUA (ORGUA) had been following the case of two Guatemalan men, Roberto Girón and Pedro Castillo Mendoza, who had been tried, convicted, and sentenced to death for allegedly raping and killing a four-year-old girl. The indignant public saw the crimes as symptomatic of general insecurity and breakdown of law and order in the waning years of the civil war. MINUGUA knew that there was strong public support for the executions. Yet ORGUA's investigation pointed to a serious lack of due process during the trial. Among other things, the men had not had a competent defense attorney. The men were scheduled to be executed on September 12, but on the night of September 9, MINUGUA got word that the men would be killed by firing squad the next morning.

Presumably acting on information from MINUGUA, the Inter-American Commission on Human Rights in San José, Costa Rica, faxed urgent letters that night to President Alvaro Arzú, Foreign Minister Eduardo Stein, and Judge Gustavo Gaitán Lara, asking the Guatemalan state and judiciary to take "precautionary measures" in favor of the two prisoners, pending further judicial review. Stephen sent ORGUA regional coordinator Rosemarie Bornand to the prison where Girón and Castillo were being held to "verify respect for the right to due process and, if the execution indeed took place, the right to life."[33] Responding to international pressure, the Supreme Judicial Court intervened, staying execution for a few days.

By the time MINUGUA stepped in to delay this execution, there had already been growing political opposition to MINUGUA's monitoring of Guatemalan police, military, and courts. In August, a pamphlet had circulated widely in Guatemala City that characterized Stephen as "an English pirate . . . hiding behind the façade of MINUGUA, [who] has arrived to inspect and police the honourable and free people of Guatemala, when it would be more appropriate for him to check up on human rights in Ireland or in his own country."[34] When word got out about the stay of execution in the Girón/Castillo case, nationalist elements in Guatemala mobilized against what they portrayed as an outrageous foreign intervention in domestic affairs. Threats singled out Bornand personally. MINUGUA's Guatemala City regional office began to receive phone calls calling the mission "accomplices of assassins," and saying, among other things, that "if the woman who defended the two disgraceful murderers had children and if she placed herself in the role of the mother of the child who was killed, she wouldn't speak of human rights. . . . You should go home to your countries." The next day, another caller asked for Bornand, and when told she was not available, said, "tell her not to continue involving herself in the matters of Guatemalans. Tell her to be careful because something can happen if she continues. This will not stay as it is. . . . Tell her to be careful, we want MINUGUA to disappear." Yet another call later in the day, claiming to be from the "White Hand" organization (a death squad name previously used by state forces) said that they would "finish her." Someone fired a few pistol shots at the MINUGUA headquarters. No one was hurt.[35] MINUGUA staff in other parts of the country received threats as well, signaling either generalized public outrage or a coordinated campaign.

There had been outbursts of animosity toward the mission in the past, but the intensity of these threats was greater than usual. MINUGUA restricted the movements of mission personnel for a few days, and took special measures to protect Bornand. On Friday, September 13, perfunctory judicial reviews were complete and the two men were executed. The national press broadcast the executions on TV, complete with "full detail" video footage of a final gunshot to the head of one of the men. The executions brought catharsis—or perhaps removed an opportunistic basis for attacking the mission—and the campaign against MINUGUA suddenly ended.

Further Debate on the Future Verification Mission

About a week later, Stein met with Goulding in New York and expressed his concern about how MINUGUA had handled the Girón/Castillo case, using it as leverage to insist on a softer UN presence in the future. Among Stein's complaints was that the mission had focused on the use of an unlicensed law student as the defense "attorney" and judged this a violation of due process. According to Stein this was commonplace in Guatemala. Stein wondered why the mission had intervened so heavily in this case when it had not even written it up in any human rights reports, and had not taken it up through its liaison committee with the government. He suggested that perhaps some people in the mission were overstepping their instructions. He expressed concern about how Guatemalans might respond to similar cases in the future. With the sour mood of the public, a MINUGUA member could be "severely beaten up." Goulding responded that if the government had concerns about the handling of human rights cases, it should raise these with the head of mission, who was responsible for MINUGUA's verification policies.

Stein then brought up (again) the mission's future. If in fact the peace talks concluded by the end of the year, MINUGUA, or its successor, would soon be asked to verify the full set of the peace accords (not just the human rights accord). Stein argued that a highly intrusive mission could not be tolerated. He claimed there was deep internal opposition to "an alternate government dressed in blue." He suggested that perhaps the United Nations Development Programme (UNDP) could do verification.[36] The Arzú government wanted the United Nations to be a partner, not a policeman.

In this and later conversations with representatives of the Guatemalan government, Goulding made clear that the United Nations would not go along with such an arrangement. The UNDP, as a development agency, is responsible for working *through* governments to help them implement the policies that the government selects. Questioning state policy is not part of its repertoire. A peace verification mission was completely different: it must hold both the government and the former rebels at arm's length. Criticizing the government's conduct was an unavoidable feature of peace verification: as Goulding told Stein pointedly during the September meeting, "in-situ verification requires 'interference.'"[37]

The government's stance seemed to have an effect on Stephen. In a lengthy memo sent to Goulding at the end of October, Stephen backed dramatically away from his original idea that a verification mission should control international aid programs. He stressed that relatively little of the mission's work in the future would be based on receiving and investigating individual complaints. As the mission took on such tasks as verifying the socioeconomic and civilian power accords, its role would shift largely to assessing overall patterns of state institutional performance, and the direction and extent of institutional reforms. Stephen also noted that the government had expressed a strong preference for "'positive' or 'pro-active' (*propositivo*) verification." The government even seemed inclined to reject appointment of a special representative of the Secretary-General. They did not want "judgemental" verification.[38] Yet "positive verification" would bring the work of the mission very close to the kind of development work done routinely by the various "UN system" development agencies in Guatemala, all of which operated under the leadership of the resident coordinator, who headed the UNDP office in the country.

These considerations led Stephen to suggest a hybrid design for UN peacebuilding in Guatemala that would incorporate some characteristics of a more typical peace mission with a beefed-up development agency presence. He proposed the creation of a United Nations Peace Commission (Comisión de las Naciones Unidas para la Paz [CONUPAZ]) under the "joint and alternating chairmanship of the Resident Coordinator and the Director of MINUGUA." The commission would include the agencies and programs of the UN system, the international financial institutions, and, as observers, representatives of regional organizations and the European Union. Stephen did not propose incorporating the friends states into the commission, a puzzling omission. The goal would be to achieve coordination between verification and development activities.

It is somewhat difficult to see how this model would have worked in practice. As it was, there had been tensions between MINUGUA and UNDP regarding who spoke for the United Nations in Guatemala. While these tensions had eased considerably under Stephen's leadership, in part because of his more confident personality compared to Franco's, the problem would return and intensify later in the peace process, even with a UN SRSG heading MINUGUA and unambiguously in charge of the overall effort. The proposed "joint and alternating chairmanship" of CONUPAZ would certainly have generated conflict and incoherence. While his specific proposal might not have been workable, Stephen's overall assessment of the changing direction of MINUGUA's work was prescient.

Discussion of these issues was temporarily placed on hold in October by the crisis surrounding the Novella kidnapping (discussed in Chapter 2). In November, as the talks got back on track, the question of what future UN verification would look like resurfaced. Stephen wrote Goulding in late November asking that he reconsider his earlier orders not to discuss future verification issues with Guatemalan authorities. He remarked that "the Guatemalans, despite their protestations that they can and will do everything themselves, do need help." He suggested that a noncommittal conversation would not do any harm, noting that "The Minister knows, in any case, that the future mandate of the Mission will come from the GA and not from the Mission staff."[39]

Goulding gave him the go-ahead to have those conversations, but with some limits. He stressed that the Framework Agreement from January 1994 made clear that the United Nations would verify implementation of all the agreements, and although conversations had been held and would continue with the parties about the modalities, "verification is primarily a UN responsibility." Goulding noted that in some ways, the government's preferences were in line with those of the UN, particularly with regard to keeping the mission small. "We respect that wish, not least because of the Organization's financial difficulties. But, as we pointed out when the Framework Agreement was under negotiation, we expect the parties to allow the United Nations to judge what it needs in order to carry out the tasks entrusted to it by them." The bottom line was that Stephen should not allow the impression to form that "the informal donors' group or other meetings between the Government and the Diplomatic Corps are fora in which decisions can be taken on how the United Nations will carry out its verification functions." Stephen could talk about his ideas in his private capacity, but should insist "verification is a political function and therefore one that is primarily for the United Nations itself." Stephen could remind his counterparts that development agencies depend on a close relationship with government and are "often reluctant to undertake verification functions which could involve criticism of the Government for non-fulfilment of its commitments."[40]

▌ Verifying the URNG's Demobilization and the China Veto

Of course none of these issues would matter if the war did not formally end. By November, it became clear that final accords would indeed be signed by the end of the year. But the United Nations faced a constitutional issue regarding the status of MINUGUA: there was little precedent for military personnel—even unarmed observers—to be deployed under a General Assembly mandate. The Secretariat leadership felt it was important to preserve the unique role of the Security Council in authorizing such deployments. Thus, the Secretariat envisioned dual mandates for MINUGUA: a continued General Assembly mandate for the overall verification mission and a Security Council mandate for the small military observer team (planned at about 150 officers) that would oversee the separation of forces, the URNG's concentration, and its disarmament and demobilization.

China, however, as a veto-wielding permanent member of the Security Council, signaled that it would block any resolution to deploy military observers to Guatemala. Guatemala had maintained a cozy relationship with Taiwan and had spoken in favor of Taiwan in the General Assembly. China considered these actions hostile to its sovereignty. Even after the implications of this for the peace process were well known, the Guatemalan government persisted in provoking China. For instance, Guatemala conspicuously invited a Taiwanese representative to attend the final peace accord signing ceremony in Guatemala City. Then the president of Congress, Carlos Alberto García Regás (a member of Arzú's party who later joined his administration) traveled to Taipei for a weeklong visit, where he spoke in favor Taiwan's entry into the United Nations, and declared "Although Guatemala is a small country, as a sovereign and free state, it will never surrender before any power in its pursuit of democracy and peace."[41] In mid-January 1997, Guatemala decorated a Taiwanese military officer.[42]

In the face of such obvious China-baiting, it was difficult not to suspect that the Guatemalan government was attempting to exercise a veto of its own—over any Security Council mandate for MINUGUA.[43] This impression was reinforced by the government's decision to allow only one representative of MINUGUA (the head of mission) to attend the final accords signing ceremony in Guatemala City, despite repeated requests for additional passes for mission staff, as well as Arzú's failure to mention MINUGUA at all during his remarks, "a clear snub."[44]

The China veto presented the Secretariat with a set of unattractive options. One option would be to go straight to the General Assembly and bypass the Security Council completely. This would involve increasing the number of "military liaison officers" in the mission and more or less pretending that they were not military observers with military verification responsibilities. This would be questionable from a UN "constitutional" point of view. It would also present significant budgetary problems, since a General Assembly–mandated mission would have to operate within existing resources (which were scarce to nonexistent) and beefing up the "military liaison" staff would be costly. A second option would be to present the issue to the Security Council and, after the expected veto, ask the Security Council to deflect the matter to the General Assembly under the precedent of the Uniting for Peace resolution.[45] This would respect precedent within the United Nations, but would also involve a rarely used and controversial mechanism that had previously been used only in very urgent situations. A third option would be to go to the Security Council, but ask it to deflect the issue to the General Assembly under Chapter 4, Article 11, of the UN Charter, which allows the General Assembly to take up issues related to peace and security when these are brought to it by the Security Council. The last two options could potentially preserve the principle that a military observer operation would be funded under the peacekeeping scale of assessments.[46] None of these were particularly good options, and any of them would make the United Nations beholden to the Guatemalan government for its political cooperation.

Beyond the United Nations, people were thinking even further outside the box. Guatemalan press commentators suggested that Taiwan could fund an observer mission that would be carried out by the OAS. Some nationalists chimed in approvingly about this idea, since at least OAS personnel would be able to speak Spanish (as if MINUGUA's overwhelmingly Latin American staff did not!). The government liked this line of argument and had been shopping around the idea that either the OAS or the European Union could undertake the military verification mission. Foreign Minister Stein remarked that he didn't expect China to reconsider its position, fretted about how long a General Assembly resolution would take, and speculated about how quickly an OAS mission could be mounted. A member of Congress called for a Central American regional observer group. Only the URNG and the ASC pushed strongly for a UN mission, and even the URNG signaled, through Pablo Monsanto, that it was open to "any possibility for verification."[47]

Goulding had been doing everything he could to counteract this kind of speculation and to insist upon the proper UN role in military verification. He wrote to Arnault in late November instructing him to notify the parties in strong terms that the United Nations was opposed to the kind of mixed verification the government was proposing. There were issues of both principle and practicality at stake. Arnault was to tell the parties "If the UN is not able to verify the accords in their totality, as established by the Framework Agreement, we would be most reluctant to undertake verification at all." It was not clear how to solve the Chinese veto. As a result, in drafting the final accords, the parties should be very careful to avoid using any language that would rule out designations other than "military observer," thus leaving open the door to the stretched "military liaison officer" concept.[48]

Since none of the alternatives looked very promising, Secretary-General Kofi Annan decided to take the issue to the Security Council and, in effect, force the issue. Predictably, on January 10, 1997, China vetoed the resolution for establishing a 155-man military observation mission in Guatemala. Having expressed its displeasure with Guatemala, however, ten days later China relented and joined in the unanimous Security Council Resolution 1094 (1997) authorizing the observer group.[49] According to a Chinese foreign ministry spokesman, Guatemala agreed to comply with the UN resolution that establishes that there is only one China. Though this was never publicly confirmed by the Guatemalan government, it would have the effect of preventing any further Guatemalan advocacy for Taiwan's admission to the UN.[50] I have been unable to learn what concessions the Guatemalan government made during the intervening ten days, if any. Observers have speculated that it involved promises not to promote Taiwan's case for membership in the United Nations. What is clear is that the impasse was damaging to both the Guatemalan and Chinese governments. Guatemala was seen as having acted in bad faith to undercut UN verification efforts, while China was seen as having put its concerns about symbolic actions regarding Taiwan ahead of final settlement of a long and bloody civil war. These reputational concerns seem to have been enough to convince both countries to set aside their differences.[51] In retrospect, the Secretary-General and his senior staff were wise to insist on the correct mandate in this case.

▌ Logistical Preparations

In the midst of all of this uncertainty about the mandate for the military observers, MINUGUA had to ensure that logistical preparations were made so that there would be camps ready to receive URNG combatants under whatever verification regime was ultimately chosen. In mid-December 1996, after the signing of the Ceasefire Accord, MINUGUA established a Logistics Support Commission (Comisión de Apoyo Logístico [CAL]) that brought together the numerous agencies whose help would be needed. The commission included representatives of the URNG; the Presidential Peace Commission; the National Commission for Refugees, Repatriated, and Displaced Persons (CEAR); the National Peace Fund (FONAPAZ); the European Union; UNDP; the OAS; and USAID.

The demobilization deadline would come early: the parties and the United Nations expected to sign the final accords by the end of the year, and planned on a definitive ceasefire (D-day) to be set for sometime in February. Then demobilization of the URNG was to be completed within sixty days from D-day. Thus within about two months, camps had to be ready to house about 3,000 combatants under "austere and dignified" conditions. This implied construction and equipping of dormitories, kitchens, eating areas, latrines, showers, and health clinics; provision of electricity, telephone, running water, road access, and helicopter landing areas; and arrangement of basic services for medical and dental care, psychological counseling (focused on adaptation to civilian life), vocational training, remedial education, and documentation. There would be eight camps, two of which were colocated with other camps, so six locations had to be selected and access negotiated with landowners.[52]

MINUGUA obviously did not have this kind of logistical capacity in place, so the Logistics Support Commission divided up tasks. For example, CEAR was in charge of design of the buildings; FONAPAZ was to negotiate with landowners to get permission to use their properties for the camps and would arrange road access. The International Organization for Migration handled the contracting with Guatemalan firms for construction. The European Union arranged the medical, dental, and sanitary services, using Médecins sans Frontières as a main contractor. Remarkably, this very distributed approach worked well, and despite delays related to difficulties with contracts, landowner agreements, and heavy rains, the work was completed in time for D-day to be set for March 3, 1997.[53]

The MINUGUA portion of each of these camps was set up separately (only waste facilities were shared) and these preparations had to be carried out by the mission itself. This put considerable strain on the limited administrative and logistical capacity of the mission, and Stephen wrote to all the regional offices in late January warning them that although they would not be involved in verifying URNG demobilization (which would be handled through a centralized UN military chain of command), they could expect that vehicles and airlift normally available to them would be diverted to prepare for the military observer contingent.[54] Maintaining this logistical separation indeed involved some rather absurd logistical heroics such as delivering tents to Guatemala from a former UN mission in Angola! Because military observers needed to be present in and around the camps well before the arrival of URNG troops, the first UN observers deployed faced difficult physical conditions.[55]

■ The Verification Mission Goes to Arnault

With the signing of the final accords, and the approval of the military observer mission, the way was finally cleared for a comprehensive UN verification mission in Guatemala. In late January 1997, the Secretary-General decided that he would appoint Jean Arnault as SRSG to Guatemala, with an appointment date of March 1, 1997. Both the Guatemalan government and the URNG had expressed a strong preference for Arnault. Both parties knew Arnault well, they were confident in his knowledge of the process and the contents of the accords, and they thought his appointment would reduce the risk of misunderstandings. He had created a "positive, procedural environment" during the talks, and had worked extensively with the other social sectors involved in the process. In making this appointment, Annan noted that it was unusual to appoint a mediator as verifier, "simply because different talents were required for each job." Foreign Minister Stein responded that Arnault's negotiating talents might still prove very useful, a prescient and in retrospect rather sly remark.[56]

Annan's decision put David Stephen in an awkward position. His contract as head of MINUGUA extended until March 31, and as the incumbent, he was at least in the running for the SRSG position. Now he was to be replaced a month before the end of his contract, something that was rare within the UN personnel system and often seen as a sign of problems with job performance. Rumors swirled within the mission and in the diplomatic community that Arnault had somehow used his influence to maneuver for the job, although there appears to be little if any factual support for that view.[57] Foreign Minister Stein and URNG Commander Monsanto leaked the news of Arnault's appointment before the United Nations issued a formal announcement. Stung by the leak, Stephen wrote to headquarters asking that a proper announcement be issued as soon as possible.[58]

▌ Police Problems

While adjusting to being passed over for the SRSG post, Stephen had to deal with serious new challenges. First, he had to move quickly to complete preparations for the military mission. The delays in obtaining an SC resolution meant that staying on track now required very compressed preparations for the concentration sites, the encampments themselves, and all the planning and logistics these arrangements entailed. There were pressures to determine D-day as soon as possible—that is, to set the date on which the definitive ceasefire would formally begin and the agreed timetable would be set in motion for separation of forces, cantonment of the URNG, and so forth. Stephen had to balance the urgency to begin the process as soon as possible with realities such as rain delays in preparing one of the encampment sites.[59]

Meanwhile the government pushed through Congress on January 29 a law reforming the police. The way this happened, and the contents of the law, marked an inauspicious start to implementation of the broader peace accords. First, the government was supposed to have presented the draft legislation to the Follow-Up Commission (which is also referred to in UN documents as the Accompaniment Commission). That commission had not been created yet, but the government went ahead with the legislation without the required consultations. As was the case earlier in 1996, when the government signed an agreement on police reform with the Spanish government *before* completing negotiations on the Agreement on the Strengthening of Civilian Power, the new police law seemed calculated to preempt a more fulsome discussion of police reforms. Moreover, the law omitted important points. It did not provide the constitutional reform required to ensure that civilian police had a monopoly over internal security. It omitted any mention of the inclusion of indigenous people within the police. It did not require that all members of the police receive training at the academy, nor did it address the educational and background requirements for new recruits. It was silent on conditions for promotions. It empowered the director general of the new National Civil Police (PNC) to establish the career path, leaving open the likelihood of an arbitrary process favoring existing police commanders or personal cronies. In a sense, the law was the culmination of the expedient and evasive strategy regarding police development chosen by Arzú's government from the outset. It posed significant risks that the PNC would merely be the old National Police in new uniforms with insufficient vetting, background checks, retraining, and new leadership to be meaningfully different from the old force.[60]

The government's timing was astute. Stephen was a lame duck and the government knew it before he did. Arnault was preparing to transition to his new role and exhausted by the final push to complete the talks. The URNG could do little to protest government noncompliance. As a result, the first major legislation to implement a critical element of the substantive accords was seriously deficient, and handled at variance with the procedures laid out in the implementation and timetable agreement. MINUGUA recommended to New York that once it had an appropriate mandate, the mission should bring the many problems with the law to the attention of the Follow-Up Commission (once it formed). For now, there was nothing else MINUGUA could do.

To further complicate what must have been a rough week for Stephen, about one thousand members of the Mobile Military Police (PMA) mutinied as soon as they figured out that the new police law did not hold out any employment opportunities for them. They demanded US$13,500 each in severance pay. They justified their claims on the basis that the URNG combatants would be getting a resettlement package and that their own should be at least as favorable. The military referred to the incident blandly as "indiscipline" rather than as a mutiny, but this was a serious breach of the military hierarchy.[61] The army's counteroffer was far less, on the order of US$860 for enlisted men. The PMA mutineers took captive the second-highest-ranking officer in the army when he came to negotiate with them. Arzú's government informed MINUGUA that they saw this as a must-win situation, because of the dangerous precedent it could set, and expressed concern about whether the army command would stand up to the mutineers.[62] In the end, the army surrounded the PMA barracks with tanks and buzzed it with aircraft. A few shots were exchanged, and then the mutineers put down their weapons and agreed to return to normal duties and await the government's final offer.

Almost eclipsed by all the drama was MINUGUA's release of its sixth human rights report, covering the period from July 1, 1996, through December 31, 1996. It marked a significant improvement in conditions compared to the previous reporting period. Incidents of violations of the right to life were down significantly, and most of the cases admitted were violations of due process rights. In parallel with these changes, the report found that the army and PACs no longer figured as prominently in complaints, whereas the police and the public prosecutor's office were the most common wrongdoers. MINUGUA had admitted a much smaller percentage of claims presented compared to earlier periods. Increasingly members of the public were bringing claims that related not to human rights issues per se, but rather to agreements for which verification had not yet begun (such as the socioeconomic agreement).

The report described in some detail the serious and risky efforts by the government to arrest alleged members of a powerful criminal organization within the military and gave the government significant credit for these undertakings. This included the arrest in September 1996 of Alfredo Moreno Molina and seizure of a massive stash of information and physical evidence indicating extensive involvement of "senior army officers, prominent businessmen, political leaders, and Government officials in smuggling" (paragraph 33). The government had dismissed a significant number of military officers, as well as members of the police and prosecutor's office, for alleged involvement in crime. The purge had been more profound in the military than in the police.

Despite these positive steps, serious problems remained, as highlighted by the poor performance of police and prosecutors with respect to due process. The police reform process had been seriously deficient up to this point, and despite salutary efforts to manage the public prosecutor's office more effectively (such as the shocking innovation of establishing shifts so that at least some prosecutors were on call at all times!) these institutions still fell short of the needed professional performance.

▌ The Transition Begins

By early February, the military observer team had arrived in the country, including 131 military observers and a twelve-person medical team under the command of Brigadier-General José Rodríguez (Spain). Seventeen countries contributed personnel to the mission. Seven individual observers did not have the requisite language skills and were sent home. The team was treated well in the press, and there was little nationalist outcry, perhaps because the observers were *unarmed* and thus posed no imminent threat to sovereignty. Once in the country, the observers received some quick training, and then deployed to the various concentration areas and buffer zones.

The Follow-Up Commission met for the first time on February 8. It was composed of Jean Arnault (as observer); Gustavo Porras and Raquel Zelaya (for the government); Pablo Monsanto and Arnoldo Noriega (for the URNG); and Rodolfo Orozco, Manuel Salazar Tezahuic, Eduardo González, and Gert Rosenthal (representing civil society). Congress had not yet chosen its representative, and Rosenthal did not attend the first meeting pending approval by the Secretary-General (Rosenthal was executive secretary of the Economic Commission for Latin America, a UN agency). Rosenthal's presence on the Follow-Up Commission was especially welcome from the United Nations' point of view, as he was a skilled diplomat who was highly competent on economic development issues, had extensive experience within the UN system, and had deep knowledge of the various political currents within the Guatemalan elite. Fortunately, at the first meeting, the government promptly agreed to present the police law to the Follow-Up Commission for review, and to supplement it as needed to comply with the accords. The Follow-Up Commission committed to reviewing it promptly and providing a response by February 19.[63]

In a less auspicious gesture, however, in late February President Arzú threw a "petulant fit" toward the press, stomped out of an official event, and refused to accept further questions on the grounds that his answers "would be distorted." In one of Stephen's last communications before stepping down, he wrote to Goulding expressing concern that this kind of behavior could present a problem for the peace process. Arzú faced difficult problems with crime and the resulting public fear. Press coverage on these issues, though flawed and somewhat inflammatory, basically reflected this reality. "Instead of understanding the situation in political terms, Arzú seems to be taking the criticism personally, and lashing out irrationally. Increasingly there is talk in political circles here of Arzú as an 'authoritarian' personality, potentially erratic and unpredictable." With peace implementation just getting under way, Arzú needed to have a working relationship with the press or things could deteriorate quickly.[64] Close advisers tried to step in and soften the president's position, but this incident ushered in a new political tone for the Arzú administration, and signaled significant political weaknesses that would soon be exploited skillfully by the farther right FRG party.

∎ Reflections on the David Stephen Period

A senior MINUGUA staff member described Stephen's time at MINUGUA as a "period of transition that never got past the transition" ("periodo de transición que no salió de la transición"). Stephen had led an intense process of internal discussion within the mission regarding how to reshape the mission's organization and its role. But this effort had, in my informant's view, been undercut by the contents of the timetable agreement in December 1996, which handed a central role to the weak Follow-Up Commission and called on MINUGUA to play a good offices and advisory role on all aspects of the peace process: "We are partners" ("vamos de socios") in the peace process.[65] The full implications of this arrangement would become clear over the next few years.

While Stephen made some critical missteps during his first weeks at MINUGUA, betraying perhaps some overeagerness combined with a not yet fully developed understanding of the political situation, he deserves credit for engaging seriously and energetically with the question of what should come next. This was an appropriate role for MINUGUA to play, even though it was technically outside of the human rights verification mandate. Decisionmakers in New York were far away from the practicalities and details of verification work in Guatemala. Arnault, who within the United Nations was best informed about the content and requirements of the accords, had at this point little direct verification experience (he had been a political officer in the UN mission in Western Sahara, where, sadly, there had been little to verify). MINUGUA needed to contribute to the discussion, and there appears not to have been a strong mechanism for dialogue between the mission leadership, the moderation, and DPA regarding how verification would actually be done. Stephen chafed against the constraints on the mission's role in facilitating military-URNG contacts on the ground in Guatemala, and one wonders whether the constraints imposed on these activities were really necessary. His proposed actions would in all probability have established a valuable on-the-ground mediation role for MINUGUA at a critical time, and given the extent to which Guatemalan field commanders were taking the lead in establishing confidence-building measures in the country, the actual risks to the United Nations, and the Guatemalan forces, were minimal. Stephen and his staff deserve credit for supporting the remarkably rapid preparation of the URNG assembly and demobilization areas.

Goulding distinguished himself during this period. Although his role was not as visible as it had been in El Salvador (where he was widely admired for having authoritatively dressed down Salvadoran generals who challenged his presence in their country), his work behind the scenes was critical in staving off the Guatemalan government's persistent efforts to prevent the creation of an effective verification mission. Goulding conceded that the mission would not grow significantly (which was a financial necessity for the United Nations in any case), but he insisted effectively that the United Nations and the United Nations alone would verify the accords, that verification was distinct from development work, and that verification would at times be intrusive. He told the government that they had better get used to it. He, along with Alvaro de Soto, successfully guided Secretary-General Annan's decision to seek a conventional Security Council resolution for the military observer deployment, and contributed to the behind-the-scenes negotiations with China that led to its passage on the second try. Through all these efforts Goulding prevented a substantial watering-down of the mission's standing that, as we will see in future chapters, would have left Guatemala with essentially no effective defender of the peace process as elite opposition grew in subsequent years.

■ Notes

1. In a thorough review of DPA's MINUGUA files, I found no comparably detailed instructions for the other heads of missions/SRSGs.

2. David Stephen, "Considerations," to Marrack Goulding, October 31, 1996.

3. David Stephen, "Request to MINUGUA from Guatemalan Army," to Marrack Goulding, June 26, 1996.

4. Marrack Goulding, letter to David Stephen, May 30, 1996.

5. Ibid.

6. David Stephen, "First Contact with Government Authorities," to Marrack Goulding, June 6, 1996.

7. Marrack Goulding, "Note to the File, Guatemala: Conversation with the Foreign Minister," June 11, 1996.

8. Marrack Goulding, "Contacts with Guatemalan Government," to David Stephen, June [1]4, 199[6] (NY Cable 1646). This document is misdated. It is marked "4 June 1995," but clearly responds to Stephen's cable of June 6, 1996. It also conveyed, as an attachment, a "note to the file" dated June 11, 1996. I believe the correct date is June 14, 1996.

9. David Stephen, "Request to MINUGUA from Guatemalan Army," to Marrack Goulding, June 26, 1996.

10. Marrack Goulding, "Request to MINUGUA," to David Stephen, June 28, 1996.

11. David Stephen, "Your 1857—Request to MINUGUA," to Marrack Goulding, June 29, 1996.

12. "MINUGUA Weekly Situation Report 16–29 April 1996."

13. Author interview, General Julio Balconi, Guatemala City, June 1998.

14. I will use the more common abbreviation PAC throughout, except where quoting directly from UN documents. The United Nations' use of the CVDC abbreviation amounted to buying into the government's claim that the committees were "voluntary," in the face of ample evidence that they were not. Thus the government's Orwellian terminology was incorporated into all official UN documents, despite the fact that the question of whether the committees were voluntary was a task requiring verification under the Comprehensive Agreement on Human Rights. See Margaret Popkin, *Civil Patrols and Their Legacy: Overcoming Militarization and Polarization in the Guatemalan Countryside* (Washington, DC: The Robert F. Kennedy Memorial Center for Human Rights, 1996).

15. "MINUGUA Weekly Situation Report 16–22 July 1996."

16. David Stephen, "Disarming of the CVDCs (ex-PACs)," to Marrack Goulding, July 30, 1996.

17. David Stephen, "Official Announcement of Dissolution of CVDC," to Marrack Goulding, August 15, 1996.

18. Most of the weapons were World War II–vintage rifle and carbines in poor condition. They had little military value, but could certainly be used in abuses against unarmed civilians.

19. "MINUGUA Weekly Situation Report 6–19 August 1996."

20. "MINUGUA Weekly Situation Report 27 August–10 September 1996."

21. If the military had been fully transparent about weapons inventories, and if there had not been credible reports that the army was forming new armed groups, this might not have been such a problem.

22. "MINUGUA Weekly Situation Report 15–21 October 1996."

23. "MINUGUA Weekly Situation Report 18–24 November 1996."

24. "Sixth Report of the Director of the United Nations Mission for the Verification of Human Rights and of Compliance with the Commitments of the Comprehensive Agreement on Human Rights in Guatemala," A/51/790, January 31, 1997.

25. "MINUGUA Weekly Situation Report 24 September–7 October 1996."

26. David Stephen, "Further Contacts with Government Authorities," to Marrack Goulding, June 7, 1996.

27. "MINUGUA Weekly Situation Report 4–10 June 1996."

28. "MINUGUA Weekly Situation Report 18–24 June 1996."

29. David Stephen, "Weekend Developments," to Marrack Goulding, July 1, 1996.

30. David Stephen, "Contacts with the Press," to Marrack Goulding, July 1, 1996.

31. David Stephen, "Analysis of Reactions to MINUGUA's Fifth Report," to Marrack Goulding, September 4, 1996.

32. "MINUGUA Weekly Situation Report 25 June–8 July 1996."

33. David Stephen, "Repercussions of Temporary Suspension of Execution," to Marrack Goulding and Kofi Annan, September 10, 1996.

34. The term "pirate" was a historical reference to the presence of British privateers along the Caribbean coast of Belize and parts of Guatemala during the colonial era. Guatemala had long asserted a sovereign claim to Belize, but had been unable to exert control over the region. Thus the presence of a British head of MINUGUA could be tapped to stir up nationalist rhetoric.

35. Ouziel (MINUGUA), "Spate of Security-Related Incidents," to Sevan (UNSECOORD) and Goulding (DPA), September 13, 1996.

36. Marrack Goulding and David Stephen, "Meeting with Foreign Minister," September 24, 1996.

37. Ibid.

38. David Stephen, "Considerations," to Marrack Goulding, October 31, 1996.

39. David Stephen, "Financing the Guatemalan Peace Programme: Informal Meeting of Donors," to Marrack Goulding, November 19, 1996.

40. Marrack Goulding, "Verification," to David Stephen, November 22, 1996.

41. David Stephen, "Statement of the President of Congress of Guatemala on Official Visit to Taiwan," to Marrack Goulding, January 8, 1997.

42. "MINUGUA Weekly Situation Report 13–19 January1997."

43. Teresa Whitfield, "Note for the File, Mr. Goulding's Meeting with Ambassador Martini," November 19, 1996.

44. "MINUGUA Weekly Situation Report 23–29 December 1996," observations and comments section.

45. The Uniting for Peace Resolution (UN General Assembly Resolution 377A, 1950) established a mechanism under which the General Assembly could act on peace and security issues if the Security Council refused to or was unable to. It had been used in response to the Suez crisis in 1956, and to impose economic sanctions against South Africa for its involvement in Namibia.

46. Alvaro de Soto, "Note for the file, Consultations on Military Observers in Guatemala," November 29, 1996.

47. "MINUGUA Weekly Situation Report 30 December 1996–12 January 1997."

48. Marrack Goulding, untitled FAX to Jean Arnault, November 27, 1996.

49. Resolution 1094 (1997), S/RES/1094 (1997), January 20, 1997, accessed at www.un.org/Docs/scres/1997/scres97.htm.

50. Evelyn Blanck, "Listos para el desarme," *Crónica* (January 24, 1997): 13.

51. Farhan Haq, "The China Veto and the Guatemalan Peace Process," *Interpress Service,* January 20, 1997, www.globalpolicy.org/component/content/article/196/39935.html (accessed June 29, 2009).

52. Comisión Nacional de Atención a Refugiados, Repatriados, y Desplazados (CEAR), "Desmovilización de la Guerrilla en Guatemala" (Guatemala: CEAR, September 1997). The camps were constructed of lightweight construction materials that could be expected to last for the sixty days of demobilization and then be easily dismantled and donated to communities to meet local needs. Designs of the buildings were adapted to climate. In the hot, humid lowlands of the Petén (Sacol), buildings were built from thatched palm leaves. In temperate zone camps, metal roofs were combined with cardboard liners to keep temperatures down, and walls were plastic sheeting that could be rolled up for ventilation. In the cold highland camps, the buildings had chipboard walls.

53. Ibid.

54. MINUGUA, "Tareas y labor de la Misión en la desmovilización de la URNG," Circular del Director no. 01/97, January 28, 1997.

55. "MINUGUA Weekly Situation Report 17–23 February 1997."

56. Denise Cook, "Note of the Secretary-General's Meeting with Mr. Eduardo Stein, Foreign Minister of Guatemala, Held at United Nations Headquarters at 10:30 on 27 January 1997," January 28, 1997.

57. Confidential interview, UN official, New York, June 2007.

58. David Stephen, "Director of Verification Mission," to Marrack Goulding and Iqbal Riza, January 30, 1997.

59. Teresa Whitfield, "Note to Messrs Goulding and de Soto: Telephone Conversation with Jean Arnault," February 12, 1997.

60. David Stephen, "Police Law," to Marrack Goulding for Jean Arnault, January 31, 1997. This cable conveyed an untitled analysis of the law prepared by the Institutional Strengthening division within MINUGUA, as well as a letter from congressional representatives, who raised many of the same issues.

61. David Stephen, "Mutiny in the Military Police," to Marrack Goulding, January 30, 1997.

62. David Stephen, "Military Police Mutiny: Developments," to Marrack Goulding, February 1, 1997.

63. Jean Arnault, "Note to Messrs. Goulding and de Soto: Summary of Peace Process-Related Developments in Guatemala," to Marrack Goulding and Alvaro de Soto, February 8, 1997.

64. David Stephen, "Political Situation of President Arzú," to Marrack Goulding, February 21, 1997.

65. Confidential interview, MINUGUA official, Guatemala City, June 1998.

5 | Verifying the Full Accords, 1997–2000

ON MARCH 1, 1997, Secretary-General Kofi Annan appointed Jean Arnault as his special representative and head of MINUGUA. With the passage of General Assembly Resolution 51/198 (on March 27, 1997), MINUGUA became the United Nations Verification Mission in Guatemala. Its mandate was extended for a full year, and the mission immediately took on the much more complex task of verifying all of the peace accords. Following on the successes of the human rights verification phase, MINUGUA's new role would prove more challenging and its achievements more ambiguous. After an encouraging start with the brisk and uneventful demobilization of the URNG, implementation of the political, institutional, and socioeconomic aspects of the accords soon faltered. The parties that had signed the accords lost much of their power, and the Guatemalan political system veered toward more overt opportunism and corruption. The Arzú government backed away from its commitments to raise taxes and maintained close ties with shadowy military intelligence structures that perpetuated impunity for human rights crimes. The defeat of constitutional reforms in a popular referendum in May 1999 drove a stake through the heart of the peace accords. The new government elected in December 1999 represented the far-right FRG party and engaged in corruption on an epic scale. MINUGUA lacked the power and strategy to counteract these adverse events. Its own inadequate public communications effort failed to shift public opinion in support of the reforms enumerated in the accords, so the government had few political incentives to carry them out. At the outset of the comprehensive verification phase, MINUGUA stumbled into an international scandal when it appeared that it had helped the Arzú government cover up the forced disappearance of a rebel in the waning months of the war. Managerial, organizational, and morale problems reduced the mission's effectiveness. MINUGUA spread itself thin trying to cover all aspects of the accords, failed to identify and focus on politically achievable goals, and established a

131

pattern of resorting to consensus-building meetings among elements of civil society in lieu of more directly and effectively influencing the government.

To verify the government's compliance with its diverse commitments under the accords, the mission needed to develop expertise and procedures to investigate and assess social and economic policies, tax policies and implementation, land tenure and markets, gender and racial discrimination, labor rights protection, and cultural and linguistic rights, while maintaining its ongoing and still-necessary human rights work. To give a sense of the scope of work, the Timetable Agreement listed at least forty-three different government measures regarding socioeconomic conditions. Some were quite sweeping, even absurdly so: "Sponsor legislative changes that will make it possible to establish an efficient decentralized multi-user land registry system that is financially sustainable, subject to compulsory updating and easy to update."[1] MINUGUA would also have to verify the functioning and implementation of a complex set of extraordinary advisory commissions. These commissions had been tasked with working out solutions to some of the stickiest policy questions—such as how to reform the judicial system or how to incorporate indigenous languages into education and public administration.

The new mandate fundamentally altered the way the mission worked. Wheras previously it had verified human rights conditions using a case-by-case methodology with clear legal points of reference, now the mission needed to become a socioeconomic and political research organization capable of assessing progress on a wide range of social conditions, including social equity and overall economic growth. These tasks required a very different skillset. Moreover, MINUGUA was expected to accomplish this internal transformation with no additional resources or personnel over the baseline established during its human rights phase, all the while maintaining its capacity to mediate immediate social conflicts, build state capacity, and verify human rights.[2]

The Timetable Agreement also called on MINUGUA to inform the public about the content of the peace accords. To gain public acceptance, MINUGUA also needed to inform the public about its own new role, a task made more difficult by the headquarters decision to keep the same name despite the change in mandate. There would inevitably be a nationalist backlash against MINUGUA from those sectors that would see it as an "alternate government dressed in blue."[3] MINUGUA would need an advertising campaign, as well as closer and more effective relations with the national press corps, to offset the negative influence of private media outlets that were skeptical of the need for the reforms within the peace accords. Broadcast stations and newspapers catered to the frustrations and insecurities of their mass audience, serving up a steady diet of inflammatory rhetoric. As a counterweight to the media resources concentrated in a few private hands, MINUGUA devoted only on average 1 percent of its annual budget to public information in all forms from 1996 to 2000.[4]

The importance of having an effective public information program was highlighted by the adverse and deteriorating political climate. While the Arzú government demonstrated a desire to promote major reforms through its participation in the negotiating process, by the time the implementation phase began in early 1997, the government had already begun to lose political support, and the president had begun sparring acrimoniously with the national press. The Novella kidnapping, described earlier, had undercut the URNG's standing. The general public showed little interest in the peace process, since comparatively few people had been directly affected by the war during its final decade. There was a widespread perception that the peace accords were a project of the PAN and the URNG, and that these parties would try to appropriate any political advantages to be had.[5] Other parties were understandably less than enthusiastic about supporting the accords' implementation. The Arzú government faced a basic problem of political motivation: while the benefits of implementing the peace accords would be widely dispersed across the population and would pay off in greater social equity and stability over decades, the political costs of implementing the accords would be borne immediately by the PAN if it went ahead. Powerful groups in business, the armed forces, and the media were opposed to the changes to which the PAN had committed; at the same time, public knowledge of and support for the accords was weak.[6]

Here, ironically, was a disadvantage of the fact that Guatemala's state had emerged from the civil war fully intact. In many peacebuilding contexts, the collapse or near collapse of the state presents UN peace missions with basic challenges of helping to restore order and governance. This vastly increases the resources required to be successful as well as the risks of outright failure. But it also creates opportunities: since existing institutions are disrupted, radical changes are more possible.[7] Guatemala presented the opposite problem: on the up side the United Nations did not have to provide governance. However, Guatemala's institutions were major obstacles to changes agreed to by the government and rebels. Determined, antireform constituencies vetoed reforms, brought suits before the courts, impeded reform legislation, and promoted counterlegislation in Congress. If that failed, they used the media to manipulate the very large pool of uninformed voters who could collectively veto reform because constitutional changes required passage by popular referendum. Moreover, in a context in which social peace was fragile, the armed forces suddenly withdrew from its traditional role in suppressing social protests. Even relatively modest antireform mobilizations, especially if they became violent, could force the government to retreat from its promises under the accords.[8]

Given this political situation, it was predictable that the government would have difficulty or would decide against delivering on many of its commitments. How could MINUGUA ensure that the government followed through? As noted in the previous chapter, David Stephen proposed unsuccessfully that MINUGUA should have a political veto over international aid programs so it could give the government financial incentives to carry through on its commitments, or conversely, impose sanctions if it did not. Faced with intense government opposition to this idea, as well as possessing no mechanism for establishing such authority over the various donor agencies, Stephen retreated.

In any case, Arnault was in charge of the implementation phase and he did not believe in strong aid conditionality. In a 2001 conference paper looking back on the MINUGUA experience, Arnault argued that verification was basically coercive and depended for its effectiveness on the threat of economic sanctions (usually in the form of conditionally withholding foreign aid). Yet if a UN verification mission were to fail to actually impose hurtful sanctions, the mission's credibility and leverage would evaporate.[9] Arnault felt that unless donor states were really willing to walk away from Guatemala in its hour of need—which he doubted—there was no point in making conditionality threats. The international community viewed the accords as an "aspirational agenda that deserve[d] international community support." Thus, it made more sense to position the mission as a helpful collaborator and advocate.[10] This philosophy matched the multiple, collaborative roles laid out for MINUGUA in the Timetable Agreement, and also dovetailed with the government's preference for a less intrusive role for the United Nations. It was less likely to trigger a nationalist backlash. But it also meant that if the government fell short on implementation, the mission had essentially no leverage other than criticism.

In this context, it appears that MINUGUA leadership did not fully appreciate that the mission's strongest potential resource was not verification, but its authority under the Timetable Agreement to communicate directly with the public. Unless public opinion swung strongly and actively in favor of the accords, elite resistance would predictably win any postconflict contest over what would or would not be implemented. However, running a peace mission as a public relations firm was outside the norm for the United Nations, and MINUGUA's organizational design reflected more its verification roots, as well as the United Nations' usual style of maintaining a low profile, depending on carefully cultivated relationships with key political actors and communicating through formal and diplomatically worded press releases. With the benefit of hindsight, a radically different, media-heavy approach was needed, but there was little if any precedent for this.

The mission also seems to have been late to appreciate the importance of properly done public opinion survey research. It depended mainly on polls conducted by others for other purposes, and when it did commission a survey in 1999 shortly before the popular referendum on constitutional reforms, it appears the survey contractor did a poor job of sampling or compensating for the fears of respondents who were nervous being interviewed by strangers. The poll gave the mission a misleadingly positive view of the strength of public support for the constitutional reforms. The mission lacked information about the public's views and extent of ignorance, and depended too heavily on its established "interlocutors" in government and civil society, who had agendas of their own.

Throughout Arnault's term, the mission continued to do its human rights work and helped support the efforts of the separate Historical Clarification Commission, which issued a very powerful report in 1999 concluding that government forces had committed acts of genocide during the civil war. As had happened in previous stages, there were tensions between the human rights role of the mission and its other goals, and the Guatemalan right frequently accused the mission of coddling criminals when it insisted on due process. Arnault and the mission itself were accused of covering up a major state crime when MINUGUA failed to investigate a disappearance that coincided with the operation to rescue Mrs. Novella from her kidnappers. The mission also faced the dark responsibility of monitoring the government's response to the ghastly murder of a Catholic bishop, Juan Gerardi, who headed the Church's independent human rights truth commission.

These challenges were all the more difficult because MINUGUA was not operating at top efficiency. Both Arnault and his deputy chief of mission Pierre Jambor (November 1997 through March 1999) described significant administrative problems that were never fully resolved. One key problem was the diversity of labor relations systems within the mission (UN Volunteers, career UN staff, temporary contract employees, and so forth), which meant that personnel quality varied widely, as did salaries, with too little correlation between the two. The mission recruited some exceptionally bright and well-educated staff at lower levels, yet there was no mechanism to provide those who showed promise with incentives and opportunities for "in-mission career development." Direct promotion from UNV positions into international staff positions was prohibited. The training and experience of some of the police officials was irrelevant to their jobs in MINUGUA, which contributed further to potential frictions between civilian and police personnel within regional offices. The mission's professional staff regrettably included some individuals who shunned hard work, feigned health problems to finagle transfers to the capital, or simply quit because they could not handle the austere conditions that prevailed in regional offices. In one bizarre incident, a staffer falsely reported being the victim of an armed robbery. In accordance with the General Assembly–mandated policy of "gender mainstreaming" in peace operations, MINUGUA placed women in charge of regional offices and in other positions of authority whenever qualified candidates could be found. This was all to the good, but a few male subordinates, primarily from South American countries, rebelled against these arrangements, making spurious complaints about authoritarian conduct by their female superiors, and openly mocking gender sensitivity and sexual harassment training programs.

In combination, these frictions—some avoidable, some not—contributed to tensions within the mission and to staff turnover. Some contract personnel did not perceive career prospects in the organization, and thus had weak incentives to adhere to the organization's goals and priorities. This undercut unity of effort and team building. Given the high turnover rates, training was a constant tax on senior staff time that could have been spent more productively. In his report to the Brahimi panel, Arnault suggested that the United Nations needed to provide centralized training on the basics of working within the United Nations, leaving only context-specific training to missions. On top of these problems, when staff did manage to move from one type of contract to another, some endured prolonged periods without pay because of snafus in New York.[11]

In a 2008 interview, Arnault noted the substantive impact of MINUGUA's diverse composition:

> Aside from the administration, and besides me, there were only 2 other regular UN staff in the mission. People were brought together for this one project—it was a collection of individuals. Yet they had to act as one single political actor. This is usually the task of national teams who come from the same schools, same culture, etc. That makes embassies cohesive, yet even they don't always get it right. . . . When you talk to "MINUGUA staff" you are going to get all kinds of things—because they all have varied perspectives, experiences. Anybody in the business of being effective would tell you that the last thing to do is to bring together people of such diversity with the intent that they work together.[12]

The diversity of backgrounds produced sharply differing assessments of how verification should be handled. Many staff involved in verification and institutional development work expressed frustration with what they saw as Arnault's collaborative approach to working with the government. Perhaps reflecting experiences during the human-rights-only phase or their own previous backgrounds in opposition politics or human rights advocacy, they wanted to take a hard line with the government and more aggressively document the many ways in which government actions fell short of the criteria set out in the accords.[13] This internal friction found its most damaging expression in the scandal that erupted around MINUGUA's failure in 1996 and early 1997 to investigate the disappearance of a URNG member. Frustrated MINUGUA staff leaked information and expressed suspicions to the press in a manner that was very damaging to the mission's reputation.

There were also rumblings within the mission that Arnault was so engaged with high-level political maneuvering that he did not attend to the nuts and bolts of running a large organization. This allowed strange patterns of authority to develop within the mission, which one interviewee referred to as "parallel powers," in an ironic reference to the dark, secretive forces that dominated the Guatemalan government from behind the scenes. For example, an individual in administrative services assumed the authority to screen all press releases and other written communications coming out of the mission, usurping the authority of the mission spokesman and causing delays.[14]

Indeed, it appears that management was not a particularly high priority for Arnault and he did not have experience running a large organization. Recall that when the Guatemalan parties asked for him to be the "moderator" in 1996, UN headquarters was concerned that he lacked the management experience to direct a large negotiating effort. As a result, they placed a more senior official, Gilberto Schlittler, above him. As it turned out, the negotiating process remained lightly staffed, Schlittler's role was limited, and most of the time Arnault and one desk officer in New York managed the negotiations with relatively little input from above. The downside of the very streamlined negotiating staff was that when Arnault assumed command of a large and very complex field mission, he still did not have large-organization management experience or training. While there can be no question about Arnault's political and diplomatic acumen, it does seem that he needed to have a very effective and empowered support staff around him, including people willing to correct serious administrative and personnel issues.[15] Arnault's deputy, Jambor, wrote in his end of mission report (coinciding with his retirement) that the Secretary-General needed to consider administrative ability in selecting future SRSGs: "The COM must not only possess the required intellectual, negotiating and political skills to fulfill his/her responsibilities: He/she must also possess essential management skills: the larger the Mission, the more complex it is and the more these skills will be of the essence for the ultimate success or failure of the Mission."[16] Another way of viewing this is that if a peace process requires a head of mission who is primarily a diplomat, not a manager, the United Nations needs to appoint an especially strong deputy or team of deputies and provide them with broad managerial powers and support from New York, so that the head of mission can focus on political affairs without detriment to the functioning of the mission.

A contributing factor in management difficulties within MINUGUA was the reporting structure for mission administration: the chief administrative officer (CAO) reported to the Field Administration and Logistics Division (FALD) of DPKO, and all administrative staff at all levels of the mission reported to the CAO. Meanwhile, all the substantive staff of MINUGUA reported through the SRSG to DPA. As a result, the administrative division of the mission sometimes worked at cross-purposes with the substantive side, refusing to provide specific kinds of material and administrative support required in the field and overruling substantive staff requests on issues small and large. One small but illustrative example cited by Jambor was that the CAO, ignoring feedback from the field, insisted on purchasing a fleet of less expensive replacement four-wheel-drive vehicles that were incapable of handling the atrocious roads in the Guatemalan highlands. As a result of this false economy, the mission had to continue operating older vehicles, despite reliability problems and maintenance costs, because they had the clearance and traction to traverse mountain tracks. FALD's role was particularly problematic with respect to hiring. Senior positions were left vacant for excessive periods and FALD took into account extraneous considerations such as trying to place personnel from other missions whose contracts had run out.[17]

The problem of split reporting channels had been noted earlier by Franco in his end of mission report, and had not been resolved. Arnault was less alarmed about these problems than Franco, or Jambor, both of whom came out of the UNHCR, where field operations were more "seamless." Arnault was used to how UN headquarters operated.[18] The underlying problem was that DPA, unlike DPKO, was not organized as an operational division. It did not make sense to duplicate FALD within DPA, but there needed to be some way to make the mission CAO more fully and consistently accountable to the SRSG/COM, while making FALD accountable to DPA for providing adequate support to DPA's missions such as MINUGUA. Arnault suggested in his response to the Brahimi panel that the way to address this was to decentralize administration down to the mission level, so that missions—and by implication the SRSG in charge—would have direct authority over the mission's main budget and be able to authorize financial transactions, hiring, and purchasing.[19] Doing this would have solved many problems for MINUGUA.

The need for decentralization was especially evident with respect to trust fund projects that supported "Institutional Strengthening" projects. One UN official interviewed referred to "trust fund" as "my most hated word."[20] MINUGUA and DPA staff who dealt with the trust fund projects reported considerable frustration with the glacial response time of the controller's office, the rigidity of the budget, the difficulty of moving money between categories as project needs evolved, and high overhead charges (13 percent) that offended donors. During 1998, MINUGUA negotiated with UN headquarters about transferring trust fund projects to the United Nations Office of Project Services (UNOPS). UNOPS charged only 5 percent overhead and was "more operational," since financial and management decisions could be made by the field office in Guatemala, not in New York.[21]

UNOPS had less restrictive budgetary procedures so it could move money across spending categories to meet on-the-ground needs. An agreement was finally reached in January 1999, but officials in New York, seemingly in an act of spite, threw out many of the details that had been worked out regarding a graduated transfer of projects to UNOPS. Instead, New York handed over all of the trust fund projects to UNOPS with only two weeks' notice. Unfortunately, this abrupt handoff coincided with the startup of a critical effort by MINUGUA, financed through the trust fund, to educate the public about constitutional reforms in advance of a popular referendum. UNOPS dealt with the challenge successfully, but with a great deal of "improvisation." The timing and handling of the UNOPS handoff did not help MINUGUA carry out a timely and effective public education campaign.[22]

▌Demobilizing the URNG

The comprehensive verification phase began with important successes: the separation of armed forces, the concentration of URNG forces in assembly areas, and their disarmament and demobilization in accordance with a rapid timetable. This task was facilitated by the comparatively small size of the URNG's forces and by the confidence-building steps previously taken by the URNG and the army before the official ceasefire began. As noted in the previous chapter, eight camps had been quickly set up in six locations around the country.[23] The Ceasefire Accord called for the establishment of a six-kilometer security radius around each of the camps, from which the Guatemalan army (and its allied paramilitaries) would be excluded. No overflights were permitted in these areas. Government forces could move through an additional concentric six-kilometer "coordination zone" as long as they had prior permission and were accompanied by UN military observers. Overflights of the outer ring were permitted with prior notice. Police could enter if accompanied by MINUGUA.

On D-day, March 3, MINUGUA hosted a ceremony at the Claudia estate (one of the URNG assembly areas near Escuintla) to mark the beginning of demobilization. The UN military observer group confirmed that government forces had withdrawn from the security areas around URNG assembly camps and the next day UN observers began escorting rebel columns to the camps, following a staggered timetable. The UN observers had spent a few days with their assigned URNG troops, establishing rapport. URNG units were already based at two of the assembly sites, and were joined by additional combatants once the official ceasefire began. The other sites were not URNG bases, so UN observers joined rebel advance teams to establish a presence in the camps before other groups moved in on foot or in convoys. UN military observers escorted all URNG columns to the camps and accompanied URNG personnel any time they needed to leave the camps to collect weapons from caches, destroy explosives or minefields, or seek medical treatment.[24]

The troop movements took place without incident, probably aided by the virtual lack of fighting since late March 1996. Top officials in the URNG, as well as field commanders, felt confident after months of direct meetings with army commanders. The top URNG commanders had remained in Guatemala after the signing ceremony at the end of 1996 and could be seen traveling in Guatemalan army helicopters to inspect and approve the concentration sites. For rank and file members of the URNG, however, who had not directly interacted with the army outside of combat, demobilization was a leap of faith, and an act of obedience to the party as well as the URNG's military command structure.[25]

One concern regarding demobilization had to do with the changeable number of combatants reported by the URNG. On D – 15 (February 16) the URNG had provided a list of 3,570 combatants to be demobilized, but by the deadline for URNG forces to concentrate (D + 21 or March 24) only 2,928 rebels had appeared at the concentration points. One document from the military observer group stated that there had been some confusion and duplication on the original list because some URNG combatants initially provided only their noms de guerre on the list. But this was not the correct explanation. A subsequent press briefing by MINUGUA's chief military observer General José Rodríguez stated that between 400 and 500 URNG members had simply decided to go home or take jobs rather than concentrating.[26] After review by MINUGUA, both sides agreed to the reduced list. Even the reduced list included quite a few people who were not actually combatants, including political cadres, children and domestic partners, some "old-timers" who remained loyal to the URNG but were no longer active fighters, and "kids sent by old-timers to get benefits and with the blessing of the organization."[27]

Initial press reports on the concentration process were favorable. However, both army and the press questioned whether the URNG was turning in all its weapons. The URNG had presented an arms inventory of only 1,818 weapons. The newspaper *La Republica* published a list, supposedly obtained from army intelligence, reporting 2,831 arms under the control of the URNG, plus some 500 additional arms they could easily access. Given the experience in El Salvador, where the FMLN rebels were found—after their formal demobilization—to have retained enough weapons to rearm virtually their entire force, the reduced number of weapons disclosed by the URNG raised concerns in some circles, especially given the fact that the rebels had registered about a thousand more "combatants" than guns.[28] The arrest on February 22 of four ORPA combatants traveling in a pickup truck full of AK-47 rifles and ammunition reinforced the perception that the URNG might be stashing guns, although the combatants claimed to be merely relocating them from one encampment to another.[29] General Rodríguez shared the army's concerns, in part because the quantities and calibers of ammunition reported by the URNG did not line up well with the calibers of the weapons in the inventory.[30]

As a practical matter, there was little risk that a failure to collect all the URNG's arms would lead to a renewed war. Neither side wanted that. In El Salvador the rebels had kept weapons as a kind of insurance policy to reassure rank and file combatants, not as part of a plan to resume the war. The same would almost certainly have been the case in Guatemala, if in fact the URNG were systematically stashing arms at all. The Guatemalan defense minister acknowledged as much by framing his concerns largely in terms of the risk of increased crime if weapons remained in rebel hands.[31] That is, even the Guatemalan army did not claim that the URNG posed a threat of renewed war. As UN military observers and relief workers saw the "combatants" assembling at the concentration points, it became clear that only a minority of them were regular soldiers—perhaps as few as 500 to 600. Thus the URNG's weapons inventory was probably close to what they actually possessed.

In light of the questions raised in the press, General Rodríguez reiterated to the URNG *comandancia* the importance of being fully forthcoming regarding their weapons. The United Nations escorted URNG personnel to dig up caches, collect firearms, and destroy explosives in situ.[32] These redoubled efforts eliminated a substantial quantity of explosives, but in the end, only half a dozen small arms were added to the original inventory. On balance, it was both reasonable and unavoidable to accept the URNG's inventory. When MINUGUA handed over the URNG's weapons and ammunition on May 17 to the minister of the interior, the minister signed off on the certificate, formally accepting its accuracy.

Unlike other insurgencies, the URNG had made minimal use of landmines and demining had not been envisioned in the ceasefire accord. However, the URNG did have a minefield that protected a radio transmitter on the Tajumulco volcano in the department of San Marcos. The rebels succeeded in digging up and destroying 378 mines, with MINUGUA supervision and assistance. This was believed to be all or nearly all of the mines that had been deployed. Unfortunately, nothing could be done to systematically eliminate other kinds of unexploded ordnance around the country, and for the next few years there were occasional deaths and injuries when people came in contact with previously unexploded mortar rounds.

The URNG handoff of personal weapons and receipt of credentials as former combatants was very rapid. Both the army and the URNG wanted the accelerated timetable. The army did not like having its movements restricted, so the sooner the demobilization was done, the better. The URNG was concerned that the many noncombatants and political cadre who were concentrating at the camps would be unwilling to wait for months to demobilize. Since many of its political affiliates were farmers, it was important that they be able to plant their corn early enough for it to be well established before the heavy rains came.[33] The United Nations also favored a rapid demobilization, largely for considerations of cost as well as the risk that a longer military observer mission would have been an easy target for Guatemalan nationalists. As a result, the whole demobilization process was complete in an astonishing eighteen days. This contrasted sharply with the gradual phased demobilization in El Salvador, which had allowed the FMLN to leverage fuller compliance by the government. The URNG ceased to be an armed force before the Guatemalan government did much of anything to implement the agreement. The rapid demobilization also made it much harder to reintegrate the former rebels, a task that proved more difficult than their small numbers might suggest.

■ Reintegration

The Agreement on the Legal Integration of the Unidad Revolucionaria Nacional Guatemalteca addressed how to integrate former URNG members back into society. This included "extinguishing" legal liability for individuals who participated in the insurgency, registering the URNG as a political party, providing personal documents for ex-combatants, and restoring their civic and political rights. It also included provisions to help ex-combatants develop new skills, livelihoods, households, and connections to communities. The failure in Nicaragua to adequately prepare former combatants for civilian life had led to sporadic combat there in the early 1990s, as ex-FSLN soldiers and ex-Contra guerrillas took arms, sometimes jointly, to demand benefits. International donors wanted to be sure not to repeat that mistake in Guatemala. The agreement assigned decisionmaking authority about implementation to a Special Integration Commission, which was made up of representatives of the government, the URNG, and four major aid donors.

Over 80 percent of the formally demobilized URNG members were indigenous, and thus already suffered the highest rates of extreme poverty, illiteracy, and poor health as a social sector.[34] Moreover, some of the ex-combatants were extremely difficult to place in the predominantly indigenous areas of the country, which had been profoundly altered by violence. During the war, the army had forcibly relocated many people from the conflict areas to break up the potential support base for the URNG. Mass killings, some committed directly by the army and others by PACs from neighboring communities (under army coercion), had sewn deep distrust and social instability. Many people ended up landless, living far from their ancestral homes. Even those who did have opportunities to settle on new lands faced extremely tenuous incomes, land tenure, food security, and access to basic needs. The army exercised intense social control and ideological influence in many resettled communities, and blamed the URNG for much of the suffering of the past decades. These strategies were at least partly effective, and while the URNG clearly had dedicated supporters in some areas, they were just as clearly unwelcome in others.

Over four hundred combatants had no communities to return to, or if they did, the fighters were unlikely to be welcomed back. Most of these were long-term, regular fighters for the URNG. This core group had been together as a fighting force for many years, and they wanted to live together. The Special Integration Commission recognized that this was a particularly vulnerable group and decided to establish four shelters at locations around the country as a temporary measure until permanent resettlement arrangements could be made. The shelters were heavily supported by aid programs directed at providing these individuals with job training and various kinds of assistance. At one of the four sites, relations with locals were hostile and the shelter had to be relocated. Resettling the shelter population required an intensive, prolonged effort to arrange financing, purchase land, and construct housing and other facilities. The last members of this small group were not resettled until November 1998, and even then lacked land and access to markets to be self-sufficient.[35]

Another group of URNG combatants who found themselves unable to go home comprised members of the Ixcán Grande cooperative in Quiché. They chose to demobilize as combatants, triggering a very negative response from other cooperative members who felt it was unfair for the URNG group to receive greater benefits. The cooperative's general assembly decided to expel the former combatants. The ex-combatants learned of the situation and tried to delay their demobilization and remain at the assembly camp. The Special Integration Committee sent MINUGUA, government (FONAPAZ), and NGO representatives to escort them back to Ixcán Grande. This did not work. Three out of four communities rejected them, and at the village of Pueblo Nuevo community members took the demobilized combatants hostage, along with personnel from MINUGUA and FONAPAZ. The mission negotiated a nonviolent exit for the hostages, but the rejected ex-combatants had to return to the demobilization camp to be resettled elsewhere.

In general, the genuine former combatants were ill prepared for reintegration. The concentration and demobilization process was so rapid that although the URNG fighters received a good deal of remedial medical care and dental work, they received only minimal vocational counseling and training. As a result, much of the work of reintegration had to be done after ex-combatants had dispersed to many different communities around the country. The logistics of delivering services to this population were thus made much more complex than they would have been had the pace of demobilization been more gradual, begging the question of whether the United Nations should have taken steps to slow down the process.

The URNG formed a new nongovernmental organization, the Guillermo Toriello Foundation (FGT), which the European Union deputized to do a needs assessment survey.[36] The FGT got off to a rocky start, as UNDP (always mindful of its relationship with the host government) was reluctant to channel funds through an organization that was explicitly linked to the URNG. Eventually FGT gained donor acceptance and collaborated with the OAS and International Organization for Migration to implement a major aid program from donors including USAID, UNDP (which administered funds from Sweden, Denmark, and Norway), Spain, and the European Community.[37]

Despite the generosity of donors, there were problems with timing. In late November 1997, the government announced that it had around US$6 million for land purchases, but was reluctant to start buying because the EU "productive projects" funding was not expected until mid-1998.[38] There was also difficulty obtaining international funding to support projects to help the four to five hundred people who had chosen not to concentrate. They remained on the "B" list for reintegration programs.

Despite the good overall security climate for URNG ex-combatants, there were occasional episodes of violence against them. In November 1997, MINUGUA reported a series of apparently unrelated attacks against demobilized URNG combatants, including three killings. Unknown men were shadowing URNG commander Rolando Morán. MINUGUA began random patrols around the residences of the top URNG commanders.[39]

■ "The Perception of a Dirty Deal": The Mincho Affair

Even as MINUGUA was carrying out the rapid and ultimately successful demobilization of the URNG, the mission was drawn into a scandal that dominated news in Guatemala, invited negative press coverage in Europe and the United States, and required months to die down.[40] In October 1996, the Presidential General Staff (Estado Mayor Presidencial [EMP]) caught two members of ORPA (a branch of the URNG) who were trying to negotiate the ransom for Olga Alvarado de Novella, an octogenarian and family friend of President Arzú kidnapped in late August. One of the guerrillas, "Isaías" (Rafael Baldizón Nuñez), was exchanged for Mrs. Novella. The other, at this stage unidentified, disappeared. The EMP, the Public Ministry, and ORPA commander Rodrigo Asturias all denied that there had been a second kidnapper captured. However, in early 1997, credible reports were published in the press claiming that a second guerrilla had been "disappeared" by state forces. In March 1997, newspapers obtained additional information, from a combination of military intelligence sources and disgruntled midlevel ORPA operatives, identifying the second guerrilla as Juan José Cabrera Rodas, known as "Mincho."

In mid-April, *Prensa Libre* reported the added detail that Arnault had known since October 1996 about the existence of a second URNG militant captured in connection with the Novella kidnapping. Since Arnault was by this point in charge of MINUGUA, this begged the question of why MINUGUA had not more aggressively investigated the case. The newspaper *elPeriódico* went a step further and accused MINUGUA of a cover-up, suggesting that Arnault had concealed the disappearance as part of the negotiations that brought the government back to peace talks in November 1996. MINUGUA immediately issued a letter from Arnault refuting the paper's claim.[41] The accusation was particularly stinging since among Guatemalan newspapers, *elPeriódico* was generally the one least inclined to side with knee-jerk conservative positions. Its editor, José Rubén Zamora, had endured death threats and at least one assassination attempt because of the paper's reporting.

Publicity prompted Cabrera's family members to come forward and make a formal complaint to the mission regarding his disappearance. MINUGUA reported this to New York, noting that, "As both the Government and ORPA have denied his existence until now, the release of MINUGUA's findings are likely to have a significant political impact," suggesting some foreknowledge of what the findings were likely to be.[42]

A story in *elPeriódico* on April 24 continued the campaign, labeling Arnault "the verifier/accomplice."[43] The next day, an editorial charged that Arnault had a conflict of interest as verifier, since he could not be expected to expose flaws in the accords that he had brokered. The writer declared it "puerile" to think that Arnault had not known about Mincho.[44] Phil Gunson of the *Guardian* in London echoed these charges, assembling quotes from leaders of Guatemalan human rights NGOs, as well as anonymous informants from inside MINUGUA, to depict a deliberate cover-up in which unnamed "superiors" had held up the investigation and relevant files had supposedly been deleted from mission computer systems.[45] Over the next month, similar stories appeared in *El País* in Spain and in the *Miami Herald*. In late May, the US-based NGO Human Rights Watch announced that it would look into the situation.[46] The *New York Times* published a story that quoted Guatemalan human rights activists faulting Arnault for not having investigated the case much sooner.[47] Arnault was, of course, not responsible for human rights investigations until March 1997, so this specific criticism was absurd. But it still left the question of why the mission had not begun to move on the case until after Cabrera's relatives made a formal complaint on April 16. The Mincho case was of singular importance: human rights violations had declined dramatically with the end of the fighting and greater international scrutiny, yet here was an apparent disappearance, and one committed by a unit of the army that was particularly notorious for abuses and closely linked to the presidency.

MINUGUA issued a statement that there had been no cover-up and that there was no linkage between the Mincho case and the government's decision to resume negotiations in November 1996. The government had returned to the negotiations after the URNG accepted responsibility for the kidnapping, stopped armed propaganda operations, and—most importantly—removed Asturias from the negotiations. Arnault acknowledged knowing about Mincho in his capacity as moderator. He denied, however, having influenced MINUGUA's verification activities prior to assuming the SRSG position.[48] This did not satisfy critics, however, and rumors circulated in Guatemala that the United Nations would launch an internal investigation, rumors the United Nations publicly and disingenuously rejected. In fact, the Secretary-General sent to Guatemala two high-ranking officials, Horacio Boneo (Spain) and Aracelly Santana (Ecuador), to look into the allegations and assess the performance of Arnault as well as MINUGUA in dealing with the case. The team arrived in Guatemala on May 28 and left June 3, and also conducted interviews in New York. In brief, the team found:

> (a) No grounds to criticize the conduct of Mr. Arnault, and we believe that his explanation concerning the extent of and circumstances in which he acquired his knowledge about the Mincho case, as well as on the way in which it was handled is credible and convincing.
>
> (b) The handling of the Mincho case by MINUGUA presents several deficiencies, including problems of communication, feedback and transparency within the Mission. However, we do not find any evidence suggesting that there was malice or attempts to "cover-up" in the behaviour of MINUGUA.[49]

So why didn't the limited information available to Arnault and others about Mincho fuel a more serious and timely investigation by MINUGUA? The first piece of an answer relates to the firewall between the "moderation" effort and MINUGUA. Arnault had been instructed to minimize contact with MINUGUA. When the URNG approached him about the case, he provided his "good offices" to contact the government and inquire about the unnamed second guerrilla. When told firmly that government forces did not have the second kidnapper, he communicated this to the URNG, which chose not to pursue it further. It would have been up to USG Goulding to communicate the information to MINUGUA if necessary, but none of the senior staff of DPA recalled discussing the case at that time.[50] When the kidnapping initially occurred, the government of Guatemala did not notify MINUGUA, instead contacting Arnault in New York to ask him to intervene with the URNG to clarify the intellectual authorship of the kidnapping.[51]

Following the public announcement on October 28, 1996, of the kidnapping as well as the capture and exchange of Baldizón, the Guatemala

City regional office of MINUGUA (ORGUA) opened a case file on the Novella kidnapping, but not on Mincho. At this point there were rumors within the NGO community pointing to the presence of a second kidnapper. Two newspaper reports referred to two kidnappers having been captured. However, the EMP, the URNG, and the Public Ministry all emphatically denied the existence of a second combatant. People close to Mincho did not come forward, and even privately the URNG refused to provide enough information to allow an investigation to start. They thought that Cabrera might still be alive and did not want to precipitate his execution by generating too much scrutiny. With few leads to pursue, the case remained in the "pre-verification" phase, during which the mission's goals were to establish whether a human rights violation was likely to have occurred. Relatively little effort went into this.

It was during this phase that a key breakdown occurred within the mission. On November 5, 1996, Arnault was briefly in Guatemala and had a chance to speak with MINUGUA's head of human rights verification, Jaime Esponda, about the kidnapping and the possible disappearance of the second kidnapper. At this point, the involvement of the URNG in the kidnapping was politically very sensitive and the government had not yet returned to the negotiating table. A substantive investigation was needed and the frustrated investigators from ORGUA sought guidance from their superiors. They received none, other than being told to maintain a low profile, for which no explanation was given.[52]

On November 23, during a meeting in Mexico, ORPA leader Rodrigo Asturias asked for a private meeting with Jaime Esponda as well as the mission's military liaison officer. Asturias and another ORPA commander told the UN officials that a second guerrilla (Mincho) had been captured along with Isaías and had disappeared, but that ORPA would not make a formal denunciation because Mincho might still be alive. They did not provide enough information (such as Mincho's identity) to launch a substantive investigation.[53] Esponda reported this information to David Stephen, but it was not mentioned in the record of the meetings in Mexico, and Esponda did not pass it on to the verification team at ORGUA.[54] In effect, MINUGUA allowed its ability to investigate the case to be held hostage to ORPA's preference for confidentiality.

On January 12, 1997, *elPeriódico* published a story that a second combatant with the nom de guerre of Mincho had been captured along with Isaías. ORGUA at this point opened an ex officio disappearance case on Mincho, that is, an investigation carried out on the basis of the mission's mandate, in the absence of a formal complaint from a victim or survivor. The investigation moved slowly, however, remaining in the "pre-verification" stage, and the case was therefore not mentioned in the sixth report on human rights published at the end of January. On February 5, the military adviser, in a side conversation during another meeting in Mexico, asked Asturias for more information. Asturias declined, once again citing concerns that Mincho could still be alive. This information was reported to Esponda, but again was not conveyed to ORGUA (possibly moot, since Asturias did not provide any valuable leads).

ORGUA separately arranged a meeting with two high-level ORPA commanders "Martín" and "Santiago," which took place on February 18. The two rebel commanders laughed at the MINUGUA investigators, saying, "Your boss was at the meeting. He knows all about it. Why don't you ask him?"[55] Martín and Santiago were referring to the November 23 meeting in Mexico and the "boss" was Esponda.[56] The ORGUA team wrote a memo asking for a meeting between ORGUA and the human rights division to discuss the issue.[57] The ORGUA meeting with the ORPA commanders had revealed two things: first, Esponda had prior knowledge; but second, ORPA *still* would not provide substantive information that could have enabled MINUGUA to move ahead with the investigation.

Probably the most discomfiting detail in the Boneo and Santana report is their suggestion that Esponda felt he was under "strict instructions" that limited the human rights area's ability to pursue the case, although they don't say who instructed him. They argue that he should have taken a more assertive role in calling for a "full verification of the case," and should, at a minimum, have put his concerns in writing, as did the verification officer from ORGUA. They also fault Esponda for an unhelpful public statement he made on April 13 that fueled speculation in the press and among human rights groups about the possibility of a cover-up. Asked by the press why MINUGUA had not done more on the case, Esponda said there had been "no serious complaint" presented to the mission. The only information the mission had was from the press, he said, and MINUGUA "acts on the basis of the presentation of a serious complaint, as a part of a formal procedure." Representatives of human rights groups immediately jumped on this statement since it was either untrue or represented a departure from the mission's past policies. It was clearly part of the mission's mandate to investigate possible human rights violations ex officio, regardless of whether victims or family members came forward.[58] Phil Gunson of the *Guardian* commented on Esponda's statement, "It defies belief that Mr. Esponda—a respected Chilean human rights lawyer of vast experience—simply made a mistake."[59] It seems more likely that Esponda was caught between two irreconcilable mandates: to verify human rights and avoid a political backlash that could disrupt the peace process.

The limited information available suggests that MINUGUA moved cautiously on the Mincho case at the outset, reflecting the lack of solid information as well as the risk that the case could cause the government to balk in the final stages of the negotiations. It had always been understood that MINUGUA's human rights mission would require a deft political touch, and that the mission's activities could derail the peace process (as discussed in Chapter 2). Given the incendiary nature of the Novella case, it is plausible that the mission leadership—with or without guidance from Arnault—thought it appropriate to maintain a low profile on the case. At a minimum, Boneo and Santana report that Esponda felt he had been directed to proceed cautiously, although they never clarify who gave him this direction.

What seems less understandable is the fact that once the peace accords were signed and there was less likelihood that the Mincho case could scuttle the peace process, the mission did not more aggressively delve into the case until after the Guatemalan press began to publicize it. A likely contributing factor was the changeover in mission leadership. Just two weeks after the January press report on Mincho, Arnault was appointed to succeed Stephen. During the remainder of his term, Stephen's attentions were focused on a series of urgent matters including a potentially violent police mutiny and preparations for the URNG's concentration and demobilization. Arnault, by then finished with the negotiations, was involved in preparations for a consultative group (donors) meeting in Brussels. He was central to the efforts in New York to secure a Security Council mandate for the military observer component, a longer and broader General Assembly mandate for the mission, and an adequate budget. He was also, according to people who worked closely with him during this period, physically and emotionally exhausted after the marathon effort to reach the final accords. There is no evidence that Arnault was even aware of the mention of Mincho in the Guatemalan press in January. And though he arrived in Guatemala on March 1 to assume his post as SRSG and head of mission, he left again shortly thereafter to continue preparations for the General Assembly meeting and resolution on MINUGUA's new mandate. He did not return to Guatemala until early April, and the accusations of a cover-up hit about a week later. Thus he had essentially no opportunity to redirect what the mission was doing with respect to Mincho.

Notwithstanding the withering press attack on MINUGUA, the Guatemalan parties were the ones that engaged in overt wrongdoing in the Mincho case. Having in all likelihood approved the Novella kidnapping in the first place, Asturias made himself increasingly ridiculous by denying the existence of Mincho in the face of mounting evidence and dissent within the URNG and even within ORPA itself. It was not until September 1997 that he finally admitted Cabrera's involvement. From the outset the Estado Mayor Presidencial (EMP), acting with typical arrogance and impunity, left other state agencies out of the loop. The Interior Ministry—in charge of law enforcement—did not learn about the captures until after Isaías had been exchanged for Mrs. Novella on October 20, 1996. The EMP also kept the Defense Ministry in the dark until after the trade. The Public Ministry, responsible for criminal investigations and prosecutions, learned about the case the same day the public did—October 28.[60]

The EMP and Ministry of Defense continued to stonewall the investigation, with help from the minister of the interior. Only the Public Ministry made efforts to investigate, but they were completely stymied. When the Public Ministry asked the EMP for information, the EMP referred them to the general staff of the army. The general staff refused to respond to the inquiry. On July 3, the head of the EMP during the Novella operation, Julio Espinoza, became chief of staff of the army, and was thus in a position to completely block any further inquiry into the agency he previously headed. His brother-in-law succeeded him as head of the EMP, surely not a coincidence. The Public Ministry also asked the Ministry of Defense to provide information regarding Mincho, and the minister of defense directed them back to the EMP.[61] The Interior Ministry issued an untrue statement that "security forces from this office" (a nonexistent "antikidnapping commando" made up of both civilian and military personnel) had carried out the detention, as would have been legally required.[62] It was a perfect runaround and a demonstration of the mechanisms of impunity that had operated for decades.

Ironically the state gained nothing by denying Mincho's death. Rather, it seems to have been a habitual response. The Historical Clarification Commission report published in 1999 concluded that Cabrera most likely suffered fatal injuries at the moment of his capture (when witnesses report he was struck in the head with a bat). Given that the two kidnappers were presumed armed, and both were highly experienced urban combatants (Cabrera had been a guerrilla since 1980), it was appropriate for state officials to use considerable force during the arrest to prevent their escape, especially since, as noted in Chapter 2, a botched arrest could have resulted in Mrs. Novella's immediate execution. No doubt the capture could have been better handled with better training in the use of nonlethal equipment, but the apparently accidental death of a presumed-armed kidnapper during an arrest might have been accepted even in democratic countries with strong human rights protections. There was, of course, the broader procedural problem that the EMP had no legal basis for conducting law enforcement activities of any kind. However, this was a well-established practice, the EMP was scheduled to be dissolved under the accords, and at the time of this encounter the role of the EMP as the premier antikidnapping unit in the country was widely accepted despite its illegality. This need not have been a crisis for the Arzú government, but was made into one when the EMP converted Mincho's probably accidental death into a disappearance.

The government supplemented its skillful runaround with yet another diplomatic offensive against MINUGUA for having "exceeded its mandate" when it announced that the EMP was probably responsible for disappearing

Mincho. The government claimed that MINUGUA had crossed the line to a judicial investigation, a patently ridiculous charge, given the mission's mandate to investigate human rights cases. Foreign Minister Stein met with Secretary-General Annan in mid-June to present his complaints, and President Arzú followed a fortnight later. They presented the tired refrain that the United Nations must not be too intrusive. Yet the real wrongdoing was the other way around: the government was systematically lying and MINUGUA had the gall to point this out.[63]

After a month of relative calm, in August 1997 the Mincho case heated up once again. In June the weekly news magazine *Crónica* had obtained a photograph of a corpse buried in a city dump and passed it on to MINUGUA in July. The corpse in the photo indeed looked like previous photos of Cabrera when he was alive, so MINUGUA, after considerable background checking to verify the authenticity of the photo and to determine the exact location where it was taken, contacted state authorities to arrange an exhumation. The mission in its public statements tried to lower expectations. Ronalth Ochaeta from the Archdiocesan Human Rights Office (ODHA) once again attacked MINUGUA for withholding information, suggesting that it had held on to the photo and delayed the disinterment to further a cover-up. The exhumation took place on August 5, and the corpse turned out not to be that of Cabrera.[64] He has never been found.

▋ The Meaning of Mincho

Obviously the United Nations' handling of the Mincho case was clumsy, but the Boneo and Santana report argues credibly that there was no malfeasance. Doing human rights verification coincident with peace negotiations did involve risks. These could have been mitigated through more fluid and bidirectional communication within the mission as well as between the mission and the negotiating team. Despite the ostensible firewall between the mission and the moderation, it appears that somebody delivered a politically motivated message to Jaime Esponda that he should go slowly. A key problem was that the "Guatemala Unit" in New York, which had consisted of Arnault plus a junior political officer and a secretary, needed senior-level support and oversight to determine what information should flow between the negotiations process and the mission. By default, that responsibility rested with Goulding. As head of DPA, however, there were limits to how much attention he could pay to the details of Guatemala. At the time of Mincho's disappearance, it seemed to be an isolated event, surrounded by great uncertainty, and none of the principals anticipated its great impact. For reasons that remain unclear, the mission locked into a mode of political caution in handling the case until the story hit the press. Adequate support and better management might have prevented this, hardly a novel finding.

The one unique contributing factor was the appointment of the former moderator as the SRSG in charge of verification. The arrangement made Arnault as verifier responsible—in the public's eye at least—for acting on information he had obtained in confidence while serving as mediator. Arnault, and the mission as a whole, were made vulnerable to the widespread perception of scandal. The Mincho affair intermittently sidetracked the mission from April through August 1997, precisely the time period during which MINUGUA needed to establish its visibility and authority as verifier of the overall accords. An obvious lesson is that the advantages of assigning a former mediator as verifier, such as that person's deep knowledge of the parties and the agreements, are accompanied by significant risks.

Arnault summed up the broader meaning of the Mincho case in a cable to New York in April. Describing the *elPeriódico* allegations, he wrote, "The salient point is that I was not accused of being pro-Government or pro-URNG but 'pro-parties' and contaminated by the illegitimacy inherent in both signatories of the peace accords."[65] The persistence of the Mincho scandal, and particularly the range of different constituencies that joined in criticizing the mission, signaled just how illegitimate the government and the URNG had become. The United Nations, by appearing to have sacrificed principle to support "the parties," became a lightning rod for popular discontent toward those parties. The Mincho scandal signaled just how politically weak the parties were, and thus how difficult the implementation phase would be. Arnault wrote in the same memo that the Mincho case, the government's hostile relationship with the press, and rising conflicts within both the PAN government and the URNG, "highlight the need to build up support for the implementation of the peace accords at the grass-roots level." There were various sources of "social support that can be tapped at local and national level."[66] Arnault's response to the Mincho scandal articulated the mission's primary strategy for dealing with implementation: work around the weakness of the parties, deal directly with Guatemalan constituencies, and build enough "social support" to make implementation desirable for the government and its successors.

▌ The Death of Seven

The cost of building peace was driven home by the tragic death of six MINUGUA staff and their pilot in a helicopter crash on March 17, 1998. The crash occurred as the mission's chartered twin-engine Bell 212 approached to land at Pajuil País, a small village in the department of Huehuetenango. MINUGUA representatives had arranged a meeting with villagers, who were waving a Guatemalan flag to signal the helicopter from near the center of the intended landing zone at about 8,700 feet. During the final approach, the pilot rejected the landing because the villagers were too close to the touchdown area. Unfortunately, the helicopter, which could carry a prodigious load near sea level and had only nine people aboard, was nonetheless at or above its weight limit for such a high-altitude landing (where both engine power and aerodynamic performance are degraded).[67] When the pilot attempted to pull up to abort the landing, the rotor blades slowed and the helicopter continued to settle. The pilot attempted a last-ditch ninety-degree turn westward toward lower ground, but the rotor blades struck trees and the chopper crashed and burst into flames. Five MINUGUA staff members were killed immediately: Omar Aguirre, Luis Escoto, Pablo Gorga, Lisa Malone, and Celso Martínez. Both the pilot Rolando Palacios and MINUGUA staff member Pedro Ruz later died from their injuries. Two other passengers, Peter Kolonias and Byron Pérez, survived.

A board of inquiry found no evidence of negligence, determined that the pilot (who worked for a charter company contracted by the mission) was highly experienced and qualified to carry out the flight, and found no evidence of any inappropriate pressure on the pilot by MINUGUA personnel to land at the site. In fact, the pilot had expressed concerns to his passengers about the weight for landing at Pajuil País, and MINUGUA's Pablo Gorga had suggested that they could change the sequence of the flight, drop some passengers at the sub-regional office in Barillas, and return to Pajuil País at a lower weight. The pilot nonetheless stuck to the original flight plan despite his concerns. Going to Barillas first would probably have changed the outcome.

What the accident demonstrated was that, despite the precautions taken by the United Nations to ensure that the contractors providing aviation services are appropriately equipped and qualified, flying in a country such as Guatemala with high-altitude terrain is unforgiving and inherently riskier than other settings. In this case, an apparently minor error in flight planning, combined with the need to abort a landing (which should be a routine maneuver), resulted in a major loss of life. This was the second fatal aviation accident involving MINUGUA, the first having been the crash of the mission's Twin Otter airplane during Franco's term. That crash had occurred in low visibility conditions—another risk of high-altitude aviation in the subtropics—and the pilots appeared to have been too determined to make their landing in marginal conditions.

This is obviously an unacceptably high rate of serious accidents, especially for a peacebuilding mission in which it was seldom critical to complete any given flight on a given day.[68] The loss of life in this case was of course devastating to morale within the mission. The United Nations also handled the payment of compensation to victims awkwardly, in part because the victims were operating under such different terms of employment (UNV, military liaison, UN services, locally hired services, and so forth). Over a year later some aspects had still not been addressed. On the anniversary of the crash, the mission found itself having to prepare evasive talking points in case anyone from the press might ask questions about the status of payments. The victims and their dedication to the people of Guatemala are commemorated by a children's park in Huehuetango.

■ The EMP Strikes Back: The Assassination of Monseñor Gerardi and the Politics of Fear

On the afternoon of Sunday, April 26, 1998, auxiliary bishop Juan José Gerardi Conadera joined friends at a gathering to celebrate the publication two days earlier of *Guatemala: Never Again,* the four-volume report of the Recovery of Historical Memory (Recuperación de Memoria Histórica [REMHI]) project.[69] This was the Catholic Church's own "truth commission" report, which had used the social networks of the Church to collect testimony from survivors of mass violence during the civil conflict. The project, directed by Edgar Gutiérrez, operated through ODHA, which Gerardi founded and oversaw on behalf of the archdiocese. Not surprisingly, the report found the army and other state forces responsible for the vast majority of the violence during the war. The REMHI report established a credible Church-sanctioned account of violence during the war. Those involved in the project felt a sense of accomplishment, but were also aware of the risk of retaliation by the army. After the press conference announcing the report, Gerardi asked ODHA director Ronalth Ochaeta whether he had made preparations for his family to leave the country. Apparently Gerardi, a senior cleric nearing retirement, was less concerned about his own safety. Gerardi was certainly not naïve about the dangers facing clergy: as bishop of El Quiché in 1980 he had closed the entire diocese to protect his priests from being killed by the military.[70]

At about 10:00 p.m. Gerardi returned alone to San Sebastián and parked his Volkswagen Golf in the garage of his house adjoining the church. Inside the garage, at least one assailant was waiting. As Gerardi exited his car, the assailant(s) struck him in the face repeatedly with a chunk of concrete (and possibly also a heavy pipe), killing him.[71] Witnesses described a muscular, shirtless man with a military haircut leaving the garage and entering the park. It was a cool night, so the man's lack of a shirt was memorable. One witness later described him as hyperventilating and pumping his arms, as if "trying to expel his euphoria."[72] Over the course of three years of fitful investigations, evidence emerged that the EMP—the same unit involved in the Mincho disappearance—was responsible for killing Gerardi. A number of officers and operatives associated with the EMP were seen outside the crime scene, entering and leaving the garage, and altering the crime scene. A license plate registered to a military base was observed on a car that dropped off men at the parish house. Witnesses from within

EMP headquarters—just two blocks from the San Sebastián church—described movements of personnel and vehicles consistent with EMP involvement in a covert operation that night. There was also evidence that Gerardi's assistant priest and housemate Mario Orantes had played a role in the crime and destroyed evidence before notifying the authorities.

In light of the possibility that state agents were involved in the crime, the court gave ODHA standing as auxiliary prosecutor (*querellante adhesiva*), and ODHA investigators took on a key role in locating witnesses and convincing them to testify in exchange for protection and opportunities to go into exile.[73] In response, EMP personnel broke into the home of ODHA director Ronalth Ochaeta and held his maid and his four-year-old son at gunpoint. After eating and drinking the contents of Ochaeta's refrigerator, they left a box containing a chunk of concrete and a threatening note. The attack seemed to confirm that the EMP had something to conceal.[74]

Witnesses included vagrants who slept in front of Gerardi's garage or in the park, a taxi driver, and lower-ranking enlisted men who worked in the EMP.[75] The sister-in-law of retired colonel Byron Lima Estrada came forward with hearsay-based claims that Lima's wife had overheard him conspiring with others to carry out the murder. Several of the vagrants who became witnesses had at some point served as informants for military intelligence or had family ties to police officials. Higher-ups in the security apparatus have maintained silence. Other potential witnesses of marginal social status were killed or vanished over the year following the crime.

ODHA and prosecutors—perhaps with the best of intentions—encouraged some of the reluctant witnesses to suppress implausible-sounding elements in their testimony, some of which later turned out to have been true.[76] *The* key witness, Rubén Chanax Sontay, whose testimony placed active-duty EMP personnel at the scene, was a vagrant who had previously served in the military, had received intelligence training, and admitted to having been in the employ of military intelligence to spy on Gerardi. Chanax gradually added more details to his account as he became more assured of his personal safety. His changing story raised questions about his veracity. He may have witnessed the crime or participated in it more directly than he admits.[77]

Four people were eventually convicted of the somewhat vaguely defined crime of "participation in extrajudicial execution": an active-duty captain in the EMP, Byron Lima Oliva; his father, retired colonel Byron Lima Estrada; EMP sergeant Obdulio Villanueva; and Father Mario Orantes. The convictions withstood repeated legal challenges up through the Supreme Judicial Court and the Constitutional Court. As of early 2013, only Lima Oliva (the son) remained in prison. His father was released in 2012 due to advanced age, and Orantes was released in early 2013 for good behavior. Fellow prisoners beheaded Villanueva in 2003, the day after the

Supreme Judicial Court upheld his conviction.[78] It was clear that the Limas, Villanueva, and Orantes were not the masterminds of the crime. The trial court called for further prosecutions of higher EMP and other officials. None have occurred. The actual killer(s) have never been identified. Some of the witnesses claimed the shirtless man (and presumed killer) was "Hugo," an assassin associated with the EMP also known as "Multicolores" for his use of disguises. Civilian prosecutors have not been able to determine his actual identity.

Journalists Maite Rico and Bertrand de la Grange, the latter of whom was MINUGUA's spokesman (June 1999 to July 2000), wrote a book and numerous newspaper columns arguing that the case against the Limas and Villanueva was a frame-up—a sort of Dreyfus affair—involving a conspiracy of other military factions, the ODHA, and a criminal gang associated with high church officials.[79] Their alternative theory, though skillfully told, is unconvincing, especially since they provide no information regarding their sources.

In the immediate aftermath of the crime, there was very little credible information. MINUGUA human rights investigators and political staff immediately suspected that it was a political crime and the mission issued a statement to that effect. The timing and savagery of the murder seemed calculated to send a message that the military would destroy anyone who tried to hold them accountable.

The murder was a tremendous blow to the Arzú government, which had staked its political reputation on the peace process and its promise of transition to a more peaceful society. Arzú's initial reaction was characteristically prickly and defensive. He declared in an interview with *Prensa Libre* that just a few days earlier a priest involved in social work had been murdered in New York. "Why should the image of our country be stained and not that of the United States, when these two acts are equally reprehensible and painful?"[80]

It was particularly problematic for Arzú that suspicion fell on the EMP. Arzú's administration, though aggressive in its suppression of some corrupt factions within the military, was very entangled with the EMP. Moreover, he had a personal debt to some of the individuals connected to the Gerardi murder. Early in his presidency, Arzú and his wife had been "saved" by the EMP's Captain Byron Lima and Sergeant Obdulio Villanueva during a violent incident in Antigua Guatemala. Arzú and his wife were horseback riding in February 1996 when a drunken milkman, Pedro Haroldo Sas Rompiche, drove his truck directly toward the president and first lady. Sas Rompiche had apparently confused Arzú with a local landowner with whom Sas Rompiche was feuding. Captain Lima—who as part of the security detail was also on horseback—rode his mount into the path of Sas Rompiche's vehicle, suffering a broken leg in the process. Sergeant Villanueva leapt forward and shot Sas Rompiche to death. A court subsequently ruled that Villanueva used excessive force and sentenced him to three years in prison.[81] Arzú objected to the punishment of Villanueva for, in Arzú's view, simply doing his duty.

In the Mincho case, the EMP identified and captured the kidnappers of Arzú's family friend Olga Novella. Arzú was both vulnerable to political damage if further evidence of EMP abuses came out, and so beholden to the unit that it would be difficult for his administration to move against them. It also appears that in some instances, Arzú depended on the EMP to do political dirty work: MINUGUA's tenth human rights report included an instance of two journalists who were warned to stop criticizing the president. The journalists subsequently noted that they were being followed in vehicles, one of which MINUGUA verified as belonging to the EMP.[82] Author Francisco Goldman also reports that Arzú's sons were vulnerable to blackmail, making the president beholden to the discretion of the EMP and its domestic intelligence network.[83] Arzú's secretary of the presidency, Gustavo Porras, became so angry about the allegations of EMP involvement that he and REMHI director Edgar Gutiérrez almost came to blows during a high-level meeting about the case. Arnault reportedly stepped in bodily to prevent a fight.[84] Perhaps not coincidentally, the case did not move forward decisively until Arzú was out of office.[85]

The implications for MINUGUA were complex. The political context made it particularly likely that if this were a political crime it would be covered up. The prosecutors and courts would find it very difficult to handle the case. As verifier of human rights protection and due process, MINUGUA would have to be vigilant, while at the same time avoiding the appearance of interference in judicial processes—a chronic sore point with the nationalistic Arzú administration. From a political point of view, the mission's interests in promoting the peace process were best served by supporting the Arzú administration and the PAN, which embraced the peace process to a greater extent than the more right-wing opposition. However, as human rights verifier, the mission had to uphold due process while seeking to mitigate the fear and divisiveness caused by the killing. MINUGUA investigator Cecilia Olmos (Chile) remarked that if the UN mission couldn't help Guatemalans solve the Gerardi case then she didn't see what reason it had for being in the country.[86] Arnault, reflecting on the case, was more circumspect: "Simply being impartial does not mean that you get to the truth."[87]

This is especially true when much of the physical evidence is destroyed in the first twenty-four hours after a murder. About two hours elapsed between Gerardi's death and Orantes's first telephone call to archdiocesan administrator Efraín Hernández. Nearly an hour after that, Orantes called the fire department to claim the body, and only then did he call the police. The court later concluded that between the time of the murder and his first calls for assistance, Orantes had destroyed evidence. Hernández arrived at the scene well before the police did, accompanied by his housekeeper's daughter Ana Lucía Escobar (widely assumed to be Hernández's illegitimate daughter). Escobar had a history of arrests for both property and violent crimes, but no convictions. She was widely suspected of being a principal in a criminal gang. Her prompt arrival at the scene, combined with her strange behavior during subsequent questioning, triggered speculation about ecclesiastical/organized crime involvement.[88]

Human rights activists, friends, and relatives began to arrive at the scene, where they ran into personnel from the EMP who were photographing and videotaping the scene. The EMP staff falsely claimed they were from the police. When the real police finally arrived, they utterly failed to protect the crime scene as onlookers wandered through the garage and the house. At least one attorney present objected, to no avail. The next morning, police and investigators abandoned the scene and Orantes and the housekeeper Margarita López thoroughly washed down the house and the garage, in the process erasing remaining physical evidence. The significance of these lapses became clear later when US Federal Bureau of Investigation (FBI) investigators using Luminol found residual blood in numerous locations around the house, including Gerardi's office and Orantes's bedroom.[89]

The initial prosecution was a farce. The prosecutor in charge, Otto Ardón, ordered the arrest of a broken-down, drunken vagrant named Carlos Vielman for the crime and spent time bellowing at him, dictating to him details of the crime to which he wanted Vielman to confess. Vielman was bewildered. He could barely move one of his arms, so he obviously could not have wielded the cement block that killed Gerardi. Moreover, he had a solid alibi. Nonetheless, it took three months to clear him. Based on the work of a retired and rather eccentric Spanish forensics professor, José Manuel Reverte Coma, as well as the Luminol tests showing blood in the house, prosecutors then ordered the arrest of Orantes, the housekeeper Margarita López, and Orantes's German shepherd dog Baloo. The arrest itself was a comedy of errors, as sixty police officers in tactical gear surrounded the San Sebastián parish. Orantes, who was not home at the time, arrived from outside the cordon and was told he couldn't come in.[90]

The working theory was that Orantes had commanded Baloo to attack Gerardi, and had then stomped on Gerardi's head. The facts that Orantes was corpulent, timorous, and physically weak, or that his dog was geriatric and had bad hips, undercut this theory. Yet Orantes's very strange behavior the night of the crime had raised suspicions that he knew more about the crime than he admitted. Orantes denied having heard anything at the time the crime occurred, but claimed to have been awakened two and a half hours later by a light in the hallway. He kept repeating in an animated fashion that he had found Gerardi's body but had not recognized him and thought the body belonged to a vagrant from the park. Orantes's indecently prompt request to be promoted to parish priest of San Sebastián after Gerardi's death also raised eyebrows within the Church. Rumors began to circulate in Guatemala City—probably originating with military intelligence—that the crime involved some kind of homosexual encounter gone bad.[91]

In September 1998, coroners exhumed Gerardi's body to determine whether some of his wounds reflected dog bites. His remains were in poor condition, but X-rays helped to clarify the nature of the blunt trauma injuries. Dr. Reverte Coma asserted that he had found dog bites, while other observers saw no such thing. Moreover, Reverte's methods damaged what physical evidence remained. Amidst this circus, Dr. Reverte tried (unsuccessfully) to retain one of Gerardi's body parts as a souvenir. In the press conference after the examination, he play-acted the roles of Orantes, Baloo (!), and Gerardi to the amazement of onlookers. He announced, "They've wanted to give this the appearance of a political crime. Lie! This is a domestic crime and that is extremely clear!"[92]

In this surreal context, MINUGUA maintained a low profile but sought to support state efforts to solve the crime, while taking steps to ameliorate anxiety on the part of human rights activists and the Church. Arnault went to the crime scene early on the morning of April 29 (two and a half days after the crime), accompanied by Cecilia Olmos and Rafael Guillamón (Spain). Guillamón became the lead investigator for MINUGUA, supported by other primary investigators and three field teams. He developed his own leads, while tracking the work of the police, state prosecutors, and ODHA. Institutional Strengthening (FORIN) advisers in the Public Ministry monitored the investigation there as best they could. The prosecutor would not allow MINUGUA access to the actual case files, which made verification difficult.[93]

Arnault began chairing a daily meeting that brought together Marta Altolaguirre (head of COPREDEH), Gustavo Porras (secretary to the presidency), as well as representatives of ODHA, the Myrna Mack Foundation, and the PNC to review the status of the case and ensure exchange of information. Inexplicably, the Public Ministry did not participate. In parallel, President Arzú appointed a "High Level Commission" to monitor the investigation. MINUGUA sent unarmed civilian police and human rights staff to maintain watch at the residences and offices of some senior Catholic clerics who had suffered threats, and also deployed frequent patrols as a signal of support for Edgar Gutiérrez, Ronalth Ochaeta, other staff of ODHA, and a staff member of the CEH who had been threatened. In this context, a reasonable degree of cooperation emerged between ODHA and the mission, a refreshing change from ODHA's past recriminations, though Ochaeta continued his pattern of publicity seeking.[94] MINUGUA's efforts to protect Ochaeta intensified after the attack on his home. His family moved to Costa Rica, and his son later recognized one of the attackers from a newspaper cover photo: it was Obdulio Villanueva.[95]

MINUGUA also provided a safe haven for potential witnesses, in cooperation with ODHA. Arlene Cifuentes, a cousin of Captain Byron Lima, came forward with information indicating that the Limas had a long-lasting vendetta against Gerardi. Afraid for her safety after approaching MINUGUA, she and her children took shelter in Arnault's private residence. Unfortunately, her intent and whereabouts were leaked in the press. She responded with a press statement disowning any knowledge of anything related to the Gerardi case, and returned to her private life "and silence."[96]

In December 1999, Otto Ardón resigned as prosecutor in charge under public pressure from MINUGUA, and was replaced by Celwin Galindo. In February 1999, the judge in the case ordered the provisional release of Orantes (and his dog) for lack of evidence, and Galindo refocused the investigation on the possibility of state involvement. With progress once again possible, Arnault spoke first with Gustavo Porras, and then directly with Arzú, to convey that MINUGUA needed to see a serious effort by the executive to facilitate the investigation, regardless of where it led. He warned that MINUGUA could not sustain its public position that blamed only the prosecutor for the failure to investigate state involvement. In fact, Arnault said, the mission knew that the presidency itself had been obstructing the inquiry. For example, people claiming to come from the presidency had offered Ardón money not to look beyond Mario Orantes. Key members of the investigative effort answered directly to Arzú, and senior justice officials were interfering with the investigation, apparently at the behest of state intelligence agencies. At best these actions signaled "an unacceptable bias"; at worst, "an outright cover-up." Arnault told the president that the mission would work closely with Galindo, and MINUGUA expected active cooperation from the executive. As if to illustrate Arnault's point, the Ministry of Defense dodged a subpoena on behalf of a senior EMP official, claiming that no such person existed. Arnault warned that he was about to denounce this publicly. The Defense Ministry produced the witness the next day, but the incident apparently angered Arzú, who maintained that the Gerardi killing was a frame-up against officers loyal to him, being carried out by officers associated with the corrupt elements he had purged from the military in 1996. While this theory was not out of the question, evidence was mounting that the EMP was in fact involved. Whatever the case, MINUGUA insisted that there needed to be an impartial investigation.[97]

Under this pressure, Arzú announced that he would ask the UN Secretary-General to appoint an independent expert to look into the government's conduct in the case. This would, of course, conflict directly with MINUGUA's existing mandate, and was a repeat of Arzú's (and Stein's) established practice of asking New York to dilute the mission's authority any time MINUGUA asserted itself. Arzú backed off and gave a speech calling more generally for the United Nations to look into the administration's conduct without specifying what form this should take. His challenge to the mission soon faded.[98]

Unfortunately, the Gerardi case was not resolved during the rest of Arnault's time as head of mission. The Arzú government became increasingly uncooperative as political campaigns heated up in 1999, his attorney general provided little support, and threats against prosecutor Celvin Galindo and his family intensified. Galindo eventually fled the country with the case still incomplete, and it would fall to a little-known assistant prosecutor, Leopoldo Zeissig, to complete the prosecution during the next presidential administration. The Limas, Villanueva, Orantes, and López were eventually convicted in June 2001. MINUGUA's work helped to keep the possibility of a prosecution alive by keeping a number of the witnesses alive. The mission imposed some limits on the absurdities that the first prosecutor could engage in, and provided information, protection, and moral support to the Guatemalans who pushed the case forward. In a positive sign that the fear engendered by Gerardi's killing had dissipated, between 35,000 and 40,000 people appeared at an event commemorating the first anniversary of his killing. This contrasted with the fewer than 5,000 who appeared at his funeral.[99]

■ Historical Clarification

Amidst the spasm of fear created by the Gerardi murder, the staff of the Historical Clarification Commission (CEH) was busy trying to complete its collection of testimonies from people around the country. The commission was a separate entity, and MINUGUA played only a secondary role in supporting its work. Senior human rights staff such as Jaime Esponda assumed top positions at the CEH, and MINUGUA helped facilitate the CEH's initial deployment. Some CEH staff—like many leaders in the Catholic Church—received death threats in the aftermath of Gerardi's death, and MINUGUA deployed observers around CEH offices and staff residences.

The CEH's mandate was to prepare a full and detailed account of violence during the war and to recommend possible forms of reparation. It was not to assign individual responsibility or have any judicial intent or effect. The CEH was supposed to begin work immediately after the final accords went into effect, but it took some time to get organized. The parties originally wanted Arnault to head the CEH, but that was impossible once he was appointed SRSG. Instead, the Secretary-General appointed German law professor Christian Tomuschat. Tomuschat enjoyed strong support from the government, the URNG, and UN headquarters. Only one right-wing grow-ers' association raised objections, calling him "contentious" and complain-ing that in his previous role as independent expert on human rights in Guatemala he had not done enough to protect private property (not his job, of course).[100]

Tomuschat appointed Mayan education scholar Otilia Lux de Cotí and legal scholar Edgar Alfredo Balsells Tojo as fellow commissioners, passing over Ronalth Ochaeta who had been lobbying hard for the position.[101] UNOPS was selected to provide administrative support, on Arnault's rec-ommendation. Despite everyone's best efforts, and in part because of donor delays, the commission was not inaugurated until July 1997 and began ac-cepting declarations in September 1997. The commissioners agreed from the outset that six months was not enough time to investigate over thirty years of violence. They planned to collect testimonies and investigate cases for ten months, then wrap up by the twelve-month deadline. In actuality, the commission collected evidence for the full twelve months and needed addi-tional months to prepare the report.

The CEH hired a highly qualified staff that peaked at two hundred in-dividuals, including a mix of internationals and Guatemalans. It opened fourteen field offices, each headed by an international staff member to en-sure impartiality. In addition to accepting testimony from individuals who came to the regional offices, the CEH began field excursions to communi-ties to hold meetings and encourage people to give statements, even in very remote, roadless areas.[102]

The commission struggled financially throughout its existence, as donors, especially Japan and the EU, were slow to provide promised funds. The United States, Sweden, the Netherlands, and Guatemala itself (which contributed almost US$1 million) picked up the slack, but the commission found itself by early 1998 on the verge of not being able to pay its bills.[103] MINUGUA stepped in to help, lending vehicles and helping to locate space for regional offices. Because of funding shortfalls, the commission had to cut back on security arrangements, which seemed acceptable until the Ger-ardi killing.

As the CEH began to accept testimony, response by the public varied. Tomuschat noted that in northern El Quiché province, most people had lost their fear and came forward readily. In other areas, including the east and west, the south coast, and the capital city, fears were still rampant "to such a degree that people may avoid any contact with the Commission or need special encouragement to testify." People expected that the lawlessness of the 1980s and 1990s could return at any time. In some places, CEH staff re-sorted to taking collective rather than individual declarations.[104] This could, of course, introduce factual inaccuracies because of group dynamics. But it was almost certainly the only way for some terrorized people to contribute to the process and was likely an empowering and healing experience. In some areas bordering Mexico, villagers had not heard that the war was over, and accused the CEH members of being guerrillas, since the URNG also used to come and talk about human rights![105]

The commission's work was particularly difficult in areas in the western piedmont where many people worked on commercial coffee plantations. In such areas, state repression and counterinsurgency networks were interwoven with local authority structures designed to prevent labor organization. Rebel groups had been defeated quickly and decisively in these areas, and many noncombatants had been killed. It took a great deal of careful preparation, working with local leaders, to convince witnesses to come forward. In some places it simply proved impossible to obtain testimonies.[106]

The government was even more reluctant to cooperate: Tomuschat reported a runaround comparable to that experienced by investigators in the Mincho case. Under both the Oslo agreement and the National Reconciliation Law, the government was obligated to cooperate with the CEH by providing all requested information regarding actions during the conflict. In practice, the Ministry of Defense routinely misrouted and ignored correspondence from the CEH. When Tomuschat contacted President Arzú to demand a response, Arzú promised that the ministry would cooperate. The army then responded that (1) it had no after-action reports or other documents related to alleged human rights violations (certainly a lie); and (2) any documents it did have were protected by confidentiality laws (ditto). Tomuschat was not impressed: "This is hardly an outcome which we could call satisfactory after three months and two weeks." He met with Foreign Minister Stein, and "hinted that the Commission might have to consider terminating its work if the Government did not live up to its commitments. It is obvious that such a decision would not be taken lightly." This was a bluff; the government ignored it and never came through with the requested information.[107]

Ultimately the CEH worked around this problem by collecting denunciations from survivors, while also incorporating evidence provided by REMHI as well as another retrospective data collection effort by the International Center for Human Rights Investigations (Centro Internacional para Investigaciones en Derechos Humanos [CIIDH]).[108] There were inherent obstacles to developing a comprehensive record of human rights violations during the conflict. First, there were not always survivors left to tell the story, since in some regions, communities had been completely eradicated. Moreover, survivors and witnesses had scattered to Mexico, the United States, and elsewhere in Central America. There were few contemporaneous records of violations from the 1980s because the military had bombed the offices of human rights monitoring groups and forced most of their staff into exile early in the conflict. Only later were Guatemalan groups able to directly monitor and take testimony about abuses. Thus, the CEH's investigation depended on finding witnesses who could come forward about acts committed from up to three decades earlier, and of course many of the people who might have done that were now dead. Not everyone who had a complaint was willing or able to report it to the CEH; some were still afraid, and some had already given their testimony to REMHI or CIIDH. Thus no single retrospective truth-telling effort was likely to have the whole picture.

Given that the CEH, REMHI, and CIIDH went about their data collection in different ways and depended on different social networks to communicate with potential witnesses, it was striking that there was very high agreement among the three sources on the timing of the violence (that is, when the worst months of violence occurred), locations, ethnicity of victims, and the proportion committed by the state as opposed to the URNG.[109] The CEH itself identified over 42,000 deaths from the testimonies it collected. By determining the extent of overlap between its data and that of other groups, the CEH was able to use multisource estimation techniques to yield a total death toll estimate in excess of 130,000 between 1978 and 1996.[110] For the whole duration of the conflict from 1962 forward, the CEH estimated the toll at 200,000 dead.

The CEH presented its report on February 25, 1999, and much of the public was surprised by the strength of its conclusions. The report itself exceeded three thousand pages in length, but there was an eighty-four-page summary of findings and recommendations that was more widely available. The CEH attributed 93 percent of the violence against civilians during the war to the armed forces and 3 percent to the URNG. It identified 626 massacres committed by state forces versus 32 by the guerrillas. It documented horrific abuses including large numbers of children killed, as well as frequent use of torture, mutilation, and rape. Eighty-three percent of individually identified victims were indigenous people, and 17 percent Ladino.

The most politically and legally consequential finding was that the state forces had committed acts of genocide against groups of Mayan peoples in four regions, based on criteria from the 1949 Convention on the Prevention and Punishment of the Crime of Genocide. It also made clear that the Guatemalan state had merged anti-Communist ideology with explicit racism in carrying out genocidal actions. The army defined entire peoples and cultures as the enemy, and then sought to destroy them.[111]

There is no statute of limitations on genocide under international law, and genocide was specifically excluded from the limited amnesty provided under the National Reconciliation Law. The CEH findings therefore increased the likelihood of future prosecutions, despite the putative limit imposed by the Oslo agreement that the CEH would have neither judicial aim nor effect. Driving this point home after the CEH report was released, the

Guatemalan NGO Center for Human Rights Legal Action (CALDH) immediately announced that it would be bringing cases against Generals Romeo Lucas García and Ríos Montt. Rigoberta Menchú soon filed a case in Spain against Ríos Montt for atrocities in the early 1980s.[112]

The CEH also made eighty-four recommendations for measures to preserve the memory of the victims, compensate victims, foster a culture of mutual respect and observance of human rights, strengthen the democratic process, further peace and national harmony, and create a government entity responsible for implementing these recommendations. Among the proposed measures to promote democracy and human rights was a commission that would investigate the conduct of individual military officers during the conflict: that is, a commission that could do "what the Commission itself was barred from doing."[113]

The government's response was tepid: it said that the peace accords provided all the measures needed to address the events described in the CEH report. Foreign Minister Stein remarked that the CEH had overstepped its mandate with some of its recommendations, especially the commission to investigate the armed forces. In the government's view, this was already covered in the Comprehensive Agreement on Human Rights. Moreover, the military had already undergone a major renovation and no further purge was required.[114] Not until the Portillo government was inaugurated in January 2000 did the government accept that additional institutional changes, and reparations, were in order, although as we will see, Portillo's implementation was spotty at best.

Overall, the CEH was a surprisingly successful truth-telling effort that converted a comparatively weak mandate into a powerful report that potentially set the stage for long-term accountability. It is less clear how broad its impact was on Guatemalan society. While members of politically engaged interest groups certainly knew about and commented on the report, the broader public had limited access. Even the eighty-four-page summary was a challenging read for individuals with limited education. One indication of the report's limitations was that only a few months after its release, a majority of voters rejected a set of constitutional reforms that would have helped prevent future repetitions of the genocide (see section on constitutional reform, below).

▌ Human Rights and Public Security

Despite the shift to a much broader mandate beginning in early 1997, human rights verification remained at the core of MINUGUA's mandate. It was also the task for which the mission was best prepared given its existing staff and structure. The seventh report on human rights covering the first half of 1997 was cautiously laudatory. "The duty to provide guarantees . . .

involves organizing the State machinery so as to enable it to ensure the full enjoyment or exercise of human rights. This is a legal requirement with which the State is gradually and progressively improving its compliance."[115] The operative word here was gradually, and even this proved optimistic. After a decline during the first months of Arnault's term, the rate of violations rebounded and three subsequent reports were increasingly bleak in their assessment of the government's efforts to correct systemic impunity.

Official abuses during the initial postwar period more often appeared to be individual acts, or acts of small groups, rather than reflections of an overall state strategy of repression. In contrast to the war years, there were comparatively few cases of clearly politically motivated state killings (though of course the Gerardi murder had a heavy impact). Instead, the perpetrators were typically military, police, or municipal authorities that used grossly disproportionate violence to capture, punish, intimidate, or extract confessions from suspects. Sometimes the violence swept up bystanders, witnesses, or individuals presenting complaints, revealing official arrogance or simply poor training and judgment. Many cases involved personal revenge, efforts to eliminate rivals, or drunkenness mixed with firearms.[116] One typical example, unfortunately involving the "new" National Civilian Police, was reported in the tenth human rights report:

> On 20 February, in the Santa Luisa housing estate, zone 6 of the capital, National Civil Police officers Gerson de Rosa Rodríguez and Neftali López Salguero . . . went in pursuit of Noé Vicente Gómez and another unidentified man who had allegedly just robbed a bus. In their flight the men burst into a butcher's shop where Gómez threw a revolver behind the counter. The officers arrested Gómez and the other suspect, but they also arrested Santiago Rafael Ruiz, who happened to be doing some shopping, and put them all in the police car. Witnesses heard two shots and saw Santiago Rafael Ruiz with his face covered in blood. The men were taken to a place known as Joya de Zabahú, where witnesses saw the officers hit Ruiz; the witnesses were then threatened and were compelled to leave. Shortly thereafter they heard a number of gunshots and saw other police units arrive. The victim, gravely wounded, was taken to San Juan de Dios General Hospital where he died. The Mission established that the immediate superiors of the two officers, far from seeking to clarify what had happened, gave an account of the incident describing it as a confrontation between "maras" (gangs) and that the officers were not punished. Following an internal investigation carried out by the National Civil Police Office of Professional Accountability, the officers were suspended from their duties and brought before the court.[117]

MINUGUA described another appalling piece of police work from the same period:

Among the cases of cruel, inhuman or degrading treatment [that] have been confirmed by the Mission and for which the National Civil Police is responsible, one which occurred on 31 December 1998 at Puerto San José, Escuintla, stands out. At 10:30 in the morning, officers Edwin Gaitán Hernández and Franco Rodas de León arrested Moisés Rivas Morales and took him to the National Civil Police citizens service office on the pretext that they had to meet an officer from that police station. The Mission confirmed that the individual in question did not enter the cells until more than six hours later. When he was placed in the cell his hair had been hacked off with scissors and he had head injuries; according to eyewitnesses these injuries had been inflicted with a leather whip by Deputy Inspector Álvaro Nájera Castro. The man was transferred to Escuintla National Hospital where his injuries were found to be very serious. In the police report the arresting officers stated that Moisés Rivas had been arrested on charges of disorderly conduct and drunkenness. The criminal court determined that the arrest had been unlawful and ordered that the man be released immediately. The Office of Professional Accountability concluded that Deputy Inspector Álvaro Nájera Castro and officers Oswaldo Gaitán Hernández, Franco Eduardo Rodas de León, Carlos Hernández Ceballos and Aníbal Contreras Tobar, among others, were responsible for the arbitrary arrest and the very serious injuries and for the ill-treatment of other prisoners who were at the time in the police cells at Puerto San José. The Office found the instruments used to ill treat the arrested persons, including the leather whip and a pair of scissors, in the possession of the officers.[118]

A final example of police action shows how deeply the practice of excessive force was established within Guatemalan security forces. In this case, the perpetrator was an officer in the PNC who had transferred from the old National Police.

On 6 July, in a court in Amatitlán, Guatemala City, defendant José Hernández Martínez took two judicial officials hostage, threatening to detonate a grenade. The National Civil Police, using proper police procedures, made strenuous efforts to free the hostages and capture the defendant. The following day, Hernández obtained a vehicle in which he managed to reach the road leading to Puerto Quetzal. There, the police negotiated the release of one hostage and agreed to hand over a pistol, with the firing pin disabled and containing a single bullet, in exchange for the release of the second hostage. The defendant then detonated the grenade inside the vehicle . . . ; immediately thereafter, a senior national Civil Police official approached and fired over 25 shots, according to subsequent expert reports.[119]

The PNC subsequently awarded the official a formal commendation for his "valor" in shooting a defenseless man who had already effectively committed suicide.

In two of the three cases just cited, the perpetrators were to some extent held accountable. This was more the exception than the rule: in most cases, the police and military actively covered up violations. Prosecutors failed to follow up, and the courts—especially lower-level courts—exonerated state officials or imposed ridiculously light sanctions. These repeated failures to hold officials responsible reflected a broader failure on the part of the Arzú government and Congress to remedy an integrated and mutually reinforcing set of institutional flaws and weaknesses that were well known at the time. First, the police were especially weak with respect to criminal investigations and internal controls. Second, many prosecutors were individually incompetent and the Public Ministry as a whole was poorly organized with respect to information, workflow management, and oversight. Third, lower-level judges were poorly educated and lacked training, while higher-level judges varied greatly in their skills and ethical commitments; some showed great courage in challenging impunity while others were actively complicit in preserving it.

At the base of the criminal justice system was the old National Police, which was in the process of being phased out during Arnault's term. The National Police was mostly made up of individuals who were simply not qualified to enforce laws in a democracy. Basic-level police officers had little education and received virtually no training. Their officers generally came from the military, and the National Police had been operated as a neglected subsidiary of the army, with a chronic lack of budgetary and material support. Morale was low, mechanisms of control and discipline were weak, and the force typically used brutality as a substitute for police work.[120]

In the National Civil Police, which began its gradual deployment in 1997, there were at least some minimum educational standards, and police received some training before being sent out to work. Pay was better than in the National Police, and the number of police posts in rural areas increased where previously there had been no police presence at all. Unfortunately, however, the Arzú government's expedient approach created serious deficiencies. In haste to field a large police force quickly and thereby avoid a postwar public security vacuum, Arzú and his interior minister Rodolfo Mendoza missed a unique opportunity to start fresh with a dramatically different and better model of policing. Instead, early efforts focused on recycling existing National Police personnel into the PNC. The government failed to advertise and recruit widely for the PNC, and the academy therefore had to lower admissions standards to have enough candidates. Applicants with less formal education were inexplicably given an easier admissions test, which biased selection in favor of the less educated. The officer corps was drawn entirely from the existing National Police, and there was no route for highly educated civilians to gain access to the top ranks of the new police. Civilians could enter only at the noncommissioned officer ranks after a prolonged training program and then work their way up. It would take a generation for a significant number of civilians from outside the old police regime to achieve command rank. Moreover a number of specialized units including a special weapons and tactics group (Special Police Forces [FEP]) and the antinarcotics police (Department of Anti-Narcotics Operations [DOAN]) were brought over wholesale from the National Police, bringing with them a culture of brutality and corruption.

The internal disciplinary regime was modeled on that of the Spanish Civil Guard (GCE). It was complex, gave all the power to unit commanders, and provided no mechanisms for police personnel to bring complaints about the conduct of their superiors. The PNC inherited the National Police's Office of Professional Responsibility (ORP), which had been created with advice from the US FBI, but it had no formal standing within the disciplinary code. The GCE oversaw the overall PNC development project (as discussed in Chapter 2) while the US International Criminal Investigations Training and Assistance Program (ICITAP) was tasked with preparing the criminal investigations division. Yet the selection process for trainees was outside ICITAP's control, and most of those selected by the PNC lacked the education and vocation to be investigators. In fact, background checks were deficient and some investigators turned out to have criminal affiliations. The result was an investigative division that was almost completely incompetent and was often consigned to regular policing tasks. Few of the detectives who had been trained at considerable international expense remained in the corps a few years later.[121]

For criminal cases to advance to the courts, the Public Ministry needed to direct investigations and then bring cases. Because the Public Ministry did not trust the PNC investigators (generally with good reason), the Public Ministry created its own investigative service, hiring former military and police personnel in a rather secretive process. Law allowed the Public Ministry to have experts, not investigators, and it was unclear what role this group could play in presenting evidence in court. A more basic problem was that, faced with a given case, most Public Ministry prosecutors did not know how to identify the relevant facts and points of law, or how to move a case forward through the courts. MINUGUA's FORIN group worked hard to advise Public Ministry prosecutors, but the scope of the problem required a level of outside help that was infeasible, both financially and politically.[122] It proved critical that Guatemala's Criminal Procedure Code allowed for private prosecutors in cases where state agents might be implicated. Most of the high-level human rights cases that were successfully prosecuted—like the Gerardi case—involved a private *querellante adhesivo*.

The courts were run by judges who were often overloaded by cases, who allowed low-level administrators to make substantive decisions, and who in some instances continued to operate as if the old Criminal Procedure Code were still in effect, most likely because they did not know how to apply the new one. Judges often issued decisions devoid of legal reasoning or facts. Things improved at higher levels of the court system, though even there, the quality of jurisprudence was highly variable.

Poor management of information afflicted all levels of the system. International donors exacerbated these problems by going forward with pet computerization projects without interagency coordination. This resulted in police and prosecutorial database systems that could not be linked, as well as special systems for specific investigative areas such as narcotics enforcement that were incompatible with other judicial information systems.[123]

In many cases with possible state involvement, prosecutors, judges, and their families faced death threats. Given that Constitutional Court president Epaminondas González Dubón had been murdered just a few years earlier, these threats had to be taken seriously. The lack of judicial protection created a vicious cycle, since it contributed to the overall weakness of the system, which in turn weakened de facto judicial protection. The same applied to witness protection, which also made it difficult to pursue cases involving the state. Witnesses often made statements and then fled the country, as seen in the Gerardi case. Prosecutors and judges often did the same thing, pushing cases as far as they could until the threats became too serious, then going into exile, leaving others to carry on. Defense lawyers routinely brought frivolous motions to stall proceedings, sometimes generating years of delays. They faced no sanctions for doing so.

Besides systemic impunity, MINUGUA documented three other trends in its reporting during the Arnault period. First, mob lynching of suspected criminals intensified during the period, from around five instances per month in early 1997 to over eight between January and November of 1999. Moreover, the death rate per month rose from three per month to over four by late 1999. MINUGUA complained in the ninth human rights report that the PNC had failed to adopt mission-recommended measures to defuse potential lynchings. Finally, in the period covered by the tenth human rights report, the death rate dropped below one per month. MINUGUA gave credit to the PNC for these improvements.[124]

Prevention by the PNC is probably part of the story, but it is suspicious that the rate of lynchings dropped so suddenly after the election of Alfonso Portillo of the FRG to the presidency. There are a number of factors that suggest that lynching was at least partially a political phenomenon. Most lynchings were in response to property crimes—sometimes very petty ones—rather than violent crimes. The areas most affected were *not* the areas of highest crime; rather, they were areas that had the strongest civil patrols infrastructure during the war. In investigating individual cases, MINUGUA was able to confirm that often lynchings were not genuinely spontaneous but were instigated by former civil patrollers. Perhaps not coincidentally, the FRG had particularly strong political ties to these remnants, and was in a position to mobilize ex-PAC members for political reasons.

A second problem, related to lynching, were "social cleansing" killings that appeared likely to involve state agents. Generally the targets were individuals accused of property crimes, and in some instances they were killed by mobs when on their way to the police to seek "protection" against what they claimed were false accusations.[125] In the far northern department of El Petén, MINUGUA found that a local social cleansing group included former army officers and ex-civil patrollers. Bodies were being dumped in areas where the army had recently stepped up its patrols, suggesting ongoing cooperation between the army and patrollers, but for the new mission of eliminating "marijuana smokers and thieves."[126]

A third priority flagged by MINUGUA in its reporting was the loss of life and liberty often associated with land and labor conflicts in rural areas. A 1996 law had allowed individuals and firms who claimed to own a given piece of land to call in the police to evict alleged squatters, without having to first prove ownership to a court. This unfairly privileged de facto landholders, many of whom had usurped control of land by overrunning peasant plots with cattle, sending in armed thugs to force peasants out, or literally moving their fences to enclose more ground not actually belonging to them.[127] Much usurpation had taken place during the armed conflict, and some land conflicts therefore involved returning refugees who wanted to reclaim lands that belonged to them. The people affected were unlikely to passively give way to police forces sent to evict them, especially if the history of the property in question did not support the usurpers' ownership claims. MINUGUA reported a number of deaths resulting from evictions that were probably illegitimate in the first place.[128]

The mission also found that landowners were bringing trumped-up criminal complaints against labor organizers on commercial plantations, and that prosecutors and lower courts were acting on these complaints, despite a complete lack of evidence. In one illustrative case in Izabál, MINUGUA confirmed that arrested labor leaders could not have been at the place where the alleged crimes had occurred.[129]

MINUGUA did not have the capacity or authority to fix these deeply systemic problems. While it maintained some FORIN projects (which moved over to UNOPS administration in 1999), these were small-scale in comparison with the Spanish Civil Guard development project for the PNC. Most of the institutional development projects for the justice system were in the hands of donors or UNDP. Unfortunately, donors generally did not allow MINUGUA to lead or coordinate their justice sector projects, and many of these projects did not adhere to performance criteria based on the peace accords. Moreover, the European Union (the key donor with respect to the police), refused to use aid conditionality in any way. Ultimately, MINUGUA was limited to exposing these ongoing problems and hoping to generate enough domestic and international political pressures to compel the government to address weaknesses in the police and the Public Ministry.

Unfortunately, the issue of crime was easily manipulated by the media and by right-wing groups opposed to reforms to the justice system. The Arzú government, always worried about its political right flank, went with the flow of both mass and elite opinion rather than taking steps that would have long-term benefits for the country. Media hype about crime dovetailed with politically motivated provocation by the organized base of the far right (evident in some lynchings). Many landowners liked being de facto authorities in their areas, and were not interested in having a functioning and accessible justice system. The public was easily swayed by charges from right-wing groups and media commentators that due process coddled criminals.

Thus with respect to human rights, MINUGUA could not escape the basic dilemma that its authority to verify facts did not give the mission power to solve the problem. That authority lay with the Guatemalan government, legislature, and courts. To the extent that international actors had a role to play in the reform of those institutions, they did so in an uncoordinated way that, if anything, undermined MINUGUA's leverage. MINUGUA's dedicated work on human rights during the Arnault period produced solid historical documentation of conditions in Guatemala, and it certainly deterred some abuses, but it could not correct the systemic problems that allowed abuses to occur and go unpunished.

▌ The Fiscal Impasse

One of the most obvious flaws in the Guatemalan political system was the weakness of the state: Guatemala took in less in tax revenue, and spent less money on public goods and services per capita, than any Latin American country. In view of high poverty rates, extreme inequities, and very low human development scores (based on child mortality, life expectancy, and literacy), the Guatemalan state clearly needed to spend more on education, health, and assistance to vulnerable sectors of society such as rural indigenous farmers. As noted in Chapter 2, even the International Monetary Fund (IMF)—usually an advocate for public sector austerity—supported a tax-and-spend policy in Guatemala. In addition to the commitments to greater education and health spending spelled out in the socioeconomic accord, strengthening civilian authority clearly implied higher spending on the police and the judiciary. Increasing the strength of the public sector fit with Arzú's modernizing agenda, and had potential to generate positive political payoffs for the PAN with the broader public.

The problem was that some core constituents of the PAN were very resistant to increased taxes. While some figures within industrial, commercial, and financial sectors were willing to contemplate increased taxes in exchange for a more functional state, this faction was unable to convince more traditional groups that were content with a weak state. As Aaron Schneider has written, emerging business groups that would actually benefit from a stronger state tended to accommodate themselves to the traditional sectors, in part because so many new firms and developments were actually funded by family-based capital groups that also had traditional interests (agrarian and monopolized industries).[130] The prevailing discourse within the traditional elite was that the state was incompetent, it wasted what money it did have, and increased taxes would just result in further corruption and waste. An additional complaint was that so much of the Guatemalan economy was either informal (that is, not registered, not legally recognized, and not tax-paying) or outright illegal (drug trafficking, contraband, and related financial flows) that taxes would fall disproportionately on the legitimate firms in the formal sector. Of course the prevalence of informality and criminality in the economy were to a large extent the result of the weakness of the state, so the status quo involved a vicious circle: private sector elites resisted taxation, keeping the state weak, which in turn created grounds for their ongoing resistance to paying taxes.

As verifier, the United Nations had to insist that the government do something that was nearly impossible: Arzú's government was very close to the private sector and could not afford to alienate these allies. The government also had to be concerned about middle-class views: the PAN's margin of victory in 1996 had been only 32,000 votes. It could not afford to alienate any significant part of the middle class.[131] For Arzú, the rational strategy was to be seen attempting to raise taxes, but to fail to do so. The attempt would get the United Nations and the international donors off his back, while failing to actually raise taxes would avoid a rupture with business elites.[132]

In April 1997, the Finance Ministry outlined plans to remove some exemptions to the value added tax (VAT) and incorporate tax violations into the criminal code. CACIF initially responded favorably to broadening the VAT: this would be better, from their point of view, than increasing rates, especially for higher earning individuals and firms.[133] CACIF strongly opposed, on the other hand, the criminalization of tax evasion. The first Secretary-General's report on peace implementation in Guatemala noted that the proposed measures were positive but would produce results very slowly. Dramatic changes were needed to meet the ramp-up targets for revenue collection set out in the accords.[134]

An IMF "technical mission" to Guatemala in August 1997 made these concerns more specific: the government's plans would result in revenues of about 9 percent of GDP in 1998, short of the 10 percent benchmark in the accords. Worse, revenues would probably fall to 8.5 percent in 1999, versus the 11 percent benchmark. The IMF team concluded that from a technical point of view the plan was deficient and recommended that the government own up to reality and ask for an extension.[135]

The September consultative group meeting provided an opportunity for MINUGUA, the IMF, and the Inter-American Development Bank to get on the same page. Arnault urged the IMF to use the meeting to build momentum and political pressure to adopt the necessary measures, rather than accept postponement of the tax targets. Arnault's initial assessment was that the meeting had been successful, but that strong international follow-up would be crucial. He recommended that the United Nations take advantage of the president's scheduled meeting with Secretary-General Annan later in the month to drive home the importance of stronger fiscal measures.[136]

Unfortunately, Annan did not get the memo, so his meeting with Arzú and Foreign Minister Stein was limited to pleasantries. In a meeting three days later with a reduced Guatemalan delegation (unfortunately Arzú had left), undersecretary-general for political affairs Kieran Prendergast (who had replaced Marrack Goulding in July 1997) sought to salvage this missed opportunity. Prendergast pushed Stein to recognize that the international community could not be expected to finance the peace process if the Guatemalans themselves would not. Stein acknowledged this fact as "annoying but irrefutable" ("molesto pero imbatible"). The government was caught between resistance from the business community to income and corporate tax increases and the political costs of a VAT increase that would hurt the public at large. Stein hinted that Arzú was unlikely to raise taxes and that the United Nations needed to adjust its expectations.[137]

In November, the government brought a plan to the IMF that was little improved: the government acknowledged a shortfall of 1 percent by 2000, while the IMF's analysts projected a 2 percent shortfall. The government wanted to confirm IMF support for a request to the Follow-Up Commission to reschedule the fiscal targets. Arnault opposed the government's request. To accept it would reward CACIF for stonewalling, undercut international credibility, and discourage all those sectors of society that were to benefit from the accords.[138]

Prendergast visited Guatemala in late November to signal both the United Nations' support for the peace process and its determination to see the government meet its fiscal targets. The visit coincided with an outbreak of divisions within the government. Labor minister Héctor Cifuentes (also the Secretary-General of the PAN) declared that the government had "reached its limits in tax collection and that the only option left [was] to review the Peace Accords." He dismissed the peace accords as a foreign creation and declared them unrealistic.[139]

Arzú's finance minister struck a similar pose.[140] He stated that the IMF, not MINUGUA, should verify fiscal commitments. Although the IMF had been well aligned with the UN Secretariat during the peace negotiations process, IMF headquarters in Washington was drifting from full support for the accords. For technical reasons, the fund's experts thought it was not practicable for Guatemala to achieve "the overall progressiveness of the tax system," and for political reasons questioned the 12 percent target for 2000. Arnault wrote Prendergast "one important factor in the equation is the Minister's feeling that he has support from IMF. I think time has come to make sure he has not." He urged Prendergast or Alvaro de Soto to "pay a visit to IMF in Washington" to "raise the level and achieve a clearer understanding on this part of the Guatemalan peace process."[141]

While the United Nations and IMF debated positions, the FRG party was mobilizing its base against the new Uniform Property Tax (Impuesto Único Sobre Immuebles [IUSI]). The law, which Congress had passed hastily, contained some design flaws: the rate structure was not particularly progressive, and the law required municipalities to collect the monies without guaranteeing them a share. Moreover, the law allowed confiscation of lands of individuals who did not pay their taxes, which, in the context of distrust toward the government at all levels, was very frightening to small landowners. This made the IUSI a beautiful wedge issue for the FRG, which carried out an aggressive disinformation campaign against the law that quickly gained traction within poor indigenous communities.[142] Surprisingly, local branches of the URNG also mobilized supporters against the IUSI, while Nobel Prize winner Rigoberta Menchú and Pablo Monsanto of the URNG spoke out against it. The Mayan group COPMAGUA argued that the IUSI should be revised not derogated. Other indigenous groups and leaders simply distanced themselves from the issue, leaving Arzú and the PAN isolated. MINUGUA's field offices were caught unprepared for the national importance of this issue and the need to help build public awareness. The mission did little if anything to publicize the positive aspects of the tax or its importance for the overall peace process, leaving the FRG a clear field to agitate against the bill.[143]

Some violent protests occurred, mainly in the department of Quetzaltenango, and MINUGUA narrowly rescued a government police officer who was about to be lynched. Instead of trying to correct the misinformation being spread about the law, the government asked Congress to derogate the law in the name of "social peace."[144] A MINUGUA report to New York remarked "the Property Tax issue revealed, on the one hand, the low capacity of the Government to inform the public and convey a credible and persuasive message on an important, but delicate aspect of the Peace Agreements, and, on the other, it showed how easy it was to manipulate and mobilize significant segments of the population, already frustrated by the precarious economic situation."[145] Two weeks later, Arnault's assessment had become even bleaker: the protests and the government's about-face on the IUSI "have created a new situation and serious concern about the political and financial sustainability of the peace process over the next two years."[146]

The collapse of the IUSI stripped US$25 million out of the government's expected tax revenues for 1998, putting them at around 8.5 percent of GDP, well off the 10 percent target. The gap would widen in 1999. This, in turn, would impede implementation of social programs and improved public security. Despite the adverse effects for the peace process, the PAN was unwilling to attempt a revised version of the bill. The party was completely isolated on the tax issue. Polling done by the PAN showed the party trailing the FRG.[147] Arnault concluded that "PAN alone, with its limited capacity to communicate and its fraying constituency, cannot alone bear the burden of the peace agenda in a pre-electoral context." Arnault added, "the risks and benefits of continuing the process should be shared with other actors, among political parties and civil society organizations." Yet in fact the Guatemalan institutions of government, as well as the accords themselves, imposed all the risks on the incumbent party, while benefits would be broadly distributed over society and would mostly accrue in the future. In view of this distribution of costs and benefits, it was rational and predictable for the government to simply opt out of the more politically challenging measures.

The impasse demonstrated just how weak the United Nations' position in Guatemala was: the only alternative that Arnault could propose was to use the Follow-Up Commission as a consensus-building forum to convince the public of the importance of the peace process, and then reschedule the implementation timetable to avoid the precedent of outright noncompliance. He then proposed a series of less controversial peace-related measures that could "regain gradually political momentum until we can reopen the fiscal issue." But there were no incentives for other political parties to help the PAN rebuild its political standing, and it was unlikely that all of this could play out before the end of Arzú's term.[148] Arnault's proposal depended on support from a relatively small group (the commission members, especially Zelaya and Porras) that was willing to promote major reforms, but whose reformist goals were increasingly at odds with the president's political priorities.

A consultative group meeting was scheduled for June, and the government needed to have an agreement in place with the IMF before that meeting since other donors would probably hold back if they did not. Yet the IMF (with some encouragement from the United Nations in New York to hold the line) would not approve any plan that did not increase revenues, and also insisted on prior approval of any plan by the Follow-Up Commission. MINUGUA stepped in to craft a compromise. It would draft a tax plan that would increase revenues by less than 1 percent, thereby meeting the

IMF's minimum standard.[149] In exchange, the Follow-Up Commission would postpone the 12 percent target from 2000 to 2002.[150] The consultative group meeting was pushed back until October to buy time for this deal to take shape.[151]

Once the consultative group meeting was done, however, the PAN's incentives to deliver evaporated. The government presented the tax amendments to Congress as promised, but then withdrew the bill as soon as PAN deputies resisted, reneging on its promises. Congress did manage to act with at least some independence from business interests, extending the tax on commercial and agricultural businesses (IEMA) for five years. With revenues projected to be below targets, the budget for 1999 had to be cut, raising concerns about future social spending and institution building in areas related to the accords.[152]

With national elections planned for late 1999, it became clear that the PAN would not be raising any taxes that would take immediate effect. As a sop, it formed the Preparatory Commission for the Fiscal Pact that would plan tax measures to be carried out by the next administration and Congress. But then the PAN allowed a series of measures that worsened the deficit. Representatives of international creditors flew into Guatemala City to warn the government against deficit spending, echoed by local think tanks and CACIF.[153] The country's balance of payments was already under pressure because of a drop in prices for export commodities, making devaluation (and resulting inflation) more likely.[154]

Stalemate persisted through 1999: the deficit grew, the value of the quetzal sank, and no new taxation was forthcoming. During meetings between various Guatemalan politicians and the UN Secretary-General's head of cabinet Iqbal Riza in October 1999, the representative of the World Bank spoke of a "forthcoming economic crisis" that could "endanger the sustainability of the peace process and the political stability of Guatemala."[155] At this point, though, there was little that MINUGUA or the international financial institutions could do until a new government was in place. CACIF busied itself during 1999 trying to obtain a temporary tax forgiveness policy, in hopes that members could clean up their books before penalties for tax evasion became operational.

The Preparatory Commission for the Fiscal Pact eventually issued a series of 100 recommendations to be taken up by the next government. After the inauguration of Alfonso Portillo as president on January 14, 2000, the international community resumed pressuring the government to present sustainable tax legislation to Congress by mid-April.[156] By February 2000, however, the IMF had already lost patience with the fiscal pact process and encouraged other international players to distance themselves. This sharply contradicted the mission's position of using the process to build a broader state-building consensus but it might have been more realistic. The IMF had no confidence that the process could produce anything other than delays. Arnault wrote New York in early March that the mission would be meeting with World Bank and IMF officials in Washington to convince them to stay the course.[157] The tax pact would not reach fruition during Arnault's term, and the fiscal issue would bedevil Guatemala and MINUGUA for the duration of the mission.

■ The Defeat of Constitutional Reform

Beyond the end of fighting and demobilization of the URNG, the most important step for the peace process was the ratification of constitutional reforms outlined in the peace accords. Without constitutional reforms, it would be difficult if not impossible to subordinate the military to elected civilian authorities and civilian courts, suppress the military's internal security roles and transfer these authorities to civilian police and intelligence organizations, strengthen the autonomy and professionalism of the judiciary, institutionalize multilingualism in official state business, and formally recognize Guatemala as a multicultural and multiethnic state. Without these basic changes, there wasn't much in the accords that could address the long-term institutional defects of Guatemalan democracy.

The Guatemalan constitution of 1985 provided for two paths to constitutional revision. First, a constitutional assembly could be formed similar to the one that wrote the 1985 constitution in the first place. This would require direct popular election of delegates, and the resulting assembly would have the power to reform any part of the constitution, with unpredictable results. The second, more feasible and ordinary, path involved approval of the reforms by a two-thirds majority of Congress, followed by a popular referendum in which the reforms had to earn a simple majority of those voting. There was no procedure under which the constitution could be reformed simply by an act of Congress. Of Latin American countries other than Guatemala, only Uruguay and Venezuela also require a popular referendum. This was a particularly challenging threshold in a country with very high illiteracy rates, a powerful media apparatus, and extreme concentration of wealth.[158]

Yet MINUGUA was initially complacent about the prospects for constitutional reform. Cables sent in 1997 and even 1998 expressed little if any doubt that once the reforms got past hurdles in Congress, the referendum would be unproblematic. Most of the political parties seemed likely to favor the reforms, as did most of the popular organizations that had made up the ASC. The mission seems to have made the assumption that the parties and civic groups accurately represented public opinion, and moreover that despite a history of low turnout for nonpresidential elections, these groups would successfully turn out enough voters to carry the referendum. Not until late in 1998 did the mission's reporting begin to raise questions about the certainty of passage. Moreover, the mission's efforts to educate the public—though nationwide—were decidedly small scale, emphasizing meetings and talks at the local level, printed materials, and relatively little use of mass media.

Just getting to a popular vote was a long and tangled process during which elite partisan and interest group politics dominated the process, perhaps distracting the mission's attention from the need to build a base of popular support for the eventual referendum itself. The Arzú administration wanted to cover its right flank, so the PAN agreed to the FRG's demand to form a Multi-Party Commission (Instancia Multipartidaria) to thresh out the details. The Multi-Party Commission, which had no basis in law, differed from Congress in that it incorporated unelected party functionaries. Not surprisingly, this made the negotiating dynamic intensely partisan.[159] Debates focused on a series of measures that the rightist FRG particularly wanted—measures that would allow its perennial presidential aspirant Efraín Ríos Montt to run. (Ríos Montt was prohibited by Article 186 of the existing constitution from becoming president because he had participated in a coup d'état in 1982 and was the de facto president in 1982–1983.) The PAN steadfastly opposed any change that would allow him to run.[160]

As had occurred with much of the peace process, the consensus-building logic in the Multi-Party Commission led to a tremendous expansion of the constitutional reform agenda, as various interest groups reached out to the parties to push for specific changes. The list of reforms swelled from the twelve submitted by Arzú to fifty. Only the original twelve were required by, and central to, the peace accords.[161]

The Mayan group COPMAGUA negotiated directly with the PAN to reform Article 203 to recognize indigenous customary law. In September they reached an agreement on that issue. But the PAN, nervous about the political risks of pushing through the reforms on its own authority, kept seeking consensus with the FRG. The FRG floated a number of alternative proposals regarding Article 186, including one that would allow Ríos Montt's wife to run in his stead. Failing that, the FRG asked to change Article 281, which lists constitutional articles that may not be revised (including 186). Dropping 186 from that list would at least open the door to future constitutional revision that could someday permit the presumably immortal Ríos Montt to run.[162] With these questions once again in play, COPMAGUA suddenly radicalized its position and began demanding reforms beyond those envisioned in the peace accords. The entire process threatened to collapse.[163]

By October, however, the parties reconverged on most points, leaving disagreements only on whether the number of deputies should be capped, and whether there should be term limits. MINUGUA's weekly report for the first two weeks of October described these as "minor issues," a view that most political scientists would strongly disagree with since district magnitude and term limits fundamentally affect legislative behavior. These were, however, less intensely controversial than other issues before Congress, and MINUGUA cabled New York expressing confidence that the reforms would pass. The list of reforms had once again swelled to fifty-two, yet somehow these did not include some of the consensus recommendations for reform produced by the various commissions established under the accords, such as the Commission on the Strengthening of the Justice System. Instead, political parties had set the priorities.[164]

With near agreement on the content, Congress debated procedure. At issue was whether Congress could approve the whole package by three "readings" and votes, or whether each individual measure would have to obtain the needed two-thirds vote as the FRG wanted. Various groups purporting to defend the constitution came forward to threaten members of Congress with criminal sanctions if they followed the wrong procedure. Looming over all of this was the consultative group meeting scheduled for late October. Facing this deadline, Congress passed a package of fifty reforms, despite the FRG's last-minute withdrawal of its support.

With this much accomplished, MINUGUA expected the referendum to be held in early 1999, and was sanguine about the outcome. MINUGUA cabled New York:

> The likelihood of reforms being approved in the referendum is very high, considering the support of all major political parties (if things stand as they are), the URNG, COPMAGUA, and other indigenous organizations and various other civil society actors. CACIF, the main business grouping, which had declared its opposition because of the introduction of an article regarding monetary policy, may support the reforms now that the article has been withdrawn. Opposition from minor groups will certainly not be sufficient to defeat this broad coalition in support of the reforms.[165]

What is striking is the mission's view that an agreement negotiated among party elites, with the participation of unelected interest groups, constituted a "broad coalition" of actual voters. This could have been avoided had the mission made better use of survey research tools to sound the views of likely voters. The mission seems to have been misled by its intensive daily contact with the various political parties. It mistook them as representative of the broader public.

On the eve of the October 1998 consultative group meeting, MINUGUA again cabled New York detailing the contents of the reforms approved by Congress, as if these were already the law of the land. For example, the mission wrote, "the Constitution now recognizes the 'norms, principles, values, procedures, traditions and customs of the indigenous peoples for the regulation of their internal coexistence, as well as the validity of their decisions . . .' (art. 203)."[166] Actually, the Constitution would say no such thing unless the reforms were ratified by popular referendum. In fairness, the cable did acknowledge that success of the popular referendum was "not totally certain given the late change of heart of the main opposition party, and misgivings of various other groups." However, the balance of the cable stressed the positive.

Just a week after that cable, however, Arnault began to signal serious concerns about the referendum. In a speech to the consultative group meeting, Arnault said that the Guatemalan parties would need to inform the public about the content and value of the reforms. He said, "while consensus building has been one of the strengths of the Peace Accords, communication has been, up to this point, the weakness." Thus the referendum would be "a real challenge," and all of those present, "governmental and non-governmental actors, political parties and social organizations, indigenous groups and professional associations" needed to put in motion "an intense explanation and motivation campaign" to make the importance and "tangible results" of constitutional reform clear to the public.[167]

Unfortunately, the actual commitment of the Guatemalan parties to the reforms was soft. With the consultative group meeting behind him and no more scheduled for his term, Arzú faced little further international accountability for his political actions.[168] And although one might think the constitutional reforms would be a centerpiece accomplishment for the party, many elite sectors were actively opposed to their passage. Pushing harder in favor of the reforms would have a political cost for the PAN. As a result, in the words of presidential adviser Gustavo Porras, "the President never committed" ("el Presidente nunca le puso").[169] Although all of the political parties formally announced their support for passing the reforms (even the FRG), none except perhaps the leftist New Guatemala Democratic Front (FDNG) really mobilized their party machinery to motivate and turn out supportive voters. Congress failed to publish the accords in the Official Gazette, and also failed to have the text published in the leading Spanish and Mayan-language newspapers as promised. MINUGUA stepped in to print 13,000 copies of the package of reforms, but Congress's inaction signaled the low level of party commitment.[170]

At this point, the referendum ran into further delays. First, the government declared a state of emergency following heavy rains and flooding from Hurricane Mitch in November 1998, suspending constitutional rights to freedom of movement and freedom from detention without due process. These measures were completely unnecessary: Guatemala had been lightly affected compared to neighboring countries, none of which imposed similar measures. The government then extended the needless emergency status into 1999. The Supreme Electoral Tribunal (TSE) refused to schedule the referendum until the emergency was lifted. The delay pushed the likely date of the referendum ever closer to the November 1999 general elections, further increasing the risk that partisan maneuvering would affect the outcome.

By December 1998, MINUGUA headquarters was beginning to worry about the referendum. The mission's work plan document for 1999 pointed out a number of areas of risk. First, peace implementation up to that point had not encouraged popular participation, and the pace of implementation had not produced any short-term gains in public security and living standards. In this context, "putting the peace process to a vote is not the most favourable test." Voter turnout was likely to be low (it had been 16 percent in the last referendum in 1993), and sectors hostile to the peace process "could conceivably mount a successful effort to defeat the peace process at the polls." Two major newspapers were already campaigning for the "no" vote. Various right-wing organizations including CONAGRO, the Association of Army Veterans, and the Pro-Fatherland League were rounding up funds for a "no" campaign.

In January 1999, the Center for the Defense of the Constitution (CEDECON) brought suit before the Constitutional Court challenging the use of a single question for a package of fifty reforms. The court responded with a temporary stay on the referendum. The mission could only express concern about the potential for delays without expressing a view on the substance of the suit. The Follow-Up Commission did, however, do some lobbying of the court. The Guatemalan political parties descended into squabbling about the procedural questions, shifting attention completely away from the substance of the reforms. Even the PAN split between Arzú's loyalists and those close to the party's presidential candidate, Oscar Berger.[171] Sensing that at least public interest in the reforms had increased, MINUGUA finally launched its public information campaign (such as it was) in February.

The court ruled in February that the single question did not provide voters with enough choices. The court proposed that the questions be grouped thematically. Congress responded with uncharacteristic swiftness, writing four questions that grouped the reforms under the labels of Nation and Social Rights, Legislative Function, Executive Function (which included the reforms on the military and police), and Judiciary and the Administration of Justice.[172]

This formula proved acceptable to the court, and the referendum was scheduled for May 16. The court dismissed other legal challenges. MINUGUA commissioned a survey in March to gauge public support, and the results suggested that the "yes" was ahead by at least 11 percentage points on all four questions. Without detailed information about how the survey was conducted by the contractor, it is impossible to diagnose why it proved to be so wrong. Most likely part of the problem related to turnout. That is, the contractor may not have had a good model for identifying likely

voters. The fact that the survey showed strongest opposition to military reforms among people in the areas most harmed by the war (the opposite of
the actual results in May) suggests significant sampling error, or, perhaps,
the effects of fear on what people were willing to say to the surveyors.
Overall, the study gave MINUGUA false assurance that public opinion was
favorable.[173] Other polls reported in the press in April were less reassuring,
showing a narrow margin of victory, and, on some questions, a lead for the
"no" vote. As of early April, MINUGUA had detected "no wide-scale organized campaign against the reform," although there were some dissenting
voices among conservative commentators and evangelical churches. Even
the FRG belatedly and tepidly announced that, despite having voted against
the reforms in Congress, it now supported the measures. MINUGUA wrote
to New York expressing concern that "there is no wide-scale campaign for
the yes vote either." Efforts by local NGOs and civic groups were "scarce
and poorly organized," and the political parties were sitting it out. Parties of
the left (including the URNG) were focused on developing their electoral
platform and were paying little attention to preparing for the referendum.[174]

By the end of April, the opposition campaign suddenly got under way
in earnest. The newspapers intensified their attacks, as did several radio stations. The CEO of the nearly monopolistic television conglomerate that
controlled three of the main TV channels banned "yes" spots on his network in an astonishing abuse of media power. The most powerful labor
union came out against the reforms, the Pro-Fatherland League helped form
a network of opinion leaders against the reforms, and the Catholic Church
limited its stance to encouraging participation in the vote. The business association CACIF did not at this point take a position, but many prominent
businessmen expressed particular concern about reforms that would remove
the military from internal security roles. The president of the Supreme Judicial Court announced complacently that he saw no need for the judicial reforms. Claims in the media that multiculturalism would lead to ethnic conflict appeared to resonate particularly with urban voters.[175] TV and radio
spots suggested that indigenous Guatemalans would be able to assert claims
to Hispanic Guatemalans' property, and Hispanics would be forced to learn
Mayan languages. This line of argument tapped into deep-seated racist fears
still prevalent in the middle and upper classes. Commentators in the press
argued that the best reason to vote against the reforms was that the political
parties were in favor of them, exploiting widespread disenchantment with
the political system. Three days before the vote, both CACIF and the Evangelical Alliance suddenly came out publically against the reforms.

MINUGUA had limited capacity to offset this negative campaign, and
it did not make optimal use of the capacity that it did have. While the mission obviously could not openly campaign for the "yes," its existing mandate did authorize it to communicate with and educate the public. There

was no legal impediment to a massive public education campaign through the broadcast media. There were several other constraints, however. First, the mission had received pledges of US$235,000 for public education on constitutional reform questions.[176] In the context of other MINUGUA-led trust fund projects, this was a considerable sum, but it was far outmatched by the opposition campaign. With the benefit of hindsight it is a shockingly small figure given the overall costs of the mission (over US$30 million per year), the centrality of the referendum to the entire peace process, and the obvious need for far more public information on the constitutional measures. The fact that the entire public education effort depended on voluntary contributions, rather than being a budgeted strategic effort, raises questions about mission planning.[177]

One must also ask why public education efforts on the reforms did not begin earlier. With the repeated postponements of the *consulta,* there had been many months for the mission to get the word out. Of course, the specific format and content of the questions could not be known until Congress was done wrangling and the Constitutional Court had ruled on all the procedural questions. But it had been expected all along that the core twelve reforms would be included, and MINUGUA could have laid a foundation of public knowledge about these months before the vote. This omission—very obviously in retrospect—is probably attributable to the mission's earlier misplaced confidence that support for the referendum was assured.

The mission also handicapped itself by initially committing to "work with national institutions toward making the contents of the constitutional reforms known by the general public . . . and promoting participation on election day."[178] This sounds appropriate and consistent with a strategy of enhancing rather than displacing local capacity. Yet working through national institutions in this instance was a risky strategy given the weakness of local counterparts. As an illustration, all the Follow-up Commission could think of was to publish a pamphlet. This was not surprising: it had not been set up as a public education body. That was MINUGUA's job, as well as a responsibility of the PAN and the URNG as the main signatories.

To a large extent, MINUGUA dealt with the public education challenge by falling back on what it already knew how to do: hold meetings at the local level with community groups and distribute printed literature. The mission headquarters sent guidelines to the regional offices calling on them to do everything possible to educate the public about the reforms, especially those of greatest "transcendence," but cautioned them to keep the mission's efforts separate from those of other organizations that might be explicitly calling for the "yes" vote.[179] While this effort was no doubt helpful in educating some members of the public, it was no match for the overwhelming ignorance and apathy of most voters, the opposition media juggernaut, and the grassroots-level disinformation capacity of the old counterinsurgency networks. The whole public education effort was too little, too late. Unsurprisingly, polls showed an increase in the proportion of "undecided" voters, reaching 50 percent by the end of April, an ominous sign.[180]

The results of the referendum were disastrous. Only 18.54 percent of registered voters turned out, only slightly better than the referendum in 1994. All four questions were defeated. Surprisingly, the question that came closest to succeeding was on indigenous rights (despite all the media fulmination about ethnic conflict), while reform of Congress lost by the biggest margin, followed by reforms to government, including the army.[181] The reforms were approved in ten departments of the country (mostly in the north and the highlands—the most heavily indigenous areas), and were voted down in the more populous capital city, as well as the coastal and lowland departments of the southwest and east, which are majority Hispanic.[182] President Arzú responded to the result by announcing tersely that the "Government had fulfilled its commitments under the Peace Agreements regarding constitutional reform, which were to submit it to Congress." The US State Department issued a statement that the vote was a setback for the peace agreements. The media and Guatemalan politicians attacked this obviously true statement as "interference in Guatemala's affairs." *Siglo XXI* columnist Armando de la Torre wrote that the vote represented "for the grotesque militancy of the MINUGUA, a lethal warning: leave Guatemala, and if you return, do so as individuals, pay your taxes, and agree to stay here and live with the consequences of your recommendations."[183]

The magnitude of the referendum defeat took some time to fully appreciate, in part because the Guatemalan actors sent such contradictory signals in the aftermath. There also seems to have been a measure of denial. MINUGUA sent an assessment to New York that opened with a quantitative analysis enumerating those reforms that could still go forward. Of seventy-two commitments remaining in the peace timetable, only fourteen were affected by the defeat of the referendum. This was, of course, ridiculous given the qualitative importance of those fourteen. The cable acknowledged that from a qualitative point of view the picture was bleaker, but softened even this admission with a strained argument that some demilitarization measures could move forward. Ultimately, the report labeled the referendum outcome a sort of "Rorschach test," in which "every school of thought tends to read their [*sic*] expectations into the referendum results." The mission recommended that the United Nations "not rush to conclusions" and allow time to assess the overall impact on the peace process.[184] Following this bizarrely agnostic account of the referendum results, USG Prendergast called Arnault to New York for consultations.[185] Meanwhile, MINUGUA's Office of Technical Cooperation wrote one of the saddest documents in the MINUGUA archives, asking the Programme Planning and Budget Department in New York to transfer trust fund contributions to UNOPS—to pay for the public education campaign on the constitutional reforms that had been defeated two weeks earlier.[186]

Two months after the referendum, political party leaders began to talk about using simple legislation to substitute for some of the defeated constitutional measures. With this news, Arnault reported too optimistically "conditions are ripe for reform on key issues of the peace agenda."[187] USG Prendergast wrote back, thoroughly unconvinced:

> It is difficult to resist viewing this evolution with some suspicion. For the political parties it is convenient to disregard the outcome of the referendum with hindsight now that, by their inaction or barely veiled opposition to the proposals contained therein, they have helped assure that fundamental elements of the peace accords cannot move forward. In other words, they are able to take this elegant and superficially progressive new stance freed of the political consequences of having taken it when they could have made a difference, and in the comfort that it will not lead very far. . . . If, nevertheless, your analysis is correct, perhaps we should abandon our postmortem aloofness on the results of the referendum and look for ways to exploit the political parties' apparent remorse and translate it into a movement to do something concrete about it. Can they be herded into some action, or commitment to action after the elections? Should they be tested on this? What would courses of action be? . . . Can you please provide us with elements of a strategy? Or do you recommend that we continue to stand by?[188]

For the remainder of Arnault's time in Guatemala, the mission stood by. There was really nothing else it could do. In the subsequent presidential administration of Alfonso Portillo, the mission was able to extract formal commitments from the major parties to carry forward with the peace accords. But the defeat of the referendum gutted the peace accords and the most important institutional changes await a new reform process, probably in the distant future.

▮ The 1999 Elections and the Rise of the FRG

In contrast to the constitutional referendum surprise, MINUGUA had plenty of warning about the electoral demise of the PAN and the rise of the FRG. Polling by Borge and Associates, the think tank ASIES, as well as CID-Gallup all showed PAN candidate Oscar Berger trailing the FRG's Alfonso Portillo by 12 percent or more in the months leading up to the vote. Despite its accomplishments in bringing peace, the PAN had presided over a period of economic stagnation and high crime. Predictably the public had swung away from the incumbent party, opening an opportunity for the FRG.

Like most Guatemalan political parties, the FRG was built around a few strong personalities. The dominant figure was former dictator Efraín Ríos Montt, who really, really wanted to be president but was proscribed by constitutional Article 186. Ríos Montt represented traditional, agrarian, pro-authoritarian values with a strong overlay of fervent anticommunism and evangelical fundamentalist Christianity. Though extremely conservative, he was no friend of big business. Since Ríos Montt could not run, the party's presidential candidate was Alfonso Portillo, whose political style was more populist. Earlier in his life, Portillo had flirted with the revolutionary left and ended up in exile in Mexico. His rhetoric appealed to the lower classes and he postured as an opponent of oligarchic business interests. He stressed the importance of building a stronger and more effective state, and called for accountability for past human rights crimes. Yet he was personally notorious as a successful fugitive from Mexican justice for having killed two men in "self-defense" during a bar fight. In Guatemala where much of the public approved of lynching accused criminals, a presidential candidate willing to kill to ensure his own safety had a unique appeal. Less noticed during the campaign was the fact that Portillo also seemed to have connections to corrupt and criminal enterprises. His party also had strong ties to the most reactionary sectors of the armed forces, which overlapped heavily with the most corrupt sectors. Both factors became very significant once he was in office.

There was obviously nothing that MINUGUA could or should have done about the impending FRG victory. The mission's attention focused for the second half of 1999 on its existing mandate to verify political rights. It planned to monitor whether public officials were abusing their positions (and budgets) for partisan purposes, whether indigenous and rural communities had fair and equal access to register and to vote, and whether the campaigning and elections took place without violence and intimidation. MINUGUA did not have a mandate to supervise vote counting or investigate claims of fraud.

The UN organization with that expertise was the Electoral Assistance Division (EAD) of DPA. Unfortunately, EAD combined very limited resources with a General Assembly–mandated impulse to take ownership over any election-related activity. EAD officials expressed concern that MINUGUA's exercise of its mandate to verify political rights impinged on the EAD's turf. Yet it was not clear what services EAD itself could offer, and MINUGUA did have a mandate to verify political rights. The result was a dispute over turf and an unwelcome distraction. EAD made promises to Guatemalan officials that it lacked the staffing to deliver, planned a preparatory mission to Guatemala without notifying MINUGUA, and potentially duplicated the efforts of other organizations.[189] Arnault appealed repeatedly to New York to encourage EAD to identify an appropriate role and not interfere with MINUGUA's exercise of its own mandate.[190] He recommended that EAD train observers and make preparations for a "quick count" that would sample ballots at various locations and establish a benchmark against which official election results could be compared.[191] (A quick count in El Salvador in 1994 had helped dissuade the incumbent ARENA government from wrongly declaring a first-round victory in the presidential race, heading off an outbreak of election-night violence.) Arnault's recommendations won support from Americas and Europe Division Director Angela Kane and ASG Alvaro de Soto, and were put into effect.[192] The Guatemalan Human Rights Ombudsman's Office (PDH) proposed that it could carry out the quick count. The PDH had enough personnel and volunteers around the country to make this work, so MINUGUA helped arrange for EAD to train PDH staff, an appropriate role given EAD's expertise but sparse resources.[193] Meanwhile, the OAS, EU, and other actors arranged to deploy dozens of observers around the country on election day.

Anticipating that the FRG would win and that it would be an unreliable agent of peace implementation, the central challenge for the United Nations was how to increase the likelihood that the peace process would survive. Experience had shown that the first year of the FRG administration would be the key moment for making any progress. Thereafter, political resistance was likely to consolidate. Moreover, the United Nations was beginning to contemplate its exit from Guatemala, which added to the urgency of consolidating some gains in the first months of an FRG administration. The Secretary-General's chef de cabinet Iqbal Riza traveled to Guatemala in October to meet with a range of different political actors and seek firm commitments from the major parties to follow through with the accords, regardless of the outcome of the election. Riza pushed particularly on the reform of the army and the justice system, fiscal reform, electoral and educational reform, implementation of the recommendations of the CEH, and the lack of progress on the Gerardi case.[194]

In the end the elections were acceptably administered, but were marred by more violence and intimidation than had been seen in recent elections. The OAS and European Union deployed jointly about 110 observers, the PDH deployed over 400 domestic volunteers, and MINUGUA deployed 200 two-person teams to oversee polling conditions and respond to complaints, focusing its efforts in the most conflicted areas. The EAD provided technical support to the PDH.[195] Despite the deterrent observer presence, MINUGUA confirmed thirty-seven "electoral conflicts" focused mainly around the Guatemala City metropolitan area and in Quetzaltenango. There was one confirmed case of vote buying. There were no signs of systematic fraud, however, and the TSE performed well overall. The results went unquestioned except in a few municipal races.

The congressional race yielded a major victory for the FRG, which won 64 out of 113 seats making it possible to legislate without forming a coalition. PAN won only thirty-six seats, and the leftist New National Alliance (ANN), which included the URNG, won nine seats. The DCG, once the most powerful party in the country, was reduced to only one seat, along with two other minor parties. Six parties (including the FDNG) did not earn the 4 percent required to remain in legal existence. The presidential race resulted in a plurality (47.7 percent) for Alfonso Portillo (FRG), 30.4 percent for Oscar Berger (PAN), and 12.3 percent for Alvaro Colóm (ANN). It was obvious that Portillo would win the second round, and Berger hardly campaigned after the first round. The second round on December 26 was comparatively free of conflict. Turnout was lower (as expected), and Portillo won a decisive 68.3 percent versus 31.7 for Berger.[196]

With the results in hand, the United Nations needed a strategy to support the peace process during the first year of the Portillo government. One thing the United Nations could do right away was to issue a strong fourth Secretary-General's report in December—before Portillo's inauguration—that provided an extensive inventory of the remaining commitments under the peace accords. This report unavoidably reflected poorly on Arzú's record, but was necessary to lay out the international community's expectations of Portillo. The report noted that even those changes to the armed forces that could be carried out despite the failure of the constitutional referendum (such as redeployment and closure of the EMP) had not been done. The report also noted that while spending on the justice system had increased, internal reforms and improved performance still lagged.[197] The document included two "annexes" assessing compliance on multiple issue areas. The tabular summaries on each theme showed starkly how much of the peace agenda remained unfinished.

USG Prendergast visited the country quietly in January 2000 to assess the situation. The mission held an internal retreat in Sololá to produce a series of recommendations. Participants agreed that the mission needed a more agile way to deliver feedback to the government, especially for the critical first year. The government's Peace Secretariat was weak compared to that under Arzú. With the departure from government of key figures from the peace talks such as Gustavo Porras, Raquel Zelaya, and Richard Aitkenhead, the mission could no longer leverage Arnault's strong personal relationships.

To improve agility, the mission rearranged reporting channels and created a coordinator position responsible for identifying and following through on quick feedback issues. For in-depth verification, the mission laid out a schedule of reports on issues including the prison system, "social conflicts and the state's response," agricultural land, labor relations, the National Civilian Police, children's rights, and justice and multiculturalism. These topical reports would alternate with the regularly scheduled Secretary-General's and human rights reports so that there would be a substantive, newsworthy report every month through the end of 2000.[198] This would keep pressure on the Portillo government, while also allowing the mission to more thoroughly document the status of compliance on key issues than was possible in the standard reports. The research for thematic reports would require more systematic interaction between divisions within the mission. For instance, a report on the prison system would require input from the FORIN (Institutional Strengthening), human rights, and political adviser offices.[199]

The Deputy COM, Juan Pablo Corlazzoli, would work to increase "political direction" of the UN system agencies (that is, making sure they paid attention to the accords in designing and implementing projects), while strengthening coordination with other donors. Part of this strategy involved getting the UN system agencies more involved in verification, thereby raising awareness about the need to align their activities with the accords. The responsibility of coordinating the field offices was shifted to a dedicated field coordinator.[200]

The organizational "areas" within the mission had originally been driven by the structure of the accords. Thus, for instance, assessment of justice institutions was part of the single area on Strengthening Civilian Power, while Human Rights was a separate area. The mission now reshuffled its verification offices to cluster around interlocking issues. Human Rights became Human Rights and Justice, in recognition that most of the human rights problems related to due process failures in the judiciary and auxiliary institutions. Public Security and Army were combined, as were the sections on Socioeconomic and Resettlement and Incorporation (of ex-combatants), the latter reflecting the fact that most resettlement and incorporation issues were directly related to employment. The mission created an Indigenous Affairs Unit as well as a Women's Unit, made up of people from various areas trained specifically on these cross-cutting themes.[201] All of these changes made so much sense that it begged the question why some of them had not been implemented earlier.

It became clear within a few months of Portillo's inauguration that MINUGUA's efforts to strengthen verification were both necessary (for the mission to play out its role as well as possible) and perhaps futile (because of the low likelihood of compliance by the government). The incoming administration's intentions and capabilities were initially difficult to read. Portillo's appointments to senior positions in his government suggested a degree of connection to the left that was obviously out of step with the agenda of party chief Ríos Montt, who was expected to be president of Congress. Both the peace secretary and the technical secretary to the Peace Secretariat were former URNG members. Since these two would represent the government on the Follow-Up Commission, both sides on the commission would now be represented by former or current URNG members, a strange outcome indeed in the wake of a right-wing political victory. Portillo also selected Edgar Gutiérrez, the former head of ODHA and field director of the REMHI project, as his director of strategic analysis, and Otilia Lux de Cotí (former CEH commissioner) as minister of culture. These appointments likewise signaled a somewhat unexpected degree of political inclusiveness. Another interpretation was that Portillo was willing to cast a broad net in search of support to counteract the more reactionary agenda of much of the rest of his party. A MINUGUA cable characterized him, overoptimistically, as "using the FRG's dark image as the perfect foil to his own progressive views."[202]

Other appointments were less encouraging. He appointed a head of the PNC who had earned a very negative reputation as a judge during the war years, and his pick for finance minister (Manuel Hiram Maza Castellanos) raised immediate concerns about prospects for corruption (Maza Castellanos would end up in jail for embezzlement committed as minister). His appointee to head the central bank lasted only a few weeks. Portillo decreed the creation of the Secretariat of Administrative Affairs and Presidential Security (SAASP), which cleared the way for the elimination of the notorious EMP. But then Portillo appointed as his chief of security an individual who was widely perceived as linked to numerous gross human rights violations including at least one extrajudicial murder, a highly organized smuggling network, and an informal network within military intelligence known as the *Cofradía.* Numerous other appointments violated the law or were obviously nepotistic (involving close relatives of prominent FRG figures). Portillo also made space for political appointees by laying off technical staff from government agencies, discarding "years of technical training and capacity-building."[203] The FRG-controlled Congress elected as its representative to the Follow-Up Commission a retired army intelligence officer implicated in grave human rights violations and crimes against humanity, who had also participated in two past coups d'état.[204]

The week before the inauguration, MINUGUA issued its tenth human rights report, which found, among other things, a 700 percent increase in due process violations during the previous year. The report noted in particular an alarming pattern of politically motivated interference in judicial processes to protect officials accused of crimes. Intelligence structures were particularly involved in obstruction of justice.

Portillo was apparently sensitive to international pressures. As one MINUGUA cable to New York remarked, his inaugural address "could have been written by MINUGUA, and entire sections seemed extracted from the Secretary-General's reports on Guatemala." The mission reported that it differed with no more than 10 percent of Portillo's proposals. In particular, Portillo signaled that he would subordinate the military to civilian authority, close down the EMP, follow the recommendations of the CEH for recognition and compensation of victims, as well as help with investigations into disappearances. He also promised to move quickly on the Gerardi case, focusing on the possible involvement of state agents. The mission was a bit overly impressed by the speech, concluding that it "answers the question of the relative influence of Portillo and the FRG in the definition of Government priorities."[205] With the benefit of hindsight, this was naïve, since a speech is one thing and implementation is another.

One of the first pieces of legislation presented by Portillo to Congress signaled the problems to come. It purported to be a bill to increase the power of civilians over the army, but, while it allowed for a civilian minister of defense, it suggested the creation of a new position of chief of staff of the armed forces that would hold most of the power, making any future civilian minister of defense more of a figurehead. Portillo had also announced that to eliminate deficit spending, he would cut the government budget by 10 percent, and do so without affecting social spending. MINUGUA experts considered this impossible, given that spending was already well below targets set out in the accords. Moreover, the accords also committed the government to build and improve existing institutions in ways that would require more spending.[206] The mission moved quickly to challenge the government on these problems, as well as the illegal procedure used to appoint provincial governors.[207]

The executive soon encountered resistance from the legislature on a series of commitments that Portillo made during his inaugural address. The one area of potential agreement was taxation and economic policy. Both Portillo and Ríos Montt were willing to impose taxes and regulation on the private sector, were opposed to monopolies, and supported better wages for labor. On other issues, Portillo and Ríos Montt were completely opposed, and the resulting legislative obstructionism was so effective that Arnault later quipped that the FRG had become "the first ruling party to simultaneously constitute the main opposition party." By May, on the eve of Arnault's departure, he argued that the United Nations' expectations needed to be "revised downward."[208]

The arrival of the new government brought renewed security concerns for the mission. Not since David Stephen's term and the furor over MINUGUA's verification of death penalty cases had the mission been subject to as many direct threats, which now extended also to international donor agencies. There was a bomb threat against MINUGUA headquarters, and death threats against the EU representative and the International Organization for Migration. Two Guatemalans working for a UNDP-funded project investigating violations of environmental laws were murdered in Puerto Barrios, and a delegation led by a local judge (who was expected to have a MINUGUA escort) was ambushed causing three deaths. Arnault and his staff did not see a centrally controlled campaign behind these incidents. Rather, the mission considered two interpretations: reactionary factions in the armed forces and private sector might feel empowered by the FRG election victory, or elements of the business community were already seeking to destabilize a government that was challenging business interests. Either way, the mission began to take invisible precautions while continuing its work. It planned to be particularly careful about observing volatile situations such as land conflicts, and would ensure that the PNC was present.[209] This dovetailed with another of the recommendations of the Sololá retreat: that the mission study more systematically the circumstances giving rise to social conflicts and develop clearer guidelines regarding when, and when not, to intervene.[210]

Indeed relations between the FRG government and large business owners had deteriorated very rapidly. The Ministry of Economy reduced protectionist tariffs favored by some oligopolistic industries. Congress passed a minimum wage increase of US$16 per month in agriculture and US$11 per month in other sectors. To anyone living above the subsistence level, these certainly sound like modest increases. However, much of the Guatemalan private sector was accustomed to paying very low wages and had a self-interested and ideologically embellished commitment to preserving exploitative labor relations. In a further signal to the private sector, Portillo gave a speech in late February predicting a "critical decision in the fiscal area, that was not taken in the past 50 years." Ríos Montt gave a speech blaming "the Church and businessmen" for poverty in Guatemala. Then Portillo appointed the former second in command of ORPA (the group that had kidnapped Mrs. Novella in 1996) as head of CONTIERRA, the agency created under the peace accords to mediate land conflicts. In meetings with CACIF, MINUGUA heard that the private sector saw the government as encouraging land grabs and labor strife in a way that could lead to a resumption of war. Businessmen boasted that they weren't afraid of renewed war, and warned that radical elements within the private sector were advocating violence.[211]

In a dispute over new measures that would allow foreign competition in trucking and intercity bus transportation, the major transport companies halted service in early March. This obviously posed an immediate threat to the economy, as fuel supplies would quickly dry up and the loss of public transportation could lead to mass protests. Portillo threatened to mobilize the military and asked MINUGUA to observe these actions to verify that no abuses took place. Portillo then thought better of calling in the military. Using the police and the courts instead, he imposed heavy fines, detained twenty-four drivers, issued warrants for the arrest of company owners, canceled two companies' licenses, and temporarily took over several companies.[212] He also threatened to liberalize licensing so that other firms could enter the market. The companies "caved in and called off the strike."[213] This was an unusually bold use of state power versus private interests, and the private sector took notice.

The government also clashed with sugar growers by suddenly removing import tariffs on 400 million pounds of sugar, thereby exposing Guatemalan sugar producers to international prices. The producers ginned up a

fake demonstration by hiring large numbers of buses to line the roads in Escuintla.[214] The government compromised by reducing the amount that could
be imported duty-free, but required the producers to reduce prices to con-
sumers (which they had just raised the previous year).[215] Amid these conflicts, the mission found itself in the novel situation of responding to a request from CACIF to provide its good offices to help it communicate with
the government![216]

▌ Developing an Exit Strategy

In anticipation of Arnault's departure from the mission at the end of May,
USG Prendergast asked him to prepare recommendations on the mission's
future. Arnault convened a working group to consider different scenarios,
taking into account financial pressures on the United Nations, the prospects
for further implementation under Portillo, and the need to leave behind at
least some long-term capacity to monitor peace implementation by Portillo
and successor governments. The Secretary-General had only committed to
provide verification through 2000, and although both the government and
the URNG favored an extension of MINUGUA into 2001 and beyond (indeed Ríos Montt, tongue in cheek, declared that the mission should "become a permanent presence in the country"!), the United Nations was under
no obligation to extend the mission.[217]

Moreover, there were good reasons to be skeptical about the value of a
prolonged mission. Arnault wrote,

> nothing in the record of this Government would indicate that the Portillo
> administration will escape the pattern of past Guatemalan Governments:
> namely, that the start of its third year in power will mark the beginning of
> a prolonged lame duck period during which the willingness and ability to
> carry out serious reforms will slow to a standstill. The last two years of
> the Arzú administration go to show that there is little the Mission can do
> to maintain the momentum of the reform process once the Government
> has lost its ability to act forcefully.[218]

This view was somewhat debatable: the incapacity of the Arzú government
derived from fairly specific political circumstances (particularly the fact
that the main threat to the PAN was from the right) and there was no particular reason to think an identical pattern would occur under Portillo. In fact,
the failure mode of the Portillo government proved to be entirely different—largely related to corruption as well as the internal gap between Portillo and Ríos Montt—and it set in almost immediately rather than emerging
only in the final two years of the government. In addition to the expected
domestic obstacles, it seemed inevitable to Arnault that international donors
and the states that had been most interested in Guatemala would disengage

as time passed, making it unlikely that coordinated international pressures could somehow overcome the domestic sources of resistance to reform.

On balance, Arnault and his team concluded that while prospects for further deep reforms under Portillo were dim, there were enough possibilities that it made sense to maintain MINUGUA's specialized verification areas through 2001 in hopes of influencing government decisionmaking. There was also the risk that, given the failure to implement the elements of the accords that would have helped with rural incomes and access to land, social conflicts could increase. The Portillo government might turn to the army to contain any unrest, as he had considered doing in the bus and trucking strike. Thus even if prospects for deeper reforms were dim, an ongoing MINUGUA presence might deter authoritarian backsliding. Moreover, Arnault wrote that the mission's signature human rights verification role positioned it to follow a number of areas

> strategic to the consolidation of democracy: political rights, indigenous rights, the behaviour of the police and the army; the performance of the justice system; the right of association and related labour situations. Finally, its mandate allows MINUGUA to play a significant role in conflict prevention and resolution at a local level, while its broad geographical deployment allows it to be an effective lobby for dialogue and deterrence of repressive solutions through the country.[219]

Specifically, Arnault recommended that the United Nations continue MINUGUA through 2001 with some consolidation of its regional offices (from twelve to eight) to save costs.[220] The mission would reduce by about half its military and police observer contingents and the Office of Technical Cooperation would be eliminated, handing off all projects to UNDP or other agencies. After that, the mission should downsize further in 2002, maintaining its field presence but with further reduced staffing. It would close at the end of 2002. A key aspect of the proposal was that during 2002, MINUGUA would limit its verification activities to human rights, and the Secretary-General would establish an Inter-Agency Monitoring Project (IMP) under which other UN system agencies including UNDP, the World Bank, the IMF, and smaller agencies would provide the inputs needed for the Secretary-General's reports. UN agencies would need to increase the proportion of international staff if they could expect to act with sufficient independence from the Guatemalan government.

In 2003, the last year of the Portillo government, a small political office headed by a representative of the Secretary-General would replace MINUGUA. The office's role would be limited to preparing reports, providing public information on the status of the peace accords, and providing good offices with respect to high-level political affairs.[221] This office would have no field presence and would not be in a position to mediate social conflicts. The Office of the High Commissioner for Human Rights would take over human rights assessment, though only the Guatemalan PDH would have the field presence to do most individual casework. The general outlines of this approach reflected the positive lessons of the United Nations' mostly successful drawdown in El Salvador, where the full-scale ONUSAL was replaced by a pared-down mission called MINUSAL, which was in turn replaced by a small political verification office with no field presence known as the United Nations Verification Office (ONUV). After ONUV closed, UNDP became, as is normal, the center of the United Nations' presence.

The main challenge posed by this approach was that there were no good models for the proposed Inter-Agency Monitoring Project, and implementing this would require a dramatically different approach and different capabilities than were customary for UNDP and other UN development agencies. These agencies generally avoided political issues, and placed a priority on smooth and cooperative relationships with governments. Verification work cut against these deeply institutionalized practices, and it was uncertain how effectively such a model would work. Yet there seemed little alternative to the envisioned handoff, and there was some question whether effective verification would matter in the future anyway. As we will see in the following two chapters, for a number of reasons MINUGUA stayed on two years longer than Arnault envisioned, maintaining its full field presence until its closure. The experimental handoff of verification to other agencies never took place.

▌ Conclusion

As Arnault assumed leadership of MINUGUA, the mission was working in an unusual setting compared to most peace operations. As implementation of the full accords began, the Guatemalan state was fully intact and the country's political institutions, with their many flaws, were well entrenched. Ironically, Guatemala lacked the disruption of the institutional status quo that can open the way to more transformative reforms in post-conflict settings.[222] Moreover, it had a financially strong print and broadcast media, and well-financed elite interest groups, that were resistant to reform. After years of war, repression, corruption, and neglect, the mass public was alienated and disengaged from politics, poorly educated, under stress from poverty and physical insecurity, and easily manipulated by propaganda. Political parties were personality-based, ephemeral, and lacked nationwide organizations. Guatemala featured a pervasive set of reactionary social networks that carried over from the counterinsurgency war and were largely controlled by the armed forces and by the FRG. These networks could be activated for the purposes of distributing disinformation and could be provoked into violent actions that threatened to destabilize the government, as illustrated by the protests against the IUSI. Finally, implementation of the accords fell initially to a government whose main opposition was to its right. Any steps the Arzú government took to actually implement its agreement with the URNG potentially exposed it to withering criticism from the FRG, and even from within its own party. To mitigate international pressures to incur such political costs, Foreign Minister Stein and President Arzú routinely complained to UN headquarters in New York that MINUGUA was exceeding its mandate. He sought to dilute international influence by making development agencies, not the mission, the center of gravity for the United Nations in Guatemala.

Although senior officials at UN headquarters generally did a good job of deflecting these demands, the fact that Arzú and Stein kept making such requests suggested that they saw the mission as politically vulnerable. Indeed, one UN official referred to MINUGUA as an "orphan mission." With the signing of the final accords, senior officials in New York saw Guatemala as a success and did not pay very much attention to it.[223] In this context, it was probably not a coincidence that Secretary-General Annan was not prepared to bring up the taxation issue during a crucial meeting with Arzú in 1997, as noted above. Only with the failure of the popular referendum did New York officials seem to sit up and take notice, and by then the peace process was irrevocably damaged. MINUGUA must accept some responsibility for the lack of attention and information at higher levels: the quality of routine political reporting from the mission was variable, with a tendency to soft-pedal bad news.

Weakness was built into the fact that the mission had a General Assembly mandate. While this had the advantage of only needing to report semiannually, it meant that major powers did not need to be engaged with the situation, and the high politics authority that comes with a Security Council mandate was absent. Moreover, the final accords had written the group of friends states out of the picture, much to the chagrin of Mexico. Thus one source of international pressure that had been present during the negotiating phase was lost, leaving the mission to pressure the government basically on its own authority without strong member-state backing. This situation, combined with the persistent independence of donor countries and agencies, left MINUGUA with few points of leverage.

As a result of all these circumstances, adversaries of change had significant advantages that MINUGUA could not offset. While the mission had nearly unparalleled information about what was going on throughout the country (indeed Portillo's secretary for strategic analysis, Edgar Gutiérrez, remarked that only MINUGUA and the Guatemalan army had coherent intelligence networks), the mission had difficulty leveraging that information to shape public opinion. This was partly a result of mistakes by the mission that undercut its ability to control its own message. The mishandling of the Mincho case was particularly damaging, because it provided the press with a perfect opportunity to attack the mission's integrity as human rights verifier. This was the one area where the mission had unambiguously developed political capital and a reputation for probity during the first phase of the mission. Moreover, the timing of the Mincho scandal could not have been worse, as it placed the mission on the defensive right at the moment that it needed to clearly communicate its new, more comprehensive mandate.

A deeper and less accidental problem was the mission's general lack of attention to public information and chronic underutilization of its mandate to communicate directly with the public about the peace accords. After a visit to Guatemala in September 1997, senior officials from FALD/DPKO and DPA wrote, "There is a need for a more comprehensive media and marketing strategy to be put in place and executed both nationally and internationally. Certain important sectors of Guatemalan society are still skeptical as to the benefits of the Peace Process, particularly in view of the increase in public insecurity."[224] Despite this awareness in New York, little was done to change the mission's public information capacity or strategy. Why, for example, was the mission so late in launching a public education campaign on the constitutional reforms? Given the depths of public ignorance about the constitution and needed reforms, with the benefit of hindsight it seems very risky to have waited until the final few months before the referendum to start preparing the public to vote in an informed way on this critical element of the accords. The 1 percent of its budget that the mission committed to public information was far too small given the importance of this mandate and role. Arnault later suggested that 7 to 10 percent would have been more appropriate.[225]

None of these problems should obscure the fact that MINUGUA made significant contributions during the 1997–2000 period. Rather than high-profile breakthroughs in implementation, however, these were dispersed contributions to social peace through the mission's constant conflict-resolution efforts at the local level, as well as the generally more open political climate that the mission's presence and human rights monitoring created.[226]

The final question is whether *any* strategy or conduct by MINUGUA could have overcome the domestic political incentives for the Arzú government to stall, or the failures of the electorate to support the referendum. Unfortunately, this question cannot be answered with any confidence. It seems likely that if the mission had focused its limited leverage on a few issues (such as justice and public security), it might have been possible to induce better policymaking by the government. Even this would have been possible only with much greater willingness by donors to allow MINUGUA to set criteria for projects and aid conditionality, which did not develop until donors fully grasped the scope of failures under the Portillo administration.

It is also possible that a stronger communications strategy might have provided the public with enough understanding of the reforms to overcome the propaganda from opponents. What is certain is that the configuration of domestic political interests and institutions worked against full implementation of the Guatemalan peace accords. Perhaps the strongest lesson from this phase of MINUGUA was that in a setting of well-entrenched domestic interests, the ability of an international mission to counteract domestic political and financial incentives is limited. In such a context, a mission is more likely to be successful at dissuading violence and conflict than motivating affirmative measures.

▌ Notes

1. "Agreement on the Implementation, Compliance, and Verification Timetable for the Peace Agreements," *The Guatemala Peace Agreements* (New York: United Nations, 1998), 226, paragraph 109.

2. Carlos Luiz da Costa and Michael Moller, "Mission Report, MINUGUA, Guatemala, 16–20 September 1997," September 24, 1997.

3. Marrack Goulding, "Meeting with Foreign Minister," to David Stephen, September 24, 1996.

4. Jean Arnault, "Panel on United Nations Peace Operations," to Iqbal Riza for Lakhdar Brahimi, April 27, 2000, 2–5.

5. Luis Pásara, *Paz, ilusión, y cambio en Guatemala: El proceso de paz, sus actors, logros, y límites* (Ciudad de Guatemala: Universidad Rafael Landívar, 2003), 67–72.

6. Ibid.

7. Charles T. Call, "War Transitions and the New Civilian Security in Latin America," *Comparative Politics* 35, no. 1 (October 2002), 1–20.

8. See the discussion below on the Uniform Tax on Land and the public backlash against it. The observation about withdrawal of the military from conflict suppression roles is from "UN Peace Operations: Lessons Learned from the Experience of the United Nations Verification Mission in Guatemala (MINUGUA)," attached to Jean Arnault, "Panel on United Nations Peace Operations," to Iqbal Riza for Lakhdar Brahimi, April 27, 2000, 6.

9. Jean Arnault, "Good Agreement? Bad Agreement? An Implementation Perspective," paper presented to the Center for International Studies, Princeton, NJ, Princeton University, 2001, 10.

10. Author interview, Jean Arnault, New York, January 2008.

11. Jean Arnault, "Urgent Staff Issues," to Bernard Miyet, December 7, 1999.

12. Author interview, Jean Arnault, New York, January 30, 2008.

13. Author interviews with multiple substantive staff members of MINUGUA and UNOPS, May and June 1998, February 1999.

14. Interviews with current and former UN officials who preferred to remain anonymous commenting on management issues in MINUGUA, February and March 2007.

15. Ibid.

16. Pierre Jambor, "End of Mission Report—Observations and Recommendations," to Kieran Prendergast, March 29, 1999.

17. Ibid., and Arnault, "Panel on United Nations Peace Operations."

18. Author interview, Jean Arnault, New York, January 30, 2008.

19. Arnault, "Panel on United Nations Peace Operations," 7.

20. Interview, UN official who preferred to remain anonymous commenting on headquarters operations, New York, February 1997.

21. Ibid.

22. Four days after the referendum, MINUGUA's technical cooperation office wrote to the director of the Programme, Planning, and Budget Department in New York asking for disbursement of US$68,814 donated by Denmark for the project "Public Information on the Constitutional Reform." This was, of course, too late, and MINUGUA had to make repeated requests over subsequent months to get these and other funds released. See Thierry Delrue (MINUGUA), "Cost Plan for One Project Funded from the First and Only Disbursement of Funds from the Fourth Danish Donation to the Trust Fund Through PRODECA," FAX to Warren Sachs (Programme Planning and Budget Department), May 20, 1999.

23. The Tuluché camp in southern El Quiché province had separate facilities for two different fronts of the EGP, and the Los Blancos and Claudia camps were adjacent in the province of Santa Rosa, hosting units of the United Front (mostly ORPA) and the FAR. The other four sites received personnel from a single party within the URNG.

24. MINUGUA, "Circular informative sobre la etapa de desmovilización" (Guatemala: MINUGUA, February 3, 1997).

25. Interview, MINUGUA official who participated in demobilization and re-settlement, Guatemala, June 1998.

26. "MINUGUA Weekly Situation Report 24–30 March 1997." See also United Nations, "Report of the Secretary-General on the Group of Military Observers Attached to MINUGUA," A/1997/432, June 4, 1997.

27. Interview, MINUGUA official who participated in resettlement of ex-combatants, Guatemala, June 1998. Also, MINUGUA, "Informe del jefe de los observadores militares sobre la desmovilización," undated. Cover sheet is entitled "Evolución de la Desmovilización."

28. "MINUGUA Weekly Situation Report 3–16 March 1997."

29. The four claimed they were transporting the weapons and ammunition to their future assembly site, and had simply failed to coordinate their actions with MINUGUA, but the press reported that they had admitted to police that they were under orders to bury the arms. "MINUGUA Weekly Situation Report 17–23 February 1997."

30. Jean Arnault, "URNG Demobilization," to Kieran Prendergast, March 5, 1997.

31. Ibid.

32. Cached explosives were detonated in situ because they were too dangerous to transport, as a result of unknown age and condition.

33. Interview, MINUGUA official, Guatemala, June 1998.

34. Funcación Guillermo Toriello, "Diagnostico socio-economico: personal incorporado, Unidad Revolucionaria Nacional Guatemalteca" (Guatemala: FGT, May 1997), 2.

35. "MINUGUA Weekly Situation Report 9–15 November 1998."

36. Guillermo Toriello was a Guatemalan diplomat who served the democratically elected governments of Juan José Arévalo and Jacobo Arbenz from 1944 through 1954. He was best known for his stirring defense of Guatemala's sovereignty during the 1954 Caracas conference of the OAS, shortly before the US-sponsored coup that ended Guatemala's democratic experiment. Guillermo Toriello died on

February 24, 1997, having attended the December 1996 signing ceremonies for the peace accords.

37. Comisión Especial de Incorporación, "Balance del programa de incorporación de la URNG a la legalidad" (Guatemala: CEI, septiembre de 1997).

38. "MINUGUA Weekly Situation Report 18–24 November 1997."

39. "MINUGUA Weekly Situation Report 11–17 November 1997."

40. The quote in the heading is from Jean Arnault, who noted that there was a campaign of disinformation against the mission, "that has a lot to do with the perception of a dirty deal," Larry Rohter, "UN Is Accused of Being Part of a Cover-Up in Guatemala," *New York Times,* May 26, 1997, 3.

41. "MINUGUA Weekly Situation Report 7–21 April 1997."

42. Ibid.

43. Ricardo Miranda, "Arnault, el verificador cómplice," *ElPeriódico,* April 24, 1997, 3.

44. "Arnault quiere lavarse las manos," editorial, *ElPeriódico,* April 25, 1997, 10. This was an absurd point to make, since by this date Arnault had already publicly acknowledged that he had known about a possible second guerrilla back in October. What he disputed was the charge that he had caused a cover-up by MINUGUA.

45. Phil Gunson, "UN's Guatemala Envoy in Cover-Up," *Guardian,* May 5, 1997, 12.

46. Carlos Canteo, "Human Rights Watch enviará una investigadora para caso *Mincho,*" *Siglo Veintiuno,* May 14, 1997, 4.

47. Rohter, "UN Is Accused."

48. "MINUGUA Weekly Situation Report 7–21 April 1997."

49. Horacio Boneo and Aracelly Santana, "Report to the Secretary General: Accusations of a Cover-up Up Raised Against MINUGUA and the Former Moderators of the Peace Talks," Horacio Boneo and Aracelly Santana to Secretary Secretary-General (New York, June 10, 1997).

50. Boneo and Santana, "Report to the Secretary General."

51. Comisión de Esclarecimiento Histórico, *Memoria del Silencio,* Annexo I (Guatemala: UNOPS, 1998), 272–276.

52. Ibid.

53. Ibid.

54. Ibid.

55. Gunson, "UN's Guatemala Envoy."

56. Boneo and Santana, "Report to the Secretary General."

57. Ibid.

58. Investigations in the absence of a formal complaint were known as ex officio cases.

59. Phil Gunson, "Private View: Time for UN to Come Clean on Rebel's Death," *Guardian,* May 31, 1997.

60. Comisión de Esclarecimiento Histórico, *Memoria del Silencio,* 272–276.

61. The general staff was the top of the operational chain of command within the military, while the Ministry of Defense was the policymaking and administrative authority for the military. Neither responded constructively to inquiries about Mincho.

62. "MINUGUA Weekly Situation Report 10–16 June 1997."

63. Jean Arnault, "Political Situation and Foreign Minister's Visit," to Kieran Prendergast, June 12, 1997; Kieran Prendergast, "Note of the Secretary-General's Meeting with President Arzú," to Jean Arnault, June 30, 1997; and Jean Arnault, "MINUGUA Staffing," to Kieran Prendergast, July 6, 1997.

64. Jean Arnault, "Follow Up to the Mincho case," to Kieran Prendergast, August 14, 1997.

65. Jean Arnault, "New Developments," to Kieran Prendergast and Bernard Miyet, April 28, 1997.

66. Ibid.

67. In the subtropics, warm daytime temperatures make the so-called "density altitude" even higher, further limiting the safe carrying capacity of aircraft for take-offs and landings.

68. For long-term peacebuilding operations like MINUGUA, the United Nations might do well to adopt and enforce higher limits for visibility and cloud ceilings, lower limits for weight, and higher fuel reserve requirements than are required by the International Civil Aviation Organization or national flight regulations. Airlines and many business flight departments use such rules and have achieved very good safety records as a result. More restrictive rules would mean that in some instances flights would be canceled that probably *could* be carried out safely, and would result in fewer passengers carried on some flights. Such rules could interfere with some mission work and might not be appropriate for peacekeeping in politically or militarily volatile situations. But in missions where there are relatively few situations where a flight *must* happen at a given time, more stringent rules could reduce loss of life.

69. Francisco Goldman, *The Art of Political Murder: Who Killed the Bishop?* (New York: Grove Press, 2007), 3–11, 21–25.

70. Ibid., 8.

71. Ibid., 133.

72. Ibid., 352.

73. Guatemalan criminal procedure code allows courts to accept a "querellante adhesivo" (auxiliary prosecutor), generally a private party that joins with the state prosecutor in investigating the case, submitting motions, and in calling and questioning witnesses during trial. This is done only when there is a possibility that state agents were responsible for a crime. If state involvement has been conclusively ruled out, judges can dismiss the private prosecution. Given the institutional weaknesses of the Public Ministry, human rights NGOs have played key roles as auxiliary prosecutors in high-profile cases such as the assassinations of Gerardi and anthropologist Myrna Mack. Rico and de la Grange base their theory of the crime on claims that ODHA fabricated the entire case and generated false witnesses.

74. Goldman, *The Art of Political Murder,* 174, 198.

75. Goldman (ibid.) provides the most thorough account of the various witnesses' accounts regarding the events in Parque San Sebastián and at the EMP headquarters. A competing account completely dismisses the value of the witnesses' testimony as fabrications and constructs an alternative scenario pointing to the involvement of a criminal gang associated with Church authorities and a vicious dog; see Maite Rico and Bertrand de la Grange, *Quién Mató al Obisbo? Autopsia de un crimen político* (México, DF: Planeta, 2003).

76. See Goldman, *The Art of Political Murder,* 230, for an example of a detail excluded from testimony at the request of ODHA.

77. Goldman (ibid.) traces in detail the evolution of Chanax's testimony, his handling by the prosecutors, and his remarks in subsequent interviews by Goldman and others. Defense attorneys made much of Chanax's statement that he added details as he became more "seguro," which means both "safe" and "sure." His meaning was clear enough in context: he was referring to his personal safety.

78. Without accepting Rico and de la Grange's far-fetched theory that a Church-related gang killed Gerardi (why would they, and why would they do so the

weekend after the announcement of REMHI?), it remains somewhat implausible that a captain in the presidential guard, who was on a prolonged trip to Argentina until the day of the crime, as well as his retired father, would be so central to an operation of this scope and political sensitivity. It seems likely that other actors were more important, and that justice has yet to be served in the case.

79. Rico and de la Grange, *Quién Mató al Obisbo.*

80. Goldman, *The Art of Political Murder,* 80.

81. Villanueva ostensibly served his sentence and was still officially incarcerated at the time of the Gerardi murder. Initially this was his alibi, but credible evidence later emerged that he was frequently allowed to leave the prison and was not present and accounted for in prison the night of the killing.

82. MINUGUA, "Tenth Report on Human Rights of the United Nations Verification Mission in Guatemala," A/54/688, December 21, 1999, paragraph 28.

83. Ibid., 325–326.

84. Ibid., 90.

85. "MINUGUA Weekly Situation Report 19–25 January 2000."

86. Paraphrased by Goldman, *The Art of Political Murder,* 70.

87. Author interview, Jean Arnault, New York, January 30, 2008.

88. See Rico and de la Grange, *Quién Mató al Obisbo* for this theory of the crime.

89. Jean Arnault, "Further Developments Relating to Msgr. Gerardi's Death," to Bernard Miyet and Kieran Prendergast, May 3, 1998.

90. *Revista Envío Digital* 197 (August 1998),www.envio.org.ni/articulo/376 (accessed September 7, 2010).

91. The Goldman as well as Rico and de la Grange accounts converge on most of the details of Orantes's strange behavior. Goldman argues that the rumors likely originated in a whisper campaign by military intelligence.

92. Goldman, *The Art of Political Murder,* 133–136. According to press reports cited by Goldman, Reverte Coma had been expelled from the exhumation of the El Mozote massacre site in El Salvador for "impeding the investigation with ludicrous interpretations. All those very small skeletons were not massacred children, he had suggested, but adolescent guerrillas—young recruits from a race of small, malnourished men—killed in battle." One detects a proregime bias in Reverte Coma's "expert" opinions. Rico and de la Grange have a very different account of the exhumation and examination of Gerardi's remains, which consists mainly in mocking the poor Spanish language skills of some of the US observers.

93. Jean Arnault, "Events Related to Msgr. Gerardi's Death," to Kieran Prendergast, May 1, 1998.

94. "MINUGUA Weekly Situation Report 6–19 July 1998."

95. Goldman, *The Art of Political Murder,* 174–177, 198.

96. Ibid, 176–177.

97. Jean Arnault, "Recent Developments," to Kieran Prendergast, March 22, 1999, 1–4.

98. Jean Arnault, "Initiative by the President in the Gerardi Case," to Kieran Prendergast, March 24, 1999; and Jean Arnault, "Speech by the President," to Kieran Prendergast, March 25, 1999.

99. "MINUGUA Weekly Situation Report 21–27 April 1999."

100. Jean Arnault, "Note to Mr. Goulding, Guatemala's Clarification Commission," to Marrack Goulding, January 14, 1997.

101. The accord provided that the head of the CEH would appoint one Guatemalan with an exemplary reputation agreed upon by the government and the URNG, and a second individual from a panel of three selected by the rectors of the

main universities in Guatemala. Lux de Cotí was the choice of the government and URNG, Balsells Tojo of the rectors. "MINUGUA Weekly Situation Report 17–23 February 1997."

102. Priscilla Hayner, *Unspeakable Truths: Confronting State Terror and Atrocity* (New York: Routledge, 2001), 45–49.

103. Christian Tomuschat, untitled letter, to Alvaro de Soto, August 4, 1998.

104. Christian Tomuschat, untitled letter, to Alvaro de Soto, December 20, 1997.

105. Hayner, *Unspeakable Truths,* 47.

106. For a chilling description of these difficulties, see Daniel Wilkinson, *Silence on the Mountain: Stories of Terror, Betrayal, and Forgetting in Guatemala* (Boston: Houghton Mifflin, 2002), 216–311.

107. Christian Tomuschat, untitled letter, to Alvaro de Soto, December 20, 1997.

108. Patrick Ball, "The Guatemalan Commission for Historical Clarification: Generating Analytical Reports, Inter-Sample Analysis," in *Making the Case: Investigating Large Scale Human Rights Violations Using Information Systems and Data Analysis,* edited by Patrick Ball, Herbert F. Spirer, and Louise Spirer, 259–286 (Washington, DC: American Association for the Advancement of Science, 2000).

109. Ibid.

110. Ibid, 271.

111. Commission for Historical Clarification, *Guatemala: Memory of Silence Tz'inil na 'Tab'al* (Guatemala, February 25, 1999), conclusion, paragraphs 114–118. Consulted online at http://shr.aaas.org/guatemala/ceh/report/english/toc.html.

112. "MINUGUA Weekly Situation Report 24 February–2 March 1999," and Hayner, *Unspeakable Truths,* 49.

113. "MINUGUA Weekly Situation Report 24 February–2 March 1999."

114. "MINUGUA Weekly Situation Report 10–16 March 1999."

115. MINUGUA, "Seventh Report on Human Rights of the United Nations Verification Mission in Guatemala," A/52/330, September 10, 1997, paragraph 13.

116. MINUGUA, "Seventh Report," paragraphs 10, 11, 20, 34, 35, and 55.

117. MINUGUA, "Tenth Report," paragraph 7.

118. Ibid., paragraph 13.

119. MINUGUA, "Ninth Report on Human Rights of the United Nations Verification Mission in Guatemala," A/53/853, March 10, 1999, paragraph 18.

120. Comisión Multinacional, "Estudio realizado por la Comisión Multnacional sobre las institutciones que brindan seguridad pública en la Republica de Guatemala," undated. The mission occurred October 24 to November 4, 1994.

121. For a detailed discussion of these problems, see William D. Stanley, "Business as Usual? Justice and Policing Reform in Postwar Guatemala," in *Constructing Justice and Security After War,* edited by Charles T. Call, 113–155 (Washington, DC: United States Institute of Peace Press, 2007).

122. Ibid.

123. Ibid.

124. MINUGUA, "Ninth Report," paragraph 16.

125. MINUGUA, "Ninth Report," paragraph 17.

126. MINUGUA, "Eighth Report on Human Rights of the United Nations Verification Mission in Guatemala," A/52/946, June 15, 1998, paragraph 86.

127. See, for example, Robert G. Williams, *Export Agriculture and the Crisis in Central America* (Chapel Hill: University of North Carolina Press, 1986), 134–151.

128. MINUGUA, "Eighth Report," paragraph 19.

129. MINUGUA, "Ninth Report," paragraph 52.

130. Aaron Schneider, *State Building in an Age of Globalization: Central American Tax Regimes and Transnational Elites* (Cambridge: Cambridge University Press, forthcoming), manuscript on file with author, 236–288.

131. Jean Arnault, "Presentation of the SG's Report on the Second Phase of the Timetable: Fiscal Issue," to Kieran Prendergast, February 21, 1998.

132. Schneider, *State Building*, 242–254.

133. "MINUGUA Weekly Situation Report 6–12 August 1997."

134. United Nations Secretary-General, *The Situation in Central America: Procedures for the Establishment of a Firm and Lasting Peace and Progress in Fashioning a Region of Peace, Freedom, Democracy and Development: United Nations Verification Mission in Guatemala,* UN Doc. A/51/936, June 30, 1997; see also Milka Casanegra de Jantscher, Patricio Castro, Alberto Ramos, y Osvaldo Schenone, "Guatemala: Rompiendo la Barrera del 8 Por Ciento" (Washington, DC: Fondo Monetorio Internacional, May 1997).

135. Jean Arnault, "Notes on Meetings with the Follow-Up Commission and with Human Rights Watch," to Kieran Prendergast, September 1, 1997; and Jean Arnault, "Request for Annual Leave, Alliance Against Impunity, Fiscal Issue, Belize," to Kieran Prendergast, August 27, 1997.

136. Jean Arnault, "Consultative Group, Alliance Against Impunity, Human Rights Watch," to Kieran Prendergast, September 15, 1997.

137. Denise Cook, "Summary Record of Meeting with Mr. Eduardo Stein, Foreign Minister of Guatemala on Friday 26 September 1997," to Kieran Prendergast, Alvaro de Soto, Michael Moller, María Maldonado, and Jean Arnault, September 30, 1997.

138. Jean Arnault, "Latest Developments," to Kieran Prendergast, November 9, 1997.

139. "MINUGUA Weekly Situation Report 25 November–8 December 1997."

140. "MINUGUA Weekly Situation Report 18–24 November 1997."

141. Jean Arnault, "Recent Developments on the Fiscal Issue," to Kieran Prendergast, January 8, 1998.

142. "MINUGUA Weekly Situation Report 17–23 February 1998."

143. "MINUGUA Weekly Situation Report 3–9 March 1998." The cable reported, "The meeting of the Mission's regional Coordinators on 5 and 6/03 underscored the need for permanent close coordination, and timely definitions of the Mission's stance on important current issues such as the Property Tax bill. In a situation of political polarization and heated debate over important aspects of the peace process, the Mission's capacity to provide clear and substantiated responses must be increased."

144. "MINUGUA Weekly Situation Report 24 February–4 March 1998."

145. Ibid.

146. Jean Arnault, "Recent Developments," to Kieran Prendergast, March 10, 1998.

147. Ibid.

148. Ibid.

149. "Planteamiento de la Comisión de Acompañamiento para asegurar la sostenibilidad del proceso de movilización creciente de recursos internos necesarios para financiar la paz y el desarrollo de Guatemala," attached to Jean Arnault, "Recent Developments on the Fiscal Issue," to Kieran Prendergast, May 9, 1998.

150. "MINUGUA Weekly Situation Report 25–31 May 1998."

151. Jean Arnault, "Recent Developments," to Kieran Prendergast, May 24, 1998.

152. "MINUGUA Weekly Situation Report 16–29 November."

153. "MINUGUA Weekly Situation Report 7–13 April."

154. "MINUGUA Weekly Situation Report 21–27 April."

155. Aracelly Santana, "Mission Report of Mr. Riza's Visit to Guatemala," to Jean Arnault, October 19, 1999.

156. "MINUGUA Weekly Situation Report 12–18 January 2000."

157. "MINUGUA Weekly Situation Report 23–29 February 2000."

158. Pásara, *Paz, ilusión, y cambio,* 75–77.

159. Ibid., 77–78.

160. "MINUGUA Weekly Situation Report 27 April–3 May 1998."

161. Pásara, *Paz, ilusion, y cambio,* 77.

162. In a sign of the variable quality of MINUGUA's reporting, the weekly situation report for the first two weeks of October described FRG's positions as stemming from "principle." "MINUGUA Weekly Situation Report 28 September–12 October 1998."

163. "MINUGUA Weekly Situation Report 21–27 September 1998."

164. "MINUGUA Weekly Situation Report 28 September–12 October 1998."

165. Ibid.

166. "MINUGUA Weekly Situation Report 12–18 October 1998."

167. "Palabras del Representante Especial del Secretario General y Jefe de la Misión de Verificación de las Naciones Unidas en Guatemala, Sr. Jean Arnault, Reunión del Grupo Consultivo para Guatemala, Bruselas, 22–23 de octubre de 1998," undated, DPA files, original in Spanish, author translation.

168. There was a subsequent special consultative group meeting for Central America as a whole in December, in response to Hurricane Mitch. Guatemala was criticized for its failures on taxation measures, but most of the international largesse was directed at the countries more heavily hit by Mitch.

169. Quoted in Pásara, *Paz, ilusion, y cambio,* 79.

170. "MINUGUA Weekly Situation Report 26 October–1 November 1998."

171. In retrospect, a better outcome might have been obtained for the accords by holding the referendum after the 1999 presidential and legislative elections.

172. These did not match the way MINUGUA had grouped the reforms in its information materials, so it had to rewrite those and print another set, with help from donors.

173. "MINUGUA Weekly Situation Report 24–30 March 1999."

174. "MINUGUA Weekly Situation Report 7–13 April 1999."

175. "MINUGUA Weekly Situation Report 5–11 May 1999."

176. "Siete nocivos errores sobre MINUGUA," op-ed piece for publication on *Siglo XXI,* attached to "MINUGUA Weekly Situation Report 18–24 August 1999."

177. See Mark Alleyne, "Manufacturing Peace Through International Communication Policies: United Nations Public Information Strategy in Guatemala 1996–2004," *Communication, Culture, and Critique* 1 (2008), 163–178.

178. "MINUGUA Weekly Situation Report 19–25 October 1998."

179. "Reformas constitucionales y consulta popular: lineas de política de trabajo de la Misión," undated, DPA files.

180. "MINUGUA Weekly Situation Report 28 April–4 May 1999."

181. Comisión de Acompañamiento de los Acuerdos de Paz, "Agenda de cumplimiento de los Acuerdos de Paz de Guatemala," undated, attached to Jean Arnault, "Political Parties and the Peace Accords," to Kieran Prendergast, September 22, 1999.

182. Jean Arnault, "Referendum," to Kieran Prendergast, May 17, 1999, and "MINUGUA Weekly Situation Report 12–18 May 1999."

183. Armando de la Torre, "La lección multiple," *Siglo XXI,* May 18, 1999, appended to ibid.

184. Jean Arnault, "Implementation of the Peace Agreements," to Kieran Prendergast, May 25, 1999.

185. Kieran Prendergast, "Implementation of the Peace Agreements," to Jean Arnault, June 2, 1999.

186. Multiple documents in DPA files reflect requests for these funds from various donors for some time after the referendum, for example, Thierry Delrue, "Cost Plan for One Project Funded from the First and Only Disbursement of Funds from the Fourth Danish Donation to the Trust Fund Through PRODECA," FAX to Warren Sachs, June 2, 1999. One hopes that these requests reflect reimbursements for funds already expended prior to the referendum, but they do reflect the lateness of the public education effort.

187. "MINUGUA's Weekly Situation Report 14–20 July 1999."

188. Kieran Prendergast, "Political Parties' Disregard for Referendum Outcome: Weekly Sitrep CGN-060 Refers," to Jean Arnault, July 26, 1999.

189. Jean Arnault, "UN Involvement in 1999 Electoral Process," to Angela Kane, July 16, 1999; and Jean Arnault, "Electoral Assistance," to Kieran Prendergast, July 27, 1999.

190. Jean Arnault, "Electoral Observation," to Kieran Prendergast, July 8, 1999 (document is a facsimile, misdated June 8, 1999. From context, and from later references to this document, July 8, 1999, is the correct date).

191. Jean Arnault, "Electoral Assistance."

192. John Tyynela, "Note on Meeting to Discuss Preliminary EAD Mission Regarding Electoral Assistance in Guatemala," July 29, 1999.

193. Jean Arnault, "MINUGUA's Involvement on Election Day," to Kieran Prendergast, October 18, 1999. The EAD's positions on this interoffice dispute may have been more reasonable than they appear in the written record, which is weighted heavily toward the MINUGUA perspective. Based on the documents I was able to consult, however, it appears that EAD was overly motivated to defend its exclusive role in election monitoring, while lacking the resources and local knowledge to follow through in Guatemala. Given scarce resources, it would seem more functional for EAD to support and advise established UN field missions rather than attempting to have a more separate role.

194. Aracelly Santana, "Mission Report of Mr. Riza's Visit to Guatemala," to Jean Arnault, October 19, 1999.

195. Jean Arnault, "MINUGUA's Involvement on Election Day," to Kieran Prendergast, October 18, 1999.

196. "MINUGUA's Weekly Situation Report 22–28 December 1999."

197. United Nations, "United Nations Verification Mission in Guatemala, Report of the Secretary-General," A/54/526, November 11, 1999.

198. Jean Arnault, "Adjustments to the Mission's Structure and Programme of Work," to Kieran Prendergast, April 7, 2000.

199. Jean Arnault, "Programme of Work 2000," to Kieran Prendergast, March 16, 2000; attached to this document was MINUGUA, "Conclusiones de la Tercera Jornada de Reflexión, Sololá, 24 al 27 de enero de 2000," March 12, 2000.

200. Ibid.

201. Ibid.

202. Jean Arnault, "Current Situation," to Kieran Prendergast, January 10, 2000.

203. "MINUGUA Weekly Situation Report 2–8 February 2000."

204. Ibid.

205. Jean Arnault, "Inauguration of the New Authorities and the President's Agenda," to Kieran Prendergast, January 17, 2000.

206. Jean Arnault, "Correspondence," to Kieran Prendergast, January 19, 2000, conveying copy of letter from Arnault to Secretary of Peace Rubén Calderón, dated January 18, 2000.

207. Ibid., and "MINUGUA Weekly Situation Report 26 January–1 February 2000," conveying a second letter to Calderón.

208. Jean Arnault, "Recommendation on the Future of MINUGUA in 2001 and Beyond," to Kieran Prendergast, May 10, 2000.

209. Jean Arnault, "Recent Incidents Giving Rise to Security Concerns for MINUGUA Staff," to Kieran Prendergast, Benon Sevan, and Bernard Miyet, March 6, 2000.

210. MINUGUA, "Conclusiones de la tercera Jornada de Reflexión."

211. Jean Arnault, "Recent Developments," to Kieran Prendergast, March 6, 2000.

212. "MINUGUA Weekly Situation Report 1–7 March 2000."

213. Arnault, "Recent Developments."

214. "MINUGUA Weekly Situation Report 29 March–4 April 2000."

215. "MINUGUA Weekly Situation Report 5–11 April 2000."

216. Arnault, "Recent developments."

217. Arnault, "Recommendation on the Future of MINUGUA." Ríos's remark was reported in "MINUGUA Weekly Situation Report 8–14 March 2000."

218. Arnault, "Recommendation on the Future of MINUUGUA," 5.

219. Ibid 9.

220. Eight of the offices covered 80 percent of the human rights cases.

221. Ibid.

222. Call, "War Transitions."

223. Author interview with a UN official who preferred to remain anonymous commenting on high-level officials' attentiveness to MINUGUA.

224. Luiz da Costa and Moller, "Mission Report."

225. Jean Arnault, "Panel on United Nations Peace Operations," to Iqbal Riza for Lahkdar Brahimi, April 27, 2000.

226. Ibid.

6

MINUGUA Deals
with Portillo, 2000–2002

WITH ARNAULT'S DEPARTURE at the end of May 2000, MINUGUA entered a critical moment during which the mission needed to adapt to a new and deteriorating situation. The failure of the constitutional reforms in 1999 had already sharply limited what could be accomplished. To implement the still-viable parts of the accords the government needed to show considerable initiative and leadership. Yet the opposite was happening: the Portillo government was increasingly incoherent. By the time Arnault left, prospects for progress were nil and there was a growing risk of reversals. Political attrition been especially accelerated for Portillo. In addition to frequent cabinet turnover and increasingly obvious corruption, Portillo's executive branch faced a fundamental political problem: the FRG majority in Congress generally opposed any goal of the pseudopopulist Portillo administration, even though Portillo nominally represented the same party. The FRG in Congress was more conservative than Portillo's administration, less concerned about international reputation, and was not particularly motivated to implement the peace accords. The other emerging feature of the Portillo administration was its breathtaking level of corruption, which came into focus as Portillo proceeded with a series of obviously unsuitable political appointments to high positions.

As USG Kieran Prendergast stated in a high-level meeting on Guatemala, "A peace process does not stand still—it either moves ahead or it reverses."[1] The strategic problem was finding a way to move the process forward against what Prendergast called "forces of resistance [that] are extremely strong." The mission's existing strategy seemed to have no effect on a government that was "in office but not in power," and that "[did] not know how to govern."[2] Whether one accepts Prendergast's progress-or-bust assertion, even to achieve stagnation (prevent backsliding) MINUGUA needed a new strategy.

For reasons that are unclear, the search for a replacement SRSG got under way late, after Arnault had already left the mission. His deputy, Juan

Pablo Corlazzoli (Uruguay) filled in as HOM ad interim. Senior officials in New York discussed possible candidates, and member states recommended their nationals, seeking market share of scarce SRSG posts. Selection criteria were partly professional, partly political, weighing individuals' expertise, personality, availability, nationality, and likely reception by the Guatemalan political elite. The initial list of candidates included nine names, but all were either unavailable or not quite suitable. After further discussions, Prendergast recommended that the Secretary-General select Rafaél López Pintor (Spain). López Pintor was highly qualified, and had been involved in Central American peace processes as a specialist on electoral processes and reform. Spain pushed for his candidacy, and it seemed likely that the Guatemalan process would be helped by stronger buy-in from Spain.

Nonetheless, the Guatemalan government rejected López Pintor. Under the emerging principle of universal jurisdiction for crimes against humanity, a Spanish court had indicted the president of the Guatemalan Congress, Efraín Ríos Montt, for genocide committed during his brief dictatorship (1981–1982). Rejecting López Pintor was one way the Guatemalans could express their displeasure.[3] The Secretariat then turned to Gerd Merrem (Germany), who had retired from the United Nations in 1998 after serving in a variety of senior positions including UNDP resident representative in three different countries and most recently as SRSG to Tajikistan. Merrem had experience in Latin America dating back to the 1970s, when he had coordinated the German Volunteer Program in Bolivia (and been detained for helping fly refugees out of the country—a detail he reported on his résumé). He also owned and spent considerable time on a farm in Nicaragua. He was acceptable to the Guatemalan government. Because of his seniority, Merrem was appointed at the Assistant Secretary-General level, a step higher than Arnault and thus a status upgrade of sorts for the mission.[4] All of this took two months, and Merrem did not arrive in Guatemala until August.

Before Merrem's arrival, discussions began within the Secretariat and the General Assembly about whether to renew MINUGUA's mandate, and if so, for how long. The Secretary-General's office accepted the basic design of Arnault's original "Inter-Agency Monitoring Project," but rather than closing the mission at the end of 2002, it would run through 2003. In exchange, however, the budget would be significantly reduced earlier than originally planned, so that the mission would need to scale back its staff significantly in 2001.[5] The extension through 2003 is puzzling. It did nothing to solve the problem that with Portillo in office through 2003, MINUGUA would still be doomed to preside over stagnation if not deterioration, and would leave behind an aborted peace process. Yet the URNG argued strenuously against even the 2003 limit (they wanted MINUGUA to remain at least through 2004). In their view a departure in 2003 in the midst of what was expected to be a polarizing electoral campaign could lead to a breakdown of the electoral order.[6] After a year in the mission, Merrem would find himself agreeing with the URNG that a 2003 closure was too soon and that an extension through 2004 would allow MINUGUA to work with a new president for at least a year and perhaps leave Guatemala under better conditions. Prendergast disagreed, stressing in meetings with Merrem the importance of the 2003 closure.[7] The extension from 2002 to 2003 proved to be the thin edge of the wedge, and the mission would end up staying through 2004.

▌ Merrem's Strategy

With limited time and with foreknowledge that the mission would soon begin drawing down, Merrem set about trying to generate enough leverage to get Portillo and the FRG bloc in Congress to make progress on the accords, with particular attention to the fiscal requirements of the socioeconomic accord. Taxation would prove to be a particularly intractable issue, and, with the benefit of hindsight, not the best emphasis for a mission with limited leverage. At the time, however, Merrem and his team saw sufficient state revenue as the sine qua non for implementing all other elements of the accords. The main potential source of leverage, of course, was to get donors to make their grants and loans contingent on compliance with the peace accords, especially the taxation component. Merrem found that the IMF, World Bank, and Inter-American Development Bank (IADB), despite having initially been supportive of the peace process, had reverted to routine, technical lending criteria and had not been making peace accord compliance a priority. He sought and received help from UN headquarters to change this, and was ultimately successful in orchestrating a consultative group meeting in Washington in February 2002 at which the donors lined up at least rhetorically in support for the peace agenda, and succeeded in extracting from Portillo a series of new commitments to demilitarize the state security apparatus, improve human rights, and (apparently with his fingers crossed behind his back) to fight corruption. Within Guatemala, Merrem continued MINUGUA's established practice of depending upon extraparliamentary political dialogue, in hopes of generating a strong enough social consensus around fiscal measures that Congress would feel obliged, and able, to act.

Unfortunately, the particular configuration of political power during the Portillo government made it difficult for even a semi-unified international donor community to get results. The core FRG leadership was ideologically committed to a small state. Moreover, they disliked the idea of handing more financial resources to the executive, much of which was controlled by "Portillista" appointees who were from outside the FRG party machine and politically left-leaning. The demands of foreign donors were not persuasive to legislators who did not necessarily *want* more money from abroad.

The mission's domestic strategy of promoting extraparliamentary dialogue and consensus building produced meager results. Civil society groups were so fractured and had such tenuous claims on representing any particular sector that they could not speak with much authority. Negotiated "fiscal pacts" did little to convince or incentivize the government to act on taxes. Moreover, the business community, which publically embraced the idea of a negotiated tax pact, was amazingly two-faced—first agreeing to tax increases and then using propaganda and its lawyers to block implementation.

While the FRG had no love for the business community and was willing to increase *business* taxes, the party quickly found that the private sector mobilized effectively against such moves, in large part by using the courts to block alleged "double taxation." This left the FRG with the politically unpopular option of increasing the value added tax (VAT), which it grudgingly accepted but only after first allowing the government to become insolvent.

Nor was it feasible for MINUGUA to convince the international community to dangle increased aid packages in front of the Portillo government as a positive incentive for better peace implementation. Corruption within Portillo's executive was so extensive and notorious that few if any donors would contemplate significant increases. Punitive cuts were more likely. Donors were particularly incensed by large transfers of money from civilian ministries to the Defense Ministry. The misappropriation was starving key institutions such as the National Civilian Police, the Public Ministry (prosecutors), and the courts, and was choking off the social spending required under the accords. Since the Defense Ministry refused to reveal any detail about how it was spending the additional money (on the laughable but unfortunately perfectly legal basis that doing so would compromise national security) donors strongly suspected that much of the transferred money was being stolen.[8]

The one area of common ground between MINUGUA and Congress was that Ríos Montt supported reforms that would decentralize government. Late in Merrem's term, Congress passed a trio of decentralization laws that effectively put more authority and funds in the hands of municipalities and local development councils, a level of government at which indigenous people had far more influence than they did at the national level. These measures could be useful in the long run, as UNDP's main strategy for carrying forward the peace process after MINUGUA left was to strengthen local-level development councils.

In pushing for overall tax and spending increases, MINUGUA probably picked the wrong fight. There were too many factors aligned against success in this venture, and it probably was not the most important fight at the moment. Tax-raising efforts had previously failed even with the more sympathetic Arzú government. It is generally bad practice to reinforce failure, yet this is exactly what MINUGUA did under Merrem: faced with stalemate on the fiscal question, it devoted most of its political resources to cracking this one problem, using mostly the same strategies that had failed previously.

While MINUGUA was tilting tax windmills, the Guatemalan state was being taken over by "hidden" or "parallel" powers consisting of criminal networks with connections within the customs service, military, police, and intelligence services. These networks challenged the integrity of formal state institutions in a way that the insurgency had never succeeded in doing.[9] In contrast to Arzú's administration, which took bold, if incomplete, measures to curtail the operations of some criminal networks, Portillo's government seemed to welcome the consolidation of the hidden powers. Portillo made a series of appointments that brought back into government individuals associated with the Cofradía criminal network that Arzú's government had sought to purge. Ill-considered (if not deliberately corrupt) appointments to the Ministry of Governance and the police crippled the law enforcement apparatus, while earlier progress stalled and reversed in the Public Ministry and in the courts. This allowed international and Guatemalan criminals, many involved in conveying drugs from South America to the United States, to consolidate their hold. The weakening and criminalization of the state would have catastrophic long-term effects on the country and would become *the* central problem of governance and state reform in the final year of MINUGUA and after its departure. Yet there is no evidence that the mission at the time understood the pace of change or its importance, and there was no associated change in strategy.

Human rights attorney Patrick Gavigan has argued that MINUGUA "had neither the tools nor the mandate to confront the 'violence entrepreneurs.'" MINUGUA was not a direct law enforcement agency of the kind that the United Nations deployed in Kosovo or East Timor. Nor did it have the coprosecutor status that would later be granted to the International Commission Against Impunity in Guatemala (CICIG) in 2008. It was clearly outmatched by the scope and resources of criminal groups, especially those embedded in the police and Public Ministry. However, MINUGUA did have mandates under both the Comprehensive Agreement on Human Rights accord as well as the Agreement on the Strengthening of Civilian Authority to both monitor and strengthen national law enforcement and justice institutions. It might have been able to use these mandates to escalate this issue to the top of the international and domestic political agenda for Guatemala. Yet MINUGUA limited itself to "reproducing essentially the same critique year after year" until its presence "became increasingly irrelevant."[10] At MINUGUA's December 2001 retreat, regional office directors and senior staff of the central office discussed the need to do something about the clandestine network of former military intelligence officers that was emerging as a main threat to the peace process, but concluded that "At the same time, it would be unwise for the Mission to take up the issue because its size and extended deployment expose it to violent reprisal. The suggestion was therefore made that an international commission of experts should be created with the task of compiling a report and make recommendations. Meanwhile, members of the Dialogue Group of major donors intend to raise this issue at the Consultative Group meeting in February."[11] No such report eventuated and the consultative group meeting focused more on financial matters than on the hidden powers problem, a crucial missed opportunity. While the security concern was a real one, and MINUGUA could not pretend to be a crime-fighting organization, its investigations into human rights cases and the functioning of police, prosecutors, and courts regularly uncovered blatant wrongdoing that deserved higher visibility condemnation, forcefully communicated to donors.

Back in New York, Prendergast, as well as Angela Kane (director of the Europe and Americas Division at DPA), realized that the mission needed to seriously rethink its priorities and strategy. MINUGUA seemed stuck in a rut. Aside from the emphasis on tax increases, most of the mission's work was devoid of strategy. The mission simply tried to do a little of everything, reflecting an internal organization that promoted thematic fiefdoms. Some of the foreign embassies in Guatemala joined DPA in urging the mission to choose a few critical issues on which to apply its limited political leverage. The representative of Norway, for example, asked the mission to place less emphasis on counting the *number* of pending agreements to be undertaken, and more on making changes of paramount importance that would begin to address the core problems.[12] In the same spirit, the United States asked the mission to place much greater emphasis on human rights.[13] The mission's January 2002 "Annual Review of Objectives" included a list of thirty-seven "priorities" spread over two and a half pages, begging the question of what part of the word "priority" the mission leadership did not understand.[14] In effect, the mission was duplicating internally the consensus-based agenda-setting dynamic that led Guatemalan civil society to produce broad and toothless accords in the first place. Then, having failed to set priorities internally, MINUGUA depended externally on the same extraparliamentary consensus-building mechanisms to build political support for implementation, even when these repeatedly failed to produce changes in actual policy. Meanwhile, the mission's institution-building efforts were stagnant at best (with the exception of the PROLEY project and a few others), just at the moment when the task of developing the capacity of Guatemalan institutions became most critical.[15]

■ The Fiscal Impasse, Again

During the two-month period when Juan Pablo Corlazzoli was running the mission (June and July 2000), the mission reported surprising apparent progress on raising taxes in support of the peace process. The Preparatory Commission for the Fiscal Pact produced an agreement at the end of May that included a commitment to reach the 12 percent tax burden target by the end of 2002, while ensuring the overall progressivity of the tax code. The main new source of revenue was to be an increase in the "Peace Value Added Tax" from 7 percent to 10 percent, supplemented by higher rates on existing business taxes and measures to strengthen administration and combat evasion, review loopholes, and so forth. CACIF and its main constituent business organizations signed on, as did most of the relevant civil society organizations and think tanks. The PAN, ex-President Arzú's party, refused to sign. Corlazzoli reported on all of this to New York with breathless enthusiasm: "the Tax Pact is one of the most important achievements of the peace accords as it simultaneously assures the possibility of strengthening the fulfillment of other agreements that require adequate resources in the national budget. Indeed, its effective application will determine the establishment of a firm and lasting peace."[16]

Unfortunately for Corlazzoli's reverie, there were early signs that the pact would not do well in Congress. Deputies from the FRG were not happy about being handed a package negotiated elsewhere. The dependence on the increased VAT made the bill a tremendous political liability for the FRG because the tax would affect such a broad cross-section of the public. Here again we see a gap between self-appointed civil society groups, who accepted the increased VAT as a cost of advancing the peace process, and the sentiments of the broader public as gauged by FRG deputies who would have to answer to the electorate for their votes.

When Congress voted in favor of a three-year tax package on June 22, 2000, the mission issued a favorable press release and reported happily to New York that CACIF—often a harsh critic of the mission—had actually thanked MINUGUA for its good offices.[17] On closer inspection, however, it turned out that the bill approved by Congress was not the bill that had been drafted by the Ministry of Finance that would have implemented the terms of the tax pact. Instead, the FRG had created a different bill that omitted the VAT increase and included new taxes on financial transactions. The total revenues it would produce were well short of the 12 percent called for in the accords. CACIF immediately objected, and called on the mission to be an "honor witness" between the FRG congressional bench and other stakeholders, apparently in hopes that the mission's presence in the talks would help inhibit the FRG from abrogating agreements so readily.[18]

The legislative failure led to marathon talks, convened by Vice President Francisco Reyes López, during which the FRG leadership once again engaged with CACIF and various interest groups on such questions as reducing tax incentives for export processing zones; reducing deductions; increasing taxes on alcohol distribution and government transactions (stamp tax); and increasing the VAT. They reached a revised agreement on June 28, and again the FRG Congress issued legislation that differed on key points from what had been negotiated.[19] Corlazzoli once again cabled New York with misleadingly effusive news about the importance of the negotiations: "Dialogue among sectors heretofore hostile to one another is a monumental milestone for the political culture of Guatemala. This does not mean that dialogue will not break down—there is always that possibility. But the political scene has witnesse [sic] a major 'shift of paradigm' under the new political context. The success of the tax pact will represent nothing less than a radical structural change for Guatemalan society."[20]

Merrem arrived in early August 2000 and during a round of introductory meetings learned that no "radical structural change" was imminent. Vice President Reyes López continued to convene tax negotiations between the legislature and CACIF, but by mid-August, CACIF was threatening to walk out. CACIF demanded that Reyes López no longer chair the sessions, which meant that the Follow-Up Commission would play this role instead. This put MINUGUA in the center of the process, as the mission had temporarily taken over the task of chairing the discombobulated Follow-Up Commission and would thus be convening talks between two of Guatemala's most contentious political actors, on one of its most intractable issues.[21]

Tensions around taxes soon erupted in the form of a scandal that came to be known as "Guategate."[22] Opposition politicians pointed out that a section of the tax bill affecting beverage distributors had been altered *after* the vote had taken place. Specifically, the new excise tax on alcoholic beverages and soft drinks had been reduced after the vote, creating suspicion that the FRG had been paid off by the bottlers. In communications with New York, MINUGUA defended the FRG, stating that the change corrected a discrepancy between what had been agreed to in the fiscal pact talks (a 10 percent rate) and the version that was voted upon (20 percent). Why MINUGUA thought the fiscal pact version should trump the voted-on legislative version is a mystery, as is the mission's haste to provide political cover for the FRG. According to MINUGUA's reporting, Vice President Reyes López, upon becoming aware of the discrepancy, called Ríos Montt and another FRG party member and asked them to make the adjustment. Apparently they did so without alerting congressional colleagues who had voted on the unadjusted version. Even this charitable interpretation reveals a shocking lack of regard for legislative process.

While MINUGUA rather credulously downplayed the importance of the change, opposition parties cried foul. As they began to investigate what had happened, they found that the video recording of the debate and vote had vanished, suggesting a cover-up. A separate audio recording of the proceedings by the *La Prensa* newspaper showed no sign of a proper revision process. Congressional president Ríos Montt claimed implausibly that tape was a fake, with someone else imitating his voice. Opposition parties demanded that MINUGUA hand over any information it had on illegal actions by FRG members of Congress, and called on the Supreme Judicial Court to appoint a special prosecutor.[23] The legal wrangling went on for fifteen months, as the question of whether congressional deputies would retain immunity from prosecution eventually went to the Supreme Judicial Court (which stripped immunity from twenty-four deputies in the case, including congressional president Ríos Montt). Ultimately, a lower court found insufficient evidence of wrongdoing and acquitted Ríos Montt and another congressional officer in April 2001, and the rest of the legislators a few months later.[24]

The private sector saw an opportunity to destabilize Portillo, and the national newspapers launched an editorial campaign accusing the government, with considerable grounds, of corruption, incompetence, and incoherence. Columnists suggested that Portillo should be forced out before the end of his term. MINUGUA learned that a private sector group had assembled US$3.5 million to fund a campaign against the government, retaining a public relations firm to ensure a steady barrage of negative news about the government.[25] As calls for Portillo's ouster became increasingly strident, MINUGUA bought a full-page newspaper ad calling for respect for the legal order and democratic institutions, which seemed to calm the waters for a time.[26] While it was certainly appropriate for the mission to argue against a coup d'état, one cannot help but wonder whether Guatemala would have been better off had Portillo's term been curtailed by constitutional means. There were almost certainly adequate grounds.[27]

By September 2000, both wings of the FRG were running away from the tax pact. President Portillo gave a speech rejecting the VAT outright, and saying that neither the executive nor Congress should be "pushed" into accepting the tax pact, implicitly blaming foreigners for doing the pushing. Congressional president Ríos Montt suggested that instead of raising taxes, the budget should simply be cut by 10 percent for 2001. In combination with the 10 percent rescission already in place since March 2000, this would mean nearly 20 percent cuts to funding for housing, health, education, rural development, and administration of justice. The FRG's position was a blatant rejection of the peace accords' call for increased social spending. Even the IMF, which had shown decreasing interest in the peace accords per se, wanted to see increased taxes because it feared deficit spending would create inflation and rising interest rates. Bilateral donors became increasingly disgusted with the government, and the Canadian ambassador told Merrem that Canada would halt new aid to Guatemala. All the relevant embassies in Guatemala agreed that the consultative group meeting of donors planned for November 2000 must be canceled. Merrem delivered this news to the government.[28]

Unswayed by international pressure, Congress passed a budget in November that imposed a 5 percent across-the-board cut, and eliminated funding entirely for a series of social service entities headed by Portillo appointees.

The budget still apportioned over 105 million quetzals (around US$13 million) to the EMP, a handsome sum for an institution that was slated to be abolished.[29] It would later emerge that between 2000 and 2003, some US$25 million was embezzled through the EMP.[30]

The economic situation was complicated further in early 2001 as international coffee prices sank, jeopardizing some 800,000 jobs as well as the income of 45,000 medium and small producers.[31] This bad news was followed in March 2001 by the near collapse of several large banks, three of which were taken over by the central bank at a cost of Q3 billion, while two others remained on the brink of insolvency.[32] One of Portillo's closest associates and largest campaign contributor, banker Francisco Alvarado MacDonald, was arrested for fraud after emergency government transfers to the "twin banks" he controlled proved insufficient to cover their huge losses.[33] In the midst of this crisis, the government itself ran out of money, requiring an emergency 2 percent increase in the VAT just to keep functioning.

Government insolvency led to a new political dynamic. The executive, having just rejected tax increases in January, suddenly began to argue that the whole pact should be implemented. The FRG in Congress continued to balk, and the resulting public debate led to absurd political theater such as CACIF's "Tax Mourning Day," on which the business association flew the flag at half-mast and draped it with black ribbons. The human rights ombudsman, Julio Arango, in a spasm of opportunism, hosted a meeting of student, labor, and human rights groups to protest any and all increased taxes, as if taxation were a human rights violation.[34]

In June 2001, Merrem met with Portillo to guide him in navigating the political crisis. Merrem recommended that Portillo identify a series of "thematic alliances," issues around which a variety of different sectors might rally, creating a minimum common denominator of measures that could be above the political fray. He suggested public security and human rights measures, fully implementing the government transparency elements of the fiscal pact, increasing citizen participation and decentralization, and providing more benefits to the indigenous population. Specifically, he advised Portillo to give a speech outlining these goals, and to hold meetings with Catholic bishops, indigenous leaders, political parties, and university rectors who had been leading one of the dialogue groups. It is rather astonishing that Merrem felt it was either necessary or appropriate to give the president of a sovereign state such specific guidance on what to do, what to say, and with whom to meet. This must be interpreted as a sign of Portillo's weakness. It is difficult imagining President Arzú ever having allowed such a conversation to take place. In any case, Portillo ignored Merrem's advice.[35]

Confronted with a political impasse, MINUGUA doubled-down on dialogue, despite having previously acknowledged that the private sector was manipulating the dialogue process to constrain "the government's maneuvering room while the government is slowly but effectively forced to alter its agenda." In a special report approved by Merrem in October 2000, the mission accused the private sector of trying to use the tax pact dialogue process to reverse the results of the 1999 election, in which its preferred, more business-friendly candidate, had lost.[36] This critical insight seems to have been lost by the following year. The mission hired a consultant (Salvadoran public finance expert Alexander Segovia) to "relaunch the fiscal pact process."[37] The Secretary-General sent his chef de cabinet Iqbal Riza to Guatemala in July 2001 to meet with the various political and economic elites in Guatemala and assess the situation. Guatemalan human rights NGOs told Riza that Portillo was just using the peace process to justify tax increases for corrupt purposes, which was more or less what many international donors thought as well. Riza ended his visit by reiterating the same failed strategy that the United Nations had used on this issue previously, proposing renewed dialogue on fiscal issues, notwithstanding the fact that dialogue had already produced a reasonable package that Congress would not pass. There was no getting around the fact that Guatemala had a majority-rule system. The FRG held an elected majority of seats in Congress, and the FRG did not want to raise taxes.[38] A CACIF delegation to Washington received a somewhat more direct message from the IMF, the World Bank, and the IADB: the fiscal issue must be resolved or Guatemala would lose international support.[39]

Perhaps thinking that drama could compensate for incoherence, Portillo declared his cabinet in permanent session and prohibited its members from leaving the capital. On the eve of the congressional debate on the requested tax increases, the executive put the PNC on alert and suspended leave for all staff. The Special Police Forces (a riot control group) carried out mock antiriot operations around the National Palace. The FRG in Congress saw this as an attempt at interbranch intimidation. Ríos Montt announced he might postpone the tax vote, and Portillo announced that the effort to raise adequate taxes would be suspended "only if I die."[40] CACIF threatened a general strike if taxes were increased. Labor unions and student groups organized demonstrations. Congress finally yielded to necessity (and international pressures) and passed an increase in the VAT from 10 percent to 12 percent in late July 2001, along with a few (weak) measures to increase transparency. Employers were required to provide larger bonuses to regular workers to compensate them for the increased VAT, so it became an indirect kind of business tax. The tax hikes were not enough to reach the delayed 12 percent-of-GDP target, but at least they would help the government maintain solvency.[41]

Having threatened a general strike, CACIF went ahead, orchestrating demonstrations and closure of up to 80 percent of businesses across the country. The strike extended even into smaller cities and towns in the indigenous highlands, where the Chamber of Commerce had affiliates. The protests were probably driven more by the "administrative" measures than the tax increase per se: plans to criminalize tax evasion had created an unlikely alliance of oligarchs and chewing gum salesmen. Even street vendors saw themselves at risk of being punished for not paying taxes on their meager informal sector incomes.[42]

The struggle over the VAT increase led to yet another scandal. During the post–tax hike protests, Chamber of Commerce president Jorge Briz condemned Portillo as "inept, corrupt, and incompetent" and called on him to resign. In response, a series of posters and fliers soon appeared around the country, accusing Briz of having ulterior political motives for opposing the tax increase. Unfortunately for the government, the posters and fliers were soon traced to the Government Printing Office, and apparently Vice President Reyes López had ordered their production and distribution. Former printing office director Sylvia Reyes turned whistleblower, and after receiving death threats was spirited out of the country by MINUGUA along with her family. A cover-up ensued in the printing office as plates were destroyed and about a ton of other printed propaganda materials disappeared.[43]

The private sector opposition that Briz had been voicing was at least in part legitimate: the Portillo government was so corrupt that a portion of any taxes collected would almost certainly be stolen. Still, it is difficult not to view the private sector as having acted in bad faith. When Congress corrected the "Guategate" scandal and increased excise taxes on beverages, the bottlers challenged the new taxes in court on the grounds of "double taxation," as well as on questions about the capacity of customers to pay. They won their case. In response, Congress raised rates on existing taxes and then extended new taxes to products not previously covered (juices, yogurt, and bottled water).[44] This legislative effort was for naught: facing yet another round of legal challenges that, regardless of the outcome, would delay implementation of any taxes, Congress agreed to lower the rates again in exchange for an agreement from bottlers not to bring further lawsuits.

International financial institutions including the IMF and IADB still wanted financial reforms to ensure adequate transparency and bank oversight, and this was especially urgent in the wake of spectacular bank failures surrounded by the stench of corruption. The IFIs took matters in their own hands and directly lobbied the FRG as well as opposition political parties, while helping to draft legislation.[45] Some of the measures, because they affected the powers of the central bank and the executive, required a two-thirds majority vote, so substantial opposition party support was essential. After months of lobbying from the IFIs as well as donor country embassies, Congress finally passed measures on banks and financial institutions in January 2002 by simple majority, just before the planned consultative group meeting. The rest of the bills—those requiring the two-thirds majority—were passed in April 2002.[46]

By the end of Merrem's term, the government had increased taxes just enough to continue functioning but not enough to make any progress on the peace agenda for reducing poverty, improving rural development, or strengthening institutions like the police or the judiciary. The 12 percent/ GDP tax burden remained out of reach. Congress also passed just enough financial reform legislation to obtain a standby agreement with the IMF, although the quality of implementation remained in doubt and tax evasion appeared to have increased. Despite the repeated rejection of the fiscal pact by the FRG in Congress, the pact does seem to have provided a framework that the FRG eventually had to respond to. However, it is unclear whether the fiscal pact dialogue process so prized by MINUGUA was the best way of achieving fiscal goals. What ultimately appears to have worked was the direct pressure applied on FRG deputies by the IFIs and donor embassies. Surely there was a more direct way for MINUGUA to have facilitated such an outcome.

■ Human Rights, Policing, and the Armed Forces

Besides the necessarily temporary role of MINUGUA as human rights monitor, the accords' main mechanism for improving human rights was centered in the Agreement on the Strengthening of Civilian Power and on the Role of the Armed Forces in a Democratic Society (AFPC), with its proposed restrictions on the military's domestic policing and intelligence roles, creation of civilian agencies to handle these tasks, reforms to strengthen the judiciary and prosecutors, reforms to enhance civilian oversight of the military, and abolition of the military's system of civilian patrols that had been responsible for so many rights violations during the conflict. If thoroughly and correctly implemented, the AFPC would have provided a strong basis for the rule of law in Guatemala: with the military confined to defense against external threats, its sweeping domestic powers and impunity would have been curbed along with the corruption and abuses that grew out of these powers. If one considers that the rule of law is the minimum function required of a state even from a libertarian point of view, this agreement was foundational. Its effectiveness would determine the success of the rest of the peace process.

Unfortunately, by the time Gerd Merrem arrived, implementation of the AFPC was already imperiled, and with it prospects for acceptable human rights conditions. Through a series of expedient but shortsighted decisions, the previous government of Alvaro Arzú had missed a critical opportunity to address the underlying causes of many human rights abuses. Arzú had failed to close the EMP, whose agents—during his term in office—murdered Bishop Gerardi and probably a number of potential witnesses, while unleashing a campaign of threats and intimidation against staff of ODHA and other advocates of accountability. Arzú failed to create an adequate civilian intelligence capacity, and failed to force the military to close down their domestic spying services, as required under the accords. He had gone about creating the "new" PNC by means of recycling the old National Police en masse, retaining the existing officer corps, and using completely deficient recruitment, screening, selection, and training strategies. Faced with a postwar crime wave, Arzú had drawn the military into law enforcement roles, including investigations into kidnapping cases that in all likelihood involved criminal networks at least loosely associated with the military itself. Nonetheless, Arzú had at least clamped down on one of the most notorious mafias—that associated with Alfredo Moreno Molina of the customs service, and had cashiered a number of officers implicated in wrongdoing, including General Luis Francisco Ortega Menaldo, who had previously headed the EMP and supported the 1993 auto-coup of President Jorge Serrano.[47]

Prospects for the rule of law deteriorated further under Portillo, and it is no exaggeration to say that his policies allowed criminal elements to become entrenched within the state in a way that may prove irreversible. Portillo brought in three retired military officers to be his closest advisers: General Francisco Ortega Menaldo, Colonel Jacobo Esdras Salán Sánchez, and Colonel Napoleón Rojas Méndez. All had been associated with Alfredo Moreno's contraband syndicate and all had been cashiered in Arzú's purge.

They became the powers behind Portillo's throne, influencing among other things the selection of leaders for the Interior Ministry (responsible for internal security), the PNC itself, the Ministry of Defense, and the EMP.[48] Portillo enhanced their power of appointment by sacking all the generals in the military and replacing them with less-experienced colonels, who would then owe their positions to Ortega, Salán, and Rojas.[49]

The search warrants executed in September 1996 as part of Arzú's actions against the Moreno gang had netted documents and computer files that identified some of Moreno's associates. Portillo's early appointments to the Ministry of Interior included two of the men so linked, judge Mario Guillermo Ruíz Wong (who headed the Interior Ministry from January through July 2000) and Major Byron Barrientos (ret.), who had been cashiered from the army for participating in a coup attempt in 1989 and who replaced Ruíz Wong as interior minister from August 2000 until November 2001. Portillo had shown a brief flash of independence when he attempted to appoint a former ORPA operative named Ricardo Marroquín, rather than Barrientos, to replace Ruíz Wong. However, the minister of defense and the army chief of staff went to the President's home at 6:00 a.m. to tell him that the armed forces were in a "state of alert" because of rumors of his appointment of the left-wing Marroquín. Portillo yielded to this delicately implied coup d'état, and appointed Barrientos.[50] Barrientos sought to enhance his standing by announcing that there were three new politically motivated armed groups in the countryside that must be combated. The PNC report on which he based his claim said no such thing, and after an initial burst of press attention, his alarmism developed little political traction.[51] After Barrientos fell to a corruption scandal, Portillo appointed the defense minister, Eduardo Arévalo Lacs, to become interior minister.[52] The new defense minister was General Alvaro Méndez Estrada, who according to MINUGUA reporting was said to be "Gen. Ortega Menaldo's creation." Méndez Estrada had served under Ortega Menaldo when he was head of G2 (military intelligence) during the Cerezo administration, then moved with him to EMP. When Ortega Menaldo was ousted after the Serranazo, Méndez's career languished until Portillo came in. Now he commanded the entire military, thanks to Ortega Menaldo.[53]

Although Arévalo Lacs formally retired from the military in order to take up the interior post, he was obviously still part of the informal military hierarchy, thus militarizing this key civilian rule of law ministry to an even greater extent. Moreover, as defense minister, he had proven reluctant to implement the accords, so his arrival at the Interior Ministry did not bode well.[54] In his capacity as interior minister, he initially impressed MINUGUA officials with his grasp of issues and his shared concern about the PNC's declining budget.[55] His appointments, however, tarnished that positive impression. He brought in Colonel César Francisco Nájera Avendaño as his deputy. Nájera was part of the hard right wing of the military, having been suspended for two years for his role in the 1989 coup attempt against President Cerezo, and was reportedly close with Byron Barrientos.[56] He also appointed a new head of the PNC who had been cashiered from the old National Police after heading a unit responsible for major human rights violations.[57] Thus Portillo's appointments combined corruption and militarization in a major setback to the civilian power agreement. As interior minister, Barrientos ordered local police post commanders to report on all their activities weekly to the local military commander, effectively subordinating the PNC to the military and making it impossible for the PNC to effectively investigate criminal activities involving army personnel. Arévalo Lacs deepened military control even further, and then, like his predecessor, resigned under a cloud of suspicion for involvement in drug trafficking.[58] He had purchased two homes valued at some US$725,000 since joining the cabinet, raising questions about where exactly he was getting that kind of money.[59]

It is not clear what Portillo's motives were for bringing Ortega Menaldo's coterie back into power. While their right-wing ideology was certainly in harmony with the prevailing thinking within the FRG, it fit poorly with Portillo's own quasi-leftist and populist leanings. These appointments may have been a necessary price for Portillo to have some degree of support and acquiescence from the FRG-dominated Congress, which, as noted earlier, disagreed with parts of his populist agenda as well as his left-wing appointments to some positions. More likely, this was simply a corrupt transaction: Portillo had formal political legitimacy that the Ortega Menaldo network could never achieve on its own. He appears to have traded his formal powers and (ephemeral) legitimacy for an opportunity to be cut in on the flow of illicit cash that only a large, well-organized network could generate.[60]

Portillo and his appointees arranged massive extra-budgetary transfers to the military, and the EMP, from other state agencies. During 2001, the military spent twice as much as had been allocated by Congress.[61] Spending increased from the 0.66 percent of GDP agreed to in the AFPC to 0.83 percent in 2000 and 0.96 percent in 2001, a flagrant violation of the accords.[62] The transfers were rationalized, in part, by a series of decrees that gave the military purview over activities that were clearly civilian in nature such as protecting historical sites, perimeter security around prisons, distribution of fertilizer to farmers, delivering library books and school lunches, and childhood vaccination campaigns. Former defense minister Julio Balconi insisted in media interviews that the military as an institution had never asked for such roles. Other experienced observers of the military agreed.[63] This suggests that the expanded powers mainly served the purpose of increasing the financial throughput of the military to facilitate embezzlement.[64] The EMP proved especially important for embezzlement because of the overall secrecy that surrounded its operations, and as noted earlier Portillo transferred additional funds to it and even obtained formal budgetary increases, despite the AFPC's requirement that it be abolished. Having announced in his inaugural speech that he would abolish the EMP, Portillo soon backtracked, saying, in effect, that the situation was complex and that the international community should not pressure him. After fifty years in operation, he said, the EMP "is one of the oldest and most efficient institutions" in the Guatemalan state. He did not specify "efficient" for what.[65]

Thus, in apparent pursuit of immediate financial gains, Portillo oversaw a comprehensive remilitarization of the state, combined with an increase in the scope of involvement of the armed forces in criminal networks. This trend devastated the capacity of the police, prosecutors, and courts to hold criminal networks accountable, even if they had been motivated to do so, and vitiated most of MINUGUA's erstwhile efforts to strengthen rule of law institutions. Portillo added a layer of militarization in the wake of the September 11, 2001, attacks on the United States, in the form of a new National Commission for Security, headed by a retired general.[66] The United States appears to have acceded to these steps post-9/11, including the selection of Arévalo Lacs as interior minister, on the grounds that ex-military officers could better insure the security of the international airport, an assumption that was questionable given the military's track record.[67]

The changes at the top set a new tone within the military, such that officers began to speak openly against the peace accords, something that would have been unthinkable during the initial implementation phase when defense minister Julio Balconi was still in charge. For example, in April 2001 the regional military command in Cobán held a "human rights seminar" at which participants declared the accords "stillborn" because of the results of the 1999 referendum and argued that there was no obligation to implement accords that had been negotiated by "an illegal group, a political party devoted to self-enrichment and a handful of military officers."[68]

The results of militarization and antidemocratic backsliding are recognizable in the patterns of human rights abuses that emerged during Merrem's term, based on the two human rights reports issued under his leadership (the twelfth and thirteenth reports, issued in August 2001 and 2002, respectively). Particularly disturbing were increases in the frequency of attacks and intimidation against organizations and individuals who were investigating past human rights crimes, as well as against investigative journalists and witnesses to crimes.

Both the twelfth and thirteenth human rights reports from MINUGUA cataloged an increasing number of killings in police custody, accompanied by falsification of arrest records by or with the consent of PNC superiors to cover up police involvement in deaths, torture, and beatings. There were at least two cases of disappearances at the hands of the police and municipal officials, neither of which were properly investigated.

A number of cases from these reports illustrates the deteriorating conduct of the police, including falsification of reports:

> More than 70 per cent of the admitted complaints of torture and cruel, inhuman or degrading treatment occurred in the departments of Petén, Guatemala and Cobán. In one case, Luis Méndez, a construction worker from Belize, was severely beaten on four occasions by police in Petén. Méndez had to have his spleen removed as a result of the beatings, during which his nose was also fractured; he was threatened with death and had a pistol shoved into his mouth. The Office of the Public Prosecutor opened an investigation, but the police in Petén falsified reports to protect those responsible. The officers who took part in the beatings remain on active duty.[69]

The internal affairs mechanisms of the PNC clearly did not function in the following case:

> On 25 October 2000, in Gualán, Zacapa, Rolando Barillas Herrera was arrested by two police officers, taken to the police substation and placed in a cell at midnight. Around five o'clock in the morning, a police officer found him dead, apparently hanged. The forensic report ruled out the possibility of suicide. According to the evidence, Barillas was beaten severely and, when he was close to death, he was suffocated to make it look like a

suicide. The investigations by the Criminal Investigation Service, the PNC Office of Professional Accountability and the Public Prosecutor's Office have not identified the culprits.[70]

Only rarely do the reports show the police hierarchy doing the right thing in the face of abuses by rank and file cops, as in the following case from the twelfth report:

Once [sic] such case occurred on 31 July 2000, when PNC officers Arnoldo Alonzo Méndez, Gabriel Ramos Ramírez and Juan Martínez Reynoso, assigned to San Juan Alotenango, Sacatepéquez, arrested José Sánchez Ascencio and took him to the local substation, where they beat him, submerged him in a barrel of water and gave him electric shocks. The next day, after he had been moved to the Antigua prison, the prison governor ordered his transfer to the local hospital because of the state he was in. The medical diagnosis indicated "intense abdominal pain, blood in the urine and internal trauma to the abdomen." To cover up the incident, the police officers drew up two police reports accusing the prisoner of committing a number of crimes at different times. The PNC Directorate-General ordered the officers' suspension from duty.[71]

Military personnel also appeared to have committed killings, with connivance of the PNC, as in this case from the twelfth report:

On 25 May 2000, men in army uniform, armed with rifles and driving a Military Zone 12 military vehicle, arrested Oscar Guzmán García and José Castañeda Alvarez. Between 28 and 29 May, two human heads were found on the banks of the Guacalate river. On 31 May, two decapitated bodies were found on the Alsancía estate in Escuintla. The heads and bodies were found to be those of Guzmán and Castañeda. According to the forensic report, the heads had bullet wounds and the bodies had stab wounds. The region's military authorities gave no information to the Mission and the National Defence General Staff provided information 11 months later. Neither the PNC Criminal Investigation Service nor the Escuintla prosecutor's office investigated the possible involvement of military personnel.[72]

There were signs of very strong pressures on the police not to look into killings that might involve military personnel. For example, in May 1999, businessman Edgar Ordóñez Porta had been kidnapped and then found murdered and mutilated. A military intelligence unit launched an investigation, ostensibly assisting the victim's brother who had brought a criminal complaint as "co-prosecutor." It became clear in the course of the investigation, however, that the military was deliberately misdirecting the investigation, following a series of made-up theories involving drug gang rivalries, debts, and extramarital affairs, while overlooking the more obvious motive that Ordóñez operated an oil refinery that competed directly with one in which military officers had interests. Instead of operating independently, the PNC and Public Ministry allowed their investigation to be derailed by the illegal military one. Ultimately two local men were brought to trial despite solid alibis and the availability of eyewitnesses who saw a vehicle belonging to the Interior Ministry (but assigned to Military Intelligence) at his abduction. They were acquitted, the Public Ministry never pursued other theories of the crime, and Ordóñez's killers got clean away.[73]

It appeared that shadowy forces used political violence at the highest levels to shape state policy. Following the February 2002 consultative group meeting at which Portillo promised to take serious steps to end impunity and corruption, armed men kidnapped the Central Bank president, and killed a key witness in the National Printing Office scandal. No one was held accountable for these crimes. In 2001, gunmen attempted to murder the wife, son, and daughter of former EMP commander and Patriot Party founder General Otto Pérez Molina, who would later become president of the republic. Given the history of rivalry between General Pérez Molina and General Ortega Menaldo (Ortega had supported the 1993 Serrano coup while Pérez opposed it successfully, subsequently replacing Ortega as EMP chief), it is likely that these attacks reflected a settling of old scores by the forces around Ortega Menaldo. General Pérez's daughter and daughter-in-law were both wounded in the attacks. In one of the most despicable acts, gunmen killed Miriam Patricia Castellanos by accident while she waited in traffic just a few yards from Mrs. Pérez's car. Apparently the gunmen confused the two vehicles. Then, when Francisco Arnoldo Aguilar, the widower of Ms. Castellanos, protested politically and called for accountability for his wife's killers, he himself was murdered outside his home. Significantly, the police and Public Ministry failed to carry out serious investigations into these attacks, despite the presence of credible witnesses.[74]

Another sign of deterioration included a massive jailbreak in June 2001 in which seventy-eight prisoners escaped from the country's highest security prison (on Byron Barrientos's watch). The government promptly declared a "state of alert," and established a curfew as police and security forces searched for the fugitives. MINUGUA identified two prisoners as having been central to organizing the escape, in collaboration with "parallel structures within PNC and intelligence agencies." The two were subsequently killed, and MINUGUA publicly questioned the PNC's official account that rival drug gangs were responsible for their deaths.[75] Perhaps the most revealing incident was an urban shoot-out between army G2 (intelligence branch) operatives and PNC detectives in February 2002 that resulted in the two soldiers dead and three cops wounded, including the head of the PNC detective unit. The incident, which the government claimed was a miscommunication during a stakeout operation, turned out to have been a struggle over possession of ransom money being transferred for the kidnapped Central Bank president![76]

The former PACs continued to be a problem, especially with regard to incidents of lynching. Tensions were particularly high in the department of Quiché, where local communities rallied against efforts by authorities to arrest two people who had been indicted for leading lynchings in 1998 and 1999. Locals even pushed for the departure of MINUGUA from the area because the mission had supported the arrest of ringleaders. Investigations by MINUGUA indicated that local PAC leaders were behind the mobilization.[77] The overall rate of lynching had declined in 1999 and 2000, but then increased again at the end of 2000. Some attacks were the customary murder of suspected criminals (such as three killed in October 2001 for stealing two cases of soft drinks, some animal feed, and groceries); but more frequently than in the past the attacks were directed against police and judges. The ostensible motive for the attacks was typically dissatisfaction with the lack of state anticrime measures or, perversely, officials' efforts to hold lynch mobs accountable. In some cases, though, criminals themselves organized attacks, as in the case of a local judge in Alta Verapaz who was stoned and burned to death by a mob incited by two criminals against which he had been taking measures.[78]

Portillo did take some tentative steps toward creating civilian intelligence and presidential security organizations. He formed the Secretariat of Administrative Affairs and Presidential Security (SAASP) that included an initial cadre of presidential bodyguards and that would replace the EMP. As noted, he then expanded the resources of the EMP and refused to demobilize it. He created a Civilian Information and Analysis Department (DICAI) within the Interior Ministry, which MINUGUA found to be "marginally in line with the peace agreement," but characterized by a weak system of controls. The mission's main concern was that DICAI could engage in both intelligence gathering and criminal investigations, which made it all too similar to the functions of the old Archivo within the EMP. Moreover, there were no restrictions on its composition, meaning it would probably be staffed by recycled military intelligence operatives.[79]

MINUGUA did a good job of reporting on the deteriorating human rights situation, as well as the failure of state reforms designed to address it. However, the mission could have acted more forcefully on the political front given the critical importance of these developments. In May 2002, the newspaper *El Periódico* took the mission to task for "lethargy and lack of action" after an employee of the Menchú foundation was murdered in a capital city cafeteria while someone phoned in funeral music to his office, and after a staffer of the rights group Center for Informative Reports on Guatemala (CERIGUA) was kidnapped by armed men who picked at him with a staple remover while telling him to "stop searching under the ground." In retrospect, the mission needed to carry out more concerted political action to sound the alarm about these developments and rally international pressure against abuses. In some instances, donors began to act independently of and more decisively than the mission on human rights concerns.[80]

The mission's ability to act on the parallel powers problem was limited by its declining capacity to gather, analyze, and act on political intelligence. With the downsizing of the mission beginning in 2001 (much of the planning for which had been done by Juan Pablo Corlazzoli as interim head of mission), police and military affairs had been deemphasized, and staffing reduced, with the result that the mission had fewer connections in these key institutions and weaker political intelligence on their activities.[81] There are signs of baffling naïveté regarding the parallel powers. When confidential informants approached the mission about the parallel powers, the mission seriously contemplated presenting their confidential information to President Portillo, and felt it was necessary to ask for guidance from New York as to whether this was a good idea (obviously it was not, since doing so would expose the confidential informants).[82] The mission also seemed to have difficulty analyzing and responding to the attacks and threats against human rights activists. After a set of particularly appalling attacks, MINUGUA reported to New York that the private sector might be involved in an effort to discredit Portillo.[83] In retrospect this was implausible, even ridiculous. The threats almost certainly came from military intelligence circles, now under the control of the old-guard leaders that Portillo had brought back into power. This faction had overwhelming incentives to avoid accountability for past crimes, and the mission could and should have acted very strongly to hold the government accountable for the threats and violence against rights activists.

To have any chance of counteracting all these adverse trends, MINUGUA would first have needed to fully understand them, and would need to have developed a strategy for uniting donors in holding the government accountable for supporting the rule of law. This would inevitably have required convincing donors to make linkages across issue areas: that is, there was not enough money at stake in rule of law programs, per se, to get the attention of the government and Congress. Multiple international aid programs would need to have been made contingent on progress on the rule of law. This sounds implausible, especially since as of August 2001, none of the donors were signaling that they were prepared to cut Guatemala off.[84] Yet when the consultative group finally met in February 2002, MINUGUA and the IFIs were able to accomplish a degree of conditionality with regard to the minimum necessary tax and transparency measures. The government knew that it was on thin ice with donors, and repeatedly postponed the consultative group meeting because they feared being held to account for their shoddy performance. In August 2001, for example, Portillo tried to cancel the proposed November 2001 consultative group meeting because of adverse commentary about the state of the peace process in the European press.[85] Had the mission devoted its ability to coordinate donors to preventing the remilitarization and criminalization of the state, it might have at least blunted these trends. As it was, the mission only dutifully reported, retrospectively, on the consequences.

The potential power of donor disgust was demonstrated at the very end of Merrem's term as HOM, when Portillo suddenly announced that he would cut the army from 33,000 to 20,000 troops, using the savings to fund social programs. He also promised to demobilize all seven hundred members of the EMP by September 2002.[86] This about-face was catalyzed by a sharp confrontation with international donors over Portillo's overly generous response to protests by ex-patrollers, who had seized the vital archaeological and tourist sites at Tikal in the Petén, demanding compensation for wartime services. Portillo too eagerly promised ex-patrollers a handsome payment package. MINUGUA issued a statement denouncing any plans to pay patrollers at a time when compensation had not yet been paid to human rights victims and their survivors. Donors reacted immediately, saying, in the words of the Swedish ambassador, "not one peso."[87] Portillo's announced military cuts appeared to be an effort to restore his standing with the donors, reinforced by a two-hour meeting with the so called Group of Twelve countries during which he promised to find an alternative to the transfers to ex-patrollers.[88]

◾ Exit Strategy

With the mission slated to close at the end of 2003, and with an agreement to cut the mission's budget substantially in its final year, MINUGUA needed to develop and implement an exit strategy. Portillo clearly would not implement most of the accords, and it was impossible to know whether his successor would do more. A key period of opportunity had been missed in the first two years of peace implementation, and internal discourse in Guatemala had shifted toward viewing the accords as an agenda that would inform future development efforts rather than as a binding agreement whose terms the state needed to implement within a specific time frame. In that context, the original concept of MINUGUA as a verification mission became less relevant than its potential as a special, short-term development agency. If the peace accords were further implemented at all, it would take place on a time scale far longer than the United Nations could maintain a mission. Thus MINUGUA needed to do whatever was possible to leave behind a domestic capacity to monitor and expand human rights, improve state institutions for law enforcement and justice, and create and protect political space for the poor and marginalized to mobilize to meet their basic needs.

While clear enough in theory, actually doing this was extremely difficult. The United Nations had to work with local counterparts as they were and was usually not in a position to transform those that were not up to the tasks before them. The most important ones were the Follow-Up Commission; political parties; the PDH; various NGOs involved in human rights monitoring and prodemocratic or social advocacy; civil organizations representing various sectors and interest groups; the UNDP, which would become the central permanent UN presence in the country after MINUGUA closed; and various specialized UN system agencies. Sadly, all of these counterparts either had limited capacity or willingness to take on elements of MINUGUA's role in the long term, or were difficult for MINUGUA to cooperate with long enough to transfer any skills or capacities. This section will review each of the main potential counterparts, to illustrate both how difficult a problem MINUGUA faced as well as how the mission's own approach exacerbated tensions that might have been resolved.

As noted in Chapter 2, representation on the Follow-Up Commission privileged the URNG and the executive branch. It included two members each from these parties, a single representative of Congress, and then four other individuals who were not really representative of any constituency. During the early phase of peace implementation, the Follow-Up Commission had played a fairly important role through its authority to review legislation and reschedule commitments. But its composition had reduced opposition parties' sense of ownership over the peace process, and the Follow-Up Commission's importance had declined over time. Under Portillo, it became almost completely irrelevant. The representatives of the executive did not represent the FRG in Congress, which held veto power over almost any important measures. Meanwhile, the URNG was imploding. The different parties within the former rebel movement were in conflict, and the movement as a whole was in such a deep financial crisis that they were evicted from their party offices.[89] The URNG representatives did not reliably appear at Follow-Up Commission meetings, even when the commission was handling issues that should have been priority concerns for them. The private sector representative resigned and was not replaced, as did another of the private citizen members, and MINUGUA officials were often asked to chair sessions that barely made quorum.[90] MINUGUA ran a trust fund project to help institutionalize the Follow-Up Commission and provide it with more of a public information capacity, but the political fundamentals made the Follow-Up Commission a hopeless cause.[91]

Political parties themselves might have been advocates for long-term implementation. The PAN, as the main negotiator of the accords, ought to have had a vested interest in defending that achievement. But even the Arzú government, as signer of the final accords, had been an indifferent implementer. The political payoff was not there. During the Portillo years, the PAN splintered into multiple smaller parties, and its most credible potential presidential candidate, Oscar Berger, split from the PAN to run under a coalition of three other parties in 2003. The PAN's own candidate would gain only 8 percent of the popular vote in 2003 and the party took only 17 out of 158 congressional seats in the same year, an abrupt decline. The URNG could also have been expected to promote the accords, but the party did not even use the formal, institutional power of its seats on the Follow-Up Commission. By 2001, the URNG was in such disarray that it needed a briefing from senior MINUGUA staff regarding the content and status of the peace accords![92] Besides providing public information, there was nothing MINUGUA could do within its mandate to rescue these parties, but their demise did remove a potential base of long-term advocacy for the accords.

Since human rights protection had been central for MINUGUA from the outset, and since conditions were deteriorating under Portillo, it was particularly important for the mission to build local capacity to carry on this work after it closed. Unfortunately, the head of the PDH during this period, ombudsman Julio Arango, behaved in an increasingly erratic way. In his last two years in office, Arango was seen dismissing employees arbitrarily (while brandishing a handgun in one case), holding a conference with PDH funds to establish a political party (for himself), and eventually ordering all his subordinates to have no contact at all with MINUGUA.[93] MINUGUA responded in kind, as the head of the mission's human rights section refused to speak with Arango following earlier disputes. MINUGUA subsequently created a special committee to rebuild its connections with the PDH, but the relationship seemed poisoned. The mission would have a chance for a fresh start when a new ombudsman was selected in 2002.

Had Arango's personality not been so problematic, it might have been possible for MINUGUA to help address the structural problems of the PDH, including its lack of vehicles, access to gasoline, adequate office space, computers, and radios that could function in remote areas. There was inevitably tension between the impoverished PDH and the comparatively well-equipped MINUGUA, and if the mission could have been seen as having brought greater international aid to the PDH, this might have eased that tension. Yet it is hard to make the case that any donor should have been generous with an institution that was under such poor leadership. This was a true dilemma that was never fully resolved.[94]

Even with the problems at the top of the PDH, MINUGUA might also have taken earlier steps to, for example, colocate its offices with the PDH and work alongside PDH staff to jointly investigate cases at the local level. In practice, concerns about control over confidential data and the insulation of investigations from political considerations dissuaded MINUGUA from sharing openly with the PDH. Given the uneven quality of PDH leadership, and the risk that the PDH staff could be infiltrated by military intelligence or other organizations linked to human rights abuses, these were reasonable precautions in the early stages of the mission. But the integrity of MINUGUA's investigations came at a cost in terms of reduced prospects for building local capacity. Privileging information security was essential in the early, dicey stages of the mission, but the lack of organic linkages to the PDH became an increasingly critical obstacle to long-term effectiveness. As the years passed, it appeared to outside observers, fairly or not, that MINUGUA staff fundamentally distrusted Guatemalans and were perhaps trying to prolong their own mandate.[95] The trade-off between the integrity of investigations and the ability to develop local capacity is a basic dilemma that deserves more attention.

MINUGUA's ability to work with and help develop national NGOs was similarly handicapped. The integrity of its own investigations required MINUGUA to embargo information until it was prepared to make an official report on a given case. Local NGOs wanted to participate and contribute to investigations, and were often frustrated by the mission's unwillingness to share information. Having endured years of oppression at the hands of state intelligence structures and parallel powers, Guatemalan NGOs were prone to perceiving conspiracies and political motivations in ambiguous cases. They often accused the mission of covering up crimes or being too close to the government. In some cases it was simply a question of timing: Guatemalan groups were quick to connect the dots when potentially political violence took place, whereas MINUGUA necessarily withheld comment until it could gather more information, a policy that was often vindicated as early information proved inaccurate or incomplete. On some issues, it was MINUGUA that took a hard line, challenging and criticizing the positions of local NGOs. For example, Guatemalan NGOs reacted angrily when MINUGUA faulted them for not taking a stronger position on lynching, ethnic discrimination, and the death penalty.[96]

There was a broader political issue between the mission and local NGOs. Many NGOs loathed the Portillo government and were willing to risk disturbing the constitutional order to see Portillo removed before the end of his term. During the intense media campaign for Portillo's removal in 2000, the mission stepped in to defend the government's right to remain in office against both open and whisper-campaign calls for his premature removal. These efforts to dampen political volatility angered NGOs that positioned themselves in uncompromising opposition to Portillo. The NGOs saw MINUGUA as too cozy with the government, and criticized the mission for this publicly. It might still have been possible for MINUGUA to do more to build up the NGO sector, but these basic philosophical and policy differences created obstacles.

More broadly, MINUGUA's relationship with civil society groups was complex and ambiguous. On one hand, the mission frequently encouraged dialogue processes that involved these groups. On the other hand, the mission did not trust civil society groups and NGOs to cooperate in its efforts to steer the Portillo government toward better behavior. While planning the consultative group meeting for late 2001 (ultimately held in February 2002), the United Nations fretted that civil society groups would turn the consultative group meeting into a pillory of the government for its poor performance, rather than support the general goal of ensuring adequate (and conditional) international funds for the peace process. Civil society groups and NGOs felt that the consultative group meeting would simply help the fragile Portillo government survive, and perhaps steal more money, rather than help the country as a whole. On these grounds, they were reluctant to participate in the consultative group meeting, and were likely to be unpredictable if they did participate.[97] There was, in short, a degree of latent and sometimes overt distrust and disagreement between the mission and Guatemalan civil society.[98]

The only bright spot was the Guatemalan Congress, which surprisingly ratified eight international conventions on human rights matters, as well as other legislation broadly supportive of the peace accords. These included conventions and protocols prohibiting discrimination against women and disabled persons, prohibiting most forms of child labor, defining the rights of children, and prohibiting the fabrication and trafficking in arms. Additional measures passed during this period included a favorable municipal code as well as laws criminalizing various kinds of discrimination; strengthening antifraud and labor protections; implementing greater administrative decentralization; and supplementing the earlier-mentioned laws on financial oversight, tax collection, and enforcement. The scope of legislative achievements is all the more surprising given the often-negative posture of the majority FRG toward the peace accords. Skillful application of pressures from donors was part of the story, but substantial credit goes to MINUGUA's low-profile PROLEY project, whose job was to assist the legislature in the drafting of legislation. Guatemalan legislators were by and large inexperienced in the drafting of laws. Congressional leadership therefore welcomed technical assistance from PROLEY, which used this entrée to build lasting working relationships with legislators. Thus we see the anomaly of an ultraconservative Congress, in the midst of a disastrous presidential administration, moving ahead with legislation that was, broadly speaking, prodemocratic.

Given the overall weakness of most of the Guatemalan domestic counterparts, Arnault's Inter-Agency Monitoring Project (IMP), with its emphasis on handing verification functions over to specialized UN agencies, was still the basic blueprint for MINUGUA's exit. Yet the plan was fundamentally divorced from the realities of the UN system agencies, which were unprepared, unfunded, and unwilling to take on the roles they were being asked to inherit. The IMP would require the various agencies to collect information on government implementation of the accords, with UNDP coordinating the effort. The original IMP called for a small UN political office to replace

MINUGUA in 2003, but that had been revised already to extend the mission, with a much-reduced staff, through 2003, and there were no specific plans for a follow-on political mission. The IMP would depend on inputs from UN system agencies to issue reports on compliance and communicate with the government about any problems verified. As noted in Chapter 5, initial contacts with the agencies elicited reluctance. This reluctance persisted during Merrem's term. During meetings in 2000, government representatives expressed doubts about the feasibility of the IMP, arguing that the UN agencies did not have the capacity to take on technical cooperation tasks that were politically sensitive and based on the "verification model" as opposed to the "classic cooperative approach" of the development agencies.[99]

Despite signals from the Secretary-General that he wanted the plan implemented, it was infeasible: the most relevant agencies were UNDP, the Food and Agriculture Organization (FAO), the International Labor Organization (ILO), the UN Educational, Scientific, and Cultural Organization (UNESCO), and Office of the High Commissioner for Human Rights (OHCHR), but the latter four had "negligible or no representation" in the country.[100] They lacked the budgets to do verification work, and the Secretary-General's report on the extension of MINUGUA's mandate and the IMP made no mention of corresponding funding. It was as if the UN Secretariat expected the agencies to magically provide services that up to that point had been costing on the order of US$30 million a year. The UN resident representative (and head of UNDP) in Guatemala, Lars Franklin, wrote directly to the Secretary-General in October 2000 pointing this out. Development assistance to Guatemala was declining sharply, he wrote, and UN agencies' core budgets had been slashed in recent years. "We are scarcely able to carry out our existing obligations under the Peace Accords, let alone assume new ones."[101]

Agencies were particularly concerned that they lacked the branch offices and nationwide deployment of staff that would be essential to verify conditions in rural areas. There was also the question of whether the leadership of UN system agencies could be autonomous enough from the government.[102] In some cases, representatives of government sat on their local boards. Moreover, as Merrem pointed out in a frank meeting with UN agencies in New York, Guatemalan nationals made up most of their senior staff, and many of them had family or political ties to the national political elite. Merrem questioned whether they could reasonably be expected to objectively verify peace accord compliance and criticize government, especially since their agencies were by charter obligated to be primarily responsive to government priorities.[103] The extensive linkages between system agencies and the government could cut the other way as well. A UNDP project paid the salary from 1997 through 2002 of the government's Technical Peace Secretary, a post within the Peace Secretariat (SEPAZ). The director of the UNDP project occupied this post, and represented SEPAZ in negotiations with the URNG over peace implementation, with mediation by MINUGUA. Thus, for a time, planning for how the government would implement peace-related projects was being carried out by UNDP, the URNG, and MINUGUA, with no real participation by the government![104]

Even if the IMP had been feasible, relations between MINUGUA and UNDP were strained and cooperation hard to achieve. After her February 2001 visit to Guatemala, Angela Kane wrote "an attitude of competition remains evident despite a façade of bonhomie."[105] The façade then dissolved into open bickering, as Merrem wrote to DPA repeatedly complaining about perceived slights by Franklin, who failed to acknowledge Merrem's status as SRSG and sometimes involved UNDP in public statements on overtly political matters that were the purview of MINUGUA.[106] It is unclear to what extent this was genuine interagency competition, or whether the very experienced Franklin simply lost patience with Merrem. This situation improved temporarily when Franklin left Guatemala in March 2001 and was succeeded, at the strong urging of DPA, by MINUGUA's former deputy head of mission Corlazzoli. Once Corlazzoli was installed in an interim capacity, DPA in New York pushed UNDP hard to waive an examination that Corlazzoli would have to pass in order to become the permanent resident representative.[107] The expectation was that since Corlazzoli knew the peace accords in detail, and had served in the verification mission, he would be more supportive of that transition and more likely to cooperate with MINUGUA. As we will see in the next chapter, this proved a vain hope, as Corlazzoli rewarded DPA's support by appropriating MINUGUA's political role, eliciting outrage from Merrem's successor as SRSG.

In the final months of Merrem's term, thinking in New York had shifted somewhat regarding the IMP. DPA political officer Martha Doggett wrote a white paper suggesting that the mission stop thinking in terms of a "transfer of functions" to system agencies. Rather, MINUGUA should pick a few areas in which progress that was consistent with the peace accords could be made, and to the extent possible engage the "full gamut" of Guatemalan actors to carry these forward. The essence of the transition would be to move from verification to "accompanying Guatemalans as they become the protagonists." She recommended a succinct adjustment of expectations: "The wholesale transformation that the accords envisage will take place over the next many generations."[108]

▌ Mission Management

While MINUGUA faced a particularly daunting set of challenges during this period, it is also clear that the mission struggled in part because of internal problems that blunted its ability to adapt, create a sound strategy, and implement it. Merrem seemed unable to foster a well-functioning mission, much less an environment conducive to creative rethinking. He could come across as jovial, with a joke for every occasion, but he was also quirky, sometimes undiplomatic, prone to holding forth about Guatemala's system of "apartheid," and too often unaware of what was going on within the mission.[109] Among the problems that he should have addressed was that senior mission staff were deeply entrenched and divided into antagonistic cliques.[110] Field coordinators felt neglected by headquarters, and information still flowed poorly between the regional offices and Guatemala City, especially as staffing levels declined in the regional offices.

Merrem also had a tendentious working relationship with his deputy. When DHOM Juan Pablo Corlazzoli left MINUGUA to become the resident coordinator for UNDP, his replacement, the high-energy Laura Canuto (Italy), set about trying to get the mission to function better. This immediately generated tensions, because Merrem thought the mission was fine as it was. He disagreed with most of Canuto's assessments and her proposed remedies, some of which did indeed seem overzealous or unrealistic. Among other things, she wanted to consolidate all administrative powers in her own hands, eliminating the chief administrative officer position. She was correct in her view that the office of the CAO often failed to serve the best substantive interests of the mission (as previous heads of mission had noted), but her proposed fix would probably have so overloaded her as to interfere with her substantive duties. Canuto also strenuously disagreed with the head of the human rights section on both organizational and political questions, inevitably resulting in tensions within mission headquarters.[111] Although she accomplished important things, such as identifying US$3 million in trust fund monies that had not been tapped, her interpersonal style offended Merrem, who complained to New York about what he considered her overly harsh manner in dealing with subordinates.[112] Working in the mission at the time was, in the words of one former staffer, "like working in an asylum." Canuto wanted personal loyalty from her subordinates while Merrem stood aloof.[113] Given all the indications of problems within the mission and with Merrem's leadership, there is little doubt that Canuto had cause for impatience, yet her imperious style seems to have heightened tensions. Regardless of how one allocates responsibility, it is clear that internal divisions, rather than being resolved, became more acute and dysfunctional during Merrem's term and extended to the top levels of the mission.[114]

Angela Kane visited MINUGUA in February 2001 and came back with a disturbingly negative assessment of the state of the mission. Kane found a surprising combination of high leadership turnover (six of eight regional directors were new, as were seven heads of substantive areas) and inability to adapt. One would expect that new leadership would bring fresh perspectives, but instead there was a pattern of retaining existing personnel and transferring them to new positions, "not always in their field of substantive knowledge." Some senior staff remained from the mission's opening in 1994. Reductions of international professional staff from 142 to 87 had hit the regional offices especially hard. UN Volunteers directed most of the subregional offices, something that at an earlier stage HOM Leonardo Franco had declared unacceptable, even on a temporary basis.[115] Long vacancies, lack of consistent leadership, and increased workloads "contributed to internal disorientation, frustration and less than optimal attention given to areas such as human rights and indigenous rights. This has also provoked comments from external actors that MINUGUA is distancing itself from the peace process and that the new HOM's brief is only to shut down the mission." Kane stressed that the mission needed a high degree of cooperation and a clear strategy. "This was, however, not evident during the third day of the MINUGUA retreat that I attended, where the work plans and objectives presented were rather general and generic and where the level of frustration with the mission leadership surfaced quite openly."[116]

Cables from New York to the mission, as well as interoffice memos within DPA, suggest that Merrem's superiors did not have full confidence in his handling of the mission.[117] Prendergast and Kane repeatedly pushed Merrem to define a strategy to get the Guatemalan political actors to do more to advance the peace agenda, and to prepare the ground for MINUGUA's departure.[118] Routine mission reporting often lacked sufficient detail on key issues such as taxation and transparency, making it difficult to determine from afar when real progress was being made. Moreover some of the political reporting from the mission was absurdly rosy. After USG Iqbal Riza visited Guatemala in August 2001, for example, Merrem cabled New York objecting to a New York–produced internal report that referred to political "instability," suggesting the term "polarization" instead, though obviously "instability" was accurate. He argued for a more optimistic tone regarding the proposed fiscal pact, claiming that although the government had thus far failed to implement the fiscal pact in its entirety, "it has accepted the principle of full implementation and has not taken a position of opposition."[119] Another example of boosterism was a cable that summarized the contents of President Portillo's 2001 state of the union speech, acknowledged that almost all Guatemalan political actors and observers scoffed at Portillo's inflated claims, and yet concluded that "Nevertheless, the Mission believes that should the President succeed in implementing the ambitious plans he has laid out for 2001, it will indeed make concrete and important steps in consolidating the peace process and addressing the causes that led to the armed conflict."[120] A more realistic assessment would have been that Portillo was engaged in more "virtual" compliance with the accords, saying the words while avoiding action. From this remove, we can't know whether Merrem was overselling the Guatemalan reality because he was in denial, defending his own role, or trying to protect the mission. Regardless, there were serious flaws in political reporting. Even formal public documents such as MINUGUA's draft of the Sixth Secretary-General's verification report on Guatemala were flawed and required strongly worded corrections from New York.[121]

In multiple cables and memos, New York officials admonished Merrem for not having kept them adequately informed, not consulting on key decisions, releasing documents that should not have been released, using improper communication channels for sensitive information, and having gone against DPA advice, especially regarding personnel matters.[122] Merrem cabled back expressing offense and frustration at the questioning of his actions, complaining about overly cumbersome approval processes, and insisting that in all cases he had in fact communicated the information required.[123] In his end of assignment memo, Merrem suggested that New York focus on substantive and policy-related matters rather than administrative micromanagement, and noted that there had been frequent turnover in the desk officer position for Guatemala within DPA during his term, with the result that he lacked a consistent sounding board and point of contact in New York.[124] Most likely there were errors of perception and inadequate communication on both sides. In any case, from a strategic point of view, Prendergast and Kane did have grounds for concern. Merrem had succeeded in temporarily herding the donors into something resembling coordinated actions, but he had not succeeded in reformulating the way the mission operated.[125] As Kane remarked in a note to Prendergast in 2002, MINUGUA had been placed on notice that it needed to prepare the ground for its own departure. "This should have translated into a new way of thinking and doing business at all levels. Unfortunately, this has not happened to the extent desirable."[126] Merrem seemed satisfied with the existing staff and style, yet by any objective standard, the peace process was foundering and MINUGUA with it. In a July 2001 editorial, the newspaper *El Periódico* remarked sharply that MINUGUA had turned itself into a mere "supervisor of the formalities of the accords" and this was not wide of the mark.[127]

While New York officials were critical of MINUGUA's approach, when they themselves did get directly involved, there did not seem to be any dramatic change in strategy or increase in political leverage. Visits by Under-Secretary-General Iqbal Riza and by Prendergast had little impact. If anything, Riza's visit led to further deterioration of UN relations with the NGOs with which MINUGUA needed to work to have an effective exit strategy.[128] Because the mission's internal and strategic shortcomings were not addressed, we can never really know whether a better-operated, more strategic mission could have stemmed the tide of deterioration under Portillo. Even optimally managed, MINUGUA's political resources might simply have been insufficient to overcome the pecuniary and ideological preferences of Guatemalan political elites.

■ Conclusion

The mission's greatest success during Merrem's term was its preparation—in close collaboration with UNDP and the IFIs—of a consultative group meeting in February 2002 at which the most important international donors were unified and imposed "constructive conditionality" on the government to follow through with the peace process.[129] Of course, even strong conditionality might not sway the Portillo government, but at least, for once, the mission and the donors spoke with one voice in support of the accords. The fact that the mission's greatest accomplishment was an improved process, not an improved outcome, says much about the United Nations' limited power in Guatemala.

The more coordinated consultative group meeting was possible because things were so obviously unraveling in Guatemala that donors were more receptive to political coordination by MINUGUA. I have suggested that MINUGUA might have exploited donors' greater willingness to coordinate to apply pressure on just a few issues, and that a priority on the rule of law might have been more timely in light of the crumbling of the formal state under Portillo. Instead, Merrem took the taxation issue head on, perhaps accepting too readily the priority concerns of the IMF and the development banks. This was a losing proposition, an issue on which it was impossible for the FRG to move ahead. Meanwhile, Portillo's administration allowed core state institutions to be taken over by organized criminals, consolidating a problem of hidden powers and fundamental lawlessness that remains years later as the gravest challenge to Guatemala's future.

Merrem's term at MINUGUA illustrates especially starkly the United Nations' persistent lack of strategy in Guatemala. Perhaps influenced by a misguided formalism, MINUGUA was unable to break away from the original, quickly obsolete view that it should verify, and promote progress on, all aspects of the accords, in spite of clear evidence that comprehensive progress was unlikely and that the mission had comparatively little political leverage. MINUGUA also persisted in its seemingly reflexive dependence upon dialogue processes in the face of repeated evidence that what ultimately mattered was the willingness of the legislature to pass laws. Legislators were not much swayed by consensus building among interest groups that were not particularly representative of the electorate. Peacebuilding is ultimately a political process, and the mission too often forgot that effective politics generally implies working within existing institutions to get things done. When the mission did remember this, as was the case with the PRO-LEY project in the legislature, surprising achievements resulted.

■ Notes

1. Susan Soux, "Briefing Note to Ms. Angela Kane: Guatemala—Executive Committee on Peace and Security," to Angela Kane, November 20, 2000.
2. Ibid.

3. A few months later (December 2000), the Spanish courts waived jurisdiction, on the grounds that the Guatemalan amnesty law excluded genocide and that the case could be pursued there. This was, of course, only a theoretical possibility given the weakness of the Guatemalan courts. In 2006, Spanish courts took up the issue again, indicting Ríos Montt and other officers who were in command during the peak years of repression.

4. Arnault had been a political officer (P-5) at the time of the peace negotiations, and had been promoted by the Secretary-General to Director-1 in recognition of his exemplary service in the peace talks. He was then given a further temporary increase to Director-2 status in accordance with his scope of responsibilities in MINUGUA. Normally the head of a mission of this size would be at the ASG level, but there were limits to how far Arnault could be promoted within so short a time frame. Angela Kane, "Special Representative of the Secretary-General and Head of Mission—MINUGUA," to Iqbal Riza, June 28, 2000.

5. María José Torres Macho, "Note to Ms. Kane: MINUGUA's phase-out strategy," to Angela Kane, June 13, 2000; Kieran Prendergast, "MINUGUA's Future in 2001 and Beyond," to Juan Pablo Corlazzoli, June 16, 2000.

6. Juan Pablo Corlazzoli, "Meetings with Government and URNG Regarding Extension of MINUGUA Mandate," to Kieran Prendergast, June 25, 2000. This proved to be prescient, as significant violence erupted in mid-2003 as Efraín Ríos Montt used gangs of thugs to push for his acceptance as a presidential candidate.

7. Anonymous notes to file, "Meetings Held by SRSG. HOM Merrem and RR/RC J. P. Corlazzoli, United Nations Headquarters, New York, 15–16 October 2001," undated, apparently October 18, 2001.

8. Portillo would in fact be indicted and extradited from Mexico in 2008 on Guatemalan and US charges of embezzlement and money laundering. He was acquitted of the most serious Guatemalan charges in 2011. The Public Ministry has filed an appeal to vacate the acquittal and seeks a new trial with a different court for Portillo and two of his former ministers, Manuel Maza Castellanos and Eduardo Arévalo Lacs, whom the Public Ministry accuses of embezzling Q120 million from the Ministry of Defense. Departamento de Información Pública, "MP y CICIG piden pena maxima contra Portillo o repetir el juicio en su contra," Ministerio Publico, May 31, 2011, www.mp.gob.gt/ (accessed June 16, 2011). Portillo also faces potential extradition to face US money laundering charges. There are strong indications that Portillo's associates systematically routed public funds to banks in Panama and elsewhere. See Adriana Beltrán, *The Captive State: Organized Crime and Human Rights in Latin America* (Washington, DC: Washington Office on Latin America, 2007), 10. In testimony to Congress, Defense Minister Arévalo Lacs had the temerity to claim that the state "owes" the armed forces Q760 million, which is the amount cut from the budget since 1997 to comply with the peace accords.

9. Susan Peacock and Adriana Beltrán, *Hidden Powers in Post-Conflict Guatemala: Illegal Armed Groups and the Forces Behind Them* (Washington, DC: Washington Office on Latin America, 2003). See also Ivan Briscoe, *The Proliferation of the "Parallel State"* (Madrid: Fundación para las Relaciónes Internacionales y al Diálogo Exterior [FRIDE], 2008).

10. Patrick Gavigan, "Organized Crime, Illicit Power Structures, and Guatemala's Threatened Peace Process," *International Peacekeeping* 16, no. 1 (2009): 70.

11. "MINUGUA Weekly Situation Report 12–18 December 2001."

12. Gerd Merrem, "Meeting with Group of Friends," to Kieran Prendergast, January 15 2001.

13. Kieran Prendergast, "Notes on Meetings with President Portillo in New York," to Gerd Merrem, November 15, 2001.

14. Gerd Merrem, "Annual Review of Objectives," to Kieran Prendergast, January 16, 2002.

15. Angela Kane, "Visit to Guatemala," to Kieran Prendergast, February 20, 2001.

16. Juan Pablo Corlazzoli, "Latest Development on the Fiscal Pact," to Kieran Prendergast, June 22, 2000.

17. "MINUGUA Weekly Situation Report 21–27 June 2000."

18. "MINUGUA Weekly Situation Report 28 June–4 July 2000," and Juan Pablo Corlazzoli, "Update on the Fiscal Pact and Tax Measures," to Kieran Prendergast, July 7, 2000.

19. Corlazzoli, "Update on the Fiscal Pact and Tax Measures."

20. Ibid.

21. "MINUGUA Weekly Situation Report 6–22 August 2000."

22. Or "guarogate" after the Guatemalan slang for moonshine liquor, "guaro."

23. Robert Sandals, "Guategate Scandal Engulfs Governing Party and Former President Efrain Ríos Montt," NotiCen, September 14, 2000, https://ladb.unm.edu/publication/ViewArticle/article_id/053739; and Gerd Merrem, "Special Report: Current Political Situation," to Kieran Prendergast, October 27, 2000.

24. Robert Sandals, "Judge Dismisses Charges Against Legislators in Guategate Tax Scandal," NotiCen, November 1, 2001. Ríos Montt would later face legal problems on a different matter: his alleged intellectual authorship of genocide in the early 1980s.

25. Merrem, "Special Report."

26. "MINUGUA Weekly Situation Report 11–17 October 2000."

27. Article 165.h empowers Congress to impeach on the basis of a two-thirds vote of all members.

28. Gerd Merrem, "Meeting with Key Embassies," to Kieran Prendergast, September 20, 2000.

29. "MINUGUA Weekly Situation Report 15–21 November 2000."

30. Beltrán, The Captive State, 10.

31. Gerd Merrem, "Meeting with Group of Friends," to Kieran Prendergast, January 15, 2001.

32. Anonymous, "Notes on Meetings Held by USG Riza, Guatemala, 8–11 July 2001," undated (probably written by Susan Soux, who drafted other reports on these meetings).

33. "MINUGUA Weekly Situation Report 14–20 March 2001."

34. "MINUGUA Weekly Situation Report 23–29 May 2001."

35. Gerd Merrem, "Meeting with President Portillo," to Kieran Prendergast, June 8, 2001.

36. Merrem, "Special Report."

37. "MINUGUA Weekly Situation Report 27 June–3 July 2001."

38. Gerd Merrem, "Report on USG Riza's Visit to Guatemala," to Kieran Prendergast, August 14, 2001.

39. "MINUGUA Weekly Situation Report 4–11 July 2001."

40. "MINUGUA Weekly Situation Report 18–24 July 2001."

41. "MINUGUA Weekly Situation Report 25–31 July 2001."

42. Gerd Merrem, "Analysis of Strike and Protests by Guatemala Regional Office," to Angela Kane, August 7, 2001.

43. Robert Sandals, "Guatemala: Vice President Accused of Using Government Resources to Attack Tax-Bill Opponent," NotiCen, September 20, 2001.

44. "MINUGUA Weekly Situation Report 7–13 November 2001."

45. "MINUGUA Weekly Situation Report 24–30 October 2001."

46. "MINUGUA Weekly Situation Report 25–30 April 2002."

47. Peacock and Beltrán, *Hidden Powers*, 16–17.

48. Guatemalan observers called them the "Montesinos" of Portillo, in reference to Vladimiro Montesinos, the spymaster and éminence grise of the Fujimori government in Peru. See ibid., 36–41. Also reported in Tom Koenigs, "Background Notes for Your Visit to Washington," to Angela Kane, November 11, 2002.

49. Mark Ruhl, "The Guatemalan Military Since the Peace Accords: The Fate of Reform Under Arzú and Portillo," *Latin American Politics and Society* 47, no. 1 (Spring 2005): 69.

50. Juan Pablo Corlazzoli, "Meeting with President Portillo on 2 August on Presidential Military Staff (EMP) and Appointment of New Minister of the Interior," to Kieran Prendergast, August 7, 2000.

51. "MINUGUA Weekly Situation Report 18–24 April 2001," and "MINUGUA Weekly Situation Report 25 April–5 May 2001."

52. "MINUGUA Weekly Situation Report 2–7 November 2001."

53. "MINUGUA Weekly Situation Report 28 November–4 December 2001."

54. "MINUGUA Weekly Situation Report 13–19 December 2000."

55. "MINUGUA Weekly Situation Report 16–22 January 2002."

56. "MINUGUA Weekly Situation Report 5–11 December 2001."

57. "MINUGUA Weekly Situation Report 1–8 January 2002."

58. "MINUGUA Weekly Situation Report 13–19 March 2002" and "MINUGUA Weekly Situation Report 9–15 July 2002."

59. "MINUGUA Weekly Situation Report 23–29 January 2002." Arévalo Lacs was charged with embezzlement after MINUGUA closed, but acquitted in 2011.

60. See Briscoe, *The Proliferation of the "Parallel State,"* 14–15. Although Portillo was acquitted of corruption charges in Guatemala in 2011, such acquittals can be overturned on appeal in the Guatemalan system and there is so much circumstantial evidence of his having benefited from embezzlement that it seems likely he was involved and will eventually be convicted either in Guatemala or the United States.

61. MINUGUA, "Thirteenth Report on Human Rights of the United Nations Verification Mission in Guatemala," A/57/336, August 22, 2002, paragraphs 7–8.

62. Ruhl, "Guatemalan Military Since the Peace Accords," 72.

63. Both former president Alvaro de León Carpio and former presidential secretary Gustavo Porras approached MINUGUA with the same assessment. "MINUGUA Weekly Situation Report 3–9 April 2002."

64. Ibid., 71–72.

65. "MINUGUA Weekly Situation Report 23–29 August 2000."

66. "MINUGUA Weekly Situation Report 3–16 October 2001."

67. "MINUGUA Weekly Situation Report 28 November–4 December 2001."

68. "MINUGUA Weekly Situation Report 29 March–4 April 2001." This was, of course, also a fairly accurate factual description of the accords.

69. MINUGUA, "Twelfth Report on Human Rights of the United Nations Verification Mission in Guatemala," A/56/273, August 8, 2001, paragraph 22.

70. Ibid., paragraph 13.

71. Ibid., paragraph 21.

72. Ibid., paragraph 10.

73. Amnesty International, *Guatemala's Lethal Legacy: Past Impunity and Renewed Human Rights Violations* (London: Amnesty International, 2002), 49–51.

74. MINUGUA, "Twelfth Report," paragraphs 15–16.

75. MINUGUA, "Thirteenth Report," paragraph 56.

76. Ibid., paragraph 55.

77. "MINUGUA Weekly Situation Report 19–25 June 2000."

78. "MINUGUA Weekly Situation Report 7–13 March 2001."

79. "MINUGUA Weekly Situation Report 4–10 October 2000."

80. "MINUGUA Weekly Situation Report 25–30 April 2002," and "MINUGUA Weekly Situation Report 1–7 May 2002."

81. Juan Pablo Corlazzoli, "Peace-Building in Guatemala 2001–2003," to Kieran Prendergast, July 24, 2000. Corlazzoli wrote, "As a result of progress of the peace accords, military and police observers could be reduced to a minimum." Also, Susan Soux, "Note to the File: Mr. Merrem's Meetings in NY—31 October 2000," November 3, 2000.

82. "MINUGUA Weekly Situation Report 24–30 October 2001." MINUGUA asked DPA for guidance on this point, since one of Portillo's top advisers asked the mission to share its information on the parallel powers with the president himself. I found no response from DPA on this point, and it appears that the mission wisely demurred.

83. "MINUGUA Weekly Situation Report 6–12 June 2002."

84. Gerd Merrem, "Government's Announcement of Consultative Group Meeting in Late November," to Angela Kane, August 14, 2001, which conveyed "Dialogue Group on Consultative Group Meeting, Note for the File by M. Tarr, 14 August, 2001."

85. "MINUGUA Weekly Situation Report 15–21 August 2001."

86. Gerd Merrem, "Important Presidential Announcements," to Kieran Prendergast, July 26, 2002.

87. Ibid., and "MINUGUA Weekly Situation Report 22–31 July 2002."

88. Portillo tried to issue high-interest Eurobonds to finance the transfers over the objections of donors. However, the bonds did not sell well internationally (why would anyone buy from such a government?) and CACIF organized a boycott domestically.

89. "MINUGUA Weekly Situation Report 7–13 March 2001."

90. Gerd Merrem, "End of Assignment Report," July 30, 2002.

91. Claudia Mojica, "Updated Version 'Proyecto Fortalecimiento de la incidencia de la C. de A. y la reactivación de las Mesas Departamentales de Concertación y Seguimiento de los Acuerdos de paz,'" to Susan Soux, July 2, 2001.

92. "MINUGUA Weekly Situation Report 3–16 October 2001."

93. "MINUGUA Weekly Situation Report," April 18–24, 2001; June 13–19, 2001; November 7–13, 2001; and November 14–21, 2001.

94. "MINUGUA Weekly Situation Report 13–19 June 2001."

95. An official for the OAS offered his good offices as mediator between MINUGUA and the PDH, alleging that MINUGUA staff were so anti-Guatemalan and so interested in prolonging their own mandate that they could not work effectively with the PDH without outside help. Martha Doggett, "OAS Issue," e-mail to Gerd Merrem, May 6, 2002.

96. Susan Soux, "Note to the File: Meeting Between USG Prendergast and Deputy Head of MINUGUA Corlazzoli, New York, 22 June 2001," undated.

97. Angela Kane, "Consultative Group Meeting—November 2001," to Gerd Merrem, September 6, 2001; and Gerd Merrem, "Your Concerns Regarding the Consultative Group Meeting in November," to Angela Kane, September 13, 2001.

98. Anonymous, "Notes on Meetings Held by USG Riza, Guatemala, 8–11 July 2001," undated (presumably Susan Soux); Gerd Merrem, "Meeting with Representatives of Non-Governmental Human Rights Organizations," to Kieran Prendergast,

August 8, 2001; Aracelly Santana, "MINUGUA—Annual Review of Objectives," e-mail to Jack Christofides, February 11, 2002.

99. Juan Pablo Corlazzoli, "Meetings with Government and URNG Regarding Extension of MINUGUA Mandate," to Kieran Prendergast, June 25, 2000.

100. Angela Kane, "Visit to Guatemala," to Kieran Prendergast, February 20, 2001.

101. Lars Franklin, untitled letter to Kofi Annan, October 27, 2000.

102. María José Torres Macho, "Note for Mr. Türk's Meeting with the UN Agencies and the International Financial Institutions," June 21, 2000.

103. Denise Cook, "Note for the File: Meeting Between Mr. Merrem and UN System, New York, 14 February 2002," February 14, 2002; Gerd Merrem, "Information Regarding UNDP Locally Recruited Staff," to Angela Kane, March 26, 2002. As Merrem wrote following a retreat of UN system agencies in Guatemala, "the mandate of MINUGUA mainly consists of verification of compliance of the Peace Agreements, whereas the rest of the UN Agencies, Programmes, and Funds must support those programs and activities that the Government of Guatemala establishes as priorities. This means that, since Government priorities do not necessarily match the peace agenda, the UN system flexibility to assume responsibilities of MINUGUA's mandate is limited." Gerd Merrem, "UN System Retreat 21–22 February 2002," to Kieran Prendergast, March 13, 2002.

104. Gerd Merrem, "Meeting Regarding UNDP Project to Support the Implementation of the Accord on Firm and Lasting Peace," to Kieran Prendergast, May 22, 2002.

105. Kane, "Visit to Guatemala."

106. Gerd Merrem, "Private Letter," to Angela Kane, February 28, 2001; and Gerd Merrem, "Joint Statements by Members of International Community and Certain UN Agencies," to Kieran Prendergast, March 8, 2001.

107. Kieran Prendergast, "Resident Coordinator for Guatemala," to Heidi Swindells, May 16, 2001; Kieran Prendergast, "Note to Mr. Malloch Brown: Resident Coordinator for Guatemala," to Mark Malloch Brown, January 2, 2001.

108. Martha Doggett, "MINUGUA: Phase-Out," May 1, 2002.

109. Author interviews with individuals who preferred not to be cited commenting on a former SRSG's work performance.

110. Gerd Merrem, "Parallel Structures and the Mission," to Angela Kane, January 8, 2002. An internal assessment showed that Peruvians were not overrepresented on the staff of MINUGUA.

111. Ibid., and Laura Canuto, "Note to the File: Meeting with Ms. A. Kane, Ms. A Santana & Ms. Soux, New York, 21 November 2001," December 4, 2001.

112. Gerd Merrem, "DHOM's Management Style, Interpersonal Relations and Judgment," to Angela Kane, March 21, 2002; and Gerd Merrem, "DHOM's Management Style and Judgement [sic]," to Angela Kane, July 2, 2002.

113. Author interview with a former MINUGUA staffer who wished to remain anonymous, commenting on the former DHOM.

114. Gerd Merrem, "Departures of Mission Staff," to Angela Kane, March 1, 2002; Angela Kane, "Guatemala: Your Meeting with New HOM, Mr. Tom Koenigs," to Kieran Prendergast, May 29, 2002.

115. Gerd Merrem, "Report for the Renewal of MINUGUA's Mandate," to Angela Kane, August 28, 2001.

116. Kane, "Visit to Guatemala." Kane handwrote on the copy forwarded to Prendergast that she wished to convey some verbal remarks in addition to the report.

117. Gerd Merrem, "Comments from HQ Conveyed by DHOM," to Kieran Prendergast, June 26, 2001; Angela Kane, "Note to Mr. K. Prendergast," June 26, 2001; and Aracelly Santana, "MINUGUA—Annual Review of Objectives," e-mail to Jack Christofides, February 11, 2002.

118. Angela Kane, "Note to Mr. Prendergast, MINUGUA: Designation of a Deputy SRSG," January 7, 2002.

119. Gerd Merrem, "Report on USG Riza's Visit to Guatemala," to Kieran Prendergast, August 14, 2001.

120. "MINUGUA Weekly Situation Report 10–16 January 2001."

121. Angela Kane, "Comments on the 6th Verification Report," to Gerd Merrem, March 6, 2001. Kane notes that police, military, and justice issues are neglected, relative to emphasis on the socioeconomic agreement, on which the report "enters into a level of specificity that it almost reads as a Government document."

122. Angela Kane, "MINUGUA—Outstanding Issues," to Gerd Merrem, January 15, 2001; Angela Kane, "Appointment of a Resident Coordinator," to Gerd Merrem, May 2, 2001; Angela Kane, "Recruitment for MINUGUA," to Gerd Merrem, May 2, 2001; Aracelly Santana, "Recruitment of Spokesman for MINUGUA," to Gerd Merrem, October 25, 2001; Kieran Prendergast, "Communications," to Gerd Merrem, April 5, 2002. In one extraordinary lapse, MINUGUA sent an unencoded fax speculating on the potential problems associated with the political affiliations and family ties of locally hired UNDP staff. Gerd Merrem, "Information Regarding UNDP Locally Recruited Staff," to Angela Kane, March 26, 2002.

123. Gerd Merrem, "Various Recruitments," to Angela Kane, May 4, 2001; Gerd Merrem, "Delays in Recruitment of International Staff Members," to Angela Kane, June 11, 2001; Gerd Merrem, "Comments from HQ Conveyed by DHOM," to Kieran Prendergast, June 26, 2001; and Gerd Merrem, "Code Cable CNG-040," to Kieran Prendergast, July 15, 2002, in which Merrem wrote, for example, "I should like to point out that your request to me to refrain from taking further personnel decisions without clearing them with Headquarters is not understood, as I have constantly kept UNHQ informed of all aspects pertaining to personnel."

124. "Gerd Merrem, End of Assignment Report," July 30, 2002.

125. Former Deputy HOM Corlazzoli shared New York's view that the mission had difficulty adapting to new situations and had some long-standing problems that remained unresolved. Susan Soux, "Note to the File: Meeting Between USG Prendergast and Deputy Head of MINUGUA Corlazzoli, New York, 22 June 2001," undated, apparently late June 2001.

126. Angela Kane, "Note to Mr. Prendergast, MINUGUA: Designation of a Deputy SRSG," January 7, 2002.

127. "El Temido fracaso del proceso de paz," El Periódico, July 11, 2001.

128. Gerd Merrem, "Meeting with Representatives of Non-Governmental Human Rights Organizations," to Kieran Prendergast, August 8, 2001.

129. Denise Cook, "Note for the File: Meeting Between Mr. Merrem and UN System, New York, 14 February 2002," February 14, 2002.

7 | Trying for a Graceful Exit, 2002–2004

BY EARLY 2002, DPA knew that Gerd Merrem would be stepping down at the end of July. The timing might have been awkward, since MINUGUA was obviously headed for closure, making the mission less than a plum assignment. As it happened, German ambassador Hanns Schumacher paid a timely visit to USG Iqbal Riza and mentioned that Tom Koenigs, a German former state and municipal official with some UN mission experience, was interested in the SRSG position in Guatemala. DPA quickly agreed that he would be suitable, apparently in the absence of a formal search. Koenigs had an eclectic background, including, as noted on his CV, "publisher, manager of bookshop, welder, electronics technician, and taxi driver" in Frankfurt in the 1970s, followed by a multiyear stint as a translator of literature between Spanish and German. He had moved into public affairs as a "science adviser" to the Green Party, though he seemed not to have formal training in science. From there he held a series of appointed and elected positions in public administration and environmental affairs at the state and municipal level in Germany. His administrative experience opened the way to his first major international job as deputy SRSG of the United Nations Interim Administration Mission in Kosovo (UNMIK), where he was in charge of civil administration, police, and "joint interim administration" structures in that former province of Serbia. Thus Koenigs was a comparative newcomer to international development, diplomacy, and the United Nations itself. He did, however, have a politician's sense for image, public information, and media. Koenigs was a small and wiry man, friendly but socially awkward. While neither a great political strategist nor diplomat, he was approachable, coherent, and brought a new energy and upbeat style to the mission.

He would need plenty of energy, because the peace process and MINUGUA were struggling. Secretary-General Annan joked with Koenigs in their first meeting that Koenigs should check with DPA about conditions in Guatemala, and then decide whether he should be grateful for the appointment as SRSG.[1] Acknowledging the deteriorated situation, Koenigs questioned the United Nations' plans to close the mission at the end of 2003. Annan was noncommittal, saying only that "objective criteria" would be used in deciding when to close the mission.[2] Koenigs raised the same question about renewal through 2004 in a meeting with ASG for political affairs Danilo Türk and Americas and Europe division director Angela Kane. Türk replied that the goal was not to turn Guatemala into Switzerland, to which Koenigs replied that the peace accords implied just that! Türk felt that no more than a six-month extension could be elicited from the General Assembly, and even that was in doubt given that the United States was opposed to an extension. Member states were dubious about long-lasting missions, as these tended to foster dependency. "Missions have to end," Türk said.[3]

Within a month, however, the picture changed. Meetings with ambassadors from the friends states showed a degree of concern about post-MINUGUA Guatemala. Representatives of Norway, Mexico, Colombia, and Venezuela felt there would need to be an SRSG in Guatemala in 2004 "to continue to verify and serve as a focal point of information for the GA, especially on human rights, indigenous matters, and the military."[4] This did not necessarily mean that MINUGUA itself would continue; in fact the prevailing thinking was that an SRSG might preside over a much smaller political office rather than a field mission, following the staged withdrawal model that had worked well in El Salvador. Spain remained aloof and the United States made it clear that the mission should close as planned at the end of 2003.[5]

The fact was that having committed, perhaps unwisely, to stay through 2003, it did not make much sense to remove the United Nations' verification presence at the end of the Portillo government. Depending on who won the election, there was a chance that a new government in its first year might be willing and able to move quickly on implementing parts of the peace agreements, taking advantage of the brief window before the entrenched opponents of change would make themselves felt. Moreover, if the mission were to close at the end of 2003, it would need to start drawing down its staff and closing offices by midyear, right in the middle of what promised to be an unstable and even violent electoral campaign. When Koenigs reported for duty in Guatemala, he followed his instructions and announced that the mission would be in "full exit mode" by December 2003.[6] Yet DPA's views gradually softened in late 2002 on the question of renewal, responding to urgings from some friends states and members of the G-12 donors group.[7] Eventually, even the United States came around to the idea of extending the mission.[8]

With or without the extension, full implementation of the peace agreements during MINUGUA's term was out of reach. Given the incapacity of any of the Guatemalan political parties to articulate a long-term vision for a stable and equitable Guatemala, the peace accords still had value as a "national agenda," but this would be implemented, if at all, after MINUGUA left. Koenigs's job, then, was to leave behind some local and international capacity to monitor human rights, political, economic, and social conditions so that there might be some chance for domestic actors to push this agenda forward in the future.

The challenges facing Koenigs were mostly the same ones that had stymied Merrem: Portillo's political and managerial meltdown continued; the criminal elements that Portillo had brought into power further insinuated themselves into the fabric of the state; CACIF continued to resist taxation; the mission itself struggled to narrow its focus in accordance with its reduced budget, while suffering from infighting and low morale; and other UN agencies did little to prepare themselves for verification roles. Portillo worsened the political situation by promising severance pay to ex–civil patrollers, while denying reparations payments to victims of wartime violence or to the surviving family members of such victims. The number of ostensible ex-patrollers demanding payments mushroomed, the government remained nearly insolvent, and donors were unsupportive of paying off a group whose participation in the war had been largely involuntary but who had nonetheless often persecuted others. Any attempt to back away from the promises to ex-patrollers triggered massive and sometimes violent demonstrations. The ex-PACs had become a coercive and destabilizing force, and the government found it had no alternative but to float market-rate Eurobonds to finance the payments. Even this proved a dead end, as CACIF organized a successful boycott of the bonds domestically, and international lenders looked askance at bonds issued by an unreliable government for purposes that seemed unlikely to promote aggregate economic growth. By May 2003, only US$185 million of the planned US$700 million in bonds had sold.

PACs were not the only groups placing demands for indemnities: civic groups representing victims of wartime violence demanded reparations, as called for in the Historical Clarification Commission report. MINUGUA facilitated an agreement between the government and victims' groups on the types and scope of compensation, in the process earning the ire of groups that felt their views had not been adequately considered.[9] Congressional president Ríos Montt rejected the bill, however, and Portillo established the program by decree, with no guarantee that the needed funding would be available.[10]

In his first year, Koenigs also faced a major political crisis caused by Efraín Ríos Montt's relentless pursuit of the presidency. In July 2003, the FRG bused armed supporters into the capital city, where they engaged in two days of mob violence that resulted in at least one death. The PNC stood aside and allowed the FRG's thugs to move about the city. The street violence ultimately discredited Ríos Montt and the FRG and led to Ríos Montt's decisive electoral defeat in the first round of the 2003 presidential race, as well as to the FRG's loss of its legislative majority (it ended up with less than 20 percent of seats, a crushing reversal).

The implosion of the FRG paved the way for Oscar Berger to win decisively in the 2003 presidential elections. Berger's political constituencies were similar to those that had elected Arzú in 1995/1996, and he showed openness to implementing the accords. At a minimum, he seemed to see the Guatemalan state as something other than an opportunity for graft, and launched an aggressive anticorruption campaign that targeted prominent figures from the previous administration, including Portillo himself and his vice president. But Berger also failed to live up to the United Nations' hopes. He lacked a working majority in Congress, and even the three-party coalition that backed his presidency quickly proved brittle. His allegiance to the agrarian elite led him to use the police in increasingly violent evictions of peasants from disputed lands, setting the context for a deadly clash in August 2004 that left three police officers and seven peasants dead (some apparently executed in police custody).[11] Following the model of his predecessors, he failed to significantly raise taxes, and failed to address the critical weaknesses of the PNC and other rule of law institutions. Berger brought in a wealthy business leader, Carlos Vielmann Montes, to serve as interior minister in charge of the police and prisons. Under Vielmann's watch a series of extrajudicial killings took place, suggesting a policy of summary execution of prisoners (see A Rule of Law Epilogue below).[12] Vielmann resigned in 2007 after PNC agents murdered three Salvadoran members of the Central American Parliament and their driver, and were then themselves murdered in prison, presumably to prevent them from identifying their crime bosses. Vielmann was later indicted along with other senior officials for seven extrajudicial executions at the Pavón prison compound in 2006.[13] In sum, there was a strong odor of brutality, organized crime, and impunity around Berger's security and justice agencies. In the end, Berger's administration ultimately looked much like Arzú's: too compromised by its ties to the business community and to shady clandestine networks to be a serious and effective advocate of reform. Thus while the one-year extension into 2004 saved MINUGUA from having to leave under the cloud of Portillo's many misdeeds, it did not really facilitate the rapid implementation of peace accord provisions that had been hoped for.

Below the presidential level, however, there were other developments that gave MINUGUA a chance to carry out a partially effective transition plan. A new human rights ombudsman, Sergio Morales, took office just as Koenigs arrived, bringing a more cooperative attitude that finally made it possible for MINUGUA to transfer skills and responsibilities to the PDH. He turned out to have some of the same limitations as previous ombudsmen, including a propensity to seek publicity at the expense of basic human rights investigations, and a tendency to neglect institutional development. Nonetheless, Morales at least allowed his regional offices to work closely with MINUGUA as the PDH offices assumed primary responsibility for rights monitoring nationwide.[14] Berger appointed an internationally recognized human rights advocate, Frank LaRue, to head the Presidential Commission on Human Rights (COPREDEH), which also had monitoring functions and maintained six regional offices. Though COPREDEH played a secondary role in the mission's transition plans, having LaRue at the helm made cooperation from COPREDEH likely.

▌ Koenigs's Choices

Koenigs was in Guatemala for nearly a year before he knew whether the mission would continue into the next government. In the meantime, he had to deal with Portillo as best he could. One small point of leverage was the mission's renewal itself: Portillo wanted the mission to stay, and Koenigs told Portillo that any extension would depend on the government doing more to implement the peace accords.[15] Portillo's ambassador to the United Nations Gert Rosenthal was highly effective, however, in rallying member-state support for an extended mandate. By early in 2003 the United Nations had effectively committed to keep MINUGUA open through 2004, leaving few points of leverage with the government.

Mostly, Koenigs and his staff worked around Portillo and sought an exit strategy. During his work in Kosovo, Koenigs had developed an appreciation for the importance of building the capacity of local groups. The logic of MINUGUA's exit belatedly shifted away from "transferring functions" to UN system agencies and toward building local capacity.[16] The one exception was that the Geneva-based Office of the High Commissioner for Human Rights (OHCHR) was willing to establish a larger staff in Guatemala that would monitor overall human rights conditions, with an emphasis on indigenous rights.[17] Other UN agencies would be encouraged to pay more attention to peace accord issues in assessing social conditions and government policies, but the transferring of verification work envisioned in the original Inter-Agency Monitoring Plan was effectively abandoned.

An interesting innovation was the creation of a National Transitional Volunteers (NTV) program that recruited Guatemalan nationals as UNVs with the idea that they could work alongside MINUGUA professional staff and pick up both the verification skills and the international norms–driven culture of the mission.[18] A secondary goal of this program was to incorporate more indigenous people into the personnel of the mission. Koenigs had found it ironic and inappropriate that one could walk into any MINUGUA office and see the walls decorated with photos of indigenous people wearing the colorful traditional clothing (*traje*) of the highlands, but would find few indigenous people actually working in the mission.[19] By incorporating indigenous NTV staff into the regional offices, MINUGUA achieved a kind of "descriptive representation" of indigenous people, but it was less clear how substantive this change was. In retrospect, the NTV program started at least a year too late. By the time the program was under way, MINUGUA was dramatically reducing its international staff, leaving fewer experienced mission officials to train and mentor the NTVs. An earlier start might also have allowed greater success in arranging assignments for NTVs within Guatemalan government agencies such as the PDH, where the mission ran into numerous administrative and political obstacles to NTV placements.[20]

In its final two years MINUGUA tried to improve its public education efforts, running TV and radio spots, as well as producing longer video features, designed to educate the public on the value of the accords, democratization, human rights, and greater social equity. Koenigs published a number of op-ed pieces in the Guatemala City papers. The mission produced a series of booklets on the status of implementation of various themes in the accords, intended as roadmaps for future efforts by Guatemalan protagonists to use the accords as an agenda for reform.[21] Less widely distributed, but nonetheless available to Guatemalan and international policy advocates through the mission's excellent website, were a series of "closure reports" from the mission's internal "advisory" groups, which detailed what had and had not been accomplished with regard to socioeconomic reforms, human rights, the strengthening of civilian power, and indigenous affairs. As it became clear that the mission would be extended into 2004, one strategic question was whether to attempt to maintain the mission's field presence throughout the country, or follow Arnault's May 2000 proposal to convert the mission in its final year into a mostly capital city–based political/diplomatic office of the kind used successfully in El Salvador after the closure of ONUSAL. The DPA desk officer for Guatemala, Martha Doggett, argued for the latter. In her view, MINUGUA should focus on applying effective diplomatic pressure on the next government and giving it technical support on key elements of the accords. Only senior-level experts would have the standing to advise and cajole counterparts in the new government on such issues as public security and demilitarization, socioeconomic affairs, and indigenous rights. With the inevitable budget cuts, maintaining a large number of field offices headed by international staff would leave insufficient funds to retain high-level policy staff at mission headquarters. Doggett argued that scarce resources would be better spent on strengthening the mission's capacity to provide technical support and build government capacity rather than extending a field presence that could provide little more than ongoing "accompaniment."

Koenigs, in contrast, had a philosophical commitment to maintaining the field presence. Everyone knew that MINUGUA was leaving, but he felt that actually closing the field offices would have devastated mission morale and public image. "We would have been a dying duck," as Koenigs put it. USG Kieran Prendergast visited Guatemala in early July 2003, and after hearing the competing arguments from Doggett and Koenigs, he deferred to Koenigs as SRSG and allowed him to retain the field offices. Once this decision was made, Koenigs shifted logistical resources to the field offices, for example, ensuring that the newest vehicles were deployed there, while the worn-out jalopies were transferred to mission offices in the capital. "My view was that if a car collapses for me in Guatemala City, I can take a cab. If a car collapses out in the field, you can walk for 2 days."[22]

In retrospect, Koenigs's arguments for maintaining the field presence were not convincing. By itself, one more year of the mission's field presence was neither here nor there and tended to reinforce existing dependence on outsiders to provide rights monitoring, mediation, and conflict resolution services in outlying areas. Moreover, perpetuating the existing structure of the mission did not help the mission staff rethink how they should function in the final year. Instead, it helped lock in existing patterns.[23] As part of a transition plan, however, it may have had value. As described in more detail below, the mission's transition strategy focused on training PDH personnel throughout the country, in part by jointly carrying out human rights casework alongside PDH staff in rural regional offices. This may or may not have been the most efficient way to work, but direct training by MINUGUA at the field office level was the only mechanism available, for reasons explained below. Maintaining the field presence also helped make the NTV program more viable, since national volunteers could build at least some relevant experience by participating in the daily work of the regional offices. A smaller, more capital city–focused mission would have provided fewer opportunities.

The internal management problems that had plagued the mission eased somewhat in its final two years. A veteran DPA division head, Maria Maldonado, took over as DHOM in early 2003, ensuring smoother communication with New York and solid management. A few other senior international staff members were reassigned within the mission, and MINUGUA veteran Jared Kotler was brought back to handle political reporting. Despite some renewal of the senior staff, Koenigs still encountered bureaucratic entrenchment in the mission, and wrote Secretary-General Annan suggesting more frequent staff rotation in future missions to prevent the kind of rigidities he had found in MINUGUA.[24]

MINUGUA created a new position of transition coordinator and hired Marcie Mersky, an experienced development worker who knew Guatemala well. Mersky came up with the idea for the NTV program as well as other mechanisms for building local capacity. Impending closure finally helped the mission break out of its entrenched mode of operation and by 2004 it had finally narrowed its scope of work with an emphasis on building local capacity. Though this was done too late, it did provide a test run for how future peacebuilding missions might go about working themselves out of a job.

Though management improved overall, there were significant gaps between MINUGUA's ostensible transition strategy and what it actually did. For example, the transition plan stated that human rights and demilitarization were priorities, but staffing decisions did not reflect those priorities.[25] In the final year and a half, the most experienced human rights staff were let go, and the few international staff to continue in the final stages—heads of regional offices—did not always have human rights expertise. Thus there was essentially no one left in the final stages to provide training and transfer know-how. The military advisory was weak, and there was no one in the mission's senior staff with particular expertise on public security matters. While the plan stressed the importance of building Guatemalan institutions, in practice what the mission was doing through its NTV program was focusing on giving individuals experience without knowing what institutions they might subsequently serve.[26]

These gaps between plan and implementation reflected a general resistance to reassessing strategically what the mission might do differently. Some of the cables sent to New York under Koenigs's name reveal a tendency toward unfounded optimism that practices that had so far yielded few results might work better in the future. In the lead-up to the May 2003 consultative group meeting (discussed below), MINUGUA drafted a very detailed and unflattering report on the lack of progress since the 2002 consultative group meeting. After receiving a draft copy, USG Prendergast cabled Koenigs, pointing out that the concluding paragraph in the draft report was too upbeat and appeared to contradict the assessment that "little tangible progress has been made." More importantly, he once again suggested that the mission needed to ask serious questions about its focus and approach.[27] Koenigs replied with a cable that might have been written by Willy Loman: "I regret that the draft report left an impression that MINUGUA is pessimistic," and then spent two paragraphs papering over the mission's concerns and pointing optimistically to the coming elections, which "may generate a somewhat better political scenario next year." Koenigs argued that progress or lack thereof in the peace accords was not indicative of "MINUGUA's effectiveness or lack thereof. . . . The Mission is only one factor in a complex environment. Though of little consolation, Guatemalans who support the Mission often say they believe the situation would be far worse without MINUGUA." Koenigs observed that both the mission and the international community had been weak during the recent period. "If one of our priorities next year is to lobby the new government for continuing with the peace accords, we must ensure we have the [sic] sufficient technical and political resources to do so effectively." He did not explain how this might be accomplished.[28] He seems to have been unaware that his own policy of maintaining the mission's field offices, and thus depriving the mission of high-level expertise in the headquarters, contributed to stripping the mission of the "technical and political resources" it would need to lobby the new government.

▌ The 2003 Consultative Group Meeting: One Step Forward, Two Steps Back

The 2003 consultative group meeting was not a pledging meeting, but rather an opportunity for donors to express their disgust with all of the FRG's failures and to lay down some performance standards that ought to guide the next government. Because the meeting was held in Guatemala City as national political parties were positioning themselves for the November elections, it was inevitably more politicized. It also gave rise to a bizarre initiative by the OAS, the IADB, and UNDP to reinitiate the kind of consensus-building dialogue process that had been unfruitful for MINUGUA. Ill-considered as it was, this initiative was a sign that other international agencies were looking beyond MINUGUA and trying to position themselves for the next phase.

MINUGUA had taken a soft approach toward Portillo around the end of 2002, "in the hope this would give the government an incentive to make further progress before the CG." By April 2003, however, Koenigs and his advisers considered it "more important to deliver a cold hard evaluation that sets a solid standard for acceptable progress."[29] The mission released its report to the press and the diplomatic corps in early May, outlining a series of familiar failures including neglect of the PNC while the military continued to gobble resources; failure to raise taxes; failure to increase spending adequately in health, housing, education, and rural development; failure to follow through with the legislative agenda agreed to at the last consultative group meeting; failure to address indigenous rights through legislation and required spending; failure to pass legislation and appropriate money to address land conflicts; and many others.

Most of the two-day consultative group meeting consisted of donors lining up in support of MINUGUA's negative assessment and making clear that future assistance would be conditional on progress in implementing the accords. The United States pushed for demilitarization measures, while the European Union announced that it was already "reorienting" its assistance. Before the meeting, Portillo had lashed out at MINUGUA for what he claimed was an overly negative assessment. During the consultative group meeting itself, however, he was meek and compliant, "pleading only that credit be given for advances, 'however small they may be.'"[30]

The meeting ended on a bizarre note, however, that undid most of the clear messaging that occurred during most of the meeting. In a closing statement that was supposed to represent the consensus of the participants, the president of the meeting, Miguel Martínez of the Inter-American Development Bank, called for a national dialogue organized jointly by the UNDP and the Organization of American States. The resident coordinator of UNDP, Juan Pablo Corlazzoli, mentioned the same thing in his closing statement, so obviously there had been collusion. As Koenigs reported to New York, "The proposal took participants by surprise, but since the CG ended with Martinez' statement, there was no opportunity for reaction." The IADB immediately gave a press conference reiterating the proposal, "and the headlines in the next day's papers read: 'Consultative Group Calls for National Dialogue.'"

Koenigs saw several problems with this. First, it represented an end run by UNDP and IADB around MINUGUA and the SRSG. Quite aside from any personal or institutional pique, it completely undermined the political impact of the consultative group. Instead of having conveyed that there were objective performance standards that the government must meet in exchange for international financial support, the consultative group ended with the message that "as long as the government shows willingness to engage in dialogue over the coming months, it can claim to be addressing the concerns of the consultative group even if it does not also produce tangible results in implementing the peace agreements." Koenigs and MINUGUA, it seemed, had finally recognized the hazards of endless dialogue in the absence of concrete measures. Yet just at the moment that the mission had orchestrated an unprecedentedly clear call for concrete actions, UNDP and IADB rushed in to revive the utterly failed strategy of national consensus-building dialogue. Even worse, Koenigs feared that the call for dialogue could open up a renegotiation of the peace accords, while undercutting the work of the commissions appointed under the peace accords to address difficult topics such as indigenous rights and justice system reform.[31] Koenigs was not alone in his objections. Americas and Europe division director John Renninger wrote a note to Prendergast entitled "UNDP Ambush," and indicated that DPA should take the issue up with higher levels of UNDP.[32] Prendergast cabled Koenigs that he also saw the dialogue proposal as a threat to the "good working relationships that have been built within the international community."[33]

The involvement of Corlazzoli in this national dialogue gambit must have been galling to senior MINUGUA and DPA staff. Recall that a couple of years earlier, Gerd Merrem and DPA had pushed very hard for UNDP to give Corlazzoli the resident representative job. Since Corlazzoli was at the time the deputy head of MINUGUA, they hoped his placement as resident representative would ensure a closer working relationship between UNDP and the mission. Once comfortably positioned at UNDP, however, Corlazzoli had no compunction about pursuing his own agenda and undermining

MINUGUA at a critical moment.[34] Questioned by Koenigs, Corlazzoli sent a six-page memorandum attributing the initiative to Miguel Martínez from IADB but then describing in detail the various meetings and statements that led to and justified Martínez's initiative. The gist of the explanation was that CACIF had proposed a vision for a "minimum national agenda" that seemed to open the way to a new consensus. It is difficult to see how someone who had been following Guatemala for the previous two years could have been taken in by such specious rhetoric.[35] In the end, strong opposition from MINUGUA with the backing of DPA and most of the dialogue group donors brought an end to this initiative.

■ Political and Social Instability

Koenigs's first full year at MINUGUA was a period of profound instability. The FRG's effort to buy votes and civil peace by promising ex-PACs an indemnity of US$2,600 quickly backfired. There was no money in the budget for the promised indemnities. Although an IMF standby agreement provided an emergency credit line of US$120 million, it also limited deficit spending and prohibited side payments of the kind envisioned. As noted earlier, the government's market-rate "peace bonds" attracted few buyers. In the face of violent actions by ex-PAC groups, especially in the Petén, Portillo eventually bargained down to a payment of US$650 per man, which would in turn have to be paid out in three installments—one in 2003 and two envisioned for 2004. The government then announced a list of eligible ex-patrollers that included fewer than one-third of the estimated 600,000 persons who participated in the patrols. This triggered violent demonstrations by those not on the list. While ex-patrollers were sincerely upset about the lack of indemnities, it also appeared that leaders of the protest movement had "links to a variety of political and military figures," and that the violent incidents were being manipulated for broader political effects.[36] While some ex-PACs clearly supported the FRG, others distanced themselves from the party. The PAC issue became a potential threat to the elections when a group of ex-patrollers who were not on the list for indemnities took seven people hostage and refused to release them until they received payments. Koenigs traveled through the night to Huehuetenango to help intercede with the hostage-takers. This was a politically complex step for MINUGUA to take, because it could have been misinterpreted as support for the payment of indemnities to ex-patrollers. Koenigs felt that the humanitarian situation demanded that the mission act.[37] He was successful in convincing the ex-patrollers to release their hostages in exchange for an opportunity to present their claims. The government then failed to pay those eligible in a timely way.[38]

Despite the FRG's dominant position in the legislature in 2003, its power was vulnerable as elections approached. The FRG's reputation had suffered major setbacks as newspapers broke the story of a US$38 million embezzlement from the Social Security Institute (the public health system) leaving Portillo to blubber on camera that he was "only human." A two-month teachers' strike also took a toll. Congress refused to meet out of fear that demonstrators might take over the session. Much of the public supported the strike, putting the FRG in an awkward position. Portillo dropped out of sight, leading to speculation that he was undergoing treatment for alcoholism or negotiating an early withdrawal from office. An opposition group filed a writ of habeas corpus on suspicion that the EMP was holding Portillo captive!

As previously noted, congressional president and FRG head Efraín Ríos Montt wanted to run for president, but the Constitutional Court had rejected his claim under Article 186, which barred former dictators from the presidency. No other FRG figure had Ríos Montt's power, and he was determined to run. In May 2003, the party chose him as their presidential candidate. Ríos Montt's megalomaniacal campaign slogan was "I am Guatemala." A broad Civic Front (Frente Cívico) formed against his candidacy, replying to Ríos Montt with the slogan "We are all Guatemala," and filing a series of legal challenges to Ríos Montt's eligibility based on his history as a dictator.[39] Ríos Montt's campaign staff were unmoved by the opposition and took a sometimes provocative approach to running the campaign. They scheduled one of his first campaign events in El Rabinal to coincide with a ceremony to rebury the remains of victims of a massacre committed during Ríos Montt's dictatorship. Party supporters taunted townspeople participating in the ceremony and soon rocks and bottles were flying, one of which apparently struck Ríos Montt in the head.[40]

The Civic Front's legal challenges soon foundered. Constitutional Court justice and FRG confidant Guillermo Ruíz Wong (recall that he was briefly head of the PNC under Portillo) rotated into the court presidency and used that position to seat two "alternate" judges on the panel, both of whom also just happened to be close associates of the FRG. The court proceeded to vote four to three in favor of allowing Ríos Montt's candidacy to go forward. This brought an unprecedented challenge by the Supreme Judicial Court (which unlike the US version does not rule on constitutional matters), declaring the Constitutional Court's action illegal. This was a severe fall from grace for the Constitutional Court, which up to that point had shared the distinction, along with the Supreme Electoral Tribunal, of being one of two national institutions that actually functioned. The Constitutional Court's decision may ironically have been, in the long run, a good thing. Some observers, including even Berger's running mate Eduardo Stein, thought that Ríos Montt's legal claim had merit since Article 186 was being applied retroactively for actions Ríos Montt had taken before that article was written. Stein remarked that the healthiest outcome for Guatemalan society would be if Ríos Montt ran and lost.[41]

In the face of the as-yet-unresolved Supreme Judicial Court challenge to the Constitutional Court, Ríos Montt acted predictably: the FRG organized thousands of activists, bused them into Guatemala City, provided them with matching truncheons and a supply of tires to burn, and sicced them on prosperous businesses and neighborhoods.[42] The police conspicuously withdrew from the streets, leaving the rioters to pillage for two days. The PNC director later explained that sending in the police to break up the mob would only have increased the level of violence.[43] One journalist died of a heart attack while fleeing the mob. MINUGUA restricted the movements of its personnel and locked down for the duration. The attacks were widely seen as a warning and as a prelude to more lethal assaults if Ríos Montt did not get his way. Human rights activists and Constitutional Court judges reported threatening phone calls.[44]

The Constitutional Court reaffirmed its ruling and the TSE reluctantly obeyed that court's instructions to enroll Ríos Montt as a candidate. DPA political officer Martha Doggett, who happened to be in Guatemala during the Ríos Montt riots, remarked in an e-mail to New York that it "seems incredibly stupid for Rios Montt and Co. to do this, only confirming what people fear about him and what his presidency would be like."[45] This was prescient: in the November elections, Ríos Montt received only 19.3 percent of the vote, behind both Oscar Berger (from the Grand National Alliance, a loose center-right coalition) and Alvaro Colom (from the National Unity of Hope, a populist coalition). Berger then beat Colom in the December runoff. In the congressional race, the FRG fell from a solid majority position to receiving only 22 percent of the vote. Clearly the electorate had had enough of the FRG's corruption and brutality.

This decisive outcome was possible in part because of international efforts to ensure a clean election and to limit preelectoral violence. Koenigs along with DHOM Maldonado met with foreign minister Edgar Gutiérrez in early August and put him on notice of the mission's priority concern that the events of July 24–25 not be a harbinger of electoral violence and intimidation to come. Both the OAS and the European Union committed to significant electoral observation missions, and despite delays in obtaining funding and staffing, both began their assessments in August so as to be able to comment on the climate surrounding the campaign.[46] While the OAS mission was the smaller of the two, it adopted a higher profile and was publicly critical of the government's actions leading up to the election. The international and domestic observer groups ultimately reached the same conclusions: there had been intense violence but little of it appeared related to politics; there were some irregularities in voter lists but nothing that suggested a systematic fraud; and the TSE had performed well overall.[47] The US National Democratic Institute helped organize an umbrella group of national civic observers to examine registration lists, perform quick counts, and monitor campaign and voting conditions. These safeguards, combined with such procedures as marking voters' fingers with indelible ink to prevent repeat voting, were especially important to ensure some degree of public confidence in democratic institutions after the July riots, which had convinced many people that Ríos Montt and the FRG would stop at nothing to remain in power.[48] Those fears proved to be overblown, but the fact that the elections ultimately went off without major incidents or fraud was attributable in part to heightened scrutiny. It also helped that public opinion surveys increasingly showed such a big gap between Ríos Montt and the two leading candidates (Berger and Colom) that an FRG electoral victory was clearly out of reach and any fraud would have to be of a massive scale to be effective. By the eve of the election, leaders of the FRG made the rounds of international and national observer groups, reassuring observers that the party would respect the results of the vote regardless of the outcome. Anticipating their loss, they sought to salvage a bit of international legitimacy.[49]

MINUGUA contributed by monitoring human and political rights, investigating acts of violence or threats that seemed politically motivated. In one instance the mission persuaded the Ríos Montt campaign to postpone a campaign event coinciding with an exhumation at a clandestine cemetery containing the remains of persons disappeared by the army during the war. This probably prevented another incident like the stoning at Rabinal.[50] The Electoral Assistance Division (EAD) of DPA sent a "needs assessment mission" to Guatemala, which unfortunately catalyzed little more than a repeat of EAD head Carina Pirelli's earlier turf-based objections to MINUGUA's electoral activities. This time around, she singled out the PROLEY project, which had assisted Congress in drafting electoral reforms, within its broader mandate to help the understaffed Congress draft coherent legislation. There was no basis for the complaint since EAD had regularly received all of MINUGUA's reports and could not have been surprised by PROLEY's activities. With the elections approaching fast, it became clear that EAD could mainly contribute through voter education efforts, and that its greatest contribution might come after the election in helping Guatemala develop a "single ID" system that would streamline voter registration and documentation.[51]

In the end, the November election went off fairly smoothly with high turnout and only isolated incidents of violence including the nonfatal shooting of one candidate in what may have been a robbery attempt. There were also some administrative problems, including the late opening of a polling place in Chajul that resulted in the death of two women who were asphyxiated as the crowd of voters pushed against the locked gates of the polling place.[52] Rios Montt finished well behind Colom, so the presidential runoff would pit Colom against Berger. Koenigs wrote to Prendergast the next day, "If nothing else, this election has shattered the myth of Ríos Montt's political invincibility and his long held claim to be a victim of exclusion from the political process. He insisted that the people speak. Now they have."[53]

The December runoff between Berger and Colom was calm by comparison, just a "'normal' contest between two mainstream—if not inspiring—presidential options." MINUGUA did not register a single complaint of threats or violence related to the campaign. International observation continued, but mainly to monitor administrative issues.[54] Berger ran the more vigorous campaign and won decisively with 54.1 percent of the vote with higher than expected 50 percent turnout.

In the weeks leading up to the election, MINUGUA prepared for the new administration. It drafted a series of "transition papers" on various aspects of the accords, laying out the government's obligations. Berger's running mate, Eduardo Stein, who had often clashed with the mission when he was foreign minister under Arzú, met with Koenigs and adopted a conciliatory tone. Stein signaled that Berger would delegate most interaction with the international community to him, and remarked that the greatest challenge for Berger would be whether he would "operate with independence from those who financed his campaign."[55]

This would quickly be tested because Berger inherited a simmering crisis in rural areas. The emergence of Vietnam as a major coffee producer drove down global coffee prices, resulting in increased rural unemployment. Moreover, the FRG had allowed many land conflicts to fester. It cut the funding to the Presidential Agency for Legal Assistance and Resolution of Land Conflicts (CONTIERRA) and never allocated the roughly US$38 million promised for the Land Fund (FONTIERRAS). Without these mechanisms, there was no way to peaceably resolve conflicts between peasants and large growers, or among competing groups of peasants (such as people displaced by the war who returned to find other people occupying their former lands). On the positive side, the Portillo government, reflecting its populist pretenses, did not use the police and military to evict peasants.

With Berger's arrival in office, the police quickly began a series of violent evictions. This decision reflected the mixed composition of Berger's political coalition and cabinet, which included a number of old-school hard-liners who were more than willing to use the state to promote the financial interests of agrarian elites. It was by no means certain that these evictions were legal, not to mention just. In many cases, peasants had occupied lands in the first place because landowners were not paying salaries and benefits required under law. Courts often sided with commercial growers despite evidence that their claims of ownership were questionable. MINUGUA reported in July 2004 that some 1,400 "threadbare families" had been forced off lands since January. Nationwide demonstrations in June temporarily put a halt to evictions, and the Supreme Judicial Court agreed to investigate all evictions since the beginning of the year. The mission spoke out against evictions, and had a TV spot made showing dramatic footage of police stealing a peasant's possessions and burning down the homes of sharecroppers. Koenigs was especially concerned about the humanitarian impact and pushed the government to at least provide some help for evicted families to obtain shelter and food.[56]

Another source of grievance that emerged under Portillo and continued under Berger was the demand for reparations for war victims. The Historical Clarification Commission had called for such reparations, and the government was obliged under the peace accords to implement that recommendation. It was also morally offensive for the government to pay off ex-PACs, however involuntary their service had been, while ignoring noncombatant victims, especially survivors of mass killings who had lost loved ones and breadwinners. MINUGUA stepped into this challenging issue and convened a meeting in March 2003 in which various victims' groups presented their demands and negotiated with the government. This was not without risks for the mission: it had to adjudicate among many different groups' demands. Months later, indigenous activist Rosalina Tuyuc would write a letter to Secretary-General Kofi Annan, cosigned by twenty-three indigenous rights groups, decrying alleged bias by the mission against the most "representative" Mayan organizations during the negotiations and singling out human rights adviser Patrick Gavigan for particular criticism.[57] The letter did not explain how MINUGUA should have determined which groups were most "representative." Whatever the political costs to MINUGUA, the negotiations led to agreement on a reparations package, which Portillo presented to Congress. Ríos Montt (still president of Congress at that juncture) rejected it. Portillo then passed it by decree, in hopes of having something positive to show to donors at the impending consultative group meeting. This left open the question of funding and sustainability into the next government.[58] When Berger came into office, he similarly had few resources to commit to reparations, but did obtain seed funding to take some initial steps. He appointed Tuyuc to head a commission charged with making decisions about reparations.[59]

Berger did seek to rekindle the peace process by creating a new mechanism for monitoring implementation and proposing measures. As noted earlier, the Accompaniment Commission had been dysfunctional at best and had become irrelevant during the Portillo government. Berger established a new National Peace Accords Commission (CNAP) with sixteen members including representatives of the four main political parties, high-profile civic leaders including Tuyuc, a former Guatemalan ambassador to the United States, the rector of the national university, and a Supreme Judicial Court justice. Berger also appointed his own secretary of the presidency and peace secretary, ensuring that CNAP would be well connected to the executive. The URNG retained two seats as signatory to the accords, but the new composition was more in line with the actual distribution of political power.[60] Some civil society groups objected to the unilateral way the government went about establishing the commission, but it was a more functional domestic mechanism. Had something similar been done many years earlier, the political parties might have felt more of a sense of ownership in the peace accords at a point when their support might have made a difference. By the time CNAP was formed, the accords had become nearly irrelevant except as an aspirational agenda.

▌ Human Rights

The human rights situation deteriorated during the last year of Portillo's term, and the situation did not dramatically improve with Berger's arrival in office. Several dynamics were noted in the thirteenth and fourteenth human rights reports (the last the mission produced). There was a surge in fatal attacks against "human rights defenders, church workers, judges, witnesses, journalists, political activists and labour unionists."[61] One of those killed was a regional office director for the PDH. Newspaper publisher José Rubén Zamora was held at gunpoint in his home by a dozen men, stripped and bound, and told to "stop bothering higher ups."[62] The number of abuses by the police continued to rise, and antidrug operations brought a recurrence of torture practices not seen since the war ended, including the use of electric shocks during questioning.[63]

Sharp criticism from US assistant secretary of state, Otto Reich, followed in January 2003 by the US decision to "decertify" Guatemala as an ally in the war on drugs, led to fitful efforts by the government to at least seem to be addressing the problem. Portillo disbanded a police antinarcotics unit that had obviously become corrupted. Its successor proceeded to commit torture during an investigation, prompting sharp criticism from the US ambassador. An announced investigation into the activities of General Francisco Ortega Menaldo and other high officials, on the other hand, briefly won praise from Reich. Applause faded as it emerged that three of the four attorneys running the investigation had probable ties to organized crime.[64]

Incidents of lynching persisted, with frequent evidence that ex-PACs and ex-soldiers participated. Lynchings were increasingly directed against the PNC and judges for perceived injustices—sometimes for excessive lenience against accused criminals, sometimes for excessive zeal. The ex-PACs, now politically mobilized to demand payoffs from the government, engaged in political violence including hostage taking. Summary murders of street children became increasingly frequent, a semiofficial and upper-class version of lynching.[65] By 2003, the homicide rate had increased by 33 percent versus 1999 levels.[66] Only about 3.5 percent of cases were even prosecuted, with about a 60 percent success rate.[67] Thus only 2 percent of murderers were convicted, making Guatemala one of the safest places in the world for murderers but not so much for other people. Failure to protect on such a massive scale was a human rights violation in and of itself. The police and the Interior Ministry continued to suffer frequent turnover, with five interior ministers and seven PNC chiefs sacked during the first three years of Portillo's term.[68] The prison system was wracked by horrible conditions exacerbated by declining budgets, an inadequate legal and administrative framework, and political neglect.[69] Prisons experienced escapes, riots, and battles between rival gangs, punctuated by sporadic and ineffectual government crackdowns. In one instance, 1,200 police agents stormed a prison on the outskirts of Guatemala in what was supposed to be a surprise raid. Prisoners, who had obviously been tipped off, were waiting, armed with machine pistols and hand grenades. One policeman was killed, along with three prisoners.[70] Meanwhile, due process was fundamentally undercut by the government's decision to slash the budget for the public defender's office, even though it was indispensable for due process under the adversarial 1994 Criminal Procedure Code.[71]

Demilitarization reversed from 2002 onward. Stung by being decertified by the United States, the government brought the army more deeply into law enforcement roles with mixed results. Ostensibly "joint" operations between the PNC and the military were in practice controlled by the army. While PNC was starved for vehicles, fuel, personnel, and resources of all kinds, the military received 24 percent more than approved by Congress.[72] The EMP was gradually demobilized during the period, and finally closed down in October 2003, although Portillo transferred about a third of its personnel into the new civilian presidential security agency.[73] During the same period, EMP spending increased by 95 percent (some US$1.5 million) ostensibly to help it demobilize.[74] In late March 2003, ex-members of the EMP occupied the Presidential Palace to protest nonpayment of indemnities promised to them. Given the amount of money previously transferred to the EMP for just that purpose, "there [were] now questions about malfeasance."[75]

Once Berger took office, he began drawing the military down from 27,000 troops to around 15,500, which ought to have corresponded to a roughly 50 percent cut in the budget, though given the lack of transparency and congressional budget oversight, it was difficult to know how much the military was actually spending.[76] He also began a crackdown on corruption that might have had positive secondary effects for human rights since it challenged the police, prosecutors, and courts to function better. But the campaign appeared largely partisan, focusing on Portillo and people close to him. Moreover, the depth of inherited criminalization of the police and military was striking. After the Supreme Judicial Court upheld the conviction of Colonel Valencia Osorio in the murder of anthropologist Myrna Mack, Valencia Osorio escaped in the midst of an apparently staged confrontation between a military unit and the police monitoring his residence.

Berger considered his inherited attorney general Carlos de León incompetent and sacked him within a month by executive order. Berger replaced him with a congressman from the Grand National Alliance (GANA) coalition, Juan Luis Florido, which raised questions about partisanship.[77] Florido would emerge as a major obstacle to accountability and the rule of law. The PNC revealed how corrupt it had become when a group of uniformed officers robbed a discothèque in Guatemala City, and when another group of off-duty cops were "captured and nearly lynched by local residents, after being caught preparing a holdup of drivers on a road in the Western Highlands."[78]

Perhaps the most alarming development was a sharp trend toward violence against human rights workers, especially those involved in promoting accountability for past human rights crimes. Hina Jilani, the "Special Representative of the Secretary-General on the situation of human rights defenders," visited Guatemala in May and June of 2002 and issued in early 2003 a report highlighting this trend and calling for corrective action.[79]

The assault on human rights workers confirmed the presence of clandestine armed groups involving both active duty and former security forces personnel. It led a coalition of seventeen Guatemalan human rights NGOs in 2002 to propose a new step. They wanted the United Nations to join with the OAS and the Guatemalan government in an International Commission to Investigate Illegal Groups and Clandestine Security Organizations (CICIACS) that would have the authority to investigate crimes in Guatemala, with an emphasis on breaking up the parallel powers that had further infiltrated the state and consolidated themselves under Portillo. Their priority was to put a halt to attacks on the human rights community, but the idea clearly had broader implications. Koenigs was supportive of the idea but had low expectations, cabling New York, "An investigation may not lead very far, but would at least increase the public focus on the problem and provide pressure to act."[80] The mission did not want to be subject to lobbying on the question. Especially as the concept veered toward a broader attack on organized crime, Koenigs didn't want MINUGUA publicly associated with it, out of concerns for the safety of mission personnel. MINUGUA told the government and the press that any decision on such a role for the United Nations would be made in New York in consultation with member states.[81] Koenigs did, however, agree to facilitate discussions with the NGOs, the PDH (which the NGOs hoped would take the lead on behalf of the government), and the OAS.[82]

The initial vision for CICIACS was modeled on the Salvadoran Joint Group for the Investigation of Illegal Armed Groups with Political Motivations, a joint effort of the United Nations, OAS, and the Salvadoran government. The Joint Group, however, had been limited to collecting information on such groups and handing it over to prosecutors for actions. No prosecutions resulted, but the investigation itself forced the organized crime networks underground and prevented them from committing violence in the lead-up to the 1994 Salvadoran elections.

As discussions proceeded slowly over the next year on CICIACS, the concept began to grow real teeth, especially after a July 2003 DPA technical mission to Guatemala. Initially proposed as a Guatemalan executive branch initiative to which the United Nations would appoint a commissioner, the design became more international. A stronger international role would insulate the commission from domestic political manipulation. It would also make it legally possible for the commissioner and UN-deployed staff to be covered by the 1946 Convention on the Privileges and Immunities of the United Nations, which would shield them from the kinds of frivolous lawsuits that often impeded investigations.[83] By the time Portillo signed an agreement with the United Nations to establish CICIACs in January 2004 as one of his last acts in office, the proposed powers of the commission were quite robust. It would be empowered as an auxiliary prosecutor, but without the legal restrictions that usually applied. The courts would not get to choose whether CICIACS would have standing to prosecute, CICIACS could add itself to a case even after it was brought by the public prosecutor, and other parties in the case would have no standing to object to CICIACS's role. CICIACS would also have the power to request that government agencies discipline or even fire public officials who obstructed a CICIACS investigation. Finally, the commission would be empowered to make recommendations for legislation and reforms to improve the justice system.[84]

There was no exact precedent for such an arrangement. The United Nations had organized war crimes tribunals for the former Yugoslavia and Rwanda, based outside of those countries and entirely international in composition. It had developed hybrid court systems in Timor-Leste, Sierra Leone, Cambodia, and Lebanon that incorporated international personnel as judges and prosecutors, alongside local counterparts. The CICIACS proposal was for an investigative and prosecutorial role only. It was based on an assumption that if well-investigated criminal cases were brought before the Guatemalan judiciary, the courts would do their duty.

The United Nations' Office of Legal Affairs determined that there were no obstacles since technically the United Nations' role was limited to appointing the commissioner and providing logistical and administrative support. CICIACS would not have a UN mandate. Despite the legal green light, the United Nations proceeded cautiously. Prendergast kept repeating in meetings with Guatemalan officials that CICIACS was only worth doing if it were effective. Clearly the Secretariat was skeptical, having already witnessed too much of the Portillo government's grandiose talk and untrustworthy behavior. Foreign minister Edgar Gutiérrez as well as human rights ombudsman Sergio Ramírez began to apply pressure through the press as well as foreign embassies in Guatemala. The Norwegian ambassador told the mission that the government was complaining that "there is no stampede in New York or at the OAS" to get CICIACS under way.[85] MINUGUA's political reporting countered that Gutiérrez and Ramírez were creating inflated expectations.[86]

Planning accelerated following the July 2003 DPA technical mission. The United Nations signed an agreement with Portillo just before he left office in January 2004. The new president, Oscar Berger, quickly signaled his support for CICIACS. The proposal just as quickly ran into political trouble. As already noted, Berger did not have a working majority in Congress. Even members of the president's GANA coalition turned against CICIACS on nationalist grounds, egged on by former general Otto Pérez Molina whose Patriot Party later split with the government as Pérez began to position himself for his own future presidential run.[87] Congressional deputies expressed concerns about whether CICIACS was constitutional, and privately appeared to be worried about the politics of it, fearing the likely nationalist backlash against the commission's extraordinary powers. One of the committees sent the draft CICIACS legislation to the Constitutional Court for an advisory opinion. The court issued an advisory opinion that several of the powers proposed for CICIACS violated the constitution.[88]

With that, CICIACS died. Though Congress did not actually vote it down, two key committees recommended against the bill and the Berger government asked that it be returned to the executive branch without a vote. In the following months, MINUGUA pushed the Berger government to move ahead with a redrafting of the CICIACS law, along lines that would satisfy the constitutional concerns but still have "teeth." Berger took little action, despite strong pressures and offers of financial support from the United States.[89] The question was still unresolved when MINUGUA closed at the end of 2004, and not until 2007 was a watered-down version of CICIACS deployed (see Epilogue below).

There was also domestic resistance to the United Nations' proposal that OHCHR expand its presence in the country to provide continuing international human rights monitoring. OHCHR already had a small technical assistance office in the country and during 2004 MINUGUA in practice handed off the monitoring of indigenous rights to OHCHR. Negotiations then got under way between OHCHR and the Guatemalan government regarding deployment of a new OHCHR office with a staff of about thirty who would monitor overall human rights conditions, following the precedent of the OHCHR's office in Colombia. OHCHR would not expect to receive human rights denunciation or conduct investigations at the retail level nationwide. Instead, they would accept and evaluate information from other sources including the PDH, investigate exemplary cases, and provide an internationally recognized and mandated backstop for the PDH. The intent was for the OHCHR office to expand during 2004 so that there would be little if any interruption in international monitoring. DPA agreed that any monies left in the Guatemala trust fund after MINUGUA's closure could go toward the initial expenses of OHCHR.[90]

Once again, nationalists reacted against a perceived international intrusion. Some legislators wanted assurance that Guatemala would be treated as a normal country, not as a special case in need of heightened human rights monitoring.[91] Others fussed over the fact that OHCHR staff would have privileges and immunities. In a meeting with Berger, Prendergast stressed that this was "perfectly normal" and no different from any of the international embassies or aid organizations such as UNDP.[92] This reflected hard feelings on the part of Guatemalan nationalists, going back many years, about being singled out by the Geneva-based Human Rights Commission of the United Nations for special attention in the form of visits from "special rapporteurs" and "independent experts." Koenigs tried to persuade Guatemalan leaders that having an annual report from OHCHR would be an opportunity to showcase the country's improvements. They were unconvinced. In a June 2004 meeting with the acting high commissioner for human rights in Geneva, the Guatemalan ambassador to the United Nations suggested a new agreement that would delete reference to an annual report to the Human Rights Commission, and that would remove the OHCHR's power to access prisons, detention centers, and places of interrogation without prior notice.[93] This turned out not to have been discussed within the cabinet and was strongly opposed by presidential human rights commissioner Frank LaRue as well as Vice President Stein, who would soon emerge as a key advocate for the successor to CICIACS. Berger reportedly contemplated establishing the OHCHR office by presidential decree, which would obviate the need to dumb down the office's powers to satisfy Congress. Koenigs supported the presidential decree strategy, though he recognized that it could result in constitutional challenges similar to those that scuttled CICIACS.[94] In August, Koenigs held a press conference in which he made the case for the importance of the OHCHR presence and tried to debunk the various fears and alarmist nationalist rhetoric about the office.[95]

In October, the new Guatemalan permanent representative to the United Nations, ambassador Jorge Skinner-Klee, met with the high commissioner for human rights Louise Arbour, and once again pushed for an agreement that the OHCHR office would not *report* on human rights in Guatemala, begging the question of what its purpose would be. His argument was that MINUGUA's human rights reporting had been politicized, Guatemala's war was over, and the country should not be treated as a "hot spot." It would be hard to explain to some constituencies why MINUGUA was being replaced with two new monitoring and investigative bodies (OHCHR and CICIACS). He wanted negotiations held in Guatemala with opposition congressional deputies participating; Arbour replied that the government should explore implementing the agreement by decree, and that in any case the government should narrow down, in writing, the range of acceptable arrangements, after which further discussion could take place— in Geneva.[96]

Under pressure from the president as well as from MINUGUA, Congress took up the question again. The Congressional Human Rights Committee approved it, but the Foreign Affairs Committee stalled for months after two votes were canceled for lack of quorum. In the end, the OHCHR proposal was recast somewhat as a technical assistance office designed to increase the capacity of the Guatemalan state to safeguard human rights by providing education and training, providing information and advice to the Guatemalan state, and promoting a culture of human rights through public outreach. The mission would make recommendations and issue annual reports by the high commissioner "on the activities of her office in Guatemala." This wording apparently mollified congressional resistance, and Congress finally approved the agreement for OHCHR's office in May 2005. The office started its work in September 2005. In practice, the office's reports describe recent developments with respect to human rights protections in detail, and their tone and content are quite similar to MINUGUA's human rights reports. The agreement between the government and the OHCHR was renewed in September 2008, so apparently both parties are satisfied with the compromise arrangement.

▍ Building Local Capacity

Given the mission's limited leverage and the need for deep changes over a prolonged period, this inevitably meant that Guatemalan institutions needed to develop their capacity to advance the peace agenda. Specifically, the PDH and COPREDEH would need the capacity to dispassionately investigate human rights cases and produce reports that were factually and legally sound; prosecutors needed to successfully direct investigations and prosecute crimes, even crimes committed by members of the police, armed forces, or powerful criminal networks; courts needed to be able to convict and sentence in accordance with law and evidence; and civil society organizations needed the ability to conduct their own credible, factually sound, and authoritative investigations, serving as private prosecutors as needed, and monitoring the performance of state agencies. Civic groups would also need to engage the state constructively on policy questions, rather than merely denouncing as had been the wartime pattern. The special institutions created under the peace accords, such as the Peace Secretariat, needed to have sufficient technical capacity to evaluate peace accord compliance and the political ability to decide on corrective actions and guide state actions. Certainly, Guatemala would need continued international financial help and cooperation, but the leadership, and mechanisms of accountability, needed to be domestic.[97]

Back in 1994, several of the officials who arrived to open MINUGUA's first offices were veterans of ONUSAL in El Salvador, where the United Nations had been slow to undertake local capacity building. They were determined not to repeat that mistake. Yet MINUGUA found local capacity building hard to do, as discussed throughout previous chapters. Obstacles included a party system that made reformist legislation difficult to pass; personalism and corruption on the part of some Guatemalan political leaders and high state officials; short-term political tactics by national leaders that resulted in expedient decisions such as the rapid expansion of the PNC without adequate screening, training, and safeguards; nationalist rejection of the mission's criticism of government performance; and chronic jealousy on the part of Guatemalan counterparts toward the mission's much superior equipment and basic resources. The mission sometimes contributed to these conflicts by failing to communicate effectively and cooperatively with local groups.

In the first few years, it was essential for MINUGUA to be staffed by international personnel and maintain very tight control over information. But as the peace process matured, the mission's emphasis on being separate and international became increasingly dysfunctional. Since the mission would, after all, eventually leave, it needed to somehow find a way to step back and let Guatemalans and their institutions handle things, even if this resulted in procedures and priorities that differed from those of the international community.[98] The failure to hand off key roles and functions earlier, combined with the long tenures of some senior staff who had purchased property in Guatemala, created the impression that the mission had become a lifestyle. At the same time, it must be said that the performance of Guatemalan state agencies and NGOs, and the attitudes and priorities of some of their leaders, had not made it obvious how to reduce the mission's profile while ensuring that its key contributions were sustained.

As Koenigs arrived, MINUGUA faced its last opportunity to build local capacity prior to leaving. All of the factors that had blocked effective capacity building previously were still present, so MINUGUA would need creative thinking and consistent leadership to break the existing pattern. A centerpiece of the new strategy was "nationalization" of the mission's know-how, and the PDH—by then under reasonably cooperative leadership—was given special priority. Because of its territorial coverage and mandate for monitoring state human rights performance, it was MINUGUA's "most similar" counterpart. A Joint Transition Commission was formed in late 2002 to guide the process, and was divided in mid-2003 into five subcommissions working on priority issues. By the end of 2003, the mission had invested 140 work months to building up the PDH, focusing on training field staff, helping create information systems, and encouraging donor contributions. The mission produced five book-length training manuals that drew on hundreds of example cases investigated by MINUGUA over the previous nine years.[99]

Results of these efforts were mixed. Field-level training went reasonably well, although some PDH staff members lacked the educational qualifications to fully exploit the material presented. Of the roughly five hundred staff in the PDH, only eight were licensed attorneys. Because it was peer-to-peer training at the field level, MINUGUA not only imparted general principles, but also hard-won practical experience regarding how to handle and investigate cases. Once initial training was complete, the mission moved to joint investigations and analyses of human rights complaints. Working jointly soon attenuated most of the animosity or distance between PDH and MINUGUA staff. Working with mission staff also encouraged PDH field workers to take on the kind of local-level conflict resolution roles that MINUGUA had played throughout its deployment.[100] Despite the mutual good feelings, gross differences in resources persisted during the transition. While MINUGUA enjoyed vehicles, sufficient fuel, handheld radios backed up by mountain-top repeaters, and networked computer systems, at the PDH "there were no electronic information systems for substantive work or financial management; and computing, transport and communications equipment were inadequate or non-functional."[101]

MINUGUA hoped not to just train PDH field staff directly, but rather "train the trainers" so as to leave the PDH with a sustainable capacity to upgrade their current personnel and to train new hires in the future. The ombudsman agreed in principle, but never followed up. It wasn't a priority for him, and no amount of cajoling from MINUGUA could remove this obstacle. Thus the transition became a one-shot training, the effects of which could quickly wear off with personnel turnover.

MINUGUA was similarly frustrated in its efforts to build the analytical, policymaking, and administrative capacity of the PDH headquarters. For example, from late 2002 onward, the mission assigned an information technology specialist to adapt MINUGUA's database design to the PDH's needs (the PDH's mandate covered a broader range of issues than had MINUGUA). But the PDH could not define basic criteria such as the classification of violations to be included or procedures for case management. Without such definitions, of course, the data-system work could not proceed. Similarly, the mission assigned specialists on indigenous, socioeconomic, and justice system issues to the PDH, but the PDH never assigned them counterparts. By the time the PDH assigned counterparts, MINUGUA had already reduced its international staff, eliminating its specialized expertise.[102]

Overall, MINUGUA was able to accomplish more at the field office level than at PDH headquarters. The mission's preliminary "Transition

Report" drafted in March 2004 argued that the ombudsman himself had political agendas and ambitions that were distinct from and incompatible with those of the mission. While he allowed the lower-level work to go on, he refused to issue joint reports, avoided appearing jointly with the mission, and did not want high-level input into the operations of the PDH or its broader strategy for improving human rights.[103] Once he determined that MINUGUA was not about to hand over its cars, radios, and computers, he lost much of his interest in what the mission had to offer.[104]

The mission's regional offices were also successful in similar training efforts for a wide variety of civil society organizations. More importantly, the mission succeeded in building regional networks of groups, as well as a national human rights movement that combined a large number of rights-related groups, broadly defined. The human rights division of MINUGUA developed and disseminated a database system that would allow groups to collect and analyze patterns and trends in human rights abuses and aggregate the data collected by different organizations and in different regions, using the same categories and data architecture. There were also marked increases in the political sophistication and effectiveness of women's organizations, resulting in part from the mission's long-standing efforts to create political space for such groups and support them with training (especially on the potential of recently passed decentralization laws). For indigenous groups, the mission emphasized training in the contents of ILO 169, and groups responded with exploratory efforts to apply the norms of the convention in "pilot efforts to assert land and consultations rights."[105] In an effort that surely did not endear the mission to landowners, regional offices in the eastern part of the country worked closely with the Ministry of Labor and the PDH to train labor unions. The March 2004 transition report brags that "Unions trained by MINUGUA no longer require accompaniment by the Mission in carrying forth their denunciations, collective bargaining, or other actions, as they had before."[106]

The National Transition Volunteers program was, like the transition effort at the PDH, a partial success, marred mainly by its not having started a year or two earlier. In strictly reputational terms, it helped ease the nationalist resentment toward the mission as many groups were gratified to see Guatemalan nationals "exercising MINUGUA's mandated functions." As noted earlier, by the time the NTV program was up and running, the mission was drastically reducing international staff, creating fewer opportunities for on-the-job training and mentorship from experienced officials. An integral part of the program was to place NTVs as interns with state agencies and NGOs in the final stages. Ultimately MINUGUA was able to arrange internships in NGOs and government agencies for fifty-three of the fifty-eight NTVs still participating in late 2004. Unfortunately, the PDH did not participate, citing various administrative obstacles, but the internship placements were mostly with appropriate organizations including COPREDEH and CONTIERRA. About half of the NTVs received job offers from the agencies where they were interning, and six returned to their original organizations as planned.[107]

The NTV program pointed to strategies that could be used in other settings, especially in peace processes in which there is low risk of renewed fighting, and where a long-term process of institutional change is involved. Both MINUGUA staff and the volunteers themselves reported a strong positive synergy. It is indicative of the value to the NTVs that only two out of sixty dropped out of the program, and both of them did so to accept permanent positions. The NTVs were energized by working within an international organization, while MINUGUA staff were reinvigorated by working with highly motivated Guatemalans who had already demonstrated a commitment to working for social and political change. The nationals brought new perspectives, and opened doors to other civil organizations that previously kept their distance.[108]

▌ Closing Down

On the eve of the release of the ninth Secretary-General's report on the Guatemalan peace process, someone sent a tongue-in-cheek, single-page document to DPA's offices. It read, "MINUGUA's 9th Report Executive summary: Things are really bad in Guatemala . . . but much better than before!" That was, indeed, the gist of the report. The one-line summary might have added that MINUGUA had helped make things better, and would be missed. The Guatemalan press awakened in September 2004 to the reality that MINUGUA was preparing to leave. The Sololá field office closed on September 3, with Koenigs lowering the UN flag and removing the blue MINUGUA sign. It was the first of eight closures scheduled between September and November. Koenigs remarked that rural Guatemalans would be among the first to feel the impact of MINUGUA's departure, as they would "no longer be able to routinely turn to the Mission for help in resolving social conflicts." Fortunately, the PDH was taking "an increasingly active and prominent good offices role," though its capacity to fill MINUGUA's shoes remained in doubt given the government's paltry budgetary support.[109]

ElPeriódico, which had been sharply critical of MINUGUA at times, commented wistfully that although many Guatemalans considered the mission to have made key contributions to building democracy, regrettably conditions weren't much different from when the mission arrived. Among the first cases MINUGUA had investigated when it arrived in the country were violent deaths associated with land conflicts. This was still happening. "Guatemala still has a long road to travel before instituting a true State of Law and a regime that fully guarantees the rights of its citizens."[110]

Other politicians and media outlets took the mission's departure as a chance to get in a few more petty nationalist hits. President Berger accused MINUGUA of "leading" the occupation of a hydroelectric plant in Chixoy (a patent falsehood, since the local branch of the PDH had requested MINUGUA's presence as observers at the incident). Local conservative talk radio picked up this theme, and even after a corrective letter from Koenigs to Berger, the president continued to complain about the role of "foreigners," though he stopped naming MINUGUA.[111]

USG Prendergast attended the mission closing ceremonies in mid-November. He traveled first to Quiché for the closure of the regional office, an event attended by hundreds of indigenous people from the area. This was followed by an event hosted by the government in the National Palace, presided over by Berger and Stein, along with Rigoberta Menchú. The president awarded MINUGUA the Order of the Quetzal, Guatemala's highest civil honor.[112] This was followed a week later by the Supreme Judicial Court's awarding MINUGUA the Order of the Judicial Branch, the highest judicial honor.[113] Not to be outdone, the URNG held a ceremony paying special tribute to the "strong women of MINUGUA, giving a pair of earrings to each female MINUGUA staff member present." As Koenigs made farewell visits to government officials and embassies, he heard a consistent message: the mission's early work had made peace possible, and the mission's "determined, steady" work had kept alive the possibility of a more peaceful and just country.[114]

▮ A Rule of Law Epilogue: CICIG

After MINUGUA's closure, there were alarming signs of a return to old ways with respect to human rights. After nineteen prisoners escaped from the high-security Infiernito (Little Hell) prison in 2005, police summarily executed three of those recaptured and then altered the crime scenes, planted weapons on the dead men, and fabricated stories that they had attacked police.[115] Then in 2006 police and military forces invaded the much-neglected and self-governed Pavón prison compound and, despite an absence of resistance, summarily executed seven prisoners who were identified as leaders of the prison's internal government and suspected of operating criminal enterprises from inside. Once again, police planted weapons on the deceased and claimed they had fired on officers. The PDH played a valuable role in documenting official wrongdoing in this case.[116]

A key player in these events was a shadowy Venezuelan national by the name of Víctor Rivera, also known as Zacarías, who was a top adviser to Interior Minister Vielmann. In the 1980s, Rivera had done intelligence work on loan to the Christian Democratic government of Napoleón Duarte in El Salvador. He returned to El Salvador in the early 1990s and positioned himself as a sort of master crime fighter, specializing in kidnapping cases. The vice minister of public security in El Salvador at that time, Hugo Barrera, foolishly invited Rivera to form a parallel special operations unit directly under the ministry, which then ran amok and undermined police investigations. Salvadoran PNC chief Rodrígo Ávila (and many others) raised objections and Rivera was eventually forced out. He resettled in Guatemala and began the same kind of business, convincing upper-class families that only he knew how to handle delicate kidnapping situations and demonstrating *amazing* knowledge of the Guatemalan criminal underworld. When Vielmann followed Barrera's lead and appointed Rivera as a special adviser, Rivera was allowed to again form his own operational unit, referred to by other cops in Guatemala as "los Riveritas" for their comparative youth. Rivera and the Riveritas formed a close alliance with the head of the National Criminal Investigations Division (DINC), Víctor Soto Diéguez. The two bosses allegedly played a prominent role in directing and carrying out extrajudicial killings and, it would emerge later, a series of other criminal operations and cover-ups.[117]

While this new and improved criminal enterprise took root in the government, negotiations around a revised CICIACS bogged down for another two and a half years. Guatemalan politicians were afraid to move ahead with it. However, by December 2006, in part because of strong advocacy by Vice President Stein, the United Nations and the government were ready to sign an agreement for a slightly toned-down version of CICIACS, known as the International Commission Against Impunity in Guatemala or CICIG. CICIG retained most of the basic CICIACS concepts, with reduced autonomy. CICIG would be treated within the judicial system like any other *querellante adhesivo,* which meant that a court could reject CICIG as auxiliary prosecutor, CICIG would not be able to step in to shore up a public prosecution gone bad, and other parties in a case could contest CICIG's role. These limitations made CICIG more vulnerable to the conduct and decisions of the Public Ministry and, of course, the courts. CICIG still had teeth, however, including full powers to conduct investigations, require state agencies to reveal information, and to call for disciplinary action against officials who obstructed CICIG's work.[118]

Even this pared-down concept for CICIG would certainly have run into fatal political resistance from the perennially nationalistic political elite, but a singular episode of violence and impunity in February 2007 demonstrated to anyone who was paying attention that the fusion of state agencies and organized crime had gotten out of hand and that Guatemala needed outside help. Three members of the Central American Parliament (PARLACEN) representing El Salvador, and their driver, were murdered while en route to a PARLACEN meeting in Guatemala City. The bodies of the men were found beaten, gunshot, and burned. A hasty investigation by the Guatemalan authorities, pushed along by the presence in country of top-level Salvadoran police officials, placed a group of police agents from the DINC at the crime scene.[119] After an armed standoff in which the suspects mobilized the support of some sixty fellow police agents, the four primary suspects were tricked into appearing at the offices of the minister of the interior, where they were arrested. One of the men, speaking directly to Víctor Rivera, accused him of "betrayal" and warned that he would "take all of you with me." He added that "you are going to know about me . . . you and all the others . . . you will remember me."[120] The four were arraigned and a judge ordered them held at a facility near the capital city. Instead, police officials transferred them to Boquerón prison, seventy kilometers from the capital. According to an account by Salvadoran journalist Lafitte Fernandez based in part on information leaked by a disgruntled former CICIG investigator, DINC director Víctor Soto (the direct supervisor of the four accused murderers) and Víctor Rivera appeared at Boquerón at around noon the next day. A short time later, Sunday visiting hours were suddenly curtailed, and a group of heavily armed masked men arrived. They passed unchallenged through multiple locked doors, each of which required a different key, each held by a different prison guard. Upon reaching the four DINC agents, the masked men shot them, and then cut their throats. Guards interviewed after the crime claimed to have seen nothing (of course), and the government lamely attempted to blame the murder on gang members in the prison. There had in fact been a disturbance inside the prison, but this happened *after* the killings, as inmates panicked when they realized that they would be blamed for the killings.[121] As with the Pavón killings in 2006, the PDH played a key role in documenting that something very irregular had taken place.

There could scarcely have been a more thorough indictment of the police or the prison system. Congress censured Interior Minister Vielmann and he resigned the next month. Yet the full scope of state involvement was not initially known. By August 2007, the government claimed to have cracked the PARLACEN case, using what were supposedly the men's mobile phone records to implicate a former congressional deputy as the mastermind of what the government claimed to be a drug-related crime with an overlay of personal vengeance.[122] Later evidence would call all of this into question and point to more extensive involvement of state officials.

In the wake of the PARLACEN and DINC killings, the CICIG proposal took on new life. It was reviewed by the Constitutional Court and approved in May 2007. Congress dragged its feet for some additional months, and then abruptly passed the CICIG law in August, leaving the United Nations to scramble to organize CICIG and its staff.[123]

CICIG's job was to map out the "illegal armed forces and clandestine security apparatuses" (CIACS)—that is, the suspected fusion of organized crime and police/military/intelligence structures—and take steps to break them up. Measures would include effective prosecution (as *querellante adhesivo* and in collaboration with the Public Ministry); calling on state agencies to weed out members and collaborators of CIACS; and recommending laws, policies, and reforms that would give the noncriminal components of the state the upper hand. As had been the case with MINUGUA, this mandate merged elements of information collection and analysis, technical assistance to state agencies, and politics.

Initially, CICIG seemed to stumble. It did not communicate effectively to the public what its mandate was or how it would go about its work.[124] For many months, it was busy organizing itself and did not outwardly seem to be doing anything of note. The expected report on the nature and organization of the parallel powers did not materialize. Its first case, against an allegedly corrupt former prosecutor, was a failure. Indeed, CICIG initially confronted significant obstructionism by prosecutors. Prosecutors, for example, refused to let CICIG investigators see records, denied access to witnesses, and allowed police officers who were (or should have been) suspects to conduct investigations into their own crimes! One prosecutor spirited a key witness (and later suspect) out of the country without authorization.

CICIG's first commissioner, Spanish judge Carlos Castresana, decided to use CICIG's mandate to demand that the state discipline obstructionists, especially prosecutors and judges who appeared to be looking out for their own rather than following the evidence. CICIG launched a campaign of public condemnations and a few indictments to remove a dozen prosecutors, as well as a number of judges including six members of the Supreme Judicial Court.[125] It convinced the Colom government to sack the attorney general inherited from Berger. It browbeat the government into dismissing 1,700 police officers, including fifty commissioners and the director and deputy director of the police who were subsequently indicted.[126] Clearing out the deadwood created opportunities for those prosecutors, cops, and judges who wanted to do their jobs diligently and honestly. CICIG's attacks on obstructionists led to criticisms from Guatemalan observers that CICIG was doing little more than tearing down the reputation of Guatemalan institutions. Indeed CICIG's criticisms of the judiciary appear to have alienated many in the judiciary, though it is hard to see how this could have been avoided given the arbitrary behavior of some judges.[127]

CICIG's landmark achievement was its investigation of a bizarre 2009 murder that threatened to bring down Berger's successor, President Álvaro Colom, who had won the presidency under a loose center-left coalition. In 2009, an attorney named Rodrigo Rosenberg was shot to death as he set out on a Sunday bicycle ride. At Rosenberg's funeral, a friend handed out DVDs containing an amateur video in which Rosenberg himself appeared before a blue screen, announcing that if people were viewing the video, it was because "I was killed by Álvaro Colom and Sandra de Colom, with the help of Gustavo Alejos," referring to the president, first lady, and presidential chief of staff. He called for justice and an end to corruption and impunity.[128] The video quickly appeared on YouTube and went viral. Demonstrations began in Guatemala City calling for Colom's ouster, right-wing political forces mobilized opportunistically, and Colom would probably have had to step down were it not for the highly professional and lucky investigation conducted by CICIG. CICIG located witnesses, collected surveillance camera footage, analyzed phone records, and eventually identified the criminal gang involved in the actual killing. But the case then took a bizarre twist, as it turned out that the intellectual author of the crime was not the president or anyone associated with him, but rather the victim himself. Rosenberg had been distraught over the death of a woman he was involved with, Marjorie Musa, who had been murdered alongside her father, Khalil Musa. The elder Musa had clashed politically with Colom over alleged corrupt dealings by a government social fund frequently used to finance the first lady's pet projects. Rosenberg suspected that the president had had Musa rubbed out, and Rosenberg apparently reached the desperate conclusion that the only way to get justice was to frame Colom by having himself killed. After a thorough investigation, Castresana publicly announced CICIG's astonishing findings to the immense relief of President Colom.[129]

It is very unlikely the case would have been solved without CICIG's involvement, and had it remained unsolved it is likely that Colom's government would have collapsed in some not entirely constitutional fashion. Curiously, police agents tried to block CICIG's investigation and shadowed CICIG agents as they worked. In one harrowing episode, police officers attempted to snatch a potential witness away from CICIG agents, and a shoot-out was narrowly averted. Even with CICIG's efforts, nothing was done to prosecute individuals who appeared to have manipulated Rosenberg to into carrying out his self-sacrificial frame-up.[130] It turned out that Khalil Musa was involved in criminal dealings, and ironically he and his daughter had been murdered by members of the same criminal gang that Rosenberg hired through intermediaries to do himself in.[131] In the end, CIGIG's investigation saved a presidency but made only a small dent in the clandestine criminal structures that were behind the scenes.

Despite his triumph in the Rosenberg case, Castresana became increasingly embattled in the Guatemalan press. He ultimately resigned in protest when President Colom appointed yet another attorney general, Conrado Reyes, whom CICIG suspected of linkages to organized crime. Given CICIG's dependence on cooperation from the Public Ministry, trying to work through a corrupted attorney general would be fatal to CICIG's mission. In the wake of adverse publicity and Castresana's resignation, the Constitutional Court annulled the selection of Reyes and ordered a new selection process.[132] The replacement attorney general, former judge Claudia Paz y Paz, worked closely with CICIG and proved highly effective.[133]

CICIG had other successes, including a number of convictions of police officers, military officers, and former government officials. Even when it failed to convict, it often succeeded in pushing malefactors from office. In addition to the work of its own mostly international staff, it helped to build a special anti-impunity group within the Public Ministry (Fiscalía Especial Contra Impunidad [FECI]). That group worked under the direct supervision of a CICIG prosecutor, but acted with increased autonomy under Attorney General Paz. Under her leadership, the Public Ministry, acting alone, swiftly solved a number of recent crimes that in the past would have remained dark mysteries. CICIG had less luck with the troubled PNC, and an effort to vet and train some thirty PNC officers was not extended. To the relief of many observers, President Otto Pérez Molina, inaugurated in January 2012, retained Attorney General Paz, and she went on to bring former dictator Efraín Ríos Montt to trial for genocide in 2013.

CICIG faced some setbacks, however, reflecting among other things how vulnerable its mission was to the unreconstructed Guatemalan courts. CICIG's high-stakes case against former president Portillo for embezzlement resulted in an acquittal, despite overwhelming evidence of Portillo's involvement. The new CICIG commissioner, former Costa Rican prosecutor Francisco Dall'Anese, maintained a lower media profile than the showy Castresana, but even Dall'Anese had to speak out with outrage following the court's absurd ruling in the Portillo case. He did not hesitate to lambaste judges who produced shoddy jurisprudence, resulting in some polemical exchanges in the Guatemalan press.[134]

From the outset, observers had questions about CIGIC's case selection. Given the ample scope of organized crime and its penetration of state agencies, CICIG obviously needed to choose its battles, considering the centrality and importance of the crime structures involved. Perhaps inevitably, other considerations such as political timing, feasibility, and international political implications seemed to enter in as well.

Costa Rican prosecutor Giséle Rivera, who was leading CICIG's investigation into the PARLACEN case, clashed privately, and later publicly, with Castresana over his refusal to pursue avenues of investigation that seemed to point to the responsibility of high police and Interior Ministry officials. Rivera and her team of investigators assembled interviews with witnesses and other evidence pointing to the involvement of top officials including Víctor Soto, Víctor Rivera, and PNC deputy chief Javier Figueroa in both the PARLACEN and Boquerón killings. This in turn raised questions about their superiors, PNC chief Erwin Sperisen and interior minister Carlos Vielmann. In contrast to the Public Ministry's claim that the four cops from DINC were rogues, operating in league with drug traffickers outside the police, Rivera found evidence that the crime was centered in the police it-self. She claims that Figueroa knew when the Salvadoran deputies were coming and in what vehicle because the deputies themselves had requested a police escort up to the outskirts of the capital city. PNC officials also knew through criminal contacts that the car was carrying some US$5 mil-lion in cash and a stash of cocaine in a secret compartment, and decided to steal it. Rivera placed Víctor Soto and Víctor Rivera, as well as additional police officers and members of the Riveritas, at the crime scene.[135] Suspi-cions of high-level state involvement were enhanced by the extreme efforts of some prosecutors, since sacked and indicted, to obstruct CICIG's inves-tigation. Rivera grew increasingly frustrated that Castresana prevented her from doing such obvious things as pursuing leads in El Salvador as to what the Salvadoran parliamentarians had been up to prior to their murders. When Castresana wouldn't budge, Rivera resigned in frustration at the end of 2009, and the rest of her highly experienced team dispersed as well.

In late 2010, after Castresana himself had resigned, conflicts between Rivera and CICIG became embarrassingly public. On the eve of the long-delayed trial in the PARLACEN cases, and not coincidentally on the eve of the publication of a series of stories in the Salvadoran daily *El Mundo* that would call into question the Public Ministry's theory of those crimes, offi-cials of CICIG brought a "defamation" (libel) lawsuit against Rivera, the United Nations revoked her immunity, and CICIG sought an INTERPOL arrest warrant against her for obstruction of justice (though Dall'Anese claimed in the press that he was merely supporting an initiative of the Pub-lic Ministry). While she could not be extradited from Costa Rica on these charges, they were sufficient to prevent her from traveling to Guatemala and giving testimony that might have undermined the Public Ministry's (er-roneous) prosecution in the PARLACEN case. All of this was accomplished within four days, suggesting a significant effort. The basis for the criminal complaint consisted of unauthorized tape recordings of Rivera speaking by phone with a fellow CICIG investigator and with former PNC deputy chief Javier Figueroa, who was under house arrest in Austria. The alleged "ob-struction," at least as Rivera tells it, consisted of her issuing verbal assur-ances and advice to Figueroa while attempting to keep him available as a potential witness.[136]

One can certainly question Rivera's judgment in taking her disagree-ments public, releasing confidential documents, and perhaps overzealously advocating protected witness status for a central figure in the crimes (Fig-ueroa). Nonetheless, the information Rivera has presented does raise seri-ous questions about some of Castresana's decisions, which seem to have steered CICIG and the Public Ministry away from considering high state officials in these politically incendiary crimes. Moreover it appears that Dall'Anese cooperated with the Public Ministry in muzzling her.

Under Dall'Anese, CICIG and the Public Ministry eventually indicted Carlos Vielmann and sought his extradition from Spain for murder and conspiracy (in the Pavón prison killings). CICIG and the Public Ministry later retreated from trying to extradite Vielmann and asked Spanish officials to prosecute him instead, claiming that it was impossible to ensure his security while attempting to bring him to justice in Guatemala.[137] Related extradition requests languished against former PNC chief Erwin Sperisen (a dual citizen ensconced in Switzerland) and PNC deputy chief Figueroa (still in Austria). Víctor Rivera (Zacarías) was murdered in April 2008, one hour after giving an interview to a member of the press. Other members of the same alleged crime network remained at large.

Sadly, after the Vielmann indictments, former vice president Eduardo Stein, who had so strongly supported the creation of CICIG, began to complain that CICIG was "out of control" and in need of political supervision—an echo of his perennial complaints against MINUGUA.[138] As with MINUGUA, Stein's objections may signal that CICIG was doing something right.

CICIG suffered from many of the same internal challenges that afflicted MINUGUA. Faced with a huge task and limited resources, it did not have a clear strategy. Its public information strategy was weak, consisting mainly of press releases and a poorly maintained. Its hastily constructed administrative arrangements were troubled. Since it was UN-sponsored, but not a UN body per se, relations with New York were complicated.[139]

For all of its challenges, CICIG brought an unprecedented degree of accountability for wrongdoing to Guatemala. Yet it faced the same question of sustainability that confronted MINUGUA: how could it work its way out of a job that only *it* had so far been able to perform? With its mandate renewed through September 2013, and with President Otto Pérez Molina's commitment to request a further extension through 2015, as of this writing CICIG still has time to build capacity in Guatemala.[140] It is less clear how CICIG will go about this, even with its excellent entrée to work with the Public Ministry. Its transference of skills so far has been concentrated in the special anti-impunity group FECI and will need to develop a broader scope.[141] By design, CICIG's capacity is limited by the performance of Guatemalan institutions, including the police and the courts, which remain weak and compromised. Aspects of Guatemalan law make prosecution difficult, and CICIG has had relatively little success so far in getting Congress to pass new or amended law.

CICIG presents three positive lessons that may also shed indirect light on the MINUGUA experience. First, its successes to date within the formerly moribund Public Ministry suggest that an internationally sponsored commission that is required by statute to function within or in close collaboration with national institutions may have a better chance of fomenting real reform than one that is more autonomous. That is, the reduced autonomy of CICIG versus the original CICIACS concept may have been a blessing in disguise. Second, it demonstrates that it is sometimes worth the risk to very aggressively name and shame individual officeholders who obstruct justice, thereby securing their removal from office, setting new expectations for what conduct is acceptable, and creating opportunities for honest and competent national officials to do their work. Third, it shows that by focusing extensive international financial and human resources on a specific set of problems, it *is* possible to effect substantial, measurable, positive change—even in Guatemala.

▌ Notes

1. Aracelly Santana, untitled memorandum, to Iqbal Riza through Kieran Prendergast, June 11, 2002. Notes taken during the Secretary-General's meeting with Koenigs on June 11, 2002.

2. Author interview, Tom Koenigs, New York, February 7, 2007.

3. Martha Doggett, "Note to the File: Meeting on Guatemala with Mr. Tom Köenigs and Mr. Gerd Merrem," June 7, 2002.

4. Gerd Merrem, "Meeting of Norwegian Ambassador regarding the Mission's Transition Process," to Kieran Prendergast, July 16, 2002.

5. Martha Doggett, "Note to the File: MINUGUA's Future," July 26, 2002.

6. "MINUGUA Weekly Situation Report 1–7 August 2002."

7. Angela Kane, "Meeting Convened by President Portillo," letter to Kieran Prendergast, September 11, 2002.

8. Angela Kane, "Guatemala: Note to Mr. Prendergast Through Mr. Türk," to Kieran Prendergast, November 14, 2002; United Nations, "United Nations Verification Mission in Guatemala: Renewal of Mandate Report, Report of the Secretary-General," A/58/262, August 8, 2003.

9. Rosalina Tuyuc, untitled letter to Kofi Annan, cosigned by twenty-three indigenous and women's organizations, July 8, 2003.

10. Martha Doggett, "Mission to Guatemala, 17–21 March 2003," May 6, 2003.

11. Tom Koenigs, "Violent Land Clash in Guatemala," to Kieran Prendergast, September 3, 2004.

12. I refer to the summary executions of escapees from the "Infiernito" (Little Hell) prison in 2005, as well as those of seven prisoners at the Pavón prison compound in 2006. None of those killed resisted their arrests. See Lafitte Fernandez, *Crimen de estado: El caso PARLACEN* (San Salvador: Ediciones Aura, 2011).

13. See Lafitte Fernandez and Miguel Jara, "Crimen de diputados de PARLACEN: Los asesinaron por $5 millones," *El Mundo,* November 15, 2010; and Fernandez, *Crimen de estado,* which includes annexes with a collection of incriminating documents leaked from CICIG.

14. MINUGUA, "Transition Report" [Preliminary Draft], March 22, 2004, 3–7.

15. Tom Koenigs, "Background and Talking Points for Meeting with President Portillo," to Angela Kane, September 9, 2002; also "MINUGUA Weekly Situation Report 30 September–6 October 2002."

16. Martha Doggett, "2 August 2002 meeting of the Friends of Guatemala," to Tom Koenigs, August 23, 2002.

17. MINUGUA, "Proposal for a Project for the Transition of Programs for the Promotion and Protection of Human Rights in Guatemala from MINUGUA to OHCHR, 2003–2005," undated.

18. Tom Koenigs, "United Nations National Transition Volunteers Project (from mid-2003–December 2004)," to Kieran Prendergast, July 18, 2003.

19. Author interview, Tom Koenigs, New York, February 7, 2007.

20. MINUGUA, "Transition Report," 9–11.

21. The series was entitled *Retomando el camino: Tareas pendientes en la construcción de la paz* (Getting Back on the Road: Unfinished Tasks for Building Peace), and included eleven booklets on such themes as human rights and justice, security and the military, and indigenous peoples.

22. Author interview with Tom Koenigs, New York, February 7, 2007.

23. As early as May 2000, MINUGUA legal adviser Luis Pásara wrote that for 2000 and 2001, the mission should select a few themes to focus on, and then define what personnel and field presence it needed to do those tasks, rather than taking the mission's existing structure as the default. Luis Pásara, "Informe del Grupo de Trabajo subre Transición," to Jean Arnault, May 3, 2000.

24. Tom Koenigs, untitled letter to Kofi Annan, December 9, 2004.

25. Aracelly Santana, "AED's Comments on MINUGUA's Draft RBB Framework for the 2004 Budget," to James Mutiso, August 13, 2003.

26. Anonymous, "MINUGUA's Transition: Questions and Issues for Discussion," undated but filed as July 2003.

27. Kieran Prendergast, "Consultative Group Meeting," to Tom Koenigs, May 2, 2003.

28. Tom Koenigs, "More on Consultative Group," to Kieran Prendergast, May 7, 2003.

29. María Maldonado, "Consultative Group Meeting," to Kieran Prendergast, April 25, 2003.

30. Tom Koenigs, "Consultative Group Results," to Kieran Prendergast, May 16, 2003.

31. Ibid.

32. John Renninger, "UNDP Ambush: Note to Mr. Prendergast Through Mr. Türk," May 20, 2003.

33. Kieran Prendergast, "Consultative Group," to Tom Koenigs, May 21, 2003.

34. Author interview with a UN official who preferred anonymity while commenting on Corlazzoli's conduct, February 2008.

35. Juan Pablo Corlazzoli, untitled FAX to Blanca Antonini, May 30, 2003.

36. "MINUGUA Weekly Situation Report 5–11 May 2003."

37. Tom Koenigs, "Hostage-Taking by Civil Patrollers in Guatemala," to Kieran Prendergast, October 27, 2003.

38. Tom Koenigs, "MINUGUA Public Message on the Eve of the Elections; Visit by FRG Leadership," to Kieran Prendergast, November 4, 2003.

39. Michael Leffert, "Guatemala: Signs of a New Solidarity Against FRG and Efraín Ríos Montt," *NotiCen,* August 7, 2003.

40. Tom Koenigs, "Ríos-Montt Candidacy," to Kieran Prendergast, June 16, 2003.

41. Kieran Prendergast, "Note to the Secretary General: Mission to Guatemala, 3–8 July 2003," July 21, 2003.

42. MINUGUA, "Informe de MINUGUA sobre los disturbios del 24 al 25 de Julio de 2003 en la Ciudad de Guatemala," August 6, 2003.

43. Tom Koenigs, "Aftermath of Constitutional Court Decision, Disturbances in Guatemala," to Kieran Prendergast, July 31, 2003.

44. Ibid.

45. Martha Doggett, untitled e-mail to John Renninger, July 25, 2003.

46. "MINUGUA Weekly Situation Report 18–24 August 2003." The EU mission was headed by Jannis Sakellariou (Germany) with Rafael Lopez-Pintor (Spain) as his deputy, while former Peruvian interim president Valentín Paniagua headed the OAS group.

47. Tom Koenigs, "MINUGUA Weekly Situation Report 25–31 August 2003" and "Latest Pre-Electoral Developments in Guatemala," to Kieran Prendergast, October 30, 2003.

48. Tom Koenigs, "Update on Political Developments in Guatemala," to Kieran Prendergast, September 2, 2003.

49. Tom Koenigs, "Preview of Guatemala's National Elections," to Kieran Prendergast, November 6, 2003.

50. Ibid.

51. John Renninger, "Electoral Assistance to Guatemala," to Kieran Prendergast, August 22, 2003.

52. Tom Koenigs, "Guatemala Election: Midday Report," to Kieran Prendergast, November 9, 2003.

53. Tom Koenigs, "Guatemala Election Results," to Kieran Prendergast, November 10, 2003.

54. Tom Koenigs, "Second Round of Guatemalan Presidential Elections," to Kieran Prendergast, December 11, 2003.

55. Tom Koenigs, "Presidential Election Update; Meeting with Eduardo Stein," to Kieran Prendergast, December 19, 2003.

56. Tom Koenigs, "Land Conflicts," to Kieran Prendergast, July 15, 2004.

57. Rosalina Tuyuc, untitled letter to Kofi Annan, cosigned by twenty-three indigenous and women's organizations, July 8, 2003.

58. Martha Doggett, "Mission to Guatemala, 17–21 March 2003," May 6, 2003.

59. "United Nations Verification Mission in Guatemala, Reports of the Secretary-General," A/59/307, August 30, 2004, paragraph 9.

60. Tom Koenigs, "Berger Inaugurates New Peace Accords Commission," to Kieran Prendergast, March 11, 2004.

61. MINUGUA, "Thirteenth Report on Human Rights by the United Nations Verification Mission in Guatemala," A/57/336, August 22, 2002, paragraph 3.

62. Tom Koenigs, "Intimidatory Attack on Media Figure Jose Rueben Zamora," to Kieran Prendergast, June 25, 2003. Such attacks have not dissuaded Zamora in subsequent years from continuing to publish exposés on organized crime and impunity.

63. Tom Koenigs, "MINUGUA Report on Torture in Counter-Drug Operation," to Kieran Prendergast, April 11, 2003.

64. "MINUGUA Weekly Situation Report 18–24 November 2002."

65. "MINUGUA Weekly Situation Report 28 April–4 May 2003."

66. MINUGUA, "Towards a Secure Guatemala: Plan of Action for the Strengthening of Public Security," January 30, 2003.

67. Andrew Hudson and Alexandra W. Taylor, "The International Commission Against Impunity in Guatemala: A New Model for International Criminal Justice Mechanisms," *Journal of International Criminal Justice* 8 (2010): 56; see also Paul Goepfert, "The International Commission Against Impunity in Guatemala: Undoing the Legacy of Violence and Corruption," *ReVista* (Fall/Winter 2011), www.drclas.harvard.edu/publications/revistaonline/fall-2010-winter-2011/international-commission-against-impunity-guatemala.

68. "MINUGUA Weekly Situation Report 13–19 January 2003. "

69. MINUGUA, "Informe ante la Reunión del Grupo Conultivo para Guatemala," May 7, 2003, 7.

70. "MINUGUA Weekly Situation Report 14–20 April 2003."

71. "MINUGUA Weekly Situation Report 10–16 March 2003."

72. MINUGUA, "Informe ante la Reunión del Grupo Consultivo," 10–12.

73. Tom Koenigs, "Dissolution of Estado Mayor Presidencial," to Kieran Prendergast, October 29, 2003.

74. "MINUGUA Weekly Situation Report 2–8 December 2002."

75. "MINUGUA Weekly Situation Report 31 March–6 April 2003."

76. Jared Kotler, "9th Report," to Aracelly Santana and Martha Doggett, July 9, 2004.

77. "MINUGUA Weekly Situation Report 19–25 January 2004," and "MINUGUA Weekly Situation Report 23–29 February 2004."

78. "MINUGUA Weekly Situation Report 2–8 February 2004."

79. Hina Jilani, "Promotion and Protection of Human Rights: Human Rights Defenders," report by the special representative of the Secretary-General on the situation of human rights defenders, submitted pursuant to Commission on Human Rights resolution 2000/61, Addendum, "Mission to Guatemala," December 6, 2002, E?CN.4/2003/104/Add.2.

80. Tom Koenigs, "Background Notes for Your Visit to Washington," to Angela Kane, November 11, 2002.

81. Tom Koenigs, "Proposed UN-OAS-Guatemalan Commission on Clandestine Groups," to Kieran Prendergast, February 14, 2003; María Maldonado, "Note de archive: Reunión con el Sr. Edgar Gutiérrez, Ministro de Relaciones Exteriores de Guatemala," August 7, 2003.

82. Tom Koenigs, "Developments This Week on Proposed Clandestine Groups Inquiry," to Kieran Prendergast, January 31, 2003.

83. Kieran Prendergast, "Investigation Commission in Guatemala—The Role of the United Nations," Attached to "Legal Opinion on CICIACS," to Tom Koenigs, April 22, 2003.

84. "Agreement Between the United Nations and the Government of Guatemala for the Establishment of a Commission for the Investigation of Illegal Armed Groups and Clandestine Security Organizations in Guatemala, ('CICIACS')," January 7, 2004.

85. Tom Koenigs, "CICIACS Comments," to Kieran Prendergast, June 19, 2003.

86. "MINUGUA Weekly Situation Report 23–29 June 2003."

87. Martha Doggett, "Mission to Guatemala, 3–11 May 2004, CICIACS Update," May 14, 2004. Conveyed with Kieran Prendergast, "CICIACS," to Tom Koenigs, May 14, 2004. Also, regarding Pérez's presidential ambitions, Tom Koenigs, "Developments Since Your Visit," to Kieran Prendergast, May 18, 2004. Pérez finally won the presidency in November 2011.

88. Tom Koenigs, "Guatemalan High Court Rejects CICIACS," to Kieran Prendergast, August 6, 2004; Kieran Prendergast, "Commission for the Investigation of Illegal Groups and Clandestine Security Organizations (CICIACS)," to Louise Arbour and Tom Koenigs, September 27, 2004.

89. Kieran Prendergast, "Commission for the Investigation of Illegal Armed Groups and Clandestine Security Organizations (CICIACS)," to Louise Arbour and Tom Koenigs, conveying report drafted by Martha Doggett, September 27, 2004.

90. Kieran Prendergast, "Office of the High Commission for Human Rights," to Tom Koenigs, November 7, 2003.

91. Tom Koenigs, "Developments Since Your Visit," to Kieran Prendergast, May 18, 2004.

92. John Renninger, "Guatemala," to Kieran Prendergast, May 18, 2004.

93. Bertrand Ramcharan, "Meeting with the Ambassador of Guatemala," to Kieran Prendergast, June 21, 2004.

94. Tom Koenigs, "Establishment of an Office of the High Commissioner in Guatemala," to Kieran Prendergast, June 25, 2004; Tom Koenigs, "Strategy Regarding the High Commissioner's Office," to Kieran Prendergast, September 8, 2004.

95. MINUGUA, "Conferencia de prensa sobre la importancia de instalar la Oficina del ACNUDH en Guatemala, Intervencion del señor Tom Koenigs, Representante Especial del Secretario General y Jefe de Misión," August 12, 2004.

96. Giorgia Passarelli, "Note on the Meeting Between the HC and the Permanent Representative of Guteamala," to Aracelly Santana, October 5, 2004.

97. MINUGUA (presumably transition coordinator Marcie Mersky), "MINUGUA Transition Strategy 2002–2004," June 2003.

98. Ibid., 1.

99. MINUGUA, "Transition Report" [Preliminary Draft], March 22, 2004, 2–4. The following section draws heavily and quite directly from this unusually candid report.

100. Ibid., 4–5.

101. Ibid., 4.

102. Ibid., 6.

103. Ibid.

104. Ibid., 7.

105. Ibid., 8.

106. Ibid.

107. Ibid., 10; Tom Koenigs, "National Transition Volunteers Program," to Kieran Prendergast, November 9, 2004.

108. MINUGUA, "Transition Report," 10–11.

109. Tom Koenigs, "Closing of MINUGUA Field Offices," to Kieran Prendergast, September 8, 2004; Antonio Ordoñez, "Está en nuestras manos," ElPeriodico, September 7, 2004.

110. "La partida de Minugua," El Periódico, September 4, 2004 (editorial).

111. Jared Kotler, "Chixoy," to Martha Doggett, September 9, 2004.

112. "MINUGUA Weekly Situation Report 15–21 November 2004."

113. "MINUGUA Weekly Situation Report 29 November–5 December 2004."

114. "MINUGUA Weekly Situation Report 6–12 December 2004." Koenigs left the country on December 30. The chief administrative officer Neva Donalds remained in the country until mid-March 2005, overseeing the process of packing up the mission's records (which were shipped back to New York), and disposing of property.

115. Fernandez, Crimen de estado, 95–107.

116. Ibid., 108–132.

117. For a detailed account, see Fernandez, Crimen de estado, and the attached documents from CICIG investigations.

118. "Acuerdo entre la Organización de Naciones Unidas y el Gobierno de Guatemala relative al establecimiento de un Comisión Internactional Contra La Impunidad en Guatemala (CICIG)," New York, December 12, 2006.

119. See Fernandez, Crimen de estado. There were strong elements of dumb luck, including the fact that a newly purchased car driven by the murderers had been equipped with GPS tracking devices that put the cops at the scene of the crime. The fact that the victims were Salvadoran was critical, because efforts by Guatemalan

police officials to cover up the crime fell apart as Salvadoran investigators rounded up security camera video footage and witnesses implicating Guatemalan police and followed up on the whereabouts of the car. Guatemalan police cover-up efforts were sloppy: they washed the top of the car, but not the bottom, which retained soil and plants matched to the crime scene, and the Toyota Yaris had physical signs of overloading from the six beefy cops crammed inside.

120. Author translation. A video recording of this chilling conversation is on YouTube at www.youtube.com/watch?v=qrUfUc-BdII, posted by *elPeriódico* under the title "Caso Parlacen: policías capturados."

121. For a detailed account, see Fernandez, *Crimen de estado* and annexes.

122. "Guatemalan Government Says Murder of Salvadoran Parliamentarians Solved," *NotiCen*, August 2, 2007. According to Fernandez, drawing on information from Giséle Rivera, the phone record analysis was conducted under the supervision of Víctor Soto, who was very likely involved in planning the killing. He argues convincingly that these records were unreliable.

123. Marlies Stappers et al., *Cambiar la cultura de la violencia por la cultura de la vida: Los primeros dos años de al Comisión Internactional contra la Impunidad en Guatemala* (Guatemala: Impunity Watch, Centro Internacional para la Justicia Transicional, and Plataforma Holandesa contra la Impunidad en Guatemala, 2010), 16–19.

124. Hudson and Taylor, "Commission Against Impunity," 61–65.

125. Frank Bajak and Juan Carlos Llorca, "U.N.-Backed Investigators Shake Up Guatemala," Associated Press, November 14, 2010.

126. David Grann, "A Murder Foretold," *The New Yorker,* April 4, 2011; Julie López, "Guatemala's Crossroads: Democratization of Violence and Second Chances" (Washington, DC: Woodrow Wilson Center for Scholars, Working Paper Series on Organized Crime in the Americas, December 2010), 20–21.

127. For the history of CICIG's first two years, see Stappers et al., *Cambiar la cultura de la violencia;* and Julia Schünemann, *Mirando al Monstruo a la Cara: La Comisión Internacional contra la Impunidad en Guatemala y el "Contrato de construcción del Estado de Derecho"* (Madrid: FRIDE, 2010).

128. See Grann, "A Murder Foretold," for a detailed description. Rosenberg's video accusation can be viewed with English subtitles at several locations on YouTube, for example, www.youtube.com/watch?v=mC_ODpxMA10.

129. Grann, "A Murder Foretold," and Hudson and Taylor, "Commission Against Impunity," 62.

130. Grann, "A Murder Foretold."

131. See the summary of CICIG cases at http://cicig.org/index.php?page=casos.

132. Ibid. Also Latin America Data Base, "Guatemala: Head of UN Anti-Impunity Commission Resigns," *LADB*, July 1, 2010, consulted at http://ladb.unm.edu/noticen/2010/07/01-050532.

133. Steven Dudley, "Guatemala Arrests Show Something Is Working," *InSight Crime: Organized Crime in the Americas,* July 13, 2011.

134. International Crisis Group, "Learning to Walk Without a Crutch: An Assessment of the International Commission Against Impunity in Guatemala," Latin America Report no. 36, ICG, May 31, 2011, 9.

135. Fernandez, *Crimen de estado,* and Fernandez and Jara, "Crimen de diputados de PARLACEN,"

136. Fernandez, *Crimen de estado,* 179–205.

137. Paola Herrera, "MP espera que España responda sobre Carlos Vielmann," *Prensa Libre,* March 17, 2012.

138. Bajak and Llorca, "U.N.-Backed Investigators Shake Up Guatemala."

139. Martha Doggett, "Contending with Conflict: Managing Crime in Central America," *Harvard International Review* (Fall 2011): 72.

140. Interestingly, Pérez, who opposed CICIACS in the early days, has been unequivocal in his support for CICIG's presence in the country.

141. See International Crisis Group, "Learning to Walk Without a Crutch."

8 | Mandate vs. Strategy: Lessons from an Underpowered Mission

WITHIN THE GUATEMALAN SOCIAL, political, and professional elite many individuals have a vision for a better, more just, more democratic, and more stable country. Such individuals helped negotiate the peace accords, served as government ministers and as representatives on the Accompaniment Commission, and showed incredible courage as judges, prosecutors, and human rights advocates. In the general public, there were tens of thousands of people who worked hard to organize against injustice, often at considerable personal sacrifice and risk. Yet these individuals were outmatched. Reviewing the cumulative effects of decisions made by elites during MINUGUA's decade and beyond, it is difficult to escape the conclusion that the dominant elite goals have been maintenance of upper-class privilege, personal advancement and enrichment, suppression of enemies, and prevention of anything resembling a system of institutionalized legal accountability for wrongdoing. Within the general public, the majority view was disaffection from politics and ignorance.[1]

Thus the basic problem of international peacebuilding in Guatemala was that the international community, the friends states, the donors of the dialogue group, and the staff of the UN Secretariat itself were more committed to promoting social equity, the rule of law, human rights, and democracy in Guatemala than were most of the upper class and political elite of Guatemala. The international actors also cared more about specific institutional reforms than did most of the politically ill informed, alienated, and manipulated Guatemalan public.

This created a basic dilemma for the United Nations. On one hand, it could attempt to provide a counterweight to the selfish and destructive tendencies of national elites by encouraging international financial assistance that in effect replaced funds that those elites refused to provide for their own country through taxes; helping develop working state institutions that those elites had failed or refused to create for their own country, despite the availability within Latin America of numerous successful models to emulate; monitoring human rights conditions that were ostensibly guaranteed by the Guatemalan constitution but routinely violated by the Guatemalan state; and coaxing the government du jour to actually carry out policies that multiple previous Guatemalan governments had agreed were essential to long-term social peace and stability. Doing all of these things might create a chance for those members of the Guatemalan social and political elite that *did* care about building a democratic country to gain a toehold and implement some lasting changes. The downside of the United Nations' doing these things was that it enabled the reactionary elements of Guatemala's elite to avoid paying taxes, avoid compromising their selfish and sometimes criminal interests for the good of the country, and avoid confronting the international and domestic political consequences of their iniquity.

An alternative was to play hardball and stop enabling. This would have entailed the United Nations' finding a way to impose serious conditionality on everything from international aid programs to the presence of the UN mission itself. The message would be, in effect, that the United Nations will help but only if the government and the economic elite do their part. If they don't do their part, or stop doing their part, the United Nations would leave, or scale back, or in other ways impose negative sanctions. The downside of such an approach is that it would provide the most recalcitrant elements of the Guatemalan political system an opportunity to veto all reform. If they just behaved badly enough, the United Nations would pack up and leave, leaving proreform groups—and the majority of the population—to suffer in isolation. Jean Arnault questioned whether the international community had the stomach to play "truth or consequences" with Guatemala, and it is noteworthy that donors only acted with some unity when things got really bad under Portillo. There is some reason to doubt whether the Guatemalan elite would respond constructively to negative sanctions. During the late 1970s, Guatemala's military government was willing to reject US assistance and accept isolation rather than being subject to scrutiny on its human rights practices.[2]

This was a genuine dilemma, and it ran through all of the United Nations' interactions with Guatemalan politicians and business elites. In the United Nations' files, there are numerous notes on meetings in which high UN officials and representatives of donors tell Guatemalan officials that "this country cannot continue to expect the international community to contribute more than $300 million a year in development assistance without the Guatemalans paying their share of the burden."[3] Yet despite the obvious necessity of, among other things, increasing taxes enough to pay for the basic functions required of any state, three consecutive Guatemalan governments failed to do what they or their predecessors had promised, and the international community continued to enable this behavior.

The United Nations' job in Guatemala, then, was to walk a tightrope between enabling as necessary to allow positive changes to take root, while imposing negative sanctions where essential to prevent backsliding or outright obstruction of changes that, from the point of view of the international community, were essential to long-term stability. Peacebuilding was a constant process of discernment and judgment about how to calibrate and combine two basically contradictory tools—enabling or accountability—to modestly improve outcomes on specific issues.

This concluding chapter attempts to assess how successfully MINUGUA accomplished this nearly impossible mission. Attempting to draw lessons from a single case history is uncertain business. In the absence of a parallel universe in which to replay events with different choices, the best we can do is make judgments based on the preponderance of evidence, emphasizing the contemporaneous documentary record in which decision-makers' views, analyses, and omissions are in plain view and untempered by post-hoc rethinking. What follows is sometimes positive about the United Nations' performance, and sometimes critical. The criticism is not intended to denigrate the United Nations or its agents in the Guatemalan peace process, who did exceptional work under difficult conditions, but rather to identify how the organization as a whole can do better as it confronts analogous situations in the future.

There is no doubt that MINUGUA and the United Nations' support for the peace talks contributed in vital ways to ending the war in Guatemala. That war could easily have sputtered on for many years, much as Colombia's has. The URNG's small forces and sporadic operations meant that it needed relatively few weapons and supplies: with its small but dedicated support base, it could have fought on. Moreover, with the increased drug trafficking opportunities in Guatemala and the rebels' bases in remote areas, it was only a matter of time before the URNG got into that business just as the FARC did in Colombia. As Arnault has pointed out, low intensity conflicts are not necessarily easy to settle—quite the opposite. In this context, MINUGUA's on-the-spot human rights investigations and reporting after 1994 created the transparency needed for the URNG to take a leap of faith and disarm. This was essential for the peace process to get around what political scientist Barbara Walter has called "the critical barrier" to civil war settlement: rebels generally have to put down their arms while government forces keep theirs, and this puts ex-rebels at disproportionate risk.[4] While the URNG and the Guatemalan military created confidence-building arrangements of their own, that probably would not have happened if MINUGUA had not first created a context of transparency. Without MINUGUA, it is unlikely that the war would have ended when it did, if at all.

Moreover, although the United Nations invested relatively little in the moderation effort, it succeeded where the Guatemalan Catholic Church had not. Arnault's diplomatic skills were clearly central to this achievement, as were the increased visibility and political stakes for the Guatemalan parties that accompanied the United Nations' involvement. The early involvement of the international development banks and the IMF helped the parties to arrive at a socioeconomic agreement that, while not revolutionary, had the potential to bring Guatemala's institutions and policies more in line with best development practices. While the accords were overly broad and short on verifiable commitments to government action, these weaknesses were largely the result of the agenda set by Guatemalan civil society groups in the earliest stages of the peace process. With this agenda, and the limited political capacity of the negotiating parties, Arnault and DPA did about as good a job as was feasible, with one critical exception in the area of rule of law.

While the peace process achieved its minimum goals of halting the fighting and reintegrating the URNG, it also fell far short of the deeper aims laid out in the accords. The most important provisions of the peace accords were never implemented, largely because of the shortcomings of Guatemalan actors and institutions. The Guatemalan rebels lacked bargaining power once they were demobilized. Successive governments found that they either lacked sufficient votes in the legislature to implement reforms, or that short-term political costs were too high in the face of determined resistance by powerful interest groups. Profound state institutional weaknesses and design flaws carried over from the war years or even earlier. A basic institutional barrier was the requirement that constitutional reforms be approved by popular referendum in a context of illiteracy, low voter motivation, and mass alienation from politics. MINUGUA did not have the power to correct such deep, systemic problems. Guatemalans will have to find ways to fix them over the long haul.

Within this context the United Nations did excellent work, but cannot be said to have optimized its impact. For example, during the final stages of the negotiations, the United Nations arranged only belated and perfunctory guidance on the design of civilian police or justice system reforms, in contrast to the strong consulting teams brought in on socioeconomic questions. While poor decisions, appointments, and priority setting by the Arzú and Portillo governments worsened the public security crisis, this merely exacerbated the underlying institutional weaknesses of the police and justice systems that were not adequately addressed in the peace accords. Establishing and maintaining the rule of law is foundational to most other development goals; its absence subverts democracy, imposes massive economic losses, and particularly harms the lower and middle economic classes that cannot afford private protection.

The lack of international guidance on public security and rule of law issues is particularly striking because it represents an unlearning of one of the main affirmative lessons of the Salvadoran peace process, where intensive UN-sponsored guidance to the parties produced a design for a National Civilian Police force that, while not without flaws, was a revolutionary change from the unaccountable militarized police forces of the past. In El Salvador, the UN mediation team helped provide a vision of civilian policing that neither the government nor the rebels had even conceived of. In Guatemala, the question of police reforms came late in the process. The parties were exhausted, and the result was unfortunate haste.

Like the UN negotiating team, MINUGUA itself did many things right, and also made some mistakes. Its human rights investigations were careful, responsible, and impartial, enabling it to issue authoritative reports on the conduct of state agents and agencies. Its presence quickly and significantly reduced human rights violations and helped make it possible to achieve partial justice for the singularly important and repugnant murder of Bishop Gerardi. MINUGUA'S outreach to isolated and marginalized communities created political space that particularly benefited indigenous people and especially indigenous women. Some of its institutional strengthening projects made valuable contributions. For example, the PROLEY project helped guide Congress through the drafting of human rights, financial regulation, and government decentralization legislation during both the Arzú and Portillo administrations. While the mission's institutional strengthening projects were too small scale to bring the Public Ministry, the PNC, or the PDH up to a satisfactory level of performance, the mission's on-the-job training and coaching did produce some improvements. The mission's presence and calming advice helped create stability through such dangerous moments as the FRG-sponsored riots of July 2003 and the elections that followed in November. In its final year, the mission carried out an innovative project to bring young, mostly indigenous Guatemalans into the mission, helping to build skills and experience that may have long-term value for the country.

Throughout the mission, weekly reporting was replete with examples of street-level conflict resolution by the mission, as well as efforts to build the capacity of the many marginalized sectors and communities to advocate more effectively for their own interests. It is beyond the scope of this book to measure the long-term impact of such local, low-visibility empowerment. However, people who staffed MINUGUA's local offices saw qualitative changes in the willingness and ability of poor people, especially poor women, to organize and express their needs in politically effective ways. This diffuse, local-level work may have been the mission's greatest contribution to helping reverse the erosion of civil society and local-level leadership caused by decades of terror, murder, and torture directed against anyone who showed ability to mobilize and lead others.

The mission's greatest failing was its chronic lack of strategy. Given the weaknesses of the Arzú government and its successors, their many political disincentives to implementing the accords, and the near disappearance of the URNG as a political actor, much of the political burden of ensuring that the accords were implemented fell on the mission. Yet the mission had no direct authority over implementation. Given this mismatch of responsibilities and actual power, MINUGUA had two main avenues available. First, it could make maximum use of its mandate to communicate directly with the public and build broad, motivated popular support for the reforms embodied in the accords. There were limits on such an approach, including a poorly educated population, concentrated ownership of media outlets, and cost. If successful in mobilizing proreform public opinion, however, this could compel national political parties to make the accords a priority. The second avenue for the mission would be to use its verification mandate in a way that maximized its political leverage vis-à-vis government policy. This would require the mission to have at least some ability to impose aid conditionality, and to focus what leverage was available on a few issues where progress was possible. While mission reporting showed an awareness of these possible strategies, in practice it did not consistently follow either of them.

In the months leading up to the crucial popular referendum on constitutional reforms, for example, the mission was slow to recognize the risk of a negative vote, largely because it lacked high-quality, representative information on public opinion. Although it had sought voluntary contributions to the trust fund to finance public education on the constitutional reforms, it started the campaign late and spent too sparingly on broadcast media given the very high stakes. There is no way to know whether better implementation could have changed the outcome of that vote, nor is it clear what scale of effort would have been enough to sufficiently alter public opinion or voter turnout. Nonetheless, if the United Nations faces a similar situation in the future, it would improve its odds of success by obtaining accurate and current information on public opinion and making maximum feasible use of any authority it has to communicate directly with the public.

In implementing its verification mandate, the mission never really embraced advice from DPA and from some friends states to choose a few of the most important issues and focus its attention on those. Even in the final year, when the mission ostensibly focused on demilitarization and human rights, its staffing decisions did not match the strategy. Instead, most of the time the mission took its mandate to verify the full accords as obliging it to dilute its verification capacity across the full range of issues in the accords. Periodically the mission staff would discuss strategy and end up producing a work plan that "prioritized" nearly everything. This of course reflected the fact that Guatemala needed reforms in all areas, but it also pointed to an institutionalized pattern of work that seemed to be difficult for the mission to change.

There was one exception: the mission did consistently place a higher priority on pressuring three consecutive governments to raise taxes. The logic behind this was that increased state revenues were necessary to increase health and education services, address land inequalities, and undertake such costly ventures as making indigenous language translators available in the courts. Moreover, amid the many provisions of the accords, the government's promises to increase taxes and social spending were among the few that were explicit and quantifiable. But politically this was a lost cause: taxes were probably the one issue on which it was most difficult for Guatemala's fragile governments to move given private sector resistance. Other issues, including the rule of law, might have been more tractable.

Finally, the mission was late in preparing the ground for its departure. It could have begun to incorporate carefully vetted Guatemalans into its staff, even at senior levels, midway through the mission. It might also have moved earlier to a policy of co-verification in collaboration with Guatemalan institutions, either state or NGOs. Doing either or both would have built more local capacity. But co-verification would have had significant downsides: the mission would have had less control over human rights investigations, with potential for reduced accuracy and credibility, and would have faced frictions over priorities, process, and publicity. More fundamentally, there were serious problems of leadership competence, political commitments, and lack of resources on the part of all the state counterpart agencies such as the PNC, Public Ministry, and PDH. The United Nations should consider to what extent it is possible to bargain for better transition conditions on the front end, prior to deploying verification missions. It could, for example, demand specific credible commitments by the state to provide adequate financial and human resources for counterpart agencies and grant the United Nations some say over the appointment and continuation of agency heads. In Guatemala, there were probably insurmountable constitutional and political obstacles to allowing a UN mission to choose or fire attorneys general or ombudsmen, but even a formal mandate to publicly assess those individuals' performance and cooperation, and to link agency budgets to such assessments, might result in national agencies to whom the United Nations could successfully transfer skills.

■ The Downside of Consensus-Building Mechanisms

From the earliest stages of the Guatemalan peace process, efforts to build a consensus agenda through dialogue took the place of direct negotiations involving people with actual power. Civil society dialogue was much celebrated by observers who were relieved to see open public debate about important questions in a country where political participation and speech had been so brutally suppressed for so many years. There is a strong finding in

interdisciplinary research on economic and social development that outcomes are better when stakeholders participate in setting priorities and
making decisions. This is common sense, and it conforms to liberal democratic as well as social democratic political philosophies. Working to build
civil society seemed like one of the main approaches available to the mission to offset the very organized power of antireform coalitions among the
social and political elite. In the early phases of the mission, groups such as
COPMAGUA were strong enough to suggest that they could significantly
shape national politics.[5] Yet civil groups failed to coalesce around a coherent, focused message. Increasingly the participatory forums in Guatemala
did not set priorities or make decisions. Much of the time they made lists.

The first government to explore the possibility of negotiating peace,
that of President Vinicio Cerezo (1986–1991), was vulnerable to a coup
d'état and much of the army was uncompromisingly opposed to negotiating
with the URNG. As a result, Cerezo did not authorize his delegates to meet
directly with leaders of the URNG. Instead, various civil society groupings
held those meetings as part of the so-called Oslo process. Because of its
emphasis on establishing a consensus agenda, this process inevitably cast a
wide net, incorporating most of the priorities of most of the participating
groups. The resulting list of desiderata was then distilled somewhat in the
eleven-point agenda that was incorporated in the Mexico Agreement once
direct talks began in 1994. Thus the role of public dialogue at the earliest
stages of the peace process established a broad substantive agenda that the
URNG and three successive governments agreed to follow. Under some circumstances, this could have been a good thing, since the problems facing
the country were of course complex and interrelated. Comprehensive solutions were needed. But the URNG was militarily and politically weak. If
the rebels were going to extract any meaningful concessions, they would
need to focus their limited leverage on one or two achievable goals. During
the Salvadoran peace talks, the FMLN rebels focused their comparatively
strong bargaining leverage on eliminating most of the political and domestic security powers of the army.[6] In the process, they sacrificed socioeconomic goals that were important to their constituents, but more difficult to
achieve in negotiations with a private sector–oriented government. In contrast, the broad, dialogue-generated agenda in Guatemala militated against
any such strategic focusing of limited leverage by the URNG: instead, they
stuck with the broad agenda even though they were negotiating from a position of weakness with a series of governments that had little incentive to
make concessions on any issue that challenged the existing privileges of entrenched economic and military elites. Not surprisingly, the resulting accords lacked substance, depth, and political feasibility. Embedded within
the accords were further participatory mechanisms—the so-called parity
commissions and others—that generated more specific guidelines for reforms

that should be carried out. Some of these commissions completed important and valuable work, as exemplified by the deep analysis of the flaws of the justice system developed by the commission on judicial reform, or the difficult decisions made by the commission on indigenous cultural rights to prioritize which of dozens of languages the state would be obligated to support in the courts and public administration. However, the parity commissions had no independent capacity to implement reforms: they depended on legislative and executive action that was rarely forthcoming.

When MINUGUA took over the task of verifying the full range of accords, it quickly encountered the reluctance of the Arzú government to change existing institutions or redistribute assets and income. As explained in Chapter 5, it was perfectly rational for Arzú to drag his feet: the benefits of reforms would accrue to the majority of Guatemalans over decades, while the political costs of implementing reforms against elite preferences would be borne immediately—by Arzú and his party. When the Arzú government defaulted on one issue after another—failing to raise taxes, taking shortcuts on civilian policing, failing to build the capacity of the Public Ministry and courts, refusing to close down the Presidential General Staff, delaying moves to address land inequities, and only tepidly supporting the constitutional reforms—the mission tried to compensate for governmental inaction by convening civic dialogue, or encouraging the government to do so with MINUGUA as an observer. The intent was to build a consensus that would either obligate the government to act or lower the political costs to the government of proceeding with reforms. Although this approach seldom produced results during the Arzú administration, the mission persisted with the same tactic during the Portillo government, with predictably few results.

Extraparliamentary dialogue can make a difference in situations where two or more groups have been isolated from one another and need to have a frank exchange of views. It can be helpful to convene conversations that are separate from negotiations among principals. The American Friends Service Committee did this kind of work in the earliest stages of the peace process in El Salvador, helping to open political space. Once various groups' positions are known, however, and the time for legislative and executive action is at hand, further consensus-building efforts are unlikely to have much effect and may distract from the real question: Are state officials going to act, or aren't they? If a mission can find a way to apply compelling pressure on a resistant government to accept the domestic costs of going ahead with reforms, it should do that. If it cannot, then it can communicate directly with the public and try to change public opinion so that government has domestic political incentives to act. If it cannot do one of these two things, then convening yet another dialogue is neither here nor there. While mass civil movements can move elected officials to undertake difficult decisions that they would otherwise avoid or delay, public pressure has to be widespread and intense enough to convey obvious electoral risk to parties that ignore the message. Meetings and discussions among not-very-representative interest groups did not rise to this level.

Moreover, the chronic dialogue syndrome encouraged by MINUGUA as well as by Guatemalan political parties (remember the Multiparty Commission sponsored by the PAN to address the constitutional reforms) tended to reproduce the list-making dynamic that began with the Oslo process. The reasons are obvious in retrospect: if the goal of a negotiation is to create consensus, and multiple sectors are at the table, the only way to reach consensus is to include something from every group's agenda. This dynamic was especially evident in the logrolling that went into drafting constitutional reforms. The core list of twelve reforms swelled to fifty, leading to an awkward Constitutional Court ruling on the packaging of the reforms, confused voters, and the eventual defeat of the reforms in the popular referendum. Actual commitment by dialogue participants can be minimal, as illustrated by CACIF's habit of agreeing to tax increases in the fiscal pact meetings and then scuttling them through political action, propaganda, and litigation. The multiyear dialogue on tax reforms showcases the bankruptcy of this approach: at no point did these negotiations and the resulting "consensus" positions actually result in legislation, taxation, or meaningful increases in state revenue. With respect to conflicts over land tenure, similar "endless dialog exercises aimed at building consensus between landowners and peasant groups" failed to accomplish anything of note.[7]

▍Verification Strategy

Since consensus building proved ineffective, the second option available to MINUGUA was to use its verification mandate in a more targeted and assertive fashion. It was technically and legally correct for MINUGUA to verify all of the accords with equal emphasis, but doing so was politically unrealistic. The circumstances of the peace process required the United Nations not just to verify, but also to use its soft power to move the government to action. This was not written into the accords, but it was a structural requirement of the postwar political situation. With the URNG expected to disarm within two months or less, only political pressure from the United Nations could compensate for strong domestic resistance. There were individuals within the Arzú government (such as Gustavo Porras and Raquel Zelaya) who were strongly motivated to implement reforms. However, they were up against the reactionary influence of CACIF and the EMP. The president himself, though willing to move against some of the corrupt elements in the military, proved less willing to move against private sector interests or the EMP. Reformists within the government needed strong outside help.

The Arzú government quickly quashed David Stephen's idea of having MINUGUA control the aid money spigot, and there were in any case institutional obstacles within the UN system to such an arrangement in the near term. However, MINUGUA could affect the attitudes and priorities of donors by escalating politico-diplomatic pressure on specific issues. The question was what issues it should prioritize. MINUGUA twice rallied donors through the consultative group process, in both cases to focus on tax increases and transparency. In the first instance, under Arzú, follow-up by the UN Secretariat was poor, and in any case Arzú was determined not to act because of domestic constraints. In the second instance, in 2002, President Portillo responded with showmanship but no substance, while Congress did the minimum necessary to keep the donors engaged. The 2003 consultative group meeting focused on laying out performance targets for Portillo's successor, with no pledging taking place.

Guatemalan officials periodically bullied the United Nations on nationalist grounds for allegedly exceeding its mandate. Usually the complaints surfaced when the United Nations had taken or was about to take a forceful or effective action. While USGs Marrack Goulding and Kieran Prendergast deflected these nationalist outbursts skillfully, there was generally also a subtle backing off and lowering of MINUGUA's profile in the wake of government complaints. This is unfortunate, because the United Nations was consistently most effective when it stood its ground forcefully against nationalist badgering or governmental evasion of responsibilities.

During the negotiations, strong positions by the United Nations (and member states' representatives in New York) helped head off the so-called Rosada Plan that would have marginalized the URNG to the point of ending the peace talks. Marrack Goulding's February 1995 threat to reconsider the continued presence of MINUGUA renewed momentum in the talks. DPA official Michael Möller's insistence that MINUGUA have unrestricted access to government facilities in conducting human rights investigations, and that the Guatemalan government not be allowed to veto mission renewals, were critical decisions that made it possible for the mission to function. Faced with a firm "no" from the United Nations, the government retreated on these points. During the implementation phase, MINUGUA's clear and evidence-based reporting on human rights brought prompt improvements. MINUGUA's early decision to use a minor passage in the human rights accord as a basis for criticizing the URNG's continued sabotage and war tax collection proved critical to establishing the mission's impartiality. That impartiality, in turn, was essential to the military's acceptance of the accuracy and legitimacy of the mission's human rights reporting. Leonardo Franco's rebuff of nationalist criticism of MINUGUA brought a temporary halt to anti–United Nations posturing by both civilian and military officials during the de León Carpio government. A few years later,

MINUGUA's outspoken commentary on the Gerardi case, and Arnault's direct threat to expose Arzu's obstruction of justice, helped keep alive the possibility of a successful prosecution.

These examples of assertiveness stand out because they were rare. In each case the United Nations fully used the combination of soft power and mandate available to it, even stretching a technicality in the mission's favor. The United Nations usually won its point when it was clear and forceful because ultimately it was very important to the Guatemalan parties that the United Nations stay involved. With domestic institutions in crisis, with the Guatemalan Church having failed to broker a settlement, and with the country a pariah in the eyes of much international public opinion, Guatemalan actors knew they needed the United Nations, however much they might bluster against it. Most of the time, the United Nations chose not to attempt to make greater use of this soft-power relationship. The United Nations' posture was more often that of a partner, unconditionally committed to the peace process, and thus an enabler of chronically short-term, expedient, noncompliant political conduct by the Guatemalan parties.

This dynamic was especially on display during the Portillo administration, which systematically misrepresented its intentions while the United Nations continued to help. The continuation of the mission during the Portillo government was, in retrospect, questionable. What was the point of maintaining a verification mission if confronting the government with evidence of noncompliance would not affect its behavior? As the Portillo administration veered toward outright criminality and obvious incompetence, MINUGUA interpreted its role to be to stabilize the government in a context in which the government's adversaries were being strident and even cavalier with the constitutional order in their haste to remove Portillo. Criticism, though present in MINUGUA's reporting, was not as sharp as it could have been, nor did the United Nations consistently signal that it would reconsider its presence in the country if Portillo did not shape up. With the United Nations positioned as a semi-ally, the president and his ministers sometimes responded rhetorically to international concerns, but made few changes of substance. Direct lobbying by international financial institutions, backed by credible threats by donors to suspend further lending, catalyzed the only serious measures by Congress to address transparency, taxation, and decentralization. It is at least possible that the United Nations could have catalyzed improved conduct by credibly threatening to leave. Rather surprisingly, I found no evidence in DPA's MINUGUA files that the organization held internal discussions about withdrawing from Guatemala, despite the mission's apparent helplessness in the face of Portillo's egregious misrule. Recall that in his May 2000 report, Arnault had warned that in all likelihood, nothing further would be accomplished after 2001. He recommended maintaining the full verification functions of the

mission only through 2001, with closures of some regional offices and reduction in international staff. He recommended that the mission limit itself
in 2002 to monitoring human rights, and shut down at the end of the year.
Instead, the Secretary-General's office publicly committed to keeping the
mission open through 2003. This may have been the wrong signal to send.

▌ Eyewitness to State Failure

With the mission committed to staying through 2003, the only remaining
way to enhance leverage would have been to focus the mission's limited influence on a single strategic issue with high stakes and on which progress
might be possible. In retrospect, the mission would have done well to emphasize police, criminal investigations, prosecutors, and the justice system.
DPA found itself negotiating for CICIACS during MINUGUA's final two
years and, when that failed to garner political support and faced constitutional objections, established the less-autonomous CICIG well after
MINUGUA closed. This begs the question of whether a greater emphasis
by MINUGUA on fighting impunity might have ameliorated the crisis that
made CICIG necessary. A combination of factors predisposed Guatemala to
a partial state failure in the face of organized crime and MINUGUA veteran
Patrick Gavigan has argued that there was little more that MINUGUA could
have done. Guatemala's vulnerabilities included among other things the negotiating weaknesses of the rebels, the incapacity of Guatemalan political
parties to deliver reform, the weaknesses of the accords on police and justice matters, lingering counterinsurgency structures, and Guatemala's bad
luck in being astride the main drug transshipment route from the Andes to
the United States.[8] One could add adjacency to Mexico, whose cartels
began to displace their Colombian counterparts in Guatemala in the years
after MINUGUA left.[9] Even with these predispositions, and the limitations
of MINUGUA's mandate, it is also true that a series of choices by UN officials consistently led away from using the mission's resources to address
organized crime and build the rule of law.

Beginning with the limited attention devoted to the question of police
reform at the very final stages of the negotiations, the United Nations chose
not to make the rule of law central to its political strategy, despite growing
signs of trouble. One highly experienced MINUGUA veteran I interviewed
described the impact of criminal influences as a "surprise," not anticipated
by the United Nations.[10] In a March 2004 meeting with representatives of
the friends states, Koenigs announced complacently that Guatemala's
"mafias" posed "no menace to the normal economic and civil development
because they lacked a coherent concept of political destabilization," as if
they must *intend* to disrupt the political order to have that effect.[11] With
hindsight, the warning signs were clear enough. From early in MINUGUA's

deployment, HOM Franco and his senior staff were well aware of the extensive involvement of military officers in criminal enterprises. And while President Arzú cracked down on some networks early in his presidency, it was clear from MINUGUA's own reporting that Arzú's limited purge had by no means exhausted the deep well of corruption and criminal violence in the military, police, and intelligence services. If there had been any doubts or forgetfulness, the Gerardi killing, the EMP's cover-up, and the subsequent high mortality rate among potential witnesses were all reminders. Once Portillo entered office and *invited* known criminal elements (in many cases the same individuals purged by Arzú) back into positions of state power, it should have been obvious that Guatemala was on a very dangerous trajectory.

In the face of all of this information, systematically collected and analyzed by MINUGUA's human rights division, its Civilian Power Strengthening Advisory, and its political advisers, MINUGUA continued with a strategy focused on promoting dialogue and persuading the government to raise taxes. While certainly the fiscal issue would need to be addressed before the Guatemalan state could adequately address extreme distributional inequities, there was a logically prior condition that had to be met: there needed to be a functioning Guatemalan state. By focusing on a secondary issue, on which it was impossible for the mission to build a winning domestic coalition, MINUGUA missed a critical opportunity to help limit the slide toward lawlessness.

The partial successes of CICIG (discussed in Chapter 7) point to some things that MINUGUA might have done differently. CICIG's mandate was clearly more robust in key ways, especially its explicit mandate to name individual state officials who obstruct justice and call for disciplinary measures against them and its contingent standing as an auxiliary prosecutor (*querellante adhesivo*). This mandate, as well as the absolute necessity of having cooperative leadership in the Public Ministry, led CICIG to take an aggressive and partially successful stance against obstructionists in the Public Ministry, the courts, and the police, using indictments as well as public demands for administrative actions. It must also be said that in some instances CICIG was not as aggressive as it could have been, suggesting that even with the commission's strong mandate, its leaders have perceived some problems as insurmountable. While MINUGUA had no explicit mandate to call for administrative actions against individuals, there was considerable latitude for MINUGUA to take similar actions under both its human rights verification and institutional strengthening mandates. There was nothing in the accords or the mission's headquarters agreement, for example, that prohibited MINUGUA's human rights reports, press conferences, or press releases, from explicitly naming and shaming individual judges, prosecutors, or police officials who were obstructing justice. Doing so, especially if linked to a mass communications strategy, could have been effective, at least in some cases. If it had been effective, it would also have opened up opportunities for institutional strengthening efforts that were otherwise pointless.

My suggestion that MINUGUA could have done more to contain the criminal metastases within the state, like any counterfactual argument, swims against a tide of uncertainties. Even if MINUGUA had acted more assertively and a domestic political coalition had formed in support of rule of law reforms, it could easily have broken down.[12] Among the modernizing business elites who should have been the primary constituents for stronger rule of law, some apparently had illegal enterprises behind the scenes.[13] Private security had become a major industry, with powerful political allies that had a vested interest in continued chaos.[14] Even the most internationalized and "modern" of the Guatemalan elite still seemed to approve of summary executions, as demonstrated by the elite outcry when CICIG had the temerity to indict former interior minister Carlos Vielmann for the murders at Pavón prison. This ugly political reality probably contributed to the ambiguity, weakness, and self-sabotage that characterized the legal reform policies of the supposedly reformist and modernizing governments of Arzú and Berger. Disunity within the international community was a further obstacle, especially the bilateral role of Spain (and later the European Union, with Spain in the lead) regarding police reform. Finally, a major constraint on such actions was the fact that MINUGUA was deployed across the country and designed to be accessible to the public. It was therefore potentially vulnerable to violence. One need only recall the very clear threats against Guatemala regional office official Rosemarie Bornand during the death penalty/due process controversy in 1996 to recognize the potential risks. Nonetheless, on balance there was probably political space for MINUGUA to use its political agenda–setting, investigative, and communications capacity to call more specific and personal attention to wrongdoers within the state, and had it done so it might have met with at least some success.

▌ Measuring and Shaping Public Opinion

When I was conducting interviews with various actors about the peace process in 1998, I was astonished when a prominent private sector leader asserted with great certainty that MINUGUA was a human rights mission and had no business opining on other issues. This was one year after the mission assumed responsibility for verifying the full accords and his statement was inaccurate. I thought this man might be trying to mislead me, but on balance I concluded that he was probably just misinformed. He was not alone. In a nationwide probability sample survey commissioned by MINUGUA in 1998, 69 percent reported knowing nothing about the mission.[15] Of the 31 percent who claimed to know something, only one in five knew that MINUGUA was responsible for "verifying compliance with the peace accords." Knowledge of the mission was sharply lower among people with less education and income. Overall, only 4 percent of the sample reported having any contact with the mission.[16] A year after it took on comprehensive verification responsibilities, MINUGUA had not been able to communicate its role effectively to the public. More importantly, it had not effectively addressed the considerable ignorance of the public about the peace accords. Only 37 percent of those interviewed spontaneously mentioned the signing of the peace accords as the most important event in the country over the previous two years. By way of comparison, 23 percent mentioned "improved roads."

When asked what the so-called peace process referred to, 58 percent said they did not know. Of those who could define in some way what the peace process was, 37 percent could not name any of the accords, even by their general content (human rights, ceasefire, reduction of the army, and so forth). But when prompted about the peace process, respondents did have opinions about what they thought was most important for the country: 28 percent cited respect for human rights and another 15 percent stressed improved administration of justice. Other issues prioritized by respondents included rural development, indigenous identities and rights, access to land, repatriation of refugees, participation of women, and the inclusion of indigenous language interpreters in the courts. When asked what issues were most important for their families (rather than to the country as a whole), respondents shifted their priorities somewhat (the percentage responding "access to land" doubled), but respect for human rights remained the top priority for 28 percent.

Thus while people were vague about the peace accords and not predisposed to place a high value on them, there was a degree of political and institutional awareness that MINUGUA could have worked with more effectively to engage the public in valuing and supporting the peace accords. Radio was clearly the primary medium to use. In the same 1998 survey, 69 percent of respondents said their main source of local news and information came from friends and neighbors, but for regional and national news, about the same 69 percent turned to radio.[17] The 1998 survey provided enough information to know that the mission needed a massive public information campaign, emphasizing radio. This information did not translate into significant change in how the mission spent money. Public information remained a tiny share of the mission's budget. As noted in Chapter 5, the mission did not even fully expend the trust fund money allocated for education on the constitutional reforms until after the referendum had taken place.

I do not intend to trivialize the difficulty in carrying out a strong, direct public communications strategy. Even assuming that the mission did not directly advocate policies, any effort to educate the public about the flaws of existing institutions and the potential benefits of change would have triggered a nationalist backlash. It is by no means certain that the privately owned media would have accepted a much higher volume of UN educational ads, though it seems likely that the business opportunity would have outweighed at least some media owners' political scruples. It would be advisable in future negotiations for the United Nations to insist that the parties include provisions that the United Nations should have unrestricted access to purchase airtime on privately owned broadcast stations, or to have the authority to install its own temporary broadcast stations.

There would also have been institutional obstacles within the United Nations. As noted earlier, the idea of peace-mission-as-political-communications-firm was outside the political culture and experience of the United Nations. Moreover, little money had been budgeted for buying media time. A midcourse change in budget toward major spending on media would have been difficult to get through the Advisory Committee on Administrative and Budgetary Questions. Such obstacles must be overcome in the long run for the United Nations to be as effective as possible in any context where public opinion and mobilization are critical. Town hall meetings and pamphlets are not enough in a context where semi-authoritarian state structures and antireform social elites are still entrenched and in control of the national media.

The 1998 survey and the 1999 survey described in Chapter 5 (about the constitutional referendum) appear to have been the only ones sponsored by MINUGUA. Much of the time, MINUGUA was operating partially blind. Instead of the representative information it could have gotten from repeated probability sample surveys, the mission got much of its input from newspapers and meetings with people from the small politically active portion of the population. Field office staff probably had a pretty good feel for public attitudes, but it was difficult to aggregate this qualitative, intuitive sense of the "ground reality" into something useful in making overall policy and shaping a public communications campaign.

There seemed to be a general lack of appreciation within the Secretariat for basic tools of social science research, particularly the tools needed to have representative information about the attitudes and experiences of the population overall. The mission's budget did not provide for repeated public opinion surveys on key issues. For a mission with a responsibility to communicate with and educate the public, repeated surveying is essential. No modern political campaign would attempt a major ad and messaging campaign without polling first. Moreover, the mission's mandate post-1996 required it to assess general patterns of socioeconomic equity and discrimination, a task that could not be accomplished without the ability to collect representative data. It was not sufficient to depend on the mission's routine contacts with the public as a guide to public opinion, since the people that mission staff met with may have been systematically different from the population as a whole. They were likely, for instance, to be more politically aware, active, and organized.

To prevent this type of omission in the future, especially in cases where broad public opinion is critical to the outcomes achieved (such as where a popular referendum is key to whether the accords are implemented), the United Nations should incorporate a survey research specialist into the senior staff of missions, and budget for multiple surveys each year during the life of a mission. It would probably not be advisable for the mission itself to conduct the research, as the public might respond differently to mission personnel than to an anonymous interviewer, but the mission should have oversight of the content and design.[18]

■ Minding Its Own Business

While MINUGUA correctly pushed for improvements in how Guatemala was governed, it needed to do a better job of governing itself. The foregoing chapters identify a number of problems, beginning with the delegation of all administrative powers to a substructure within the mission that did not report to the head of the mission! This arrangement, combined with the fact that FALD/DPKO controlled personnel selection and that the comptroller in New York controlled expenditures from the trust fund (during early stages of the mission), often impeded the mission's work. Long vacancies in key mission positions resulted in lost time, loss of continuity, and low morale for staff members who had to do their own jobs plus the duties of the unfulfilled positions. Heads of Mission Franco, Arnault, and Merrem all remarked on these problems and recommended that more power be delegated to the mission to make decisions locally. In an ideal world, that would include the ability to promote people on the basis of merit, without regard to the type of contract they have (including UNV) at the time they join a mission.

There is much to recommend in decentralizing management authority. But its effectiveness presupposes that mission management will make such decisions competently and advisedly. The chances of this are weakened by the United Nations' intermittent disregard for the importance of management skills in the selection of mission leaders and deputies. Merrem in particular allowed a "period of unproductive infighting that had come to involve a good portion of the staff," as his successor put it.[19] The mission's deputies were sometimes highly effective, but other times not. DHOMs were often overwhelmed by an excessive scope of responsibilities, lacked the delegated authority to manage, or both. A mission that is already operating on a shoestring in a politically adverse environment cannot afford to carry the inefficiencies that result from troubled management.

MINUGUA needed to advance during just a few years through life phases that included human rights verification, verification of the full accords, and preparing its own departure. Each phase required different skills, priorities, and strategies. By the time Merrem took over the mission in 2000, leaders in New York had begun to notice the inability of MINUGUA to think outside the box, and they attributed that problem in part to entrenchment of senior staff and a propensity toward factional infighting and organizational turf. The established practice of most national diplomatic services to rotate personnel every few years so that they don't "go native" has drawbacks, including recurring loss of hard-won local knowledge and historical insight. Yet MINUGUA seems to present the opposite problem. Term limits on the order of four years would allow mission staff to build and use local knowledge, while encouraging them to work themselves out of a job efficiently. Replacement personnel would bring fresh perspectives, potentially more in tune with what a mission needs to be doing at each stage.

The difficulty of refreshing the mission's approach was also organizational. Since MINUGUA was structured around substantive areas mirroring the components of the peace accords, the mission bureaucratized the overly broad agenda established at the earliest stages of the peace process. At annual retreats to discuss priorities, the staff naturally and appropriately argued for the importance of their piece of the substantive agenda. The sum of these arguments, however, was the recurring decision to emphasize everything, regardless of political feasibility. In light of this dynamic, which seems unavoidable for a multidimensional verification mission, MINUGUA might have benefited from an external board to set strategy. Such a board, similar to those used in corporate governance to address strategic decisions, might have succeeded in identifying priorities in a climate free of any dynamic of organizational self-perpetuation.

As an outsider to the United Nations reading cables and internal memos related to hiring, I was struck by the degree of informality and personalism involved. Rather than issuing an open call for applications and nominations, senior officials "discuss names." The criteria considered include legitimate political, linguistic, and experience criteria, but also seemed to include back-channel personal recommendations and word of mouth reputations. When high visibility positions are in play, there also appears to be a great deal of jockeying for position by member states, to the point of outright interference in selection processes as in the case of Spain's efforts to impose one of its nationals as the head police adviser when a Spanish national was already the mission's chief military liaison officer. One senior UN official I interviewed summarized succinctly this combination of sloppy internal processes and member-state maneuvering in selecting top mission officials: "it sucks."[20] Until the United Nations adopts better human resources and staff selection processes, it can expect that missions will sometimes operate poorly. Particular attention should be given to selecting a leadership team that, as a whole, embodies the necessary skill sets.

Below the level of SRSG, "the personnel system had failed to weed out poor performers," as Koenigs put it in a letter to Kofi Annan. For MINUGUA to "recharge and retool" for the final stretch, UN headquarters had to replace at least five key officials in the mission.[21] The United Nations' Lake Wobegon personnel culture seems to rate everyone above average until failures become too flagrant to ignore, while failing to reward some outstanding performers.

▌ Linking Mediation to Verification

The Guatemala experience suggests that the United Nations needs to look more closely at the relationship between negotiating/mediation processes and verification missions. One of the hard lessons of the genocide in Rwanda was that because the United Nations was not involved in the negotiating process, it did not have a clear reading on the intentions of the hardline elements within the government. As a result, the proposed peacekeeping role for the United Nations was completely out of step with what would have been required to contain the violent defection of extremists within the state. In Guatemala, in contrast, the United Nations mediated the peace talks, and had good knowledge regarding the parties' intensions and capacities. But this did not translate into opportunities to shape agreements in ways that would give the United Nations greater capacity to ensure that necessary reforms took place after the fighting ended.

Key decisions had already been made during the early, agenda-setting phase of the talks, before the United Nations began mediating. The fundamental mismatch between the limited political leverage of the URNG and the sweeping scope of the negotiating agenda was already locked in before Arnault was appointed moderator. Once those earlier agreements were signed, there was probably no way to backtrack and narrow the focus of the talks to something more consistent with the URNG's minimal bargaining power. The organizational firewall between the moderation and MINUGUA may have been an impediment to shaping more verifiable agreements. As David Stephen and his team began thinking through what the mission's role would be during the verification phase and began to realize how tenuous the United Nations' position would be, they had no direct and recurring mechanism for having input into the design of the accords. In the future, as the United Nations contemplates a mediation process that could lead to a UN verification role, it could be helpful to convene a panel of officials experienced in verification missions to advise the mediation team on what features ought to be included in a peace accord to strengthen the United

Nations' hand during the implementation phase. This is especially important in any peace process that does not lead to power sharing and in which
the former rebels will lose much of their bargaining leverage after their military forces demobilize, leaving the United Nations to ensure government
compliance. There may be limits to what UN mediators can do to shape
more verifiable accords, especially if one of the parties is too weak to place
concrete demands, but to the extent feasible mediators should have institutional support in crafting the most verifiable agreements possible.

While the shadow of future verification responsibilities should shape
the work of UN mediators, mediators and verifiers should probably not be
the same person. While as moderator Arnault came to know the parties and
the agreements well, he unavoidably carried baggage from that role that en-
dangered his subsequent role as SRSG. While the specifics of the Mincho
scandal could not have been anticipated, the collision between the confidentiality required of a mediator and the transparency required of a verifier
was to some extent inevitable given Arnault's dual role. The international
press furor over the Mincho case distracted the mission and much of the
public during a crucial period when MINUGUA needed to establish its new
verification authority and educate the public about the accords. More
broadly, the fact that Arnault was seen as "pro-parties" opened the mission
up to damaging attacks in the press and a perception that it might not be impartial with respect to the interests of the nation as a whole.

■ Peacebuilding, Development, and Exit Strategy

In his parting letter to Kofi Annan, Koenigs ventured that "all United Nations missions should adopt a transition strategy, and that this kind of thinking should be present early in the mission."[22] This is sound advice, but challenging to implement. From its earliest days, MINUGUA was charged with
strengthening institutions in Guatemala, so that the mission was both verifier
and development partner. The final Secretary-General's report on MINUGUA
asserted that this combination worked well.[23] Perhaps. The combination did
provide MINUGUA with a degree of legitimacy that it might have lacked if
the mission had had nothing to offer but criticism. But there were serious
problems with the way the partnership played out. In the earliest stages,
MINUGUA found itself strengthening institutions that would soon be slated
for extinction under the accords. Then, once the postwar architecture of police and justice institutions was clear, the mission lacked decisive influence
over the most important ones. The Spanish government preempted a UN
role in developing the civilian police, and the European Union subsequently
ratified this by granting Spain leadership over an expanded aid and training
program that ignored many of the principles put forward by the accords.
The job of training the vital investigations police fell to a bilateral program

of the United States, but the Guatemalan police did such a poor job of selecting potential detectives that much of the money was wasted. MINUGUA hired trainers through the trust fund to work with the new PNC and the police academy, but their role was decidedly secondary to the bilateral donors. Throughout the rule of law effort, there was little coordination among donors, and bilateral donors often ignored the peace accords (the United States, for example, tended to fixate on drug enforcement at the expense of other priorities). The same was true of economic aid programs. The main international financial institutions intermittently supported peace accord implementation, but unless MINUGUA actively guided them, they tended to relapse into using technical criteria and setting their own political agenda. UNDP often operated without any regard for political guidance from MINUGUA, and at times contested the mission's political preeminence. Not until late 2003 did UNDP include an assessment of implementation of the socioeconomic and agrarian accord in its annual *Human Development Report* on the country, an astonishing omission that shows how disengaged UNDP was from the peace process.[24]

The lack of coordination among international development agencies is not a news flash. Moreover, it is understandable that permanent international aid organizations are reluctant to subordinate their work to a temporary mission like MINUGUA. Naturally, the aid agencies have their own ways of doing things, their own relationships with host governments, their own career paths, and their own criteria for grants and loans. Yet the costs of donor agency independence are high. If MINUGUA had been in a position to approve or disprove specific projects, and to significantly influence overall aid levels, it could have produced greater unity of effort, ensured that more development activities directly supported peacebuilding, and made the government more responsive to the mission's observations about compliance. To achieve this degree of coordination, however, the United Nations would need to make a high-level decision to require at least those agencies that are part of the UN system to accept close political and programmatic oversight from an SRSG for the duration of a peacebuilding mission. There would be institutional and political resistance to such an arrangement, but anything short of strong SRSG authority seems unlikely to work.

A second benefit of tight conditionality would be greater mission influence over key counterpart agencies and their leaders. All of MINUGUA's trust fund institutional development efforts were small scale relative to needs, and the mission's leverage over what went on in counterpart institutions was correspondingly slight. A mission with the ability to deliver major institution-building programs, or withhold them, might be able to leverage better leadership and decisionmaking in counterpart agencies like the PNC, Public Ministry, and PDH.

MINUGUA's National Transitional Volunteer program was an excellent idea, and would have had greater impact had it been implemented while the mission still had a full complement of regional offices and experienced personnel. Moreover, the success of the volunteer program begs the question of whether Guatemalan professionals could have been brought into higher-level roles. While impartiality and credibility required an exclusively international professional staff in the early days of the mission, the idea that this standard needed to continue for the whole life of the mission is unconvincing. MINUGUA could have used robust screening to select motivated and competent Guatemalans to do key elements of the mission's work. Doing so would have developed local human resources, and would have gone some way toward defusing the chronic nationalist complaints against MINUGUA, some of which, at the end of the day, were not entirely wrong.

▌ Enabling Peace, Enabling Purgatory

When the United Nations engages with a peace process, it acts as a representative of the global community. It therefore wields a kind of soft power in addition to the transparency, verification services, and good offices it can provide: the United Nations can either bestow its endorsement regarding the legitimacy of a peace process, or withhold that endorsement. Civil war adversaries face international political costs if they fail to gain the United Nations' participation, and stand to gain international acceptance and opportunities for economic recovery if they do get the United Nations on board. The United Nations has something the parties want, and this can increase its leverage to insist upon progress in negotiations and actual compliance with agreements. Unfortunately, it is easiest to wield this leverage at the early stage, when the United Nations is deciding whether to participate and at what level. Once the UN Secretariat obtains a resolution from the Security Council or General Assembly, commits to a peace process, and deploys personnel and equipment, the dynamic changes. At that point the United Nations' reputation is at stake and there are daunting political, not to mention logistical, obstacles to withdrawing. Only in extreme circumstances, where fighting has resumed (as in Rwanda and Angola), has the United Nations withdrawn or dramatically scaled back its involvement. With the decision to deploy comes the risk that the United Nations will provide the domestic parties with what they want—international legitimacy and the economic opportunities that come with that—even if the domestic parties abandon their own commitments and act in ways that fundamentally undermine the United Nations' peacebuilding intentions.

We can see this sequence play out in Guatemala. The United Nations was initially cautious, and internal correspondence showed concerns that the Guatemalan parties might be less interested in peace than the United

Nations was. The United Nations signaled its distrust through a series of deliberate half-measures and delays that in fact motivated the parties to get more serious. After the Guatemalan government barred UN observer Vendrell, the Secretary-General rejected the government's request that he appoint a senior statesman as observer, appointing the then-junior Arnault instead. Even after the parties asked Arnault to moderate the talks rather than just observing them, the Secretariat provided Arnault with little staff support and only intermittent high-level engagement from DPA. DPA was likewise cautious about deploying the human rights mission, suspecting that the final accords might be years away and not wanting to be caught on the ground with no end to the fighting.

Once committed, however, the United Nations lost some of its skeptical edge and joined in partnership with a series of Guatemalan governments, even as they acted in ways that perpetuated or even reinforced the kinds of social and political problems that led to war in the first place. Guatemala drifted into a kind of purgatory that was neither war nor peace, but rather a chronic condition of criminal violence, impunity, political instability, and corruption. If MINUGUA had been able to consolidate a few pockets of probity and competence within state institutions, then it might have been able to make significant contributions even in the midst of Portillo's misrule. Failing that (possibly unrealistic) scenario, it is difficult to discern how MINUGUA could have a decisive, durable, national-level impact on human rights, democracy, or social equity after 1999. Of course the local-level work of the mission provided benefits from 2000 onward, and many Guatemalans were grateful for the mission's presence. But these benefits were not sustainable and may even have fostered dependence. The United Nations' power to reshape war-torn societies is limited, as are its financial and human resources. It cannot afford to merely accompany a people whose national institutions are broken. Thus a final lesson from MINUGUA is that the UN Secretariat may need to more actively and frequently reassess whether a given mission is making a decisive contribution. If it is not, then the mission needs to radically change its approach, or the United Nations needs to be able to credibly threaten to withdraw. This would increase the reputational risks to host governments of being uncooperative, and increase incentives to mission staff to remain agile and jettison strategies that are not working.

Notes

1. Luis Pásara, *Paz, ilusion, y cambio en Guatemala: El proceso de paz, sus actors, logros, y límites* (Ciudad de Guatemala: Universidad Rafael Landívar, 2003).

2. Author interview, Jean Arnault, New York, January 2008.

3. Tom Koenigs, "Guatemalan Vice-President's Visit to UNHQ," to Kieran Prendergast, April 15, 2004.

4. Barbara F. Walter, "The Critical Barrier to Civil War Settlement," *International Organization* 51, no. 3 (1997): 335–364.

5. Personal communication, Jean Arnault, December 2011.

6. The FMLN maintained de facto control over significant territory, was capable of major military offensives, and in the year before the peace talks began had occupied portions of the capital city San Salvador, demonstrating the government's failure to dominate the battlefield. The URNG was never able to pose a comparable threat.

7. Tom Koenigs, "Land Conflicts," to Kieran Prendergast, July 15, 2004, paragraph 3.

8. Guatemala became a prime transshipment corridor after US radar and air defense improvements rendered direct overwater flights from Colombia impracticable. Patrick Gavigan, "Organized Crime, Illicit Power Structures, and Guatemala's Threatened Peace Process," *International Peacekeeping* 16, no. 1 (2009): 62–76.

9. Ivan Briscoe and Marlies Stappers, *Breaking the Wave: Critical Steps in the Fight Against Crime in Guatemala* (Guatemala: Clingendael Institute and Impunity Watch, 2012).

10. Author interview with former MINUGUA regional office director, Guatemala, February 9, 2011.

11. Marylene Smeets AED/DPA, "Note to the File: Meeting on Guatemala, Wednesday, 24 March 2004," April 6, 2004.

12. For an analysis of the social underpinnings of the crime problem in Guatemala, especially the complexity of elite positions, see Ivan Briscoe and Martín Rodríguez Pellecer, *A State Under Siege: Elites, Criminal Networks and Institutional Reform in Guatemala* (The Hague: Netherlands Institute of International Relations "Clingendael," 2010), www.clingendael.nl/cru.

13. As Grann points out, the murders of Khalil and Marjorie Musa that led Rodrigo Rosenberg to stage his own death probably had their roots in well-hidden criminal activities involving Mr. Musa.

14. Tom Koenigs, "Current Issues of Concern," to Kieran Prendergast, July 30, 2004, paragraph 4.

15. A probability sample is one in which every person in the country has a theoretically equal chance of being selected for the survey, with the result that the survey results can be considered representative of the population as a whole within a margin of error determined by the size of the sample. Typically, a survey of around 1,200 people has a margin of error of +/- 3 percent. Of course, actually achieving a probability sample is complex and there are many ways for things to go wrong if the sampling is poorly designed or if field interviewers are not adequately trained.

16. MINUGUA, "La población Guatemalteca y el proceso de paz," internal document, 1998, 56–57.

17. Ibid., 68–70.

18. It was originally planned that MINUGUA personnel would accompany the survey team for the 1998 poll, which would very likely have contaminated the results. Quality control needs to be achieved by other means.

19. Tom Koenigs, untitled letter to Kofi Annan, December 9, 2004.

20. Author interview with senior UN official who preferred anonymity commenting on internal procedures, New York, February 2007.

21. Tom Koenigs, untitled letter to Kofi Annan, December 9, 2004.

22. Ibid.

23. United Nations, "United Nations Verification Mission in Guatemala: Report of the Secretary General," A/59/746, March 18, 2005, paragraph 26.

24. Tom Koenigs, "Human Development Report," to Kieran Prendergast, September 4, 2003.

Acronyms

ACABQ	Advisory Committee on Administrative and Budgetary Questions
AED	Americas and Europe Division of the Department of Political Affairs, United Nations
AFPC	Agreement on the Strengthening of Civilian Power and on the Role of the Armed Forces in a Democratic Society
ANN	New National Alliance
ASC	Civil Society Assembly
ASIES	Association for Research and Social Studies (Asociación de Investigación y Estudios Sociales)
CACIF	Coordinating Committee of Associations for Agriculture, Commerce, Industry, and Finance
CAL	Logistics Support Commission (Comisión de Apoyo Logístico)
CALDH	Center for Human Rights Legal Action
CAO	chief administrative officer
CEAR	National Commission for Refugees, Repatriated, and Displaced Persons
CEDECON	Center for the Defense of the Constitution
CEH	Historical Clarification Commission
CERIGUA	Center for Informative Reports on Guatemala
CIA	Central Intelligence Agency (United States)
CIACS	illegal armed forces and clandestine security apparatuses
CIAV	International Verification and Assistance Commission
CICIACS	International Commission to Investigate Illegal Groups and Clandestine Security Organizations
CICIG	International Commission Against Impunity in Guatemala
CIDH	Inter-American Commission on Human Rights

CIIDH	International Center for Human Rights Investigations (Centro Internacional para Investigaciones en Derechos Humanos)
CNAP	National Peace Accords Commission
CNR	National Reconciliation Commission
CONAGRO	National Coordinating Committee for the Agricultural Sector (Coordinadora Nacional Agropecuaria)
CONTIERRA	Presidential Agency for Legal Assistance and Resolution of Land Conflicts
CONUPAZ	United Nations Peace Commission (Comisión de las Naciones Unidas para la Paz)
COPAZ	Presidential Peace Commission
COPMAGUA	Coordination of Mayan Peoples' Organizations
COPREDEH	Presidential Human Rights Commission
CSJ	Supreme Judicial Court
CVDCs	Voluntary Civil Defense Committees
DCG	Christian Democratic Party
DICAI	Civilian Information and Analysis Department
DINC	National Criminal Investigations Division
DOAN	Department of Anti-Narcotics Operations
DOM	Director of Mission
DPA	Department of Political Affairs
DPKO	Department of Peacekeeping Operations
EAD	Electoral Assistance Division (of DPA)
EGP	Guerrilla Army of the Poor
EMP	Presidential General Staff (Estado Mayor Presidencial)
ETP	Technical Advance Team (Equipo Técnico Preparatorio)
EU	European Union
FALD	Field Administration and Logistics Division (of DPKO)
FAO	Food and Agriculture Organization
FAR	Revolutionary Armed Forces
FDNG	New Guatemala Democratic Front (Frente Democrático Nueva Guatemala)
FECI	special anti-impunity group within the Public Ministry (Fiscalía Especial Contra Impunidad)
FEP	Special Police Forces
FGT	Guillermo Toriello Foundation
FMLN	Farabundo Martí National Liberation Front (El Salvador)
FOD/DPKO	Field Operations Division of the Department of Peacekeeping Operations
FONAPAZ	National Peace Fund
FONTIERRAS	Land Fund
FORIN	Institutional Strengthening division (Fortalecimiento Institucional)

FRG	Guatemalan Republican Front
GAM	Mutual Support Group
GANA	Grand National Alliance Party (Partido Gran Alianza Nacional)
GCE	Spanish Civil Guard
HOM	Head of Mission
IADB	Inter-American Development Bank
ICITAP	International Criminal Investigations Training and Assistance Program (United States)
IEMA	tax on commercial and agricultural businesses
IFIs	international financial institutions
ILO	International Labour Organization
ILO 169	International Labour Organization Convention 169 Concerning Indigenous and Tribal Peoples in Independent Countries
IMF	International Monetary Fund
IMP	Inter-Agency Monitoring Project
INC	National Consensus Body (Instancia Nacional de Consenso)
IUSI	Uniform Property Tax (Impuesto Único Sobre Immuebles)
MAS	Solidarity Action Movement
MICIVIH	International Civilian Mission in Haiti
MINUGUA	United Nations Verification Mission in Guatemala
MINUSAL	United Nations Mission in El Salvador
MR-13	Revolutionary Movement of November 13
NTV	National Transitional Volunteers
OAS	Organization of American States
OAU	Organization of African Unity
ODHA	Archdiocesan Human Rights Office
OHCHR	Office of the High Commissioner for Human Rights
ONUCA	United Nations Observer Group in Central America
ONUSAL	United Nations Observer Mission in El Salvador
ONUV	United Nations Verification Office in El Salvador
ONUVEN	United Nations Observer for the Verification of Elections in Nicaragua
ORGUA	Guatemala City regional office of MINUGUA
ORP	Office of Professional Responsibility
ORPA	Organization of the People in Arms
ORQUE	Quetzaltenango regional office
PACs	Community Self-Defense Patrols (Patrullas de Autodefensa Civil)
PAN	National Advance Party (Partido de Avanzada Nacional)
PAO	Public Affairs Office (United Nations)
PARLACEN	Central American Parliament

PDH	human rights ombudsman's office (Procuraduría para la Defensa de Derechos Humanos)
PGT	Guatemalan Workers Party
PMA	Mobile Military Police
PNC	National Civil Police
PRODERE	Development Program for Displaced Persons, Refugees, and Returnees in Central America
PROLEY	Program of Institutional Assistance for Legal Reform
PROPAZ	Foundation for Peace
REMHI	Recovery of Historical Memory (Recuperación de Memoria Histórica)
RENAMO	Mozambican National Resistance
SAAS	Security and Administrative Affairs Secretariat
SAASP	Secretariat of Administrative Affairs and Presidential Security
SEPAZ	Peace Secretariat
SRSG	special representative of the Secretary-General
TSE	Supreme Electoral Tribunal
UDN	Democratic National Union
UNDP	UN Development Programme
UNESCO	UN Educational, Scientific, and Cultural Organization
UNHCR	United Nations High Commissioner for Refugees
UNMIK	United Nations Interim Administration Mission in Kosovo
UNMOSA	United Nations Observer Mission in South Africa
UNOPS	United Nations Office for Project Services
UNVs	United Nations Volunteers
URNG	Guatemalan National Revolutionary Unity
USG	Under-Secretary-General
WOLA	Washington Office on Latin America

Bibliography

Alleyne, Mark. "Manufacturing Peace Through International Communication Policies: United Nations Public Information Strategy in Guatemala 1996–2004,"
Communication, Culture, and Critique 1 (2008), 163–178.

Amnesty International. *Guatemala's Lethal Legacy: Past Impunity and Renewed
Human Rights Violations.* London: Amnesty International, 2002.

Arnault, Jean. "Good Agreement? Bad Agreement? An Implementation Perspective." Paper presented to the Center for International Studies, Princeton University, 2001.

Bajak, Frank, and Juan Carlos Llorca. "U.N.-Backed Investigators Shake Up
Guatemala." Associated Press, November 14, 2010.

Ball, Patrick. "The Guatemalan Commission for Historical Clarification: Generating
Analytical Reports, Inter-Sample Analysis." In *Making the Case: Investigating
Large Scale Human Rights Violations Using Information Systems and Data
Analysis,* edited by Patrick Ball, Herbert F. Spirer, and Louise Spirer, 259–286.
Washington, DC: American Association for the Advancement of Science, 2000.

Beltrán, Adriana. *The Captive State: Organized Crime and Human Rights in Latin
America.* Washington, DC: Washington Office on Latin America, 2007.

Blanck, Evelyn. "Listos para el desarme." *Crónica,* January 24, 1997.

Briscoe, Ivan. *The Proliferation of the "Parallel State."* Madrid: Fundación para las
Relaciónes Internacionales y al Diálogo Exterior (FRIDE), 2008.

———. *A Criminal Bargain: The State and Security in Guatemala.* Madrid: FRIDE,
2009.

Briscoe, Ivan, and Martín Rodríguez Pellecer. *A State Under Siege: Elites, Criminal
Networks and Institutional Reform in Guatemala.* The Hague: Netherlands Institute of International Relations "Clingendael," 2010.

Briscoe, Ivan, and Marlies Stappers. *Breaking the Wave: Critical Steps in the Fight
Against Crime in Guatemala.* Guatemala: Clingendael Institute and Impunity
Watch, 2012.

Call, Charles T. "War Transitions and the New Civilian Security in Latin America."
Comparative Politics 35, no. 1 (October 2002): 1–20.

Canteo, Carlos. "Human Rights Watch Enviará una Investigadora Para Caso Mincho." *Siglo Veintiuno,* May 14, 1997.

Comisión de Esclarecimiento Histórico. *Memoria del Silencio,* Annexo I. Guatemala: United Nations Office of Project Services (UNOPS), 1998.

————. *Guatemala: Memoria del Silencio.* Guatemala: UNOPS, 1999.

Costa, Gino. *La Policía Nacional Civil de El Salvador (1990–1997).* San Salvador: UCA Editores, 1999.

de Jantscher, Milka Casanegra, Patricio Castro, Alberto Ramos, and Osvaldo Schenone. "Guatemala: Rompiendo la Barrera del 8 Por Ciento." Washington, DC: International Monetary Fund, May 1997.

de la Torre, Armando. "La Lección Multiple." *Siglo XXI* (May 18, 1999).

de Soto, Alvaro, and Graciana del Castillo. "Obstacles to Peacebuilding." *Foreign Policy* 94 (Spring 1994): 69–83.

Doggett, Martha. "Contending with Conflict: Managing Crime in Central America." *Harvard International Review* (Fall 2011).

Dudley, Steven. "Guatemala Arrests Show Something Is Working." *InSight Crime: Organized Crime in the Americas,* July 13, 2011.

Fernandez, Lafitte. *Crimen de estado: El caso PARLACEN.* San Salvador: Ediciones Aura, 2011.

Fernandez, Lafitte, and Miguel Jara. "Crimen de diputados de PARLACEN: Los asesinaron por $5 Millones." *El Mundo,* November 15, 2010.

Garst, Rachel. *Military Intelligence and Human Rights in Guatemala: The Archivo and the Case for Intelligence Reform.* Washington, DC: Washington Office on Latin America, 1995.

Gavigan, Patrick. "Organized Crime, Illicit Power Structures, and Guatemala's Threatened Peace Process." *International Peacekeeping* 16, no. 1 (2009): 62–76.

Gleijeses, Piero. *Shattered Hope: The Guatemalan Revolution and the United States, 1944–1954.* Princeton, NJ: Princeton University Press, 1991.

Goepfert, Paul. "The International Commission Against Impunity in Guatemala: Undoing the Legacy of Violence and Corruption." *ReVista* (Fall/Winter 2011), www .drclas.harvard.edu/publications/revistaonline/fall-2010-winter-2011/international -commission-against-impunity-guatemala.

Goldman, Francisco. *The Art of Political Murder: Who Killed the Bishop?* New York: Grove Press, 2007.

Goodfellow, William, and James Morrell. "Esquipulas: Politicians in Command." In *Political Parties and Democracy in Central America,* edited by Louis W. Goodman, William M. LeoGrande, and Johanna Mendelson Forman, 267–287. Boulder, CO: Westview Press, 1992.

Grandin, Greg. *The Last Colonial Massacre: Latin America in the Cold War.* Chicago: University of Chicago Press, 2004.

Grann, David. "A Murder Foretold." *New Yorker,* April 4, 2011.

Guillermo Toriello, Funcación. "Diagnostico socio-economico: personal incorporado, Unidad Revolucionaria Nacional Guatemalteca." Guatemala: FGT, May 1997.

Gunson, Phil. "UN's Guatemala Envoy in Cover-up." *Guardian,* May 5, 1997.

————. "Private View: Time for UN to Come Clean on Rebel's Death." *Guardian,* May 31, 1997.

Haq, Farhan. "The China Veto and the Guatemalan Peace Process." *Interpress Service,* January 20, 1997.

Hayner, Priscilla. *Unspeakable Truths: Confronting State Terror and Atrocity.* Routledge: New York, 2001.

Herrera, Paola. "MP espera que España responda sobre Carlos Vielmann." *Prensa Libre,* March 17, 2012.

Hudson, Andrew, and Alexandra W. Taylor. "The International Commission Against Impunity in Guatemala: A New Model for International Criminal Justice Mechanisms." *Journal of International Criminal Justice* 8 (2010): 53–74.

Inforpress Centroamericana. *Guatemala 1986–1994, Compendio del Proceso de Paz I: Cronologías, análisis, documentos, acuerdos.* Guatemala: Inforpress Centroamericana, 1995, 9–11.

International Crisis Group. "Learning to Walk Without a Crutch: An Assessment of the International Commission Against Impunity in Guatemala." *Latin America Report no. 36.* Brussels: International Crisis Group, 2011.

Jamail, Milton, and Margo Gutierrez. *It's No Secret: Israel's Military Involvement in Central America.* Belmont, MA: Association of Arab-American University Graduates, Inc., 1986.

Leffert, Michael. "Guatemala: Signs of a New Solidarity Against FRG and Efraín Ríos Montt." *NotiCen,* August 7, 2003.

López, Julie. "Guatemala's Crossroads: Democratization of Violence and Second Chances." Washington, DC: Woodrow Wilson Center for Scholars, Working Paper Series on Organized Crime in the Americas, December 2010.

Management Systems International. "An Assessment of the State of Democracy Consolidation and Governance in Guatemala: Late 1996." Washington, DC, 1996.

McClintock, Michael. *The American Connection: State Terror and Popular Resistance in Guatemala.* London: Zed Books, 1985.

Miranda, Ricardo. "Arnault, el Verificador Cómplice." *El Periódico,* April 24, 1997.

Ordoñez, Antonio. "Está en nuestras manos." *El Periodico,* September 7, 2004.

Palencia Prado, Tanya. *Peace in the Making: Civil Groups in Guatemala.* London: Catholic Institute for International Relations, 1996.

Pásara, Luis. *Paz, ilusión, y cambio en Guatemala: El proceso de paz, sus actors, logros, y límites.* Ciudad de Guatemala: Universidad Rafael Landívar, 2003.

Peacock, Susan C., and Adriana Beltrán. *Hidden Powers in Post-Conflict Guatemala: Illegal Armed Groups and the Forces Behind Them.* Washington, DC: Washington Office on Latin America, 2003.

Popkin, Margaret. *Civil Patrols and Their Legacy: Overcoming Militarization and Polarization in the Guatemalan Countryside.* Washington, DC: Robert F. Kennedy Memorial Center for Human Rights, 1996.

Rico, Maite, and Bertrand de la Grange. *Quién Mató al Obisbo? Autopsia de un crimen político.* México, DF: Planeta, 2003.

Rosada-Granados, Héctor. *El lado oculto de las negociaciones de Paz: Transición de la Guerra a la paz en Guatemala.* Guatemala: Friedrich Ebert Stiftung, 1998.

Ruhl, Mark. "The Guatemalan Military Since the Peace Accords: The Fate of Reform Under Arzú and Portillo." *Latin American Politics and Society* 47, no. 1 (Spring 2005): 55–85.

Salvesen, Hilde. "Guatemala: Five Years After the Peace Accords." Report for the Norwegian Ministry of Foreign Affairs. Oslo: International Peace Research Institute (PRIO), 2002.

Samford, Stephen. "IMF Lending Arrangements, Social Development Spending, and Civil War." Manuscript, Albuquerque, 2009.

Sandals, Robert. "Guategate Scandal Engulfs Governing Party and Former President Efrain Ríos Montt." *NotiCen,* September 14, 2000.

———. "Guatemala: Vice President Accused of Using Government Resources to Attack Tax-Bill Opponent." *NotiCen,* September 20, 2001.

———. "Judge Dismisses Charges Against Legislators in Guategate Tax Scandal." *NotiCen,* November 1, 2001.

Saxon, Dan. *To Save Her Life: Disappearance, Deliverance, and the United States in Guatemala.* Berkeley: University of California Press, 2007.

Schirmer, Jennifer. *The Guatemalan Military Project: A Violence Called Democracy.* Philadelphia: University of Pennsylvania Press, 1998.

Schneider, Aaron. *State Building in an Age of Globalization: Central American Tax Regimes and Transnational Elites.* Cambridge: Cambridge University Press, forthcoming.

Schünemann, Julia. *Mirando al Monstruo a la Cara: La Comisión Internacional contra la Impunidad en Guatemala y el "Contrato de construcción del Estado de Derecho."* Madrid: FRIDE, 2010.

Simon, Jean-Marie. *Guatemala: Eternal Spring, Eternal Tyranny.* New York: W. W. Norton, 1987.

Stanley, William D. "Building New Police Forces in Guatemala and El Salvador: Learning and Counter-Learning." *International Peacekeeping* 6, no. 4 (Winter 1999): 113–134.

———. "Business as Usual? Justice and Policing Reform in Postwar Guatemala." In *Constructing Justice and Security After War,* edited by Charles T. Call, 113–155. Washington, DC: United States Institute of Peace Press, 2007.

Stappers, Marlies, et al. *Cambiar la cultura de la violencia por la cultura de la vida: Los primeros dos años de al Comisión Internacional contra la Impunidad en Guatemala.* Guatemala: Impunity Watch, Centro Internacional para la Justicia Transicional, and Plataforma Holandesa contra la Impunidad en Guatemala, 2010.

Torres-Rivas, Edelberto. *Negociando el futuro: La paz en una sociedad violenta, la negociación de paz en 1996.* Guatemala: Facultad Latinoamericana de ciencias sociales (FLACSO), 1997.

Tsebelis, George. *How Political Institutions Work.* Princeton, NJ: Princeton University Press, 2002.

UN Security Council Resolution 1094 (January 20, 1997), UN Doc. S/RES/1094.

United Nations. *Statement by the President of the Security Council.* UN Doc. S/PRST/1995/9, February 22, 1995.

———. *Report of the Director of the United Nations Mission for the Verification of Human Rights and Compliance with the Commitments of the Comprehensive Agreement on Human Rights in Guatemala.* UN Doc. A/49/856, March 1, 1995.

———. "Agreement on the Implementation, Compliance, and Verification Timetable for the Peace Agreements." In *The Guatemala Peace Agreements.* New York: United Nations, 1998.

———. *United Nations Verification Mission in Guatemala, Report of the Secretary-General.* UN Doc. A/54/526, November 11, 1999.

———. "United Nations Verification Mission in Guatemala: Report of the Secretary General." UN Doc. A/59/746, March 18, 2005.

United Nations Development Programme. "UNDP Security Sector Reform Assistance in Post-Conflict Situations: Lessons Learned in El Salvador, Guatemala, Haiti, Mozambique, Somalia and Rwanda." New York: UNDP Emergency Response Division, 2001.

United Nations Office of Project Services. "Comisión de Esclarecimiento Histórico, Guatemala: Memoria del Silencio." Guatemala, 1999.

United Nations Secretary-General. *An Agenda for Peace: Preventive Diplomacy, Peacemaking, and Peace-keeping.* UN Doc. A/47/277–S/24111, June 17, 1992.

———. *The Situation in Central America: Procedures for the Establishment of a Firm and Lasting Peace and Progress in Fashioning a Region of Peace, Freedom, Democracy and Development: United Nations Verification Mission in Guatemala.* UN Doc. A/51/936, June 30, 1997.

Valdez, J. Fernando, and Mayra Palencia Prado. *Los dominios del poder: La encrucijada tributaria.* Guatemala: FLACSO, 1998.

Walter, Barbara F. "The Critical Barrier to Civil War Settlement." *International Organization* 51, no. 3 (1997): 335–364.

Ward, Ken. "The United Nations Mission for the Verification of Human Rights in Guatemala: Database Representation." In *Making the Case: Investigating Large Scale Human Rights Violations Using Information Systems and Data Analysis,* edited by Patrick Ball, Herbert F. Spirer, and Louise Spirer, 137–150. Washington, DC: American Association for the Advancement of Science, 2000.

Wilkinson, Daniel. *Silence on the Mountain: Stories of Terror, Betrayal, and Forgetting in Guatemala.* Boston: Houghton Mifflin, 2002.

Williams, Robert G. *Export Agriculture and the Crisis in Central America.* Chapel Hill: University of North Carolina Press, 1986.

Woodward, Susan. *Balkan Tragedy: Chaos and Dissolution After the Cold War.* Washington, DC: Brookings, 1995.

Index

About the Book

WILLIAM STANLEY tells the absorbing story of the UN peace operation in Guatemala's ten-year endeavor (1994–2004) to build conditions that would sustain a lasting peace in the country.

Unusual among UN peace efforts because of its largely civilian nature, its General Assembly mandate, and its heavy reliance on UN volunteers to staff field offices, the mission (MINUGUA) focused initially on human rights; beginning in 1997, however, its scope expanded to include verification of the full range of peace accords designed to end nearly four decades of civil war between the government and the revolutionary insurgency.

MINUGUA faced a challenging political context: the government that signed the peace accords proved unable or unwilling to implement them, and the progress of successive governments was modest at best. Left to do the heavy lifting politically, the mission also grappled with uncooperative political elites and persistent state corruption, organized crime, and social inequality. Stanley chronicles a series of strategic—and sometimes experimental—choices from the UN's point of view and provides a cautionary tale about the limits of international benevolence.

William Stanley is professor of political science at the University of New Mexico. His publications include *The Protection Racket State: Elite Politics, Military Extortion, and Civil War in El Salvador.*

341